IFIP Advances in Information and Communication Technology 358

IFIP – The International Federation for Information Processing

IFIP was founded in 1960 under the auspices of UNESCO, following the First World Computer Congress held in Paris the previous year. An umbrella organization for societies working in information processing, IFIP's aim is two-fold: to support information processing within its member countries and to encourage technology transfer to developing nations. As its mission statement clearly states,

> *IFIP's mission is to be the leading, truly international, apolitical organization which encourages and assists in the development, exploitation and application of information technology for the bene t of all people.*

IFIP is a non-profitmaking organization, run almost solely by 2500 volunteers. It operates through a number of technical committees, which organize events and publications. IFIP's events range from an international congress to local seminars, but the most important are:

- The IFIP World Computer Congress, held every second year;
- Open conferences;
- Working conferences.

The flagship event is the IFIP World Computer Congress, at which both invited and contributed papers are presented. Contributed papers are rigorously refereed and the rejection rate is high.

As with the Congress, participation in the open conferences is open to all and papers may be invited or submitted. Again, submitted papers are stringently refereed.

The working conferences are structured differently. They are usually run by a working group and attendance is small and by invitation only. Their purpose is to create an atmosphere conducive to innovation and development. Refereeing is less rigorous and papers are subjected to extensive group discussion.

Publications arising from IFIP events vary. The papers presented at the IFIP World Computer Congress and at open conferences are published as conference proceedings, while the results of the working conferences are often published as collections of selected and edited papers.

Any national society whose primary activity is in information may apply to become a full member of IFIP, although full membership is restricted to one society per country. Full members are entitled to vote at the annual General Assembly, National societies preferring a less committed involvement may apply for associate or corresponding membership. Associate members enjoy the same benefits as full members, but without voting rights. Corresponding members are not represented in IFIP bodies. Affiliated membership is open to non-national societies, and individual and honorary membership schemes are also offered.

Ian Wakeman   Ehud Gudes
Christian Damsgaard Jensen
Jason Crampton (Eds.)

Trust
Management V

5th IFIP WG 11.11
International Conference, IFIPTM 2011
Copenhagen, Denmark, June 29 – July 1, 2011
Proceedings

 Springer

Volume Editors

Ian Wakeman
University of Sussex
Falmer, Brighton, BN1 3TQ, UK
E-mail: ianw@sussex.ac.uk

Ehud Gudes
Ben-Gurion University of the Negev
Beer-Sheva, Israel, 84105
E-mail: ehud@cs.bgu.ac.il

Christian Damsgaard Jensen
Technical University of Denmark
2800 Lyngby, Denmark
E-mail: christian.jensen@imm.dtu.dk

Jason Crampton
Royal Holloway, University of London
Egham Hill, Egham, TW20 0EX, UK
E-mail: jason.crampton@rhul.ac.uk

ISSN 1868-4238   e-ISSN 1868-422X
ISBN 978-3-642-26877-9   ISBN 978-3-642-22200-9 (eBook)
DOI 10.1007/978-3-642-22200-9
Springer Heidelberg Dordrecht London New York

CR Subject Classification (1998): K.6.5, C.2, E.3, D.4.6, H.4, H.5

Typesetting: Camera-ready by author, data conversion by Scientific Publishing Services, Chennai, India

Printed on acid-free paper

Springer is part of Springer Science+Business Media (www.springer.com)

Preface

This volume contains the proceedings of IFIPTM 2011, the 5th IFIP WG 11.11 International Conference on Trust Management, held in Copenhagen, Denmark, from June 29 to July 1, 2011.

IFIPTM 2011 provided a truly global platform for the reporting of research, development, policy, and practice in the interdependent areas of privacy, security, and trust. Building on the traditions inherited from the iTrust and IFIPTM conferences, IFIPTM 2011 was a multi-disciplinary conference focusing on areas such as: trust models, social and behavioral aspects of trust, trust in networks, mobile systems and cloud computation, privacy, reputation systems, and identity management.

IFIPTM 2011 was an open IFIP conference. The program of the conference featured both theoretical research papers and reports of real-world case studies from academia, business and government. IFIPTM 2011 received 42 submissions from 21 different countries, including: Canada, Denmark, Finland, France, Germany, India, Israel, Italy, Japan, Kuwait, Luxembourg, The Netherlands, Norway, Portugal, Saudi Arabia, Singapore, Slovenia, Switzerland, UK, United Arab Emirates, and USA. The Program Committee selected 14 full papers and 8 short papers for presentation and inclusion in the proceedings. We categorized submissions as full or short papers based on the opinions of the Program Committee. The full papers were unanimously deemed to be worthy of inclusion, while short papers were accepted if committee members believed them likely to excite debate and discussion.

In addition, the program and the proceedings include invited papers and extended abstracts by four academic experts in the fields of trust management, privacy and security: Toshio Yamagishi, Pamela Briggs, Dieter Gollmann and Angela Sasse. Professors Sasse and Gollman provided keynote addresses at the 2011 conference, while Professors Yamagishi and Briggs provided keynote addresses at the 2010 conference. Unfortunately, timing constraints prevented their inclusion in the 2010 proceedings.

In the IFIPTM 2011 conference, as well as in previous IFIPTM conferences, we had several accompanying workshops enabling the presentation of new ideas and allowing the early exposure of ongoing research, particularly from PhD students. We believe the deep and wide profiles produced by all of the events will solidify IFIPTM as an international, multidisciplinary trust conference.

Running an international conference requires an immense effort from all parties involved. We would like to thank the Program Committee members and external referees for having provided timely and in-depth reviews of the submitted papers.

We would also like to thank the Workshop, Tutorial, Poster and Demonstration, Publications, Local Organization, Registration, Publicity, Liaison and Website Chairs for having provided great help organizing the conference.

We hope you enjoy the proceedings and the conference.

June 2011

Ian Wakeman
Ehud Gudes
Christian Damsgaard Jensen
Jason Crampton

Organization

Executive Committee

General Chairs

Christian Damsgaard Jensen   Technical University of Denmark, Denmark
Jason Crampton   Royal Holloway, University of London, UK

Program Chairs

Ian Wakeman   University of Sussex, UK
Ehud Gudes   Ben-Gurion University of the Negev, Israel

Workshops and Tutorial Chair

Daniele Quercia   Cambridge University, UK

Panels and Special Sessions Chair

Stephen Marsh   Communications Research Centre, Canada

Publicity Chair

Nicola Dragoni   Technical University of Denmark, Denmark

Program Committee

Anirban Basu   Tokai University, Japan
Elisa Bertino   Purdue University, USA
Licia Capra   University College London, UK
Dan Chalmers   University of Sussex, UK
Anupam Datta   Carnegie Mellon University, USA
Theo Dimitrakos   BT Innovate & Design, UK
Naranker Dulay   Imperial College London, UK
Sandro Etalle   T.U. Eindhoven and University of Twente, The Netherlands
Rino Falcone   ISTC-CNR, Italy
Elena Ferrari   University of Insubria, Italy
Nurit Gal-Oz   Ben-Gurion University of the Negev, Israel
Dieter Gollmann   Hamburg University of Technology, Germany
Elizabeth Gray   Accenture, USA

Jochen Haller   SAP Research, Germany
Peter Herrmann   The Norwegian University of Science and
                                Technology
Kevin Hoffman   Purdue University, USA
Roslan Ismail   Universiti Tenaga Nasional (UNITEN),
                                Malaysia
Valerie Issarny   INRIA, France
Audun Jøsang   University of Oslo, Norway
Reid Kerr   University of Waterloo, Canada
Hiroaki Kikuchi   Tokai University, Japan
Adam J. Lee   University of Pittsburgh, USA
Ninghui Li   Purdue University, USA
Emiliano Lorini   Institut de Recherche en Informatique de
                                Toulouse (IRIT), France
Pratyusa Manadhata   Symantec Research, USA
Fabio Massacci   University of Trento, Italy
Kanta Matsuura   University of Tokyo, Japan
Walter Quattrociocchi   ISTC-CNR, Italy
Kent Seamons   Brigham Young University, USA
Jean-Marc Seigneur   University of Geneva, Switzerland
Jessica Staddon   PARC, USA
Ketil Stolen   SINTEF and University of Oslo, Norway
Vipin Swarup   MITRE, USA
Sotirios Terzis   University of Strathclyde, UK
Mahesh Tripunitara   University of Waterloo, Canada
Luis Javier Vaillalba   Complutense University of Madrid, Spain
Danfeng Yao   Rutgers University, New Brunswick, USA

Sponsored by

IFIP WG11.11

Table of Contents

Extended Abstracts for Keynote Speakers

Full Papers

Short Papers

From Access Control to Trust Management, and Back – A Petition

Dieter Gollmann

Hamburg University of Technology,
Hamburg, Germany
diego@tu-harburg.de

Abstract. In security too often services are understood not from first principles but via characteristic mechanisms used for their delivery. Access control had got tied up with DAC, MAC, RBAC and reference monitors. With developments in distributed systems security and with the opening of the Internet for commercial use new classes of access control mechanisms became relevant that did not fit into the established mold. Trust Management was coined as a term unifying the discussion of those mechanisms. We view *trust* as a placeholder that had its use in driving this research agenda, but argue that trust is so overloaded that it is now an impediment for further progress. Our petition asks for a return to *access control* and proposes a new framework for structuring investigations in this area.

Denn eben wo Begriffe fehlen,
da stellt ein Wort zur rechten Zeit sich ein.
Mit Worten läßt sich trefflich streiten,
mit Worten ein System bereiten.

[Mephistopheles in Goethe's Faust 1.]

1 Services and Mechanisms

From communications security we get the important conceptual distinction between *security services* and *security mechanisms* [7]. A service describes security goals that should be achieved at a generic, implementation independent level. A mechanism is an implementation of a security service. Implementations may reflect specific requirements of a class of applications or specific features of a technology.

This distinction is useful, although sometimes difficult to maintain in practice when services become equated with the characteristic (sic!) mechanisms used for their delivery. This has led to definitions such as "authentication is what authentication protocols do". There is a further problem. In case a service is too closely tied to its 'old' mechanisms and the applications or the technology changes, the service may get renamed just to break clear of its past implementations although the security goals have actually not changed.

I. Wakeman et al. (Eds.): IFIPTM 2011, IFIP AICT 358, pp. 1–8, 2011.

In an early attempt to define the yet nascent field of informatics, Zemanek followed Mephistopheles from Goethe's Faust when making the salient point that we need words for discussing emerging phenomena *before* they are truly understood [17]. The terms coined at that stage are placeholders, yet without precise meaning, just vehicles for moving the discussion along. Zemanek concluded that the new word 'informatics' was such a placeholder. In security, a similar pattern can be observed when old mechanisms become insufficient and have to be substituted by something new, but it is not yet fully determined what the new solution should provide.

2   Access Control

Access control is one of the security services listed in [7].

Access control: provides protection against unauthorised use of resources.

From the 1970s on, the corresponding security mechanism was a *reference monitor* enforcing security policies that referred to user identities or to security labels. The former policies were called discretionary access control (DAC), the latter mandatory access control (MAC) [1]. The reference monitor was implemented by the *security kernel*. On a historic note, *trusted* operating systems in the 1980s were those that supported multi-level security based on security labels.

By the mid 1990s access control by DAC and MAC, which had deep roots in the US defense sector, showed itself unsuitable for the commercial applications that came to dominate the use of IT. In role-based access control (RBAC) security policies refer to functional roles in an organisation, not to user identities or to security labels [14].

The Internet had been opened to commercial use in the early 1990s creating opportunities for Internet-based interactions between organisations. Before, access control was a purely local service, both with respect to the setting of policies and with respect to their enforcement. Exposure to the Internet led to demands for new kinds of access control. In particular, there were fundamental changes in the enforcement of security policies.

3   Trust Management

In 1996 Blaze *et al.* introduced the term *Trust Management* for access control in this new environment [3]. As stated in [2]:

Trust management, introduced in the PolicyMaker system, is a unified approach to specifying and interpreting security policies, credentials, and relationships.

As a service, Trust Management is nothing else but access control[1]. As a mechanism, it is a distinctive departure from the past.

---

[1] The purist may complain that this service is defined by reference to a collection of mechanisms.

As a service, access control is a system for describing and interpreting policies that regulate access to resources. Policies refer to *attributes*. There is no inherent limitation on the attributes that can be used for access control. User identities and security labels were just two instances of convenient attributes. Attribute values (evidence) should not be taken on trust and have to be authenticated.

> *Authentication*: decides whether to accept or reject claimed evidence provided with an access request.

In the past the main policy attribute was the user identity. From that time, authentication can be narrowly understood as the verification of a claimed user identity. In the past, evidence was verified locally. Now, verification might be 'delegated' to some other entity which then advises on the validity of an attribute value. Attributes thus have a value and a source. Authentication is split into the verification of the attribute value, possibly performed externally, and the local verification of the source of the advice received from an external entity. The SAML specification refers to trust when discussing the use of XML Signatures for origin authentication [13].

Authentication was once reserved for origin authentication, as in *obtaining the source of the request is called 'authentication'* [12]. Now, a new term is needed for the verification of an attribute value. In code-based access control, for example, *code-identity authentication* goes beyond verifying the source of code [11].

Access control also includes the step where for a given request a decision is made based on the current policy and on the evidence presented. KeyNote calls this step *compliance checking* [2]. In the past, this step was called *authorisation*. As put famously in [12],

> access control = authentication + authorisation.

In common use of English people are authorised but requests (transactions) are approved. Hence, we may put instead

> access control = authentication + approval.

Figure 1 captures the new view of access control. A *Policy Decision Point* (PDP) receives a request together with a set of attributes. The request may arrive within a *session*. For externally verified evidence, the source of evidence has to be authenticated. Locally verifiable evidence is directly authenticated. The session identifier may associate the request with further local evidence, *e. g.* with the identity of an authenticated user who had established the session. Once authentication is completed, the PDP decides whether to approve the request.

4   Trust and Authorisation

Descriptions of access control mechanisms explain how a request will be approved in accordance with the given policy. Such explanations state how attributes are authenticated, how the applicable policy rules are found, and how those rules are to be interpreted. Such descriptions do not explain how the policy

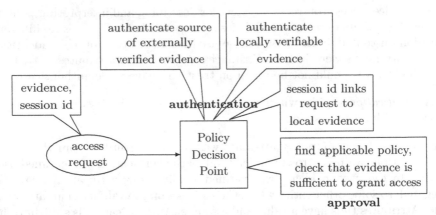

Fig. 1. A fresh look at access control

came into existence in the first place. The act of defining a policy can be called *authorisation*. A policy based on user identities can authorize a user to perform certain actions; a policy based on roles can do the same for the functional roles in an organisation. The SAML specification refers once more to trust when discussing authorisation.

> When determining what issuers to trust, particularly in cases where the assertions will be used as inputs to authentication or authorization [approval in the terminology proposed above] decisions, the risk of security compromises arising from the consumption of false but validly issued assertions is a large one [13].

An organisation has some rationale for setting its policy. A good example for such a rationale is the *need-to-know* principle; users and roles must be enabled to perform the actions expected from them. A policy is set by assigning access rights (permissions) to *principals* such as users, roles, code, web sites, *etc*. When 'trust' is used to capture the scope of access rights granted, *e. g.* as in *code with more trust is allowed to do more on your machine* [11], language suggests that access rights are granted *because* an entity is trusted in an anthropomorphic meaning of the word.

It is plausible that trust in a person or in an institution and the access rights granted are correlated. In the social fabric of an organisation decision makers will appoint people they trust to positions of responsibility. Equally, appointment of contractors will relate to trust established earlier. We are, however, departing from access control when speculating about the reasons driving decisions within an organisation. In this context, a mixture of competence, reliability, cost, and personal allegiance will play its role. There exists advice for organisations on how to best balance these various factors in their decisions, and one should note that when too much emphasis is placed on personal allegiance and family ties, trust just becomes another word for nepotism.

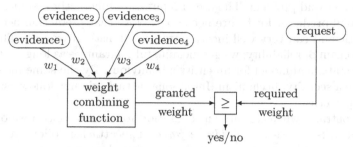

Fig. 2. Weighing evidence for access control

5 Weighing Evidence

It is desirable that a security policy should be *complete*; for each request and for each viable combination of attribute values there should be a defined decision. Moreover, all the policy rules ought in principle be accredited by management. In a setting with a rich collection of attributes dealing with each possible case individually becomes unmanageable. An alternative approach discussed in [9] structures access control as follows.

- Each piece of evidence gets assigned a granted weight; the weight may reflect the trustworthiness of evidence.
- An algorithm for combining the weights of different pieces of evidence is defined; in the simple most case, weights are just added up.
- Each request gets assigned a required weight.
- A request is approved if the combined granted weight of the evidence presented exceeds the required threshold.

The weights assigned to evidence might be called trust but this term evokes an interpretation that is not necessary. Weight of evidence is an established concept, as are decision processes that require judge or jury to move beyond reasonable doubt when finding their verdict. Practical validation of the approach to access control sketched here still is an open challenge.

6 Reputation as an Attack Vector

It has been proposed to use *reputation* (a.k.a. trust) as an attribute for access control, see *e. g.* [4,5,10,15,16]. This approach is problematic for two reasons. First, we have to deal with the authentication of this attribute. When reputation scores are computed locally we can believe what we see but still should account for imperfections in our observations. When reputation scores are received as *recommendations* from third parties, we need a policy for accepting external evidence. We may take the ratings from certain entities on trust. Alternatively, we could iterate the process and rate a party's reputation as a recommender; we could, for example, compare recommendations received with our own observations and trust recommenders that share our bias.

There is a second problem. The use of reputation inherently assumes that the past is a good predictor for future behaviour. Note that prediction need not be deterministic and can very well incorporate probabilistic reasoning. This places us in the domain of reliability; we get meaningful guarantees as long as we have a reasonable statistical model for an entity's behaviour. By the same measure, we do not have a security mechanism. Intentional attacks do not follow established statistical patterns.

To the contrary, when we rely on reputation for access control we open ourselves to attacks known as *confidence fraud*. The attacker follows a course of action that leads to a good reputation score and then strikes at a convenient moment. eBay is often quoted as an example for the successful deployment of reputation systems, usually without giving a definition for success. In reality, eBay's reputation system could be gamed and was, *e. g.*, modified in 2008 to deal with some of the more blatant misuses[2].

If reputation-based access control is to be taken seriously as a security mechanism, it has to be subjected to proper security analysis. Reputation-based systems are usually assessed via simulations, und usually the adversaries deviate at random from the correct behaviour. Such an approach is suitable for a reliability analysis. It is fundamentally flawed in the context of security. A security analysis deserving its name is a min-max method that first looks at the maximal damage an attacker can cause for a specific defence (within given assumptions on attack patterns of interest) and then searches for the defence that minimizes the maximal damage.

7 Occam's Razor

Our discussion of access control has encountered seven forms of trust:

- Trust as an indicator for multi-level security and mandatory access control.
- Trust as a synonym for access rights, such as in trusted code or in semi-trusted code.
- Trust as origin authentication (trust in an assertion)
- Trust as a policy rule to accept evidence from a third party (trust in an issuer/recommender, delegation of authentication).
- Trust as a rationale for assigning access rights.
- Trust as a weight of evidence.
- Trust as a synonym for reputation.

Occam's razor has been expressed as

> *pluralitas non est ponenda sine necessitate*
> (plurality should not be posited without necessity).

There is no necessity to use a term like trust that has such a plurality of meanings, a point that had been elaborated in more detail in [8].

---

[2] http://www.wired.com/epicenter/2008/05/ebay-feedback/

8   The Petition

Influential work on access control was published in the 1970s and 1980s. Commercial use of the Internet then changed the context for access control and it became apparent that the old security mechanism had reached their limits. Trust management was forged as a new term. As put by Joan Feigenbaum, one of its creators:

> Trust management is supposed to be an incredibly vague and provocative term invented by Matt Blaze. I don't know whether he intended it that way, but it comes natural to him [6].

The petition is then to return to *access control* as this term quite adequately captures the very nature of this security service. Challenges in access control lie in the identification of suitable policies and policy attributes, and in the authentication of those attributes, set in the context of federated (mashed-up) systems where access control functions are distributed among many players. All of this can be expressed quite elegantly without mentioning trust. Trust has served its purpose as a placeholder and catalyst in the discussion transforming access control and can be safely put to rest.

References

1. Bell, D.E., LaPadula, L.J.: Secure computer systems: Mathematical foundations and model. Technical Report M74-244, The MITRE Corporation, Bedford, MA (May 1973)
2. Blaze, M., Feigenbaum, J., Ioannidis, J., Keromytis, A.D.: The KeyNote Trust-Management System Version 2, RFC 2704 (September 1999)
3. Blaze, M., Feigenbaum, J., Lacy, J.: Decentralized trust management. In: Proceedings of the 1996 IEEE Symposium on Security and Privacy, pp. 164–173 (1996)
4. Bonatti, P.A., Duma, C., Olmedilla, D., Shahmehri, N.: An integration of reputation-based and policy-based trust management. In: Semantic Web Policy Workshop in Conjunction with 4th International Semantic Web Conference, Galway, Ireland (November 2005)
5. Colombo, M., Martinelli, F., Mori, P., Petrocchi, M., Vaccarelli, A.: Fine grained access control with trust and reputation management for globus. In: Chung, S. (ed.) OTM 2007, Part II. LNCS, vol. 4804, pp. 1505–1515. Springer, Heidelberg (2007)
6. Feigenbaum, J.: Overview of the AT&T Labs trust-management project. In: Christianson, B., Crispo, B., Harbison, W.S., Roe, M. (eds.) Security Protocols 1998. LNCS, vol. 1550, pp. 45–50. Springer, Heidelberg (1999)
7. International Organisation for Standardization. Basic Reference Model for Open Systems Interconnection (OSI) Part 2: Security Architecture, Genève, Switzerland (1989)
8. Gollmann, D.: Why trust is bad for security. Electronic Notes on Theoretical Computer Science 157(3), 3–9 (2006)

9. Jøsang, A., Gollmann, D., Au, R.: A method for access authorisation through delegation networks. In: Safavi-Naini, R., Steketee, C., Susilo, W. (eds.) Proc. Fourth Australasian Information Security Workshop (Network Security) (AISW 2006), Hobart, Australia. CRPIT, vol. 54, pp. 165–174 (2006)
10. Krukow, K., Nielsen, M., Sassone, V.: A logical framework for history-based access control and reputation systems. Journal of Computer Security 16(1), 63–101 (2008)
11. La Macchia, B.A., Lange, S., Lyons, M., Martin, R., Price, K.T.: .NET Framework Security. Addison-Wesley Professional, Boston (2002)
12. Lampson, B., Abadi, M., Burrows, M., Wobber, E.: Authentication in distributed systems: Theory and practice. ACM Transactions on Computer Systems 10(4), 265–310 (1992)
13. OASIS. Assertions and Protocols for the OASIS Security Assertion Markup Language (SAML) v2.0. Technical report, OASIS Standard (March 2005)
14. Sandhu, R.S., Ferraiolo, D., Kuhn, R.: The NIST model for role based access control: Toward a unified standard. In: Proceedings of the 5th ACM Workshop on Role Based Access Control, pp. 47–63 (July 2000)
15. Sukumaran, S., Blessing, E.: Reputation based localized access control for mobile ad-hoc networks. In: Kunz, T., Ravi, S.S. (eds.) ADHOC-NOW 2006. LNCS, vol. 4104, pp. 197–210. Springer, Heidelberg (2006)
16. Yong, H.: Reputation and role based access control model for multi-domain environments. In: 2010 International Symposium on Intelligence Information Processing and Trusted Computing (IPTC), pp. 597–600 (October 2010)
17. Zemanek, H.: Was ist Informatik? Elektronische Rechenanlagen, 157–161 (1971)

Familiarity Breeds Con-victims: Why We Need More Effective Trust Signaling

M. Angela Sasse and Iacovos Kirlappos

Department of Computer Science, University College London, UK
a.sasse@cs.ucl.ac.uk

1 Introduction

The past 10 years have seen a plethora of research on trust in online interactions. In the late 90s, the issue was whether people would be willing to trust the Internet enough to order and enter their credit card details online. Most of the academic research and commercial advice published then focused on 'how to increase user trust online' by making websites 'user friendly' and having a 'personal touch' e.g. in the form of photos of company staff. Unfortunately, much this advice on how to make your Internet presence trustworthy is now being used by perpetrators of phishing scams, who are using the latest 'trustworthy UI design techniques' to trick users into revealing authentication credentials and other personal data. A key trust issue that has emerged with the huge popularity of social networking is users' voluntary (and sometimes ill-judged) disclosure of personal information, and accidental sharing of that data by applications and other users.

Whilst many new applications and services have emerged, little progress has been made in helping ordinary users to work out who they can trust online, and who they can't. Trust is only required when risk and uncertainty are present. Since it serves as a shortcut for a full risk-benefit analysis and mechanisms to assure that a transaction partner delivers what is being promised, there are significant economic benefits to trust-based environments [1]. In online transactions, uncertainty is increased because transactions partners are separated in space, and – unless delivery is instant (e.g. when buying a music track) - in time.

2 The Importance of Trust Signaling

When deciding whether to trust, user look for signals of trustworthiness – cues about the transaction partner's ability and motivation to deliver their side of the transaction, rather than 'taking the money and run' [4]. In real-world transactions, first-time interactions are regarded as more risky, whilst a past history of interactions allow the trustor to form a reasonable expectation of the trustee's behaviour. Users transfer this behaviour to online transactions: they will trust website that they have used in the past, or rather – any site that looks, feels or sounds like one they have used successfully in the past – not realising that in online environments, attackers can more easily mimic the appearance and behavior of genuine transaction partners.

I. Wakeman et al. (Eds.): IFIPTM 2011, IFIP AICT 358, pp. 9–12, 2011.

In a recent study, we had participants buying music festival tickets under conditions of risk and uncertainty. We found that people use the following as indicator of trustworthiness:

1. **Previous experience with the website.** Users will trust websites they have used before – or rather: websites they think they have used before – and those that look or feel familiar. Small differences in appearance or behavior usually won't raise suspicion, nor do certificate warnings, because users have been de-sensitised by too many false positives.

2. **Logos and certifications.** Most of the websites display some form of trust logo, and many users them as symbols of trust. We found, however, that none of our participants could explain though what these logo signify, and why a website is secure if it has this logo. Very few participants checked whether the logo was a clickable link and what information about the merchant it was providing.

3. **Reference to other names the participants could recognize.** Websites that had affiliate programs which included known venues around the country created a feeling of trust in participants. The inclusion of the *Oxfam* charity name in a website (www.gigantic.com), and mentioning that they give 10% of their profits to it, made participants think that it cannot be fake - even though there was no way to verify whether the claims of that website were true, since no links existed that confirmed.

4. **Advertising.** Participants had mixed reactions on the presence of advertisements on websites. Adverts of well-known companies induced a feeling of trust for 14% of participants. Their main argument was *"why would a company pay them to include advertisements in their website if they were scammers?"* On the other hand, 11% of participants said that if they have a lot of advertisements, then they can be scams, and they preferred to buy from sites that displayed fewer of these.

5. **Social Networking references.** Inclusion of links to *Facebook* and *Twitter* pages can significantly affect the level of trust in a site. 19% of participants mentioned that if a retailer has a *Facebook* Page or a *Twitter* site, then they cannot be fraudulent, as their victims could post negative comments on those sites after they were scammed, deterring other people from using them. In addition, the inclusion of other user feedback in the website can also contribute in the creation of a feeling of trust and received positive comments by 11% of participants. This was strongly present in the case of a website which included pictures of the people that left feedback for its services, or other members of the website that are planning to attend an event, concurring with findings that richer media representations could lead to a positive trust bias.

6. **Amount of information provided.** The amount of information the website included on the particular event influenced 17% of participants. Although all websites included information on the event (gate opening times, facilities, instructions how to get to the venue etc), those that had that information viewable on the main event page seemed to attract the participants more. Inclusion of visual artifacts like maps increased the level of trust and made them appear more persuasive and real.

7. **Website Layout.** 19% of participants mentioned that the structure of the website design was something that looked familiar to them from other websites they are using, which are known to be legitimate. So the websites they have chosen to trust are possibly genuine as the layout is similar. Indication that a site sells tickets for a variety of events was also critical, as participants did not perceive it as a scam aiming to target a particular event audience.

8. **Company Information.** The type of information the website provided on the company behind it also affected decisions. 14% of participants mentioned that the presence of the registration number of the company, VAT numbers, direct telephone numbers, ticket delivery information and claims that they are official ticket outlets seemed to be trusted more. As with the logos (see 2), however, none of the participants knew how to verify this information though.

Our results show that trust signalling in online interactions is currently dysfunctional. Attackers have an easy game - techniques that are successfully employed in the real world are currently even cheaper and easier to online (a point elaborated by Stajano & Wilson [3]).

Information about ability and motivation of a trustee to fulfil can be inferred from signals of trust-warranting properties [2]. There are two main types of signals for trustworthiness:

- **Symbols of trustworthiness.** Symbols have an arbitrarily assigned meaning - they are specifically created to signify the presence of trust-warranting properties. Examples of symbols for such properties are e-commerce trust seals. Symbols can be protected by making them very difficult to forge, or by threatening sanctions in the case of misuse. They are a common way of signaling trustworthiness, but their usability is often limited. Because they are created for specific settings, the trustor has to know about their existence and how to decode them. At the same time, trustees need to invest in emitting them and in getting them known.

- **Symptoms of trustworthiness.** Symptoms are not specifically created to signal trust-warranting properties; rather, they are by-products of the activities of trustworthy actors. As an example, a steady gaze and firm voice may not require much effort when telling the truth, but may require some training to maintain while lying. Therefore, exhibiting symptoms of trust incurs no cost for trustworthy actors, whereas untrustworthy actors would have to invest some effort to engage in effective mimicry.

Our currently online environment has very much relied on trust symbols; but the results of our study illustrate why they do not work in an online environment – they are cheap to mimic, and users cannot tell the difference between genuine and mimicked ones. The presentation will argue that we need to shift our design efforts to supporting trust symptoms, which are impossible or expensive for attackers to forge, and provide user with richer cues that are embedded in the specific transactions.

References

1. Gefen, D.: E-Commerce: The Role of Familiarity and Trust. Omega: International Journal of Management Science 28(6), 725–737
2. Riegelsberger, J., Sasse, M.A., McCarthy, J.D.: The mechanics of trust: a framework for research and design. International Journal of Human-Computer Studies 62(3), 381–422 (2005)
3. Stajano, F., Wilson, P.: Understanding scam victims: seven principles for systems security. In: Technical Report 754. University of Cambridge (2009)
4. Twyman, M., Harvey, N., Harries, C.: Trust in motives, trust in competence: Separate factors determining the effectiveness of risk communication. Judgment and Decision Making 3, 111–112 (2008)

The Evolution of Trust

Pam Briggs

PaCTLab,
Northumbria University,
Newcastle upon Tyne, UK
p.briggs@northumbria.ac.uk

Abstract. In this paper I discuss the evolution of trust from early studies of interpersonal trust to current research on the role of trust in computer-mediated communication. I reflect on the ways in which the context for the investigation of trust has led to very different views about just what trust is and how it changes over time and I conclude with examples from my own work about the development of trust online and the potential for new trust tools.

Keywords: Trust, credibility, privacy.

1 Introduction

Trust. . . is not a commodity which can be bought very easily. If you have to buy it, you already have some doubts about what youve bought [1, page 23].

A story appeared in the news a few years ago about a circus touring in Scotland that posted an advert for a knife-throwers assistant in a local town. Twenty-three people applied for the post, but only six were brave enough to turn up for an audition, when they were asked to stand against a board while 10 knives were hurled at them at speeds of up to 45 miles per hour. The knife-thrower – a Mr Hanson – said he had never inflicted major injury although he had given people nicks and cuts in the past. He said was looking for someone who was willing to have a laugh but who also had serious qualities and trusted him. Seonaid Wiseman, a 29-year-old post-graduate student at Aberdeen University was the first of the candidates to audition. Following the ordeal she said she had been "blank with terror" when the first knife hit the board, but added: "It wasn't bad after the first one. After the first one I had every confidence in him."

Understanding the development of just this kind of interpersonal trust was one of the first challenges for early trust researchers where the focus was on the critical dimensions by which people evaluate how others will behave. In early contexts trustworthiness was defined as "the extent to which people are seen as moral, honest and reliable" [12] – a definition which while perfectly valid (although defining 'moral' is not an enviable task) says little about what trust is, nor why its perception will vary between individuals.

The term trust can imply so many different things, because it presupposes some risk, but isn't explicit about the nature of that risk. Inevitably, then,

I. Wakeman et al. (Eds.): IFIPTM 2011, IFIP AICT 358, pp. 13–16, 2011.

over time, different approaches to trust research have evolved, depending upon the trust context. Within the workplace trust presupposes risks such as loss of reputation and self-esteem, damage to career and loss of salary. Yet trust between colleagues is vital. Robert Levering, author of 'A great place to work' [4] and co-author of 'The 100 best places to work for in America' [5] has argued that "trust between managers and employees is the primary defining characteristic of the very best workplaces" and Dennis and Michelle Reina [9] described the betrayals that undermine modern working relationships – the colleague taking credit for your work, the boss failing to deliver on a promise, the assistant passing on confidential information – and have concluded that we live in an era where corporate leaders have lost the loyalty, trust and commitment of their workforce, to devastating effect.

Political philosopher Onora O'Neill has argued that trust can be lost by the very systems set up to preserve it. In delivering the 2002 Reith Lectures [8, lecture 3], O'Neill describes the ways in which various systems of public accountability have provided consumers and citizens with more information and more complaints systems, but which have ultimately built a culture of suspicion and low morale likely to generate professional cynicism and ultimately public mistrust. Thus the trend towards audit and transparency which is evident in indicators such as school league tables, University research ratings, hospital waiting lists and transport punctuality figures means that workers gear their actions towards the accountable targets, and have less time to spend on those aspects of the work that cannot be explicitly measured. In this way some of the metrics that can be used (rather unsuccessfully) as proxies for trust can start to drive organisational behaviour.

A different approach to trust was discussed by Francis Fukuyama who set trust in the context of vastly different societies and cultures [3]. He identified to 'high trust' societies like Japan, where, he argued, life can be much easier on the individual as a result of the strong social ties binding Japanese citizens together, and observed that these, coupled with relatively low instances of deviance, meant that the enhanced sense of trust within that society is palpable. However, crucial to Fukuyamas argument was that many societies are suffering an erosion of trust that is having devastating effects on both individuals and society. He cited America as an example of a society previously high in trust, in which individualism grew at the expense of community, creating a crisis of trust signalled by a huge increase in litigation and a corresponding fortress mentality. He described the effects of such a decline: 'people who do not trust one another will end up cooperating only under a system of formal rules and regulations, which have to be negotiated, agreed to, litigated, and enforced, sometimes by coercive means. This legal apparatus, serving as a substitute for trust, entails what economists call "transaction costs". Widespread distrust in a society, in other words, imposes a kind of tax on all forms of economic activity, a tax that high-trust societies do not have to pay.' [3, pg. 28].

Against this background – of interpersonal, workplace and societal trust – what can we learn from current studies of trust that take place in the context of computer-mediated communication? Certainly, in the wake of significant amounts of e-commerce research, we know that it is meaningful to talk about trust online and that there are arguably high-trust cultures that flourish online (such as early versions of eBay, where there were fewer guarantees and a greater willingness to trust in a transaction).

Furthermore the context for trust online has become extremely diverse with the rise of social networks and an increased tendency for people to use Internet-based information to inform important life decisions across a number of domains (in my own work I have explored trust decisions in the contexts of e-government [7], privacy[6] and health [10]).

Such domains of trust enquiry have led to the proliferation of trust models that capture different aspects of online trust or that model the dynamics of trust development. In my own work I have tried to capture the evolution of trust over time and consider the role of different contextual factors at early and late stages of the trust relationship [11] including an analysis of the impact of those factors – such as personalised communication – that can help cement longer-term trust.

Yet perhaps the most exciting new developments in trust research are moving beyond this simple transactional model of trust in information offered to capture a more complex set of parameters in relation to the ways in which we might use technology in the form of a trusted companion. To this end I have been working towards refining the idea of an electronic life partner – the Biometric Daemon [2] – which would be capable of not only authenticating identity across a number of different platforms, but also acting as a trust agent. Intrinsic in the Daemon model is the notion that a relationship must be sustained over time and that both parties – Daemon and individual – are capable of learning about trust from each other and are similarly capable of seeking different forms of reassurance from each other.

References

1. Arrow, K.J.: The Limits of Organization. Norton, New York (1974)
2. Briggs, P., Olivier, P.L.: Biometric daemons: authentication via electronic pets. In: Proceedings of CHI 2008, pp. 2423–2432. ACM, New York (2008)
3. Fukuyama, F.: Trust: The Social Virtues and the Creation of Prosperity. Simon and Schuster, New York (1996)
4. Levering, R.: A Great Place to Work. Plume (1994)
5. Levering, R., Moskowitz, M.: The 100 Best Companies to Work for in America. Plume (1994)
6. Little, L., Marsh, S., Briggs, P.: Trust and privacy permissions for an ambient world. In: Song, R., Korba, L., Yee, G. (eds.) Trust in e-services: Technologies, Practices and Challenges, ch. XI, pp. 259–292. Idea Group Publishing, USA (2007)
7. Marsh, S., Patrick, A., Briggs, P.: Trust in digital government – social issues. In: Anttiroiko, A., Malkia, M. (eds.) The Encyclopedia of Digital Government. IGI Publishing (2006)
8. O'Neill, O.: A Question of Trust: The BBC Reith Lectures, Cambridge (2002), available from the BBC, http://www.bbc.co.uk/radio4/reith2002/

9. Reina, D.S., Reina, M.L.: Trust and NBetrayal in the Workplace: Building Effective Relationships in Your Organization. Berret-Koehler Publishers, San Francisco (1999)
10. Sillence, E., Briggs, P., Harris, P., Fishwick, L.: Going online for health advice: Changes in usage and trust practices over the last five years. Interacting with Computers 19(3), 397–403 (2007)
11. Sillence, E., Briggs, P., Harris, P., Fishwick, L.: How do patients evaluate and make use of online health information? Social Science and Medicine 64(9), 1853–1862 (2007)
12. Wrightsman, L.S.: Measurement of philosophies of human nature. Psychological Reports 14, 743–751 (1964)

Trust and Social Intelligence

Toshio Yamagishi

Department of Behavioral Science
Graduate School of Letters
Hokkaido University, Japan
Toshio@let.hokudai.ac.jp

Extended Abstract

One of the strongest expression of generalized distrust – i.e., distrust of human nature in general – can be found in a Japanese proverb, "Its best to regard everyone as a
thief" (*hito wo mitara dorobo to omoe*). An expression of the other extreme, generalized
trust, can also be found in another Japanese proverb, "you will never meet a devil as
you walk through the social world" (*wataru seken ni oni ha nai*). I asked about these
proverbs to hundreds of students in several colleges in Japan and found that the majority
of the respon-dents considered that those who believe the former proverb are smarter
(66% vs. 34%) and more likely to be successful in life (54% vs. 46%). They believed
that distrust means social shrewdness and trust means gullibility. The results of experimental and survey research, however, provide evidences contrary to this popular belief.
Based on these findings, I will present an argument that trust and social intelligence
co-evolve, and distrust and lack of social intelligence constitute a vicious cycle. On the
one hand, generalized distrust prevents people from engaging in further social interactions. Low-trusters are unwilling to enter into potentially beneficial but risky social
interactions because they focus on the risk side of such interactions. This unwillingness
of distrusters to engage in potentially beneficial but risky social interactions deters them
from correcting their depressed level of trust. At the same time, their unwillingness to
engage in risky but potentially fruitful interactions prevents them from improving the
level of their social intelligence. The lack of social intelligence or social shrewdness, in
turn, makes them vulnerable in such risky but potentially fruitful interactions. This vulnerability will then have two consequences. First, the lack of social intelligence makes
them more gullible when they do in fact engage in such interactions. They will more
often have experiences of failure than success in such interactions, and they will further
learn to distrust others. Second, realizing this vulnerability, they will avoid engaging in
such interactions. By engaging in such social interactions, they learn to distrust. By not
engaging in such social interactions, they lose opportunities to learn social shrewdness
and improve their level of their social intelligence or the ability to understand own and
other peoples internal state, and use that understanding in social relations.

After reviewing the experimental and survey research findings supporting my claim
that high-trusters are more socially intelligent than distrusters, Ill present an argument
that the level of general trust reflects, both at the individual level and societal level, the
overall level of opportunity costs for staying in the relatively stable and secure social
relations in which untrustworthy behaviors are well controlled. We can make sense of

I. Wakeman et al. (Eds.): IFIPTM 2011, IFIP AICT 358, pp. 17–18, 2011.

these findings in terms of two general strategies to deal with social uncertainty and opportunity costs: opportunity seeking versus security seeking. Opportunity seekers look outside stable and secure relations and invest cognitive resources in developing the ability to predict other peoples behavior in an open environment. Because they accrue social skills to deal with social risks, they can afford to maintain a high level of general trust and enter into risky but potentially profitable relations. Security seekers, on the other hand, pay opportunity costs in exchange for the security that stable relations provide and invest cognitive resources in assessing the nature of interpersonal relations. They are good at detecting who would be an allyand everyone else is regarded as a potential enemy. The characteristics of high-trusters (i.e., the correlations between general trust and the perceived need to cooperate with others, the sense of self-determination, and the lack of social risk avoidance) are indicative of opportunity seekers who leave the security of commitment relations to pursue better opportunities. Conversely, the characteristics of believers in the thief proverb (i.e., the lack of a perceived need for cooperation or a sense of self-determination, social risk avoidance, and the lack of social skills) are likely characteristics of individuals who prefer not to deal with people outside of their secure relations. Which strategy people adopt depends on the opportunities open to them. An opportunity-seeking strategy is more adaptive in a social environment in which staying in the stable and secure relations entail large opportunity costs, so the social-explorer type of social intelligence is more likely to prosper there. In contrast, a commitment-formation strategy is more adaptive in a social environment in which stable and secure relations do not entail large opportunity costs, so the commitment-former or security-seeker type of social intelligence will prosper there.

Detecting and Reacting to Changes in Reputation Flows

Sini Ruohomaa, Aleksi Hankalahti, and Lea Kutvonen

University of Helsinki, Finland
sini.ruohomaa@cs.helsinki.fi,
http://cinco.cs.helsinki.fi/

Abstract. In inter-enterprise collaboration, autonomic services from different organizations must independently determine which other services they can rely on. Reputation-based trust management in the Pilarcos open service ecosystem combines shared experience information on the actors' past behaviour and the decision context to estimate the risks of a collaboration. The trust decision process is semi-automatic, with selected decisions forwarded to a human user. A particularly interesting feature of the decision process is incongruity, that is, unexpected changes in service performance. In the classical example, a previously well-behaved service turns malicious to cash in its good reputation as ill-gained monetary profit. If the reputation system swiftly reacts to such changes, it protects its user more efficiently and deters misbehaviour. We present a new model for detecting and reacting to incongruities in a reputation-based trust management system. The model is based on the concept of reputation epochs, dividing an actor's reputation into periods of internally consistent behaviour. In contrast to earlier approaches, this model provides the necessary flexibility for the trust management system to adjust to constantly changing business situations.

1 Introduction

In inter-enterprise collaboration, services from different organizational domains join together to fulfil a mutual goal. In the open service ecosystem, the services are autonomous and there is no centralized control on the collaboration process. Each service must independently determine which other services it can rely on, both in the sense of making its own resources available, and in expecting that the other collaborators do their part in realizing the joint goal. To support these decisions, it collects experience information on the past performance of other services, both first-hand and shared by other actors in the ecosystem. This experience information forms the reputation of a service. Due to the decentralized nature of open service ecosystems, reputation is subjective to the actor who has collected and analyzed the information; it is not globally agreed upon by all.

Reputation-based trust management supports making trust decisions on different services, in the context of a given collaboration and possibly a specific set of transactions within it. The decision process consists of two parts [6]: First,

I. Wakeman et al. (Eds.): IFIPTM 2011, IFIP AICT 358, pp. 19–34, 2011.

reputation information is combined with a model of the decision context in order to estimate the risks of a positive decision. Second, this estimate is compared to a risk tolerance policy for the particular type of decision in order to determine the outcome: yes, proceed; no, withdraw; or, if the result falls on a gray area between the two, forward the decision to a human user.

A semi-automatic decision process is necessary due to the complex and constantly changing business environment. Automation is perfect for handling routine cases, which we expect to form the majority of decisions. Unforeseen situations and uncertainty, on the other hand, cannot be comprehensively dealt with by exact rules, and are left for a human user to resolve. Due to this division, the trust management system must be able to detect when a decision is not routine.

Incongruities, i.e. sudden changes in service performance, are a challenge for the automated decision process. In the classical example, a previously well-behaved service turns malicious to cash in its good reputation as ill-gained monetary profit. As reputation largely depends on shared experiences, information sources can also change their behaviour, and begin to spread misinformation.

We require a reputation system to swiftly react to such changes, both to limit the losses of the decision-maker service, and to discourage misbehaviour by minimizing the gains from it. At the same time, an honest actor's reputation should not be irreparably tarnished due to a momentary outage or dishonest negative feedback. These conflicting requirements are impossible to meet with a single universal, or fixed, set of rules; instead, reputation-based trust management systems must have support for appropriately handling incongruity through policies that can be configured — and re-configured — according to the business situation.

This paper presents a new model for detecting and reacting to incongruities in a reputation-based trust management system. We build on our existing Pilarcos trust management system, presented in earlier work [7]. Our model separates reputation analysis policies from trust decision policies in order to be able to use the same reputation information in a variety of decision-making contexts. Similarly, we separate the detection of behaviour changes from how their existence should affect upcoming trust decisions.

The model is based on the novel concept of *reputation epochs*, periods of internally consistent behaviour. A detected change in the behaviour pattern causes a change of reputation epoch. To illustrate the concept, we compare a few simple algorithms for identifying a pattern and detecting when it is broken. For this, we draw inspiration from the field of anomaly detection. The power of the concept goes beyond our examples, however, and it provides unprecedented flexibility for handling incongruity in reputation evolution.

The paper is organized as follows: Section 2 presents the problem context and related work, Section 3 presents reputation epochs, and evaluates the costs and benefits of introducing them. Section 4 presents three example epoch detection policies for use in three different scenarios, and Section 5 presents simulation results on how the policies behave in practice for each scenario. Section 6 concludes the paper.

2   Background

In this section, we first introduce the context in which we utilize reputation flows to for trust management in Pilarcos. We then present related work on the topic of adjusting to changes and uncertainty in reputation flows, and relate our proposal to the existing research.

2.1   Reputation-Based Trust Management in Pilarcos

The reputation-based trust management system we propose has been implemented as a part of the Pilarcos open service ecosystem [5]. Besides trust management, the Pilarcos collaboration management tools provide automated support for setting up collaborations, including interoperability checking and contract negotiation, and runtime monitoring, including contract breach detection and recovery. For signing contracts, actors are required to have persistent identities.

The trust management process can be divided into two parts: the trust decisions, and the evolution process of the reputation information. Both are governed by their own, separate policies; this separation is necessary in order to be able to use the once-collected reputation information in different decision contexts.

A trust decision is triggered at specific points of the collaboration process, whenever resources are being committed and risk evaluation is needed. To evaluate the risk of proceeding with the collaboration, we predict the outcome it would have on different assets based on previous experiences, stored in reputation information [6]. For the purposes of this paper, we only consider the effects on the monetary asset. These effects are divided into a scale of minor or major, positive or negative effects on the asset, no effect, and unknown effect for cases when the outcome cannot be observed for all assets.

To complete the trust decision, the risk estimate is compared to a risk tolerance policy, which essentially categorizes the risk into three options: acceptable (proceed with the collaboration), unacceptable (withdraw) or uncertain (forward the decision to a human user). The risk tolerance policy defines a minimum level of certainty required for an automated decision; certainty is influenced by a set of factors, measuring the amount and quality of reputation information used in the decision. A central measure of the quality of the information is its credibility — reputation based on local observations is ultimately credible, while the credibility of external reputation information varies [6,8].

The evolution of reputation information allows the system to adjust to changes in partner behaviour. New experiences from collaborations are stored into the system from two kinds of sources: a flow of first-hand experiences from local monitors, observing parameters such as quality of service and detecting any breaches of contract, and flows of external experiences, reported by other actors through reputation networks. A reputation network is the combination of a reputation system, defining the processes of dissemination, calculation and evolution of reputation scores, and the actors using it. We expect that third-party reputation information relevant to a specific service will be scattered over a number of different reputation networks. The local trust management system will merge the reputation information from different sources, taking into account how relevant it is and how credible the source is considered to be.

The epoch detection process we are proposing will take place after reputation flows from different networks have been analyzed and merged into a single external reputation flow, and compared to the flow of local experiences. The ordering is significant in that an epoch change must be based on credible information; errors should be minimized to avoid situations where outlier experiences trigger unnecessary epoch changes. An epoch change affects both local and external reputation streams simultaneously.

2.2   Related Work on Changes and Uncertainty in Reputation Flows

While there exists a notable body of research on reputation systems [8,2], the evolution of reputation remains a largely uncharted area. A typical approach to addressing changes in behaviour is time-based discounting of old experiences [2], which ensures that newer experiences gain a greater weight in decision-making. While this does mean that bad behaviour is reflected in the actor's reputation value somewhat faster, an increase in reaction speed also directly increases the speed in which old information is lost — and any old transgressions forgotten.

Simulation experiments, used for comparing reputation metrics (e.g. [10,4]), commonly assume consistent behaviour from both the well-behaved actors and any attackers. While it is quite reasonable to expect that an attacker intelligently adjusts its behaviour to the policies in place, the simulated attacker behaviour that we have observed so far is far from optimal. It is revealing that the most simple baseline attack against reputation systems, one where an attacker first gains reputation through good behaviour and then uses it up with bad behaviour, is dubbed the "disturbing" attacker model by Schlosser et al. [10]. The name reflects how poorly the compared systems could handle strategic changes in behaviour. Our proposal directly addresses this issue.

A promising example of related work, TrustGuard, proposes a reputation calculation formula which can react to incongruity [11]. In the model, decisions on a given actor are based on a trust value calculated as a weighted sum of three factors: 1) the current experiences, i.e. reports received in a given time period, 2) the (optionally weighted) average of accumulated experiences overall, and 3) a "derivative" of the current reports, representing whether there has been a recent change for the better or worse in the reported experiences.

The TrustGuard model is one-dimensional: it assumes the experience report values are real numbers between 0 and 1, and the result is a single real number. The Pilarcos model, in contrast, is multidimensional, with reputation represented as a vector of observed outcomes in relation to different assets and a set of certainty measures. In other words, the trust score alone does not fix the decision.

TrustGuard has no concept of certainty; the calculated trust value is the sole basis of a trust decision. The first factor represents the idea that current experiences should be emphasized in the decision. However, as other time-based discounting systems, it discounts all other information equally, independent of their information content or context. The second, accumulated average factor can emphasize the time-based discounting, or treat stored experiences equally. The derivative, on the other hand, could capture sudden changes in behaviour. The larger the change, the larger the derivative value. Given a high weight, the factor could speed up reaction to a current drastic change considerably. On the other hand, it would equally strongly reward any change for the better, partially overriding even the accumulated reputation or lack thereof. Information about past changes in behaviour is not retained.

A few other reputation systems introduce certainty measures for the resulting decision. For example REGRET [9] defines a certainty measure based on the amount of information used, the variation in experience values, the subjective confidence of the recommender in the information they give, and social relationships. If the certainty of the calculated reputation value is too low, the model includes an option for calculating reputation using different approaches, such as falling back from actor-specific experiences to the reputation of the social group the actor belongs to. The amount of information stored is tracked also by e.g. Travos [12]. SECURE, on the other hand, equates certainty with the particularity of information [1]: it defines trust values as ranges between 0 and 1, and the wider the range is, the less certainty there is, as it excludes fewer values as incorrect.

Pilarcos has a computational measure for the degree of certainty [7]. As a result, specific trust decisions can be identified as needing human attention. We can also take advantage of knowing how inconsistent an actor's behaviour has been in the past. If an actor changes its behaviour all the time without a discernible pattern, a reputation system should be able to detect that the information it has is insufficient for the task at hand — it cannot predict the unpredictable actor's future behaviour.

The option to selectively involve an external human actor based on certainty is generally not used in existing reputation systems, which are designed to either be fully autonomous or to only provide supporting information for a human decision-maker [8]. Even for a fully automated system, certainty could be used for activating further levels of computation, such as REGRET does. Indeed, it is natural to divide decision processes in partially supervised systems to multiple levels as well, with a human intervention as the last option if other attempts fail. We have discussed different levels of policy in earlier work [7].

3   Tracking Changes with Reputation Epochs

When analyzing experience and reputation information for decision-making, a central concern is whether the information is up-to-date, i.e. describes the current behaviour of the actor in question well enough to be useful in trying to predict its future behaviour. When faced with ten positive experiences and two negative, it can make quite a difference if the negative experiences are ancient and the actor's recent behaviour has been spotless, or if the good experiences are mostly older and the two negative are the most recent experiences available of the actor.

Whether it is possible to detect the order or timing of actions depends on the reputation information model. Storing the ordering of experiences sets heavy requirements on the way experiences are stored and processed: treating each experience as a unique object with a timestamp, or with a position in a queue of experience objects, creates large data structures, which take an increasing time to process as the number of experiences grows. While a theoretical model of reputation can accommodate for infinite amounts of experience information, practical models must adapt to time constraints at decision-making time: either information must be compressed, which loses information, or old experiences must be purged after a while.

We have chosen to compress experience items into outcome counters. The compression tradeoff loses timing information. The basic reputation data structure places equal weight to all experiences, independent of the time they were gathered. While it would be possible to discount old information through e.g. aging factors, we find that such methods in practice steadily lose information: they form a kind of fixed-size window to the past. The main problem with fixed windows, in turn, is that they cannot be easily adjusted at the time of the decision: data is already lost while it is gathered. For example, past transgressions can be completely erased from such systems by simply flooding the network with new experiences from low-value real transactions or false experiences produced by colluding partners.

Considered against the goal of reacting to changes in behaviour, we find that time is actually *not* the optimal measure for determining the weight or value of a unit of experience at all. Instead, we should measure whether the experience brings new information; something we did not already know.

We propose to divide reputation information into reputation epochs, groups of abstract periods of a given type of behaviour. While the latest turn of behaviour is the most interesting, it is also typical that there is very little experience on it; hence information from older epochs should also be included. The weight given to the current epoch determines the speed in which the system reacts to changes in behaviour. As an example, a pessimistic decision could even be based on the worst ever observed behaviour. The number of epochs also provides a measure of the consistency of the trustee: if experiences on the trustee are divided into a large and constantly increasing number of epochs, it indicates that the trustee's behaviour is not stable — or that it is not entirely fitting into any behavioural categories the system can detect.

While reputation epochs do allow us to give less weight to old information, they are superior to time-based constant discounting in two aspects: First, as epochs are based on behaviour changes rather than strict time periods, they fit the purpose of detecting when information is outdated in the sense of not being useful for predicting future behaviour. Second, the weighing policy between new and old information can be dynamically changed, and as no information is actually discarded, the oldest experiences remain available for later analysis: the reputation system can be configured to never forget anything without straining the time-constrained decision-making process.

We assume that the number of epochs will not grow without limit, and can therefore be processed in real time. It is also possible to set up epoch pruning processes that ensure the number of distinctly stored epochs remains under control. For example, if it turns out that an actor's behaviour regularly fluctuates between two types of epochs, older epochs can be regularly merged, as the fluctuations then actually represent a different type of consistent behaviour in the long term.

4   Detecting Changes in Service Performance

As a baseline risk tolerance policy, we will use a simple additive policy that gives more weight to negative than positive outcomes (by a factor of 3), and further weight on major effects as opposed to minor effects (another factor of 3) [7]. As an example, an actor with 10 experiences stored, of which 4 represent major positive outcomes, 2 minor positive, 2 minor negative and 1 major negative, would receive a *trust score* of $(4 * 3) + 2 + 2 * (-3) + 1 * (-3) * 3 = -1$. We set the trust score threshold for a positive decision to 0, so this would result in a negative decision. Changes in behaviour are then addressed through epoch change policies: for simplicity, our simulations will use only the current epoch to calculate this trust score.

In the general case, detecting changes between reputation epochs can be approached through the reasonably well-studied problem of anomaly detection [13]. Anomaly detection algorithms are often based on an example set of "normal" values learned from earlier data, which are used to form a model of normal behaviour; anything deviating from the model is then an anomaly.

In more specific cases, even quite simple epoch change policies can be suitable. We present two example policies to achieve two different goals:

Load balancing: A service provider usually provides good service, but occasionally the service quality varies depending on the number of incoming requests. The first example policy should quickly react to a drop in the quality of service, as it also indicates a need for load balancing.

Oscillation detection: A service provider oscillates between good and malicious behaviour: first it collects good reputation, then it cuts corners in as many service transactions as it can. Whenever there is a fixed decision policy in use that is known or can be deduced by experimenting, the optimal attacker targeting the reputation system will collect just enough positive reputation to not be shut out of the community, which makes this kind of behaviour relevant to address. The second example policy should quickly react to this kind of change for the worse, but also take advantage of the service returning to normality.

In the load balancing example, we apply a simple dynamically learning algorithm: a window of n previous experiences is stored by the epoch change detector, and whenever a new experience falls outside the values present in the existing filled window, a new epoch is created. As normal service quality is indicated by the vast majority of experiences, the window is typically filled with such experiences. At the first drop in reputation, a new epoch and a new, empty learning window are created. While the disturbance goes on, the window is filling up with negative (or less positive) experiences. During this learning phase, when the epoch contains less than n experiences, new epochs are not created. In our simulations in the following section, we set $n = 10$.

If the window (n) is set to be shorter than a typical disturbance, it will be full of negative experiences by the time the service returns to normal load, and a new epoch is started when the first positive experience arrives. This leads to a swift return to the service provider when it is no longer overloaded. For a more pessimistic, slow recovery, the window (n) can be chosen to be longer than a typical disturbance, which means that reputation is slowly regained within the newest epoch. Again, once the window fills up with normal experiences, the first sign of a negative experience causes a new epoch to be started. A limitation of this policy is that if the experiences indicating normal or overloaded states have some natural variation, new epochs may be created too easily.

In the oscillation detection example, the difference between good and malicious behaviour is simple to observe, as the experiences will be polarized: positive or negative. To allow greater variation in behaviour than the previous policy, we apply a static, specification-based epoch detection algorithm. We define two behaviour profiles: "good" and "evil". The good profile covers positive experiences, the evil profile negative. Neutral experiences, or those representing unknown outcomes, fall in neither category.

Given these profiles, we define each ongoing epoch to be either good or evil, and the epoch changes if an incoming experience matches the opposite profile rather than the current one. Neutral or unknown outcomes do not change the epoch, as they match neither. Again, the ongoing epoch can in principle be given full weight in decision-making. On the other hand, the attacker may respond by oscillating on every service request: cooperate, defect, cooperate, defect. To withstand this kind of behaviour, the number of epochs or the number of experiences in the current epoch should play a part in choosing a better weight division between the current and previous epochs, or indicate that the decision should really be delegated to a human user due to high uncertainty in the reputation information.

The two above policies perform at their best when the central source of reputation information is either first-hand experience, or a single highly credible reputation network. On the other hand, sometimes experiences on an actor are only available through a low-credibility reputation network, where there may be errors in the experience information — either intentional misinformation or due to e.g. differences in measurement standards. To cover this scenario, we extend the oscillation detection case above with an additional requirement:

Conservative oscillation detection: A potentially oscillating service provider is only known through a reputation network where some experience reports are incorrect. The third example policy should be cautious in trusting reputation information that is out of the ordinary, and treat it as an outlier unless it is backed up by additional information.

For this requirement, we apply the idea of sequential hypothesis testing [14], which can be used to limit the probability of overreacting in anomaly detection [3].

In sequential hypothesis testing, a single experience out of the ordinary does not yet change the epoch. It only strengthens the hypothesis that the epoch should be changed, by a constant measure i; we set $i = 1$ for the purposes of this text. Similarly, an experience supporting the current epoch weakens the hypothesis by 1. Again, neutral and unknown experiences cause no effect. For the epoch to change, either the change must amass support exceeding a given threshold k, or during a period of t consecutive experiences there must be more support for changing it than there has been for continuing the current epoch. For our experiments in the following section, we set $k = 5$ and $t = 10$.

Combined to the oscillation detection policy, we get the following algorithm:

```
% Initialize and reset support and timer variables to 0.
for each round:
  if experience and epoch match: % (both good / both evil)
    if timer == 0:
      skip to next round;
    else:
      support--;
  if experience and epoch mismatch: % (one good, one evil)
    support++;
  timer++;
  if support >= k:
    change_epoch();      % Overwhelming support for change.
    reset_variables();
  if support < 0:
    reset_variables();
  if timer >= t:
    if support > 0:
      change_epoch();    % Majority of t votes supports it.
    reset_variables();
```

Sequential hypothesis testing can be similarly combined to the window-based load balancing algorithm, to test the need to change epochs once the learning window has been filled. However, this modification alone will not stop outliers in incoming reputation information from being stored as examples of normal behaviour during the learning process. Therefore, the algorithm would remain vulnerable to any noise in reputation flows.

5   Comparison of Epoch Detection Policies

We illustrate the behaviour of the policies proposed in the previous section by applying them to four scenarios with different experience input. These reputation

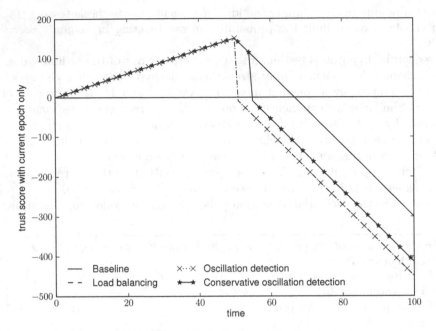

Fig. 1. Scenario 1: A change for the worse

flows are manually constructed to illustrate the kind of a situation each policy is designed to handle. For realistic applications, a combination of detection policies is likely to be better suited than any specialized single policy.

In the first scenario, a service behaves well (major positive experiences) for the first half of the time period, then misbehaves (major negative experiences) for the latter half; this situation could be caused e.g. by a service going permanently offline, getting hacked or otherwise becoming untrustworthy. For a traditional additive trust decision policy, its trust score (positives – negatives) would remain positive to the end of this simulation, the trusting service suffering considerable losses during that time. As discussed in the previous section, however, our baseline policy for comparison is already more strict: it gives more weight (x3) to negative than positive experiences. Our threshold for a positive trust decision is set to 0, i.e. when the calculated trust score drops below 0, trust decisions become negative.

The plots only follow the trust score calculated from the current epoch. As seen in Fig. 1 the two first epoch detection algorithms (Load balancing and Oscillation detection) react instantaneously to a change in behaviour; their trust scores are equal. The more conservative version of oscillation detection follows closely behind; the sequential hypothesis tester waits until 5 consecutive evidences of the change in behaviour have arrived, then triggers an epoch change. The baseline algorithm, on the other hand, patiently waits until the old good experiences are "used up" before turning negative. Even though it gives triple weight to negative experiences, it lags behind the epoch change policies in reaction speed (by 17 rounds).

In the second scenario, the monitored service generally behaves well (major positive experiences), but suffers two drops in service quality due to overload — at rounds 20 and 50, the flow outputs *minor* negative experiences to reflect e.g. a slow response time. The first disturbance lasts for 10 rounds, after which the service recovers. The second disturbance is less predictable, with two minor positive experiences arriving in the middle of it — in other words, the response time was reasonable, but the service had not actually recovered and was congested again soon after. The scenario is depicted in Fig. 2.

Using the baseline policy, the service has a positive trust score throughout the simulation. The weight on negative experiences is cancelled out due to their lesser impact: positive experiences are major, while the service quality drops produce minor negative experiences.

The epoch detection policies react quickly to the first outage; again, the Load balancing and Oscillation detection algorithms behave the same way for the first service quality drop, and immediately recover as service quality returns to normal. In the second disturbance, however, the 10-round-long learning window of the Load balancing policy is only filling up when the temporary recovery occurs, and it does not change epochs in the middle of its learning phase. On the other hand, the Oscillation detection algorithm reacts somewhat too quickly to the temporary change to positive. As before, the Conservative oscillation detection algorithm reacts with a delay while it accumulates evidence of the

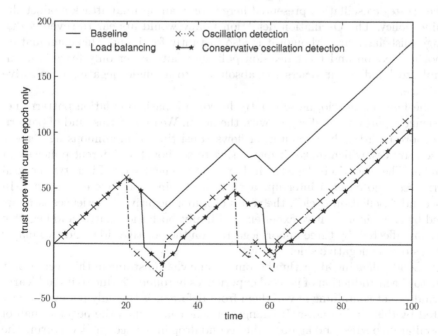

Fig. 2. Scenario 2: A need for load balancing

change; the inconsistency during the second disturbance simply delays its epoch change by two rounds.

The third scenario represents the "disturbing" behaviour pattern [10], an actor who oscillates between good and bad: the service collects just enough good reputation to not be shut out of the system when it denies service. This can also be interpreted as an opportunistic or "lazy" service provider who is ready to violate contracts to cut costs, but takes care to not burn up its reputation entirely. The length of the different oscillation phases is optimized for a given trust decision policy. In the case of our baseline policy, it behaves well 75% of the time (minor positive experiences), and misbehaves 25% of the time (minor negative experiences); as a result, its trust score is never negative with the baseline policy. This scenario is depicted in Fig. 3 on the next page.

The Oscillation detection and Load balancing algorithms react immediately to the first transgression. Their differences become apparent when the quality of service increases again: The policy optimized for regular oscillation changes the epoch in order to take advantage of the period of good service, up until the next disturbance. Meanwhile, due to the shortness of the period of low service quality (8 rounds), the Load balancing algorithm is still in its learning phase when the change for better occurs; it only changes epoch at the next drop in service quality. By then its window has filled with positive experiences (at round 56), and the current epoch's reputation has just climbed to zero, resulting in a mirror plot of the baseline policy. Finally, the Conservative oscillation detection algorithm's reactions are slightly delayed versions of those observed for the basic Oscillation detection.

The strategic oscillation presented here is only an optimal attack against the baseline policy. The Oscillation detection policy would appear to severely discourage misbehaviour, although it is also instantly forgiving. This combination of epoch detection and trust decision policies is altogether only feasible as an example to build on; it reacts too absolutely to a single negative or positive experience.

In the fourth scenario, noise is introduced to a basic oscillation pattern, i.e. experience reports which disagree with the norm. We expect this kind of pattern to be more realistic than reputation flows consisting of unanimous agreement between sources, which makes it interesting to see how the different policies can handle it. The scenario is depicted in Fig. 4 on the next page. First, two neutral experiences ("no effect") interrupt a pattern of minor positive experiences. In the second "oscillation cycle", the series of minor negative experiences is interrupted by two minor positive experiences. Finally, both the positive and negative halves are affected, by three minor negatives on the positive side, and two major positives on the negative side.

The Load balancing algorithm becomes somewhat unstable in this scenario. It reacts to the introduction of neutral experiences in round 12; due to its full learning window not containing any of them from before, it is the only policy strongly affected by this kind of noise. It changes epochs again when the negative half of the oscillation begins, and again at the second drop in service quality. During the

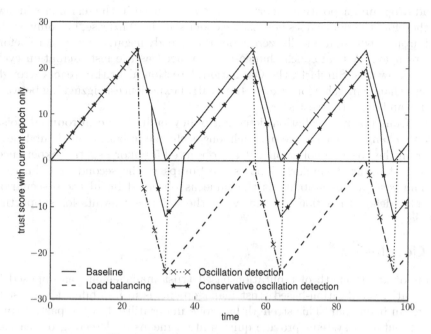

Fig. 3. Scenario 3: Oscillating behaviour

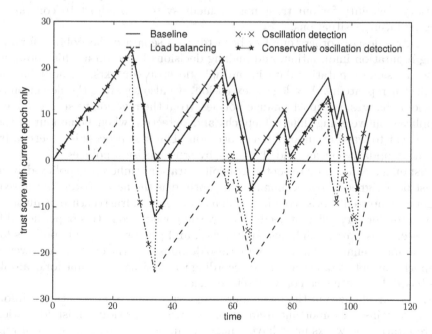

Fig. 4. Scenario 4: Oscillating behaviour with noise

second drop, minor positive experiences are introduced in the learning window, and therefore the policy does not change epochs at the third rise, but only at the third drop — which, ironically, zeroes out the already negative trust score before it drops again. A final epoch change is introduced as the last oscillation cycle turns downwards. Similarly, the Oscillation detection algorithm reacts strongly to every change in behaviour except the neutral experiences, zigzagging between positive and negative trust scores.

The Conservative oscillation detection policy endures the introduced noise, and only changes epochs once per each longer change in behaviour. It first deviates from the baseline policy once it has observed 5 minor negative experiences in the first cycle; it similarly ignores the bumps in the second and third cycle. The cost of this stability is the same as observed in all these scenarios: a slightly delayed reaction to changes, as the algorithm awaits for supporting evidence.

6   Conclusion

An important strength of reputation-based trust management, as opposed to more static, certification-based trust management, is in its ability to adjust to changes in behaviour. This strength has gone underutilized in the past, as proposed reputation systems provide quite limited means of detecting or reacting to incongruity in reputation information.

In contrast, the epoch-aware reputation model we have proposed provides the necessary flexibility for our trust management system to adjust to constantly changing business situations.

A central design cornerstone has been to keep separate the policies for updating reputation information, and making decisions based on it: this allows us to use the same reputation data in multiple decision contexts, without having to collect it repeatedly. As a logical extension, we also separate the detection of behaviour changes, i.e. epoch change policies, from the reaction to such changes, i.e. policies on weighing different epochs and detecting when behaviour is too inconsistent to warrant an automated decision. The first process is governed by reputation update policies, and the latter by trust decision policies.

Trust management for inter-enterprise collaboration is inherently policy-driven; it must be designed to be reconfigured at runtime as the need arises. As Pilarcos is a general inter-enterprise collaboration management infrastructure, it must be able to cater for very different needs. We have demonstrated in this paper how different scenarios warrant different approaches, and proposed suitable policies for four example scenarios. These scenarios also demonstrate the expressive power of the epoch concept; it can be adjusted according to the situation, while for example time-based discounting can only be set up once.

Addressing changes in the behaviour of external sources of reputation information remains an important item of future work. Spreading misinformation into reputation networks must have a negative impact on the source's own reputation. To fulfil this requirement, we are currently researching contractually governed reputation systems based on objective, verifiable experiences.

Acknowledgements

This work has been performed in the CINCO group at University of Helsinki. We thank the anonymous reviewers for their encouraging and helpful comments on improving the manuscript.

References

1. Cahill, V., et al.: Using trust for secure collaboration in uncertain environments. Pervasive Computing 2(3), 52–61 (2003),
http://ieeexplore.ieee.org/iel5/7756/27556/01228527.pdf
2. Jøsang, A., Ismail, R., Boyd, C.: A survey of trust and reputation systems for online service provision. Decision Support Systems: Emerging Issues in Collaborative Commerce 43(2), 618–644 (2007),
http://dx.doi.org/10.1016/j.dss.2005.05.019
3. Jung, J., Paxson, V., Berger, A.W., Balakrishnan, H.: Fast portscan detection using sequential hypothesis testing. In: Proceedings of the IEEE Symposium on Security and Privacy, pp. 211–225 (2004),
http://dx.doi.org/10.1109/SECPRI.2004.1301325
4. Kinateder, M., Baschny, E., Rothermel, K.: Towards a generic trust model – comparison of various trust update algorithms. In: Herrmann, P., Issarny, V., Shiu, S. (eds.) iTrust 2005. LNCS, vol. 3477, pp. 177–192. Springer, Heidelberg (2005),
http://dx.doi.org/10.1007/11429760_13
5. Kutvonen, L., Ruokolainen, T., Ruohomaa, S., Metso, J.: Service-oriented middleware for managing inter-enterprise collaborations. In: Global Implications of Modern Enterprise Information Systems: Technologies and Applications. Advances in Enterprise Information Systems (AEIS), pp. 209–241. IGI Global (December 2008),
http://www.igi-global.com/reference/details.asp?id=9648
6. Ruohomaa, S., Kutvonen, L.: Making multi-dimensional trust decisions on inter-enterprise collaborations. In: Proceedings of the Third International Conference on Availability, Security and Reliability (ARES 2008), pp. 873–880. IEEE Computer Society, Barcelona, Spain (March 2008),
http://dx.doi.org/10.1109/ARES.2007.123
7. Ruohomaa, S., Kutvonen, L.: Trust and distrust in adaptive inter-enterprise collaboration management. Journal of Theoretical and Applied Electronic Commerce Research 5(2), 118–136 (2010),
http://www.jtaer.com/aug2010/ruohomaa_kutvonen_p7.pdf
8. Ruohomaa, S., Kutvonen, L., Koutrouli, E.: Reputation management survey. In: Proceedings of the 2nd International Conference on Availability, Reliability and Security (ARES 2007), pp. 103–111. IEEE Computer Society, Vienna, Austria (2007), http://dx.doi.org/10.1109/ARES.2007.123
9. Sabater, J., Sierra, C.: Reputation and social network analysis in multi-agent systems. In: AAMAS 2002: Proceedings of the First International Joint Conference on Autonomous Agents and MultiAgent Systems, Bologna, Italy, pp. 475–482 (2002),
http://doi.acm.org/10.1145/544741.544854
10. Schlosser, A., Voss, M., Brückner, L.: On the simulation of global reputation systems. Journal of Artificial Societies and Social Simulation 9(1) (January 2006),
http://jasss.soc.surrey.ac.uk/9/1/4/4.pdf

11. Srivatsa, M., Xiong, L., Liu, L.: TrustGuard: countering vulnerabilities in reputation management for decentralized overlay networks. In: WWW '05: Proceedings of the 14th International Conference on the World Wide Web, pp. 422–431. ACM Press, New York (2005), http://doi.acm.org/10.1145/1060745.1060808
12. Teacy, W.T.L., Patel, J., Jennings, N.R., Luck, M.: TRAVOS: Trust and reputation in the context of inaccurate reputation sources. Autonomous Agents and Multi-agent Systems 12(2), 183–198 (2006),
   http://dx.doi.org/10.1007/s10458-006-5952-x
13. Viljanen, L.: A survey on application level intrusion detection. Tech. rep., University of Helsinki, Department of Computer Science (2005)
14. Wald, A.: Sequential tests of statistical hypotheses. The Annals of Mathematical Statistics 16(2), 117–186 (1945),
   http://dx.doi.org/10.1214%2Faoms%2F1177731118

Validation and Verification of Agent Models for Trust: Independent Compared to Relative Trust

Mark Hoogendoorn[1], S. Waqar Jaffry[1], and Peter-Paul van Maanen[1,2]

[1] VU University Amsterdam, Department of Artificial Intelligence,
De Boelelaan 1081a, 1081 HV Amsterdam, The Netherlands
{mhoogen,swjaffry}@cs.vu.nl
[2] TNO Human Factors, Department of Cognitive Systems Engineering,
P.O. Box 23, 3769 ZG Soesterberg, The Netherlands
peter-paul.vanmaanen@tno.nl

Abstract. In this paper, the results of a validation experiment for two existing computational trust models describing human trust are reported. One model uses experiences of performance in order to estimate the trust in different trustees. The second model in addition carries the notion of relative trust. The idea of relative trust is that trust in a certain trustee not solely depends on the experiences with that trustee, but also on trustees that are considered competitors of that trustee. In order to validate the models, parameter adaptation has been used to tailor the models towards human behavior. A comparison between the two models has also been made to see whether the notion of relative trust describes human trust behavior in a more accurate way. The results show that taking trust relativity into account indeed leads to a higher accuracy of the trust model. Finally, a number of assumptions underlying the two models are verified using an automated verification tool.

1 Introduction

When considering relations and interaction between agents, the concept of trust is of utmost importance. Within the domain of multi-agent systems, the concept of trust has been a topic of research for many years (e.g., [14,13]). Within this research, the development of models expressing how agents form trust based upon direct experiences with a trustee or information obtained from parties other than the trustee is one of the central themes. Some of these models aim at creating trust models that can be utilized effectively within a software agent environment (e.g., [11]), whereas other models aim to present an accurate model of human trust (e.g., [10,3,6]). The latter type of model can be very useful when developing a personal assistant agent for a human with the awareness of the human's trust in different other agents (human or computer) and him- or herself (trustees). This could for example avoid advising to use particular information sources that are not trusted by the human or could be used to enhance the trust relationship with the personal assistant agent itself.

In order for computational trust models to be usable in real life settings, the validity of these models should be proven first. However, relatively few experiments have been performed that validate the accuracy of computational trust models upon empirical data.

I. Wakeman et al. (Eds.): IFIPTM 2011, IFIP AICT 358, pp. 35–50, 2011.
© IFIP International Federation for Information Processing 2011

For instance, in [9] an experiment has been conducted whereby the trends in human trust behavior have been analyzed to verify properties underlying trust models developed in the domain of multi-agent systems. However, no attempt was made to fit the model to the trusting behavior of the human.

In this paper, the results of a validation experiment for two computational trust models describing human trust are reported. A trust model taken from [11], which was inspired on the trust model described in [10], has been taken as a baseline model. This model uses experiences of performance in order to estimate the trust in different trustees and is an influential model in the domain of agent systems. The second model which is validated in this study is a model which also carries the notion of relative trust [6]. The idea of relative trust is that trust in a certain trustee not solely depends on the experiences with that trustee, but also with trustees that are considered competitors of that trustee. A comparison between the two models is also made to see whether the notion of relative trust describes human trust behavior in a more accurate way.

The validation process includes a number of steps. First, an experiment with participants has been performed in which trust plays an important role. As a result, empirical data has been obtained, that is usable for validating the two models. One part of the dataset is used to learn the best parameters for the two different trust models. Then these parameters are used to estimate human trust, using the same input as was used to generate the other part of the dataset. Finally, a number of assumptions underlying the two trust models are verified upon the obtained dataset using an automated verification tool. These assumptions are useful to verify whether the humans indeed exhibit the patterns that are used as a basis for the development of trust models.

This paper is organized as follows. First, the two trust models that have been used in this study are explained in Section 2. The experimental method is explained in Section 3. Thereafter, the results of the experiment in terms of model validation and verification are described in Section 4. Finally, Section 5 is a discussion.

2   Agent Models for Trust

In this section the two types of trust models which are subject of validation are described. In Section 2.1 a model is explained that estimates human trust in one trustee independent of the trust in other trustees. In contrast, in Section 2.2 a model is described for which this relative dependency actually is important.

2.1   Independent Trust Model

This section describes the independent trust model [11,10]. In this model trustees are considered rational and are therefore thought of having no bias to calculate trust. Trust is based on experiences and there is a certain decay of trust.

For the present study, it is assumed that a set of trustees $\{S_1, S_2, \ldots, S_n\}$ is available that can be selected to give particular advice at each time step. Upon selection of one of the trustees (S_i), an experience is passed back indicating how well the trustee performed. This experience ($E_i(t)$) is a number on the interval $[-1, 1]$. Hereby, -1 expresses a negative experience, 0 is a neutral experience and 1 a positive experience. There is also a decay parameter λ_i in the model, for which holds that $0 \leq \lambda_i \leq 1$.

Given the above, trust now can calculated by means of the following formula:

$$T_i(t) = T_i(t-1) \cdot \lambda_i + \left(1 - \left(\frac{E_i(t)+1}{2}\right)\right) \cdot (1 - \lambda_i)$$

The independent trust is calculated for each trustee. Note that the experience is mapped to the domain $[0,1]$ in this equation. Eventual reliance decisions are made by determining the maximum of the independent trust over all trustees. For more details on the rationale behing the formula, see [11,10].

2.2   Relative Trust Model

This section describes the relative trust model [6]. In this model trustees are considered competitors, and the human trust in a trustee depends on the relative experiences with the trustee to the experiences from the other trustees. The model defines the total trust of the human as the difference between positive trust and negative trust (distrust) on the trustee. The model includes several parameters representing human characteristics including trust flexibility β_i (measuring the change in trust on each new experience), decay γ_i (decay in trust when there is no experience) and autonomy η_i (dependence of the trust calculation considering other options). The model parameters β_i, γ_i and η_i have values from the interval $[0,1]$.

As mentioned before, the model is composed of two models: one for positive trust, accumulating positive experiences, and one for negative trust, accumulating negative experiences. Both negative and positive trust are represented by a number between $[0,1]$. The human's total trust $T_i(t)$ in S_i is the difference in positive and negative trust in S_i at time point t, which is a number between $[-1,1]$, where -1 and 1 represent the minimum and maximum values of trust, respectively. The human's initial total trust in S_i at time point 0 is $T_i(0)$, which is the difference in initial trust $T_i^+(0)$ and distrust $T_i^-(0)$ in S_i at time point 0.

As a differential equation the change in positive and negative trust over time is described in the following manner [8]:

$$\frac{dT_i^+(t)}{dt} = E_i(t) \cdot \frac{(E_i(t)+1)}{2} \cdot \beta_i \cdot$$
$$\left(\eta_i \cdot (1 - T_i^+(t)) + (1 - \eta_i) \cdot \right.$$
$$\left. (\tau_i^+(t) - 1) \cdot T_i^+(t) \cdot (1 - T_i^+(t))\right) -$$
$$\gamma_i \cdot T_i^+(t) \cdot (1 + E_i(t)) \cdot (1 - E_i(t))$$

$$\frac{dT_i^-(t)}{dt} = E_i(t) \cdot \frac{(E_i(t)-1)}{2} \cdot \beta_i \cdot$$
$$\left(\eta_i \cdot (1 - T_i^-(t)) + (1 - \eta_i) \cdot \right.$$
$$\left. (\tau_i^-(t) - 1) \cdot T_i^-(t) \cdot (1 - T_i^-(t))\right) -$$
$$\gamma_i \cdot T_i^-(t) \cdot (1 + E_i(t)) \cdot (1 - E_i(t))$$

In these equations, $E_i(t)$ is the experience value given by S_i at time point t.

Furthermore, $\tau_i^+(t)$ and $\tau_i^-(t)$ are the human's relative positive and negative trust in S_i at time point t, which is the ratio of the human's positive or negative trust in S_i to the average human's positive or negative trust in all trustees at time point t defined as follows:

$$\tau_i^+(t) = \frac{T_i^+(t)}{\left(\dfrac{\sum_{j=1}^n T_j^+(t)}{n}\right)}$$

and

$$\tau_i^-(t) = \frac{T_i^-(t)}{\left(\dfrac{\sum_{j=1}^n T_j^-(t)}{n}\right)}$$

Finally, the total change in trust can be calculated as follows (using which the new trust value can easily be calculated):

$$\frac{dT_i(t)}{dt} = \frac{dT_i^+(t)}{dt} - \frac{dT_i^-(t)}{dt}$$

Similarly as for the independent trust model, the trustee with the highest trust value is relied upon.

3 Method

In this section the experimental methodology is explained. In Section 3.1 the partici- pants are described. In Section 3.2 an overview of the used experimental environment is given. Thereafter, the procedure of the experiment is explained in four stages: In Sections 3.3, 3.4, 3.5 and 3.6, the procedures of data collection, parameter adaptation, model validation and verification are explained, respectively. The results of the experi- ment are given in Section 4.

3.1 Participants

18 Participants (eight male and ten female) with an average age of 23 ($SD = 3.8$) were found to be willing to participate in the experiment as paid volunteers. Non-color blinded participants were selected. All were experienced computer users, with an aver- age of 16.2 hours of computer usage each week ($SD = 9.32$).

3.2 Task

The experimental task was a classification task in which two participants on two sep- arate personal computers had to classify geographical areas according to specific cri- teria as areas that either needed to be attacked, helped or left alone by ground troops. The participants needed to base their classification on real-time computer generated video images that resembled video footage of real unmanned aerial vehicles (UAVs). On the camera images, multiple objects were shown. There were four kinds of objects:

civilians, rebels, tanks and cars. The identification of the number of each of these object types was needed to perform the classification. Each object type had a score (either -2, -1, 0, 1 or 2, respectively) and the total score within an area had be determined. Based on this total score the participants could classify a geographical area (i.e., attack when above 2, help when below -2 or do nothing when in between). Participants had to classify two areas at the same time and in total 98 areas had to be classified. Both participants did the same areas with the same UAV video footage.

During the time a UAV flew over an area, three phases occurred: The first phase was the advice phase. In this phase both participants and a supporting software agent gave an advice about the proper classification (attack, help, or do nothing). This means that there were three advices at the end of this phase. It was also possible for the participants to refrain from giving an advice, but this hardly occurred. The second phase was the reliance phase. In this phase the advices of both the participants and that of the supporting software agent were communicated to each participant. Based on these advices the participants had to indicate which advice, and therefore which of the three trustees (self, other or software agent), they trusted the most. Participants were instructed to maximize the number of correct classifications at both phases (i.e., advice and reliance phase). The third phase was the feedback phase, in which the correct answer was given to both participants. Based on this feedback the participants could update their internal trust models for each trustee (self, other, software agent).

In Figure 1 the interface of the task is shown. The map is divided in 10×10 areas. These boxes are the areas that were classified. The first UAV starts in the top left corner and the second one left in the middle. The UAVs fly a predefined route so participants do not have to pay attention to navigation. The camera footage of the upper UAV is positioned top right and the other one bottom right.

The advice of the self, other and the software agent was communicated via dedicated boxes below the camera images. The advice to attack, help, or do nothing was communicated by red, green and yellow, respectively. On the overview screen on the left, feedback was communicated by the appearance of a green tick or a red cross. The

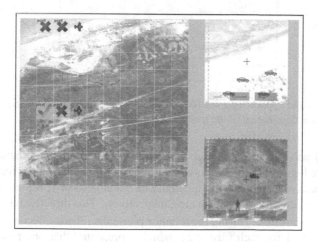

Fig. 1. Interface of the task

reliance decision of the participant is also shown on the overview screen behind the feedback (feedback only shown in the feedback phase). The phase depicted in Figure 1 was the reliance phase before the participant indicated his reliance decision.

3.3 Data Collection

During the above described experiment, input and output were logged using a server-client application. The interface of this application is shown in Figure 2. Two other client machines, that were responsible for executing the task as described in the previous subsection, were able to connect via a local area network to the server, which was responsible for logging all data and communication between the clients. The interface shown in Figure 2 could be used to set the client's IP-addresses and ports, as well as several experimental settings, such as how to log the data. In total the experiment lasted approximately 15 minutes per participant.

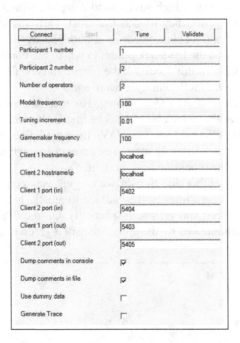

Fig. 2. Interface of the application used for gathering validation data (Connect), for parameter adaptation (Tune) and validation of the trust models (Validate)

Experienced performance feedback of each trustee and reliance decisions of each participant were logged in temporal order for later analysis. During the feedback phase the given feedback was translated to a penalty of either 0, .5 or 1, representing a good, neutral or poor experience of performance, respectively. This directly maps to the value $\frac{E_i(t)+1}{2}$ in the trust models. During the reliance phase the reliance decisions were translated to either 0 or 1 for each trustee S_i, which represented that one relied or did not rely on S_i.

3.4   Parameter Adaptation

The data collection described in Section 3.3 was repeated twice on each group of two participants, called condition 1 and condition 2, respectively. The data from one of the conditions was used for parameter adaptation purposes for both models, and the data from the other condition for model validation (see Section 3.5). This process of parameter adaptation and validation was balanced over conditions, which means that condition 1 and condition 2 switch roles, so condition 1 is initially used for parameter adaptation and condition 2 for model validation, and thereafter condition 2 is used for paramter adaptation and condition 1 for model validation (i.e. cross-validation). Both the parameter adaptation and model validation procedure was done using the same application as was used for gathering the empirical data. The interface shown in Figure 2 could also be used to alter validation and adaptation settings, such as the granularity of the adaptation.

The number of parameters of the models presented in Section 2 to be adapted for each model and each participant suggest that an exhaustive search [8] for the optimal parameters is feasible. This means that the entire parameter search space is explored to find a vector of parameter settings resulting in the maximum accuracy (i.e., the amount of overlap between the model's predicted reliance decisions and the actual human reliance decisions) for each of the models and each participant. The corresponding code of the implemented exhaustive search method is shown in Algorithm 1.

Algorithm 1. ES-PARAMETER-ADAPTATION(E, R_H)

---

1. $\delta_{\text{best}} \leftarrow \infty$
2. $X \leftarrow 0$
3. **for all** parameters x in parameter vector X **do**
4.   **for all** settings of x **do**
5. $\delta_X \leftarrow 0$
6.   **for all** time points t **do**
7. $e \leftarrow E(t)$
8. $r_M \leftarrow R_M(e, X)$
9. $r_H \leftarrow R_H(e)$
10.   **if** $r_M \neq r_H$ **then**
11. $\delta_X \leftarrow \delta_X + 1$
12.   **end if**
13.   **end for**
14.   **if** $\delta_X < \delta_{\text{best}}$ **then**
15. $X_{\text{best}} \leftarrow X$
16. $\delta_{\text{best}} \leftarrow \delta_X$
17.   **end if**
18.   **end for**
19. **end for**
20. **return** X_{best}

In this algorithm, $E(t)$ is the set of experiences (i.e., performance feedback) at time point t for all trustees, $R_H(e)$ is the actual reliance decision the participant made (on either one of the trustees) given a certain experience e, $R_M(e, X)$ is the predicted reliance decision of the trust model M (either independent or relative) given an experience e and candidate parameter vector X (reliance on either one of the trustees), δ_X is the distance between the estimated and actual reliance decisions given a certain candidate parameter vector X, δ_{best} is the distance resulting from the best parameter vector X_{best} found so far. The best parameter vector X_{best} is returned when the algorithm finishes. This parameter adaptation procedure was implemented in C#.

If for Algorithm 1 the number of parameters is μ, Γ the granularity for each parameter, N the number of trustees and B the number of reliance decisions (i.e., time points) made by the human, then the worst case complexity of the algorithm is expressed as $O(10^{\mu\Gamma}BN)$. The complexity also depends on N, since $R_M(e, X)$ results in a calculation of trust values over all trustees. For the independent trust model it holds that $\mu = 1$ (i.e., the parameter λ_i) and for the relative trust model $\mu = 3$ (i.e., the three parameters β_i, γ_i and η_i). In the current experiment it furthermore holds that $\Gamma = 2$ (i.e., steps of .01), $N = 3$ (the two humans and the software agent) and $B = 98$ (the total of classified geographical areas). This means that $2.94 \cdot 10^4$ computation steps are needed for the independent trust model and $2.94 \cdot 10^8$ for the relative trust model, which took on average 31 milliseconds for the first, and 3 minutes and 20 seconds computation time for the second model.[1]

3.5   Validation

In order to validate the two models described in Section 2, the measurements of experienced performance feedback were used as input for the models and the output (predicted reliance decisions) of the models was compared with the the actual reliance decisions of the participant. The overlap of the predicted and the actual reliance decisions was a measure for the accuracy of the models. The results are in the form of dynamic accuracies over time, average accuracy per condition (1 or 2) and per trust model (independent or relative). A comparison between the averages per model and the interaction effect between condition role allocation (i.e., parameter adaptation either in condition 1 or 2) and model type, is done using a repeated measures analysis of variance (ANOVA).

3.6   Verification

Next to a validation using the accuracy of the prediction using the models, another approach has been used to validate the assumptions underlying existing trust models. The idea is that properties that form the basis of trust models are verified against the empirical results obtained within the experiment. In order to conduct such an automated verification, the properties have been specified in a language called Temporal Trace Language (TTL) [1] that features a dedicated editor and an automated checker. The language TTL is explained first, followed by an expression of the desired properties related to trust.

---

[1] This was on an ordinary PC with an Intel(R) Core(TM)2 Quad CPU @2.40 GHz inside. Note that $31 \cdot \frac{2.94 \cdot 10^8}{2.94 \cdot 10^4}$ milliseconds $= 5.17$ minutes $\neq 3.33$ minutes computation time. This is due to a fixed initialization time of on average 11 ms for both models.

Temporal Trace Language (TTL). The predicate logical temporal language TTL supports formal specification and analysis of dynamic properties, covering both qualitative and quantitative aspects. TTL is built on atoms referring to states of the world, time points and traces, i.e., trajectories of states over time. In addition, dynamic properties are temporal statements that can be formulated with respect to traces based on the state ontology Ont in the following manner. Given a trace γ over state ontology Ont, the state in γ at time point t is denoted by state(γ, t). These states can be related to state properties via the formally defined satisfaction relation denoted by the infix predicate $\models$, i.e., state$(\gamma, t) \models p$ denotes that state property p holds in trace γ at time t. Based on these statements, dynamic properties can be formulated in a formal manner in a sorted first-order predicate logic, using quantifiers over time and traces and the usual first-order logical connectives such as $\neg$, $\wedge$, $\vee$, $\Rightarrow$, $\forall$ and $\exists$. For more details on TTL, see [1].

Properties for Trust Models. Within the literature on trust, a variety of properties have been expressed concerning the desired behavior of trust models. In many of these properties, the trust values are explicitly referred to, for instance in the work of [10] characteristics of trust models have been defined (e.g., monotonicity and positive trust extension upon positive experiences). In this paper however, the trust function is subject of validation and hence, cannot be taken as a basis. Therefore, properties are expressed on an external basis, solely using the information which has been observed within the experiment to see whether these behaviors indeed comply to the desired behavior of the trust models. This information is then limited to the experiences that are received as an input and the choices that are made by the human that are generated as output. The properties from [7] are taken as a basis for these properties. Essentially, the properties indicate the following desired behavior of human trust:

1. Positive experiences lead to higher trust
2. Negative experiences lead to lower trust
3. Most trusted trustee is selected

As can be seen, the properties also use the intermediate state of trust. In order to avoid this, it is however possible to combine these properties into a single property that expresses a relation between the experiences and the selection (i.e., the above items 1 + 3 and 2 + 3). Two of these properties are shown below. In addition, a property is expressed which specifies the notion of relativity in the experiences and the resulting selection of a trustee. The first property expresses that a trustee that gives the absolute best experiences during a certain period is eventually selected at least once within, or just after that particular period, and is shown below.

P1(min_duration, max_duration, max_time): Absolute more positive experiences results in selection
If a trustee a_1 always gives more positive experiences than all other trustees during a certain period with minimal duration min_duration and maximum duration max_duration, then this trustee a_1 is selected at least once during the period [min_duration, max_duration + max_time].

Formal:

P1(min_duration:DURATION, max_duration:DURATION, max_delay:DURATION) $\equiv$
$\forall\gamma$:TRACE, t_{start}, t_{end}:TIME, a:TRUSTEE
[[$t_{end} - t_{start} \geq$ min_duration & $t_{end} - t_{start} \leq$ max_duration &
absolute_highest_experiences(γ, a, t_{start}, t_{end})
$\Rightarrow$ selected(γ, a, t_{start}, t_{end}, max_delay)

where

absolute_highest_experiences(γ:TRACE, a:TRUSTEE, t_{start}:TIME, t_{end}:TIME) $\equiv$
$\forall t$:TIME, r_1, r_2:REAL, a_2:TRUSTEE $\neq a$
[[$t \geq t_{start}$ & t $< t_{end}$ & state(γ, t) $\models$ trustee_gives_experience(a, r_1) &
state(γ, t) $\models$ trustee_gives_experience(a_2, r_2)] $\Rightarrow r_2 < r_1$]

selected(γ:TRACE, a:TRUSTEE, t_{start}:TIME, t_{end}:TIME, z:DURATION) $\equiv$
$\exists t$:TIME [$t \geq t_{start}$ & t $< t_{end} + z$ & state(γ, t) $\models$ trustee_selected(a)]

The second property, P2, specifies that the trustee which gives more positive experiences on average during a certain period is at least selected once within or just after that period.

P2(min_duration, max_duration, max_delay, higher_exp): Average more positive experiences results in selection

If a trustee a_1 on average gives the most positive experiences (on average more than higher_exp better than the second best) during a period with minimal duration min_duration and maximum duration max_duration, then this trustee a_1 is selected at least once during the period [min_duration, max_duration+max_delay].

Formal:

P2(min_duration:DURATION, max_duration:DURATION, max_delay:DURATION, higher_exp:REAL)
$\equiv \forall\gamma$:TRACE, t_{start}, t_{end}:TIME, a:TRUSTEE
[[$t_{end} - t_{start} \geq$ min_duration & $t_{end} - t_{start} \leq$ max_duration &
average_highest_experiences(γ, a, t_{start}, t_{end}, higher_exp)]
$\Rightarrow$ selected(γ, a, t_{start}, t_{end}, max_delay)]

where

average_highest_experiences(γ:TRACE, a:TRUSTEE, t_{start}:TIME, t_{end}:TIME, higher_exp:REAL)
$\equiv \forall t$:TIME, r_1, r_2:REAL, a_2:TRUSTEE $\neq a$
[$t \geq t_{start}$ & t $< t_{end}$ &
[$\sum_{\forall t:TIME}$ case(experience_received(γ, a, t, t_{start}, t_{end}, e), e, 0) $>$
($\sum_{\forall t:TIME}$ (case(experience_received(γ, a, t, t_{start}, t_{end}, e), e, 0)) + higher_exp * $t_{end} - t_{start}$)
]]

In the formula above, the case(p, e, 0) operator evaluates to e in case property p is satisfied and to 0 otherwise.

experience_received(γ:TRACE, a:TRUSTEE, t:TIME, t_{start}:TIME, t_{end}:TIME, r:REAL) $\equiv$
[$\exists r$:REAL, $t \geq t_{start}$ & t $< t_{end}$ & state(γ, t) $\models$ trustee_gives_experience(a, r)]

The final property concerns the notion of relativity which plays a key role in the models verified throughout this paper. The property expresses that the frequency of selection of a trustee that gives an identical experience pattern during two periods is not identical in case the other trustees give different experiences.

P3(interval_length, min_difference, max_time): Relative trust
If a trustee a_1 gives an identical experience pattern during two periods $[t_1, t_1+$ interval_length] and $[t_2, t_2+$ interval_length] and the experiences of at least one other trustee is not identical (i.e., more than min_difference different at each time point), then the selection frequency of a_1 will be different in a period during, or just after the specified interval.

Formal:

P3(interval_length:DURATION, min_difference:REAL, max_time:DURATION) $\equiv$
$\forall \gamma$:TRACE, t_1, t_2:TIME, a:TRUSTEE
[[same_experience_sequence(γ, a, t_1, t_2, interval_length) &
$\exists a_2$:TRUSTEE $\neq a$
[different_experience_sequence(γ, a, t_1, t_2, min_difference)]
$\Rightarrow \exists i$:DURATION $<$ max_time
$\sum_{\forall t:\text{TIME}}$ case(selected_option(γ, a, t, $t_1 + i$, $t_1 + i+$ interval_length), 1, 0) /
$(1 + \sum_{\forall t:\text{TIME}}$ case(trustee_selected(γ, t, t_1, $t_1 + i+$ interval_length), 1, 0)) $\neq$
$\sum_{\forall t:\text{TIME}}$ case(selected_option(γ, a, t, $t_2 + i$, $t_2 + i+$ interval_length), 1, 0) /
$(1 + \sum_{\forall t:\text{TIME}}$ case(trustee_selected(γ, t, $t_2 + i$, $t_2 + i+$ interval_length), 1, 0))

where

same_experience_sequence(γ:TRACE, a:TRUSTEE, t_1:TIME, t_2:TIME, x:DURATION) $\equiv$
$\forall y$:DURATION [$y \geq 0$ & $y \leq x$ & $\exists r$:REAL
[state(γ, $t_1 + y$) $\models$ trustee_gives_experience(a, r) &
state(γ, $t_2 + y$) $\models$ trustee_gives_experience(a, r)]]

different_experience_sequence(γ:TRACE, a:TRUSTEE, t_1:TIME, t_2:TIME, x:DURATION, min_difference:REAL) $\equiv$
$\forall y$:DURATION [$y \geq 0$ & $y \leq x$ & $\exists r_1, r_2$:REAL
[state(γ, $t_1 + y$) $\models$ trustee_gives_experience(a, r_1) &
state(γ, $t_2 + y$) $\models$ trustee_gives_experience(a, r_2) &
$|r_1 - r_2| >$ min_difference]]

trustee_selected(γ:TRACE, t:TIME, t_{start}:TIME, t_{end}:TIME) $\equiv$
$\exists a$:TRUSTEE [$t \geq t_{\text{start}}$ & $t < t_{\text{end}}$ & state(γ, t) $\models$ trustee_selected(a)]

4   Results

In this section the validation and verification results are given in Sections 4.1 and 4.2, respectively.

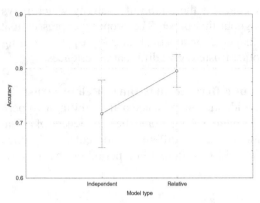

Fig. 3. Main effect of model type for accuracy

4.1   Validation Results

From the data of 18 participants, one dataset has been removed due to an error while gathering data. This means that there are 2 (condition role allocations, i.e., parameter adaptation either in condition 1 or 2) times 17 (participants) = 34 data pairs (accuracies for 2 models). Due to a significant Grubbs test, from these pairs 3 outliers were removed. Hence in total 31 pairs were used for the data analysis.

In Figure 3 the main effect of model type (either independent or relative trust) for accuracy is shown. A repeated measures analysis of variance (ANOVA) showed a significant main effect ($F(1, 29) = 7.60, p < .01$). This means that indeed the relative trust model had a higher accuracy ($M = .7968, SD = .0819$) than the independent trust model ($M = .7185, SD = .1642$).

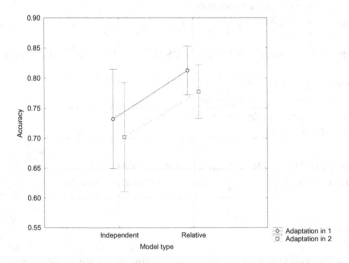

Fig. 4. Interaction effect between condition role allocation and model type on accuracy

Figure 4 shows the possible interaction effect between condition role allocation (parameter adaptation in condition 1 is referred to as adaptation 1 and parameter adaptation in condition 2 is referred to as adaptation 2) and model type (either independent or relative trust) on accuracy. No significant interaction effect was found ($F(1, 29) = .01$, $p = .93$). Hence, no significant learning effect between conditions was found. Cross-validation was not needed to balance the data, but the procedure still produced twice as much data pairs.

4.2 Verification Results

The results of the verification of the properties against the empirical traces (i.e., formalized logs of human behavior observed during the experiment) are shown in Table 1. First, the results for properties P1 and P2 are shown. Hereby, the value of max_duration has been kept constant at 30 and the max_time after which the trustee should be consulted is set to 5. The minimal interval time (min_duration) has been varied. Finally, for property P2 the variable higher_exp indicating how much higher the experience should be on average compared to the other trustees is set to .5. The results in Table 1 indicate the percentage of traces in which the property holds out of all traces in which the antecedent at least holds once (i.e., at least one sequence with the min_duration occurs in the trace). This has been done to avoid a high percentage of satisfaction due to the fact that in some of the traces the antecedent never holds, and hence, the property is always satisfied. The table shows that the percentage of traces satisfying P1 goes up as the minimum duration of the interval during which a trustee gives the highest experience increases. This clearly complies to the ideas underlying trust models as the longer a trustee gives the highest experiences, the higher his trust will be (also compared to the other trustees), and the more likely it is that the trustee will be selected. The second property, counting the average experience and its implication upon the selection behavior of the human, also shows an increasing trend in satisfaction of the property with the duration of the interval during which the trustee on average gives better experiences. The percentages are lower compared to P1 which can be explained by the fact that they might also give some negative experiences compared to the alternatives (whereas they are giving better experiences on average). This could then result in a decrease in the trust value, and hence, a lower probability of being selected.

Table 1. Results of verification of property P1 and P2

min_duration	% satisfying P1	% satisfying P2
1	64.7	29.4
2	64.7	29.4
3	86.7	52.9
4	92.3	55.9
5	100.0	58.8
6	100.0	70.6

Table 2. Results of verification of property P3

interval_length	% satisfying P3
1	0
2	41.1
3	55.9
4	67.6
5	66.7
6	68.4

The third property, regarding the relativity of trust has also been verified and the results of this verification are shown in Table 2. Here, the traces of the participants have been verified with a setting of min_difference to .5 and max_time to 5 and the variable interval_length during which at least one trustee shows identical experiences whereas another shows different experiences has been varied. It can be seen that property P3 holds more frequently as the length of the interval increases, which makes sense as the human has more time to perceive the relative difference between the two. Hence, this shows that the notion of relative trust can be seen in the human trustee selection behavior in almost 70% of the cases.

5   Discussion and Conclusions

In this paper, an extensive validation study has been performed to show that human trust behavior can be accurately described and predicted using computational trust models. In order to do so, an experiment has been designed that places humans in a setting where they have to make decisions based upon the trust they have in others. In total 18 participants took part in the experiment. The results show that both an independent [11,10] as well as a relative trust model [6] can predict this behavior with a high accuracy (72% and 80%, respectively) by learning on one dataset and predicting the trust behavior for another (cross-validation). Furthermore, it has also been shown that the underlying assumptions of the trust models (and many other trust models) are found in the data of the participants.

Of course, more work on the validation of trust models has been performed. In [9] an experiment has been presented to investigate human trust behavior. Although the underlying assumptions of trust models have to some extent been verified in that paper, no attempt has been made to fit a trust model to the data. Other papers describing the validation of trust models for instance validate the accuracy of trust models describing the propagation of trust through a network (e.g., [5]). In [12] a multidisciplinary, multidimensional model of trust in e-commerce is validated. The model includes four high-level constructs: disposition to trust, institution-based trust, trusting beliefs, and trusting intentions. The proposed model itself does however not describe the formation of trust on such a detailed level as the models used throughout this paper, it presents general relationships between trust measures and these relationships are subject to validation. Gefen and Straub [4] validate a four-dimensional scale of trust in the context of e-Products and revalidates it in the context of e-Services which shows the influence of social presence on these dimensions of trust, especially benevolence, and its ultimate contribution to online purchase intentions. Again, correlations are found between the concepts of trust that have been distinguished, but no computational model for the formation of trust and the precise prediction thereof is prosed. Finally, in [2] a development-based trust measurement model for buyer-seller relationships is presented and validated against a characteristic-based trust measurement model in terms of its ability to explain certain variables of interest in buyer-seller relationships (long-term relationship orientation, information sharing, behavioral loyalty and future intentions).

Within the domain of agent systems, quite some trust models have been developed, see e.g. [14], [13] for an overview. Although the focus of this paper has been on the validation of two specific trust models, thereby also comparing relative with absolute trust, other trust models can also be validated using the experimental data obtained in combination with parameter estimation. This is part of the future work. Furthermore, other parameter adaptation methods will be explored or extended for the purpose of real-time adaptation, which accounts for human learning. In addition, a personal assistant software agent will be implemented that is able to monitor and balance the functional state of the human in a timely and knowledgeable manner. Also applications in different domains are explorable, such as the military and air traffic control domain.

Acknowledgments

This research was partly funded by the Dutch Ministry of Defense under progr. no. V929. Furthermore, this research has partly been conducted as part of the FP7 ICT Future Enabling Technologies program of the European Commission under grant agreement no. 231288 (SOCIONICAL). The authors would like to acknowledge Francien Wisse for her efforts to gather the necessary validation data and implementing the experimental task. The authors would also like to thank Tibor Bosse, Jan-Willem Streefkerk and Jan Treur for their helpful comments.

References

1. Bosse, T., Jonker, C., Meij, L.v.d., Sharpanskykh, A., Treur, J.: Specification and verification of dynamics in agent models. International Journal of Cooperative Information Systems 18, 167–193 (2009)
2. da Costa Hernandez, J.M., dos Santos, C.C.: Development-based trust: Proposing and validating a new trust measurement model for buyer-seller relationships. Brazilian Administration Review 7, 172–197 (2010)
3. Falcone, R., Castelfranchi, C.: Trust dynamics: How trust is influenced by direct experiences and by trust itself. In: Proceedings of the 3rd International Joint Conference on Autonomous Agents and Multiagent Systems (AAMAS 2004), New York, USA, pp. 740–747 (July 2004)
4. Gefen, D., Straub, D.W.: Consumer trust in b2c e-commerce and the importance of social presence: experiments in e-products and e-services. Omega 32, 407–424 (2004)
5. Guha, R., Kumar, R., Raghavan, P., Tomkins, A.: Propagation of trust and distrust. In: Proceedings of the 13th International Conference on World Wide Web (WWW 2004), pp. 403–412. ACM, New York (2004)

6. Hoogendoorn, M., Jaffry, S., Treur, J.: Modeling dynamics of relative trust of competitive information agents. In: Klusch, M., Pěchouček, M., Polleres, A. (eds.) CIA 2008. LNCS (LNAI), vol. 5180, pp. 55–70. Springer, Heidelberg (2008)
7. Hoogendoorn, M., Jaffry, S., Treur, J.: Modelling trust dynamics from a neurological perspective. In: Wang, R., Gu, F. (eds.) Proceedings of the Second International Conference on Cognitive Neurodynamics, ICCN 2009, Advances in Cognitive Neurodynamics II, pp. 523–536. Springer, Heidelberg (2011)
8. Hoogendoorn, M., Jaffry, S.W., Treur, J.: An adaptive agent model estimating human trust in information sources. In: Baeza-Yates, R., Lang, J., Mitra, S., Parsons, S., Pasi, G. (eds.) Proceedings of the 9th IEEE/WIC/ACM International Conference on Intelligent Agent Technology (IAT 2009), pp. 458–465 (2009)
9. Jonker, C.M., Schalken, J.J.P., Theeuwes, J., Treur, J.: Human experiments in trust dynamics. In: Jensen, C., Poslad, S., Dimitrakos, T. (eds.) iTrust 2004. LNCS, vol. 2995, pp. 206–220. Springer, Heidelberg (2004)
10. Jonker, C.M., Treur, J.: Formal analysis of models for the dynamics of trust based on experiences. In: Garijo, F.J., Boman, M. (eds.) MAAMAW 1999. LNCS, vol. 1647, pp. 221–232. Springer, Heidelberg (1999)
11. Maanen, P.-P.v., Klos, T., Dongen, K.v.: Aiding human reliance decision making using computational models of trust. In: Proceedings of the Workshop on Communication between Human and Artificial Agents (CHAA 2007), Fremont, California, USA, pp. 372–376. IEEE Computer Society Press, Los Alamitos (2007); Co-located with The 2007 IEEE IAT/WIC/ACM International Conference on Intelligent Agent Technology
12. McKnight, D.H., Choudhury, V., Kacmar, C.: Developing and validatin trust measures for e-commerce: An integrative topology. Information Systems Research 13(3), 334–359 (2001)
13. Ramchurn, S., Huynh, D., Jennings, N.: Trust in multi-agent systems. The Knowledge Engineering Review 19, 1–25 (2004)
14. Sabater, J., Sierra, C.: Review on computational trust and reputation models. Artificial Intelligence Review 24, 33–60 (2005)

Composing Trust Models towards Interoperable Trust Management*

Rachid Saadi, Mohammad Ashiqur Rahaman,
Valérie Issarny, and Alessandra Toninelli

ARLES Project-Team
INRIA CRI Paris-Rocquencourt, France
{name.surname}@inria.fr

Abstract. Computational trust is a central paradigm in today's Internet as our modern society is increasingly relying upon online transactions and social networks. This is indeed leading to the introduction of various trust management systems and associated trust models, which are customized according to their target applications. However, the heterogeneity of trust models prevents exploiting the trust knowledge acquired in one context in another context although this would be beneficial for the digital, ever-connected environment. This is such an issue that this paper addresses by introducing an approach to achieve interoperability between heterogeneous trust management systems. Specifically, we define a trust meta-model that allows the rigorous specification of trust models as well as their composition. The resulting composite trust models enable heterogeneous trust management systems to interoperate transparently through mediators.

1 Introduction

With people getting increasingly connected virtually, trust management is becoming a central element of today's open distributed digital environment. However, existing trust management systems are customized according to specific application domains, hence implementing different trust models. As a result, it is nearly impossible to exploit established trust relations across systems. While a trust relation holding in one system does not systematically translate into a similar relation in another system, it is still a valuable knowledge, especially if the systems relate to the same application domains (e.g., e-commerce, social network). This is such an issue that we are addressing in this paper.

To the best of our knowledge, little work investigates interoperability between heterogeneous trust models. The closest to our concern is the work of [19], which describes a trust management architecture that enables dealing with a variety of trust metrics and mapping between them. However, the architecture deals with the composition at the level of trust values and do not account for the variety of trust models. In particular, one may want to differentiate between direct trust values and reputation-based ones when composing them. In general, what is needed is a way to formalize heterogeneous trust models and their composition. Such a concern is in particular addressed in [9,21], which introduce trust meta-models based on state of the art trust management systems. Nevertheless, little detail is given and the paper does not describe how

---

* Work supported by EU-funded project FP7-231167 CONNECT and by EU-funded project FP7-256980 NESSOS.

I. Wakeman et al. (Eds.): IFIPTM 2011, IFIP AICT 358, pp. 51–66, 2011.

to exploit the meta-model for composing heterogeneous trust models and this achieve interoperability. Dealing with the heterogeneity of trust models is also investigated in [4,20]. However, the study is for the sake of comparison and further concentrates on reputation-based models. Summarizing, while the literature is increasingly rich of trust models, dealing with their composition remains a challenge.

Towards overcoming the interoperability challenge faced by trust management systems, this paper introduces a comprehensive approach based on the definition of a reference trust meta-model. Specifically, based on the state of the art (Section 2), the trust meta-model formalizes the core entities of trust management systems, i.e., trust roles, metrics, relations and operations (Section 3). The trust meta-model then serves specifying the composition of trust models in terms of mapping rules between roles, from which trust mediators are synthesized (Section 4). Trust mediators transparently implement mapping between respective trust relations and operations of the composed models. While this paper introduces the composition approach from a theoretical perspective, we are currently implementing it as part of the CONNECT project[1] on next generation middleware for interoperability in complex systems of systems (Section 5).

2 Trust Model Definition

As in particular defined in [5]: *i.e., A trustor trusts a trustee with regard to its ability to perform a specific action or to provide a specific service.* Hence, any trust model may basically be defined in terms of the three following elements:

1. *Trust roles* abstract the representative behaviors of stakeholders from the standpoint of trust management, in a way similar to role-based access control model [3].
2. *Trust relations* serve specifying trust relationships holding among stakeholders, and
3. *Trust assessment* define how to compute the trustworthiness of stakeholders.

We further define trust relations and assessment below.

2.1 Trust Relations

We identify two types of trust relationships, i.e., *direct* and *indirect*, depending on the number of stakeholders that are involved to build the trust relationship:

Direct trust: A direct trust relationship represents a trust assertion of a subject (i.e., trustor) about another subject (i.e., trustee). It is thus a one-to-one trust relation (denoted *1:1*)) since it defines a direct link from a trustor (**1**) to a trustee (**1**). One-to-one trust relations are maintained locally by trustors and represent the trustors' personal opinion regarding their trustees [10]. For example, a one-to-one relation may represent a belonging relationship (e.g., employees trust their company), a social relationship (e.g., trust among friends), or a profit-driven relationship (e.g., a person trusts a trader for managing its portfolio).

Recommendation-based trust: As opposed to a direct trust relationship, a recommendation-based relationship represents a subject's trustworthiness based on a third party's opinion. This can be either (i) transitive-based or (ii) reputation-based.

---

[1] http://connect-forever.eu/

Transitive-based trust relations are one-to-many (denoted *1:N*). Such a relation enables a trustor (**1**) to indirectly assess the trustworthiness of an unknown trustee through the recommendations of a group of trustees(**N**). Hence, the computation of 1:N relations results from the concatenation and/or aggregation of many 1:1 trust relations. The concatenation of 1:1 trust relations usually represents a transitive trust path, where each entity can trust unknown entities based on the recommendation of its trustees. Thus, this relationship is built by composing personal trust relations [1,18]. Furthermore, in the case where there exist several trust paths that link the trustor to the recommended trustee, the aggregation can be used to aggregate all given trust recommendations [7].

Reputation-based trust relations are many-to-one (denoted *N:1*) and result from the aggregation of many personal trust relationships having the same trustee. Hence, the N:1 trust relation allows the definition of the reputation of each trustee within the system. Reputation systems may then be divided into two categories depending on whether they are (i) *Centralized* or (ii) *Distributed*. With the former, the reputation of each participant is collected and made publicly available at a centralized server (e.g., eBay, Amazon, Google, [14]). With the latter, reputation is spread throughout the network and each networked entity is responsible to manage the reputation of other entities (e.g., [7,23]).

2.2 Trust Assessment

Trust assessment, i.e., assigning values to trust relationships, relies on the definition of: (i) trust metrics characterizing how trust is measured and (ii) operations for composing trust values.

Trust metrics: Different metrics have been defined to measure trust. This is due to the fact that one trust metric may be more or less suitable to a certain context. Thus, there is no widely recognized way to assign trust values. Some systems assume only binary values. In [24], trust is quantified by qualitative labels (e.g., high trust, low trust etc.). Other solutions represent trust by a numerical range. For instance, this range can be defined by the interval [-1..1] (e.g., [12]), [0..n] (e.g., [1,18]) or [0..1] (e.g., [7]). A trust value can also be described in many dimensions, such as: (Belief, Disbelief, Uncertainty) [7].

In addition, several definitions exist about the semantics of trust metrics. This is for instance illustrated by the meaning of zero and negative values. For example, zero may indicate lack of trust (but not distrust), lack of information, or deep distrust. Negative values, if allowed, usually indicate distrust, but there is a doubt whether distrust is simply trust with a negative sign, or a phenomenon of its own.

Trust operations: We define four main operations for the computation of trust values associated with the trust relations given in Section 2.1 (see table 1): *bootstrapping, refreshing, aggregation,* and *concatenation*.

The *bootstrapping* operation initializes the *a priori* values of 1:1 and N:1 trust relations. Trust bootstrapping consists of deciding how to initialize trust relations in order to efficiently start the system and also allow newcomers to join the running system [16]. Most existing solutions simply initialize trust relation with a fixed value (e.g., 0.5 [6], a uniform Beta probabilistic distribution [8]). Other approaches include among

Table 1. Trust assessment operations

	Bootstrapping	Aggregation	Concatenation	Refreshing
One-to-One (1:1)	X			X
One-to-Many (1:N)		X	X	
Many-to-One (N:1)	X	X		X

others: initializing existing trust relations according to given peers recommendations [17]; applying a sorting mechanism instead of assigning fixed values [18]; and assessing trustees into different contexts (e.g., fixing a car, babysitting, etc.) and then inferring unknown trust values from known ones of similar or correlate contexts [16,2].

All the solutions dealing with 1:N trust assessment mainly define the *concatenation* and the *aggregation* operations, in order to concatenate and to aggregate trust recommendations by computing the average [18], the minimum or the product [1] of all the intermediary trust values. In the case of Web service composition, some approaches (e.g., [15]) evaluate the recommendation for each service by evaluating its provider, whereas other approaches (e.g., [11]) evaluate the service itself in terms of its previous invocations, performance, reliability, etc. Then, trust is composed and/or aggregated according to the service composition flow (sequence, concurrent, conditional and loop).

Aggregation operations such as Bayesian probability (e.g., [13]) are often used for the assessment of N:1 (reputation-based) trust relations. Trust values are then represented by a beta Probability Density Function [8], which takes binary ratings as inputs (i.e., positive or negative) from all trustors. Thus, the reputation score is refreshed from the previous reputation score and the new rating [14]. The advantage of Bayesian systems is that they provide a theoretically sound basis for computing reputation scores and can also be used to predict future behavior.

Finally, refreshing operations are mainly trigged by trustors to refresh 1:1 and N:1 trust relations, after receiving stakeholders' feedback.

3   Trust Meta-model

Following the above, we formally define the trust meta-model as: $TM =< \mathbb{R}, \mathbb{L}, \mathbb{M}, \mathbb{O} >$, where $\mathbb{R}, \mathbb{L}, \mathbb{M}$ and $\mathbb{O}$ are the finite sets of trust roles, relations, metrics and operations.

3.1   Trust Meta-model Formalization

As detailed below, each set of TM consists of *elements* where an element can have a *simple value* (e.g., string) or a complex value. A complex value of an element is either an exclusive combination of values (only one of the values) $\vee v$ (e.g., $v_1 \vee v_2 \vee v_3$) or an inclusive combination of values (one or more elements) $\diamond v$ (e.g., $v_1 \wedge v_2 \wedge (v_3 \vee v_4)$) of elements.

Role set $\mathbb{R}$: The role set contains all the roles r played by the stakeholders of the trust model. A role r of $\mathbb{R}$ is simply denoted by its name:

$$r =< \text{name:string} > \tag{1}$$

where: the attribute *name* of type *string* represents the name or the identifier of the role[2]. In our meta-model, a stakeholder is represented as a *Subject s*, playing a number of roles, $r_1, r_2...$and r_n, which is denoted as $s \triangleright r_1, r_2...r_n$.

Metric set $\mathbb{M}$: The metric set describes all the trust metrics that can be manipulated by the trust model. A metric is formally denoted as a pair:

$$m =< \text{name:string, type:string} > \tag{2}$$

where: *name* and *type* are strings and respectively define the name and the type. The *type* can be a simple type (e.g., probability([0..1]), label(good, bad), etc.) or a composition of simples ones (e.g., tuple (believe([0..1]), uncertainty([0..1]))).

Relation set $\mathbb{L}$: A relation set $\mathbb{L}$ contains all the trust relations that are specified by the trust model. We specifically denote a trust relation as a tuple:

$$l =< \text{name:string, ctx:string, type:string, trustor:} \vee r_i, \text{trustee:} \vee r_j, \text{value:} m_k >$$
$$\text{with } r_i, r_j \in \mathbb{R} \text{ and } m_k \in \mathbb{M} \tag{3}$$

where: (i) *name* identifies the relation; (ii) *ctx* describes the context of the relationship in terms of the application domain (e.g., selling); (iii) *type* represents the cardinality of the relation and is denoted by one of the following arities: 1:1, 1:N or N:1; (iv) *trustor* and *trustee* are roles where a trust relation relates a *trustor* role with a *trustee* role; (v) *value* is an element from the metric set and thus reflects the trust measure given by the trustor to the trustee through this relation. In the above, note that different trustors can establish the same type of relationship with different trustees. Thus, as a trust relation is binary and between a *trustor* role and a *trustee*, the exclusive combination of roles (e.g., $r_1 \vee r_2 \vee r_3$) is used to describe these elements

Operation set $\mathbb{O}$: The operation set specifies the operations that can be performed over relations by a subject, either to assess the trustworthiness of another subject or to communicate (i.e., request/response) trust values associated with desired subjects (see Figure 1). As defined in Section 2, trust assessment relies on the bootstrapping, aggregation, concatenation and refreshing operations, whereas, the communication of a trust value relies on the request and response operations. An operation is formally denoted as:

$$o =< \text{name:string, host:} \vee r_i, \text{type:string, input:} \Diamond l_j, \text{output:} \Diamond l_k, \text{via:} \Diamond l_n, \text{call:} \Diamond o >$$
$$\text{Where } r_i \in \mathbb{R}, l_j, l_k, l_n, \in \mathbb{L}, \text{ and } o \in \mathbb{O} \tag{4}$$

where: (i) *name* identifies uniquely an operation; (ii) *host* instantiates the role(s) that hosts and executes the operation; (iii) *type* defines the operation (i.e., request, response, bootstrapping, aggregation, concatenation, and refreshing); (iv) *input* gives the trust

---

[2] Note that the name can in particular be specified by an ontological concept that formally describes this role into a given trust ontology although this is not longer discussed in this paper.

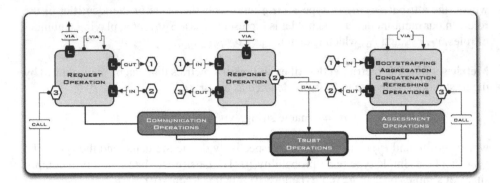

Fig. 1. Operation continuation

relations that are required to perform an assessment operation or are received by a communication operation; (v) *output* gives the trust relations that are provided, as the result of either an assessment operation or a communication; (vi) *via* specifies the trust relationship that should hold with the role with which the communication happens, while its value is *self* in the case of assessment; and (vii) *call* denotes a continuation (see Figure 1). Note that *input* and *output* are complex values, i.e., logical conjunction of one or more relations.

Trust graph TG: We associate the definition of a *trust graph* with any trust model TM for the sake of graphical representation. Specifically, the trust graph $TG(\mathbb{R}, \mathbb{E})$ associated with a given TM is a directed graph with the vertices representing the set of roles $\mathbb{R}$ of TM, and the set of edges $\mathbb{E}$ representing the relationship between roles according to $\mathbb{L}$. Hence, each edge is labeled by the referenced relation l from the set of relations $\mathbb{L}$ and the type of that relation, i.e., 1:1, 1:N or N:1.

3.2 Example

We illustrate the expressiveness of our trust meta-model by considering the specification of representative trust models associated with two selling transaction scenarios. Precisely, we introduce the specification of an eBay like centralized trust model (see Table 2) and of a fully distributed one (see Table 3). Both trust models aim at assessing transaction behaviors of sellers.

Figure 2 depicts the trust graphs of both models; the centralized trust model, i.e., TM_C (on the left in the figure), is defined with three roles, i.e., $r_S=Seller$, $r_B=Buyer$, and $r_M=Manager$, whereas the distributed trust model, i.e., TM_D (on the right in the figure), is defined with the unique role $r_C=Customer$, which can be either a seller or a buyer.

Focusing on the specification of TM_C in Table 2 , the roles $Buyer$ and $Seller$ have a direct trust relationship (i.e., l_0) with the $Manager$ that manages the sellers' reputation (i.e., l_3). Thus, any $Buyer$ can: (i) query the $Manager$ about the reputation of a $Seller$ (i.e., l_1), and (ii) provide the $Manager$ with its feedback (i.e., l_2) after a selling transaction. Hence, a $Buyer$ has to perform a request operation (i.e., o_4) to get the reputation of the seller, so that it can compute locally the trustworthiness of the

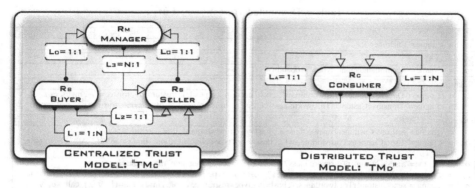

Fig. 2. Trust graphs of the centralized (TM_C) and the distributed (TM_D) trust models

seller (i.e., o_1). After a transaction is completed, a *Buyer* can provide its feedback to the *Manager* by triggering a request operation (i.e., o_8). The *Manager* in turn processes (i.e., o_9) this feedback request to compute and refresh the reputation of the concerned *Seller* (i.e., o_3).

Regarding the distributed model TM_D specified in Table 3, the role *Customer* of the distributed model can maintain a direct trust relationship with other *Customers* (i.e., l_a) and can then ask trustee *Customers* to get their recommendation about unknown *Customers* that are sellers (i.e., l_b). Hence, a *Customer* can perform a request operation (i.e., o_d) to get a recommendation of an unknown *Customer* seller, so that the requester *Customer* can compute locally the trustworthiness of the *Seller* (i.e., o_b and o_c). After the transaction is completed, the requester *Customer* can provide its feedback to other *Customers* by triggering a request operation (i.e., o_f). The recipient *Customer*

Table 2. Centralized Trust model: TM_C

Role set $\mathbb{R}$
r_S = <name="Buyer">
r_B = <name="Seller">
r_M = <name="Manager">

Metric set $\mathbb{M}$
m_0 = <name="Reputation", type="Probability">
m_1 = <name="Recommendation", type="Probability">
m_2 = <name="Rate", type= "Five Semantic labels">

Relation set $\mathbb{L}$
l_0 = < name="ServerRecommendation", ctx= "Selling", type=1:1, trustor=($r_S \lor r_B$), trustee=r_M, metric=m_1>
l_1 = < name="SellerTrustworthiness", ctx= "Selling", type=1:N, trustor=r_S, trustee=r_B, metric=m_1 >
l_2 = < name="BuyerFeedback", ctx= "Selling", type=1:1, trustor=r_S, trustee=r_B, metric=m_2 >
l_3 = < name="SellerReputation", ctx= "Selling", type=N:1, trustor=r_B, trustee=r_M, metric=m_0 >

Operation set $\mathbb{O}$
o_0 = <name="getManagerTrustworthiness", host=($r_S \lor r_B$), type=request, in=l_0, out=l_0 >
o_1 = <name="assessSellerTrustworthiness", host=r_S, type=concatenation, in=($l_0 \land l_3$) , out=l_1 >
o_2 = <name= "assessBuyerFeedback", host=r_S, type=update, in=l_2, out=l_2, call=o_8 >
o_3 = <name="setSellerReputation", host=r_M, type=aggregation, in=l_2, out=l_3 >
o_4 = <name="getSellerTrustworthiness", host=r_S,type=request, via=l_0, out=l_1, in=l_3, call=o_1 >
o_5 = <name="getSellerReputation", host=r_M,type=response, in=l_3, out=l_3 >
o_6 = <name="sendSellerReputation", host=r_M,type=response, via=l_0, in=l_1, out=l_3, call=o_5 >
o_7 = <name="getBuyerFeedback", host=r_S,type=request, in=l_2, out=l_2 >
o_8 = <name="sendBuyerFeedback", host=r_S,type=request, via=l_0, out=l_2 >
o_9 = <name="updateSellerReputation", host=r_M,type=response, via=l_0, in=l_2, call= o_3 >

Table 3. Distributed Trust model: TM_D.

Role set $\mathbb{R}$
r_C = <name="Customer ">
Metric set $\mathbb{M}$
m_a = <name="Recommendation", type="Probability">
Relation set $\mathbb{L}$
l_a = < name="DirectCustomer Trustworthiness", ctx= "auction", type=1:1, trustor=r_C, trustee=r_C, metric=m_a >
l_b = < name="TransitiveCustomer Trustworthiness", ctx="auction", type=1:N, trustor=r_C, trustee=r_C, metric=m_a >
Operation set $\mathbb{O}$
o_a = <name="getLocalCustomerTrustworthiness", host=r_C, type=request, in=l_a, out=l_a >
o_b = <name="assessCustomerTrustworthiness1", host=r_C, type=concatenation, in=($l_a \wedge (l_a \vee l_b)$) , out=$l_b$, call=$o_c$ >
o_c = <name="assessCustomerTrustworthiness2", host=r_C, type=aggregation, in=l_b , out=l_b >
o_d = <name="getRemoteCustomerTrustworthiness", host=r_C, type=request, via=l_a, out=l_b, in=($l_a \vee l_b$), call=o_b >
o_e = <name="sendCustomerTrustworthiness", host=r_C,type=response, via=l_a, in=l_b, out=($l_a \vee l_b$), call=($o_a \vee o_d$) >
o_f = <name="sendCustomerFeedback", host=r_C,type=request, via=l_a, out=l_a >
o_g = <name="setCustomerTrustworthiness", host=r_C,type=update, in=l_a, out=l_a, call=o_f >
o_h = <name="updateCustomerTrustworthiness", host=r_C,type=response, via=l_a, in=l_a, call= o_g >

can process (i.e., o_h) this feedback to refresh its relationship with the concerned *Seller* (i.e., o_g) and can also in turn propagate this feedback by calling the o_f.

4 Composing Trust Models

Given the specification of trust models, their composition relies on mapping their respective roles so that: (i) the trustworthiness of the various roles can be assessed, (ii) existing trust relations can be queried, and (iii) trust feedbacks can be propagated transparently from one trust model to another. Further, the existing trust relations and operations are extended to relate roles from the composed models, and new assessment operations are required to map trust relations from one model to another. Finally, the resulting mapping and extensions are implemented through mediation [22] so as to make composition transparent to existing systems, which leads us to introduce the corresponding *mediator role*.

Formally, the composition, denoted $\bigoplus$, of two trust models TM_x and TM_y, which introduces the trust model TM_{xy}, is defined as follows:

$$
\begin{aligned}
TM_{xy} &= TM_x \bigoplus_{\Psi^{xy}} TM_y \\
&= < \mathbb{R}_x, \mathbb{M}_x, \mathbb{L}_x, \mathbb{O}_x > \bigoplus_{\Psi^{xy}} < \mathbb{R}_y, \mathbb{M}_y, \mathbb{L}_y, \mathbb{O}_y > \\
&= \left\langle \begin{array}{l} \mathbb{R}_{xy} = \mathbb{R}_x \cup \mathbb{R}_y \cup \mu\mathbb{R}_{xy} \\ \mathbb{M}_{xy} = \mathbb{M}_x \cup \mathbb{M}_y \\ \mathbb{L}_{xy} = \mathbb{L}_x^+ \cup \mathbb{L}_y^+ \\ \mathbb{O}_{xy} = \mathbb{O}_x^+ \cup \mathbb{O}_y^+ \cup \mu\mathbb{O}_{xy} \end{array} \right\rangle
\end{aligned}
\tag{5}
$$

where:

- Ψ^{xy} is the set of mapping rules over roles that enables the composition of TM_x and TM_y;
- $\mu\mathbb{R}_{xy}$ and $\mu\mathbb{O}_{xy}$ are the new sets of mediator roles and mediation operations, respectively;

– ($\mathbb{L}_x^+$ and $\mathbb{L}_y^+$) and ($\mathbb{O}_x^+$ and $\mathbb{O}_y^+$) are the extended relations and operations, respectively.

In the following, we elaborate on the mediation process to generate the sets of mediator roles, and mediation operations (i.e., $\mu\mathbb{R}_{xy}$, and $\mu\mathbb{O}_{xy}$) and extended relations and operations (i.e., $\mathbb{L}_x^+$, $\mathbb{O}_x^+$ $\mathbb{L}_y^+$, $\mathbb{O}_y^+$).

Algorithm 1. Trust_Models_Composition(TM_x, TM_y, Ψ^{xy})

Input(s) : Trust models TM_x and TM_y
         The set of Mapping rules Ψ^{xy}
Output(s): The trust model composition $TM_{xy} = <\mathbb{R}_{xy}, \mathbb{M}_{xy}, \mathbb{L}_{xy}, \mathbb{O}_{xy}>$

1 **begin**
   // Initialize trust models sets for composition
2    $\mathbb{L}_x^+ = \mathbb{L}_x$; $\mathbb{L}_y^+ = \mathbb{L}_y$
3    $\mathbb{O}_x^+ = \mathbb{O}_x$; $\mathbb{O}_y^+ = \mathbb{O}_y$
4   **foreach** $(\psi_k^{xy} = (\psi_k^{xy} = (r_i : TM_{m=\{x,y\}}) \odot (r_j : TM_{n=\{x,y\}, m\neq n})) \in \Psi^{xy})$ **do**
5      $Relation\_Mediation(r_i, \mathbb{L}_m^+, r_j, \mathbb{L}_n^+, \odot)$
6   **if** $(\odot == " \underset{\mu r_k}{\bowtie} ")$ **then**
7   **if** $\mu r_k \notin \mu\mathbb{R}_{xy}$ **then**
8          $\mu\mathbb{R}_{xy} = \mu\mathbb{R}_{xy} \cup \{\mu r_k\}$
9        $Operation\_Mediation(r_i, \mathbb{L}_m^+, \mathbb{O}_m^+, r_j, \mathbb{L}_n^+, \mathbb{O}_n^+, \mu r_k)$
10   $\mathbb{R}_{xy} = \mathbb{R}_x \cup \mathbb{R}_y \cup \mu\mathbb{R}_{xy}$
11   $\mathbb{M}_{xy} = \mathbb{M}_x \cup \mathbb{M}_y$
12   $\mathbb{L}_{xy} = \mathbb{L}_x^+ \cup \mathbb{L}_y^+$
13   $\mathbb{O}_{xy} = \mathbb{O}_x^+ \cup \mathbb{O}_y^+ \cup \mu\mathbb{O}_{xy}$
14 **end**

4.1 Role Mapping

The mapping of roles from 2 distinct models is explicitly defined through a set of mapping rules defined as follows:

$$\psi_k^{st} = (r_s : TM_s) \odot (r_d : TM_t) \tag{6}$$

where, $\odot$ is asymmetric and maps the source role r_s of TM_s to the target role r_t of TM_t. We further refine $\odot$ into two mapping operators:

– *The See operator*, noted "$\succ$", simply associates a source role with a target role so as to define that the role r_t of TM_t is seen as r_s in TM_t. For instance, in the selling transaction scenarios, $(r_B : TM_C) \succ (r_C : TM_D)$ means that $Buyers$ (i.e., $r_B : TM_C$) of the centralized trust model are seen by the distributed trust model (TM_D) as $Customers$ ($r_C : TM_D$).
– *The Mimic operator*, noted "$\underset{\mu r}{\bowtie}$", specifies that r_s should be able to request trust values of TM_t as if it was r_t. This is practically achieved through the mediator role μr that translates r_s requests into r_t requests. For instance, the rule $(r_C : TM_D) \underset{\mu r}{\bowtie}$

$(r_S : TM_A)$ means that any customer is able to request trust values as if it was a buyer in the centralized trust management system, thanks to the mediation achieved by μr.

The computation of the composition of trust models TM_x and TM_y is detailed in Algorithm 1. The algorithm iterates on mapping rules for each of which it invokes *Relation_Mediation* (see line 5) so as to extend relation sets, namely: $\mathbb{L}_x^+$ and $\mathbb{L}_y^+$, (see Section 4.2). Then, according to the definition of *Mimic* rules, mediator roles (i.e., μr) are added to the set of mediator roles (see lines 7-8), and *Operation_Mediation* is invoked so as to perform mediation over the communication operations (see line 9) of the composed trust models (see Section 4.3).

4.2 Relation Mediation

The aim of relation mediation is to extend the trust relations of the original models to roles of the other. More precisely, for any trust relation:
$l =<$ name:string, ctx:string, type:string, trustor:$\vee r_i$, trustee:$\vee r_j$, metric:$m_k >$ of $\mathbb{L}_x$ and $\mathbb{L}_y$ of the composed models TM_x and TM_y, its *trustee* and *trustor* elements are possibly extended to account for mapping between roles.

Algorithm 2 details the corresponding extension where: (i) function $e \sqsupset v$ returns true if v is in e, and (ii) $e \xleftarrow{v_i} v_j$ replaces the value v_i in e with the value v_j. As shown in the algorithm, the extension of trust relations depends on the type of the mapping

---

Algorithm 2. Relation_Mediation$(r_s, \mathbb{L}_s^+, r_t, \mathbb{L}_t^+, \odot)$

Input(s) : Roles r_s and r_t ; Relation sets $\mathbb{L}_s^+$ and $\mathbb{L}_t^+$;
Mapping operation $\odot$
Output(s): The source and the target relation sets: $\mathbb{L}_s^+$ and $\mathbb{L}_t^+$

```
1  begin
2  |  if ⊙ = " ≻ " then          /* Ψ^xy is defined with the "See" Operator */
3  |  |  foreach (l_i ∈ L_t^+) do      /* Find relations with the trustee r_s */
4  |  |  |  if l_i.trustee ⊐ r_t then
5  |  |  |  |  l_i.trustee ←――― (r_t ∨ r_s)        /* Add r_s as a trustee */
                           r_t

6  |  if ⊙ = " ⋈ " then     /* Ψ^xy is defined with the "Mimic" Operator */
          μr
7  |  |  foreach (l_i ∈ L_s^+) do      /* Find relations with the trustee r_s */
8  |  |  |  if l_i.trustor ⊐ r_s then
9  |  |  |  |  l_i.trustee ←――――――― (l_i.trustee ∨ μr)      /* Add μr as a
                          l_i.trustee
   |  |  |  |  trustee */

10 |  |  foreach (l_i ∈ L_t^+) do      /* Find relations with the trustor r_t */
11 |  |  |  if l_i.trustor ⊐ r_t then
12 |  |  |  |  l_i.trustor ←――― (r_t ∨ μr)        /* Add μr as a trustee */
                           r_t

13 end
```

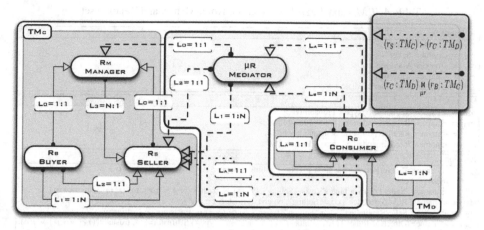

Fig. 3. Trust graph TG_{CD}

operator. The *See* operator defines which local trustee (target role r_t) corresponds to the source role (r_s). Therefore, all the relations l_i (from the source trust model) that consider the source role as a trustee ($l_i.trustee \sqsupseteq r_t$) are extended with the target role (see lines 2-5). The *Mimic* operator introduces a new mediator role that plays trustees of the source role as a trustee in the source trust model, and plays the target role as a trustor in the target trust model. This leads to the corresponding extension of the trust models relations of $\mathbb{L}_x$ (see lines 7-9) and $\mathbb{L}_y$ (see lines 10-12).

Figure 3 depicts the trust graph TG_{CD} resulting from the composition of TM_C and TM_D, while Table 4 details the associated trust roles, metric and relations where new mediator role and extended relations are highlighted in grey. The composition relies on two mapping rules that allow a *Customer* of TM_D to assess a seller of TM_C. The rule using the *See* operator represents how sellers are perceived in TM_D, while the second rule using the *Mimic* operator introduces a mediator role that enables *Costumers* to request TM_C as *Buyers*. Thus, "$r_B : TM_C \succ r_C : TM_D$" leads to extend the trustee element of l_a and l_b by replacing r_C with ($r_C \vee r_B$). The mapping rule "$r_C : TM_D \underset{\mu r}{\bowtie} r_S : TM_C$" extends the relations that sink into the role *Customer* (i.e., l_a and l_b) with the mediator role μr. In addition, all the relations that originate from the role *Buyer* (i.e., l_0, l_1 and l_2) also originate from the mediator role μr.

4.3   Operation Mediation

Operation mediation serves translating request operations from one model into requests in the other model, according to the mappings between roles defined using the *Mimic* operator. More precisely, consider a request operation by r_s for a relation:

<name="l", ctx="c", type="t", trustor="r_s", trustee="tee", metric="v"> of TM_s

where $l \in \mathbb{L}_s$, $tor \in \mathbb{R}_s$, while $tee \in \mathbb{R}_t$ and $r_s{:}TM_s \underset{\mu r}{\bowtie} r_t{:}TM_t$. Then, operation mediation first identifies the matching relations:

Table 4. TM_C and TM_D Composition: Role, Metric, and Relation sets

Roles set $\mathbb{R}$
r_S = <name="Buyer">
r_B = <name="Seller">
r_M = <name="Manager">
r_C = <name="Customer ">
μr = <name="Customer Mediator">

Metric set $\mathbb{M}$
m_0 = <name="Reputation", type="Probability">
m_1 = <name="Recommendation", type="Probability">
m_2 = <name="Rate", type= "Five Semantic labels">
m_a = <name="Recommendation", type="Probability">

Relation set $\mathbb{L}$
l_0 = < name="ServerRecommendation", ctx= "Selling", type=1:1, trustor=$((r_S \lor \mu r) \lor r_B)$, trustee=$r_M$, metric=$m_1$ >
l_1 = < name= "SellerTrustworthiness", ctx= "Selling", type=1:N, trustor=$(r_S \lor \mu r)$, trustee=r_B, metric=m_1 >
l_2 = < name="BuyerFeedback", ctx= "Selling", type=1:1, trustor=$(r_S \lor \mu r)$, trustee=r_B, metric=m_2 >
l_3 = < name= "SellerReputation", ctx= "Selling", type=N:1, trustor=r_B, trustee=r_M, metric=m_0 >
l_a = < name="DirectCustomer Trustworthiness", ctx= "auction", type=1:1, trustor=r_C, trustee=$((r_C \lor r_B) \lor \mu r)$, metric=$m_a$ >
l_b = < name="TransitiveCustomer Trustworthiness", ctx= "auction", type=1:N, trustor=r_C, trustee=$((r_C \lor r_B) \lor \mu r)$, metric=$m_a$ >

<name: string, ctx="c", type: string, trustor="r_t", trustee="tee", metric: m> of TM_t

that should be requested in the target model using a request operation of $\mathbb{O}_t$. Replies are finally normalized using the mediation operation given by $\mu\mathbb{O}_{xy}$ for use in the source trust model. Operation mediation is practically implemented in a transparent way by the mediator that intercepts and then translates r_s requests, as given in Algorithm 3. In the algorithm, the mediator interacts with r_s (see lines 2-4) and r_t (see lines 5-7). Then, the mediator computes the matching relation for each output relation (see lines 11-18) of the reply, where we assume that there is only one such relation (see lines 12-13) and requests its value using the appropriate request operation (see lines 16-18). We further consider that the mediator (μr) embeds a library of mediation functions that translate and normalize heterogeneous trust metrics, which are invoked by mediation operations μo (see lines 12-14). Finally, for each update (i.e., bootstrapping and refreshing) triggered by the response, as specified in the corresponding *call* element (see lines 19-20), the matching relations is sought in $\mathbb{L}_t$ (see line 23) and its value requested (see lines 25-28).

Figure4 depicts the basic mediation process (left hand side) and its extension with update (right hand side), as performed by the mediator. First, the mediator receives the request *in* (step 1). Then, it invokes the corresponding request in the target model (steps 2 to 4) and upon receipt of the result, it normalizes the value using the mediation operation $\mu\mathbb{O}_{ts}$ (steps 5-6). Finally, the reply *out* is returned. In the case of update (on the figure right hand side), the relation matching the one given as input is sought in the target model using the mediation operation $\mu\mathbb{O}_{st}$ (step 2), leading to invoke the corresponding update operation of the target model (step 3).

As an example, Table 5 gives the operation set $\mathbb{O}_{1,2}$ resulting from the composition of TM_C and TM_D.

The response operation o_e should be able to assess *Sellers* of TM_C since its outputs (i.e., l_a and l_b) contain relations that sink into the *Seller* role (see Table 4). To do so, o_e is extended (see lines 9-18) to enable the mediator role μr (when it performs this

Algorithm 3. Operation_Mediation($r_i, \mathbb{L}_m^+, \mathbb{O}_m^+, r_j, \mathbb{L}_n^+, \mathbb{O}_n^+, \mu r_k$)

Input(s) : Source role r_s, relation $\mathbb{L}_s^+$ and operation set $\mathbb{O}_s^+$
Target role r_t, relation $\mathbb{L}_t^+$ and operation set $\mathbb{O}_t^+$
The mediator role μr

Output(s): The source, the target and the mediation operation sets: $\mathbb{O}_s^+$, $\mathbb{O}_t^+$ and $\mu \mathbb{O}_{st}$

```
1  begin
2  |  foreach (o_i ∈ 𝕆_s^+) do              /* Find operation with the host r_s */
3  |  |  if o_i.type = "response" ∧ o_i.via.trustor ⊐ r_s then
4  |  |  |  o_i.host ←^{o_i.host} (o_i.host ∨ μr)       /* Add μr as a host */
5  |  foreach (o_i ∈ 𝕆_t^+) do              /* Find relations with the host r_t */
6  |  |  if o_i.type ≠ "response" ∧ o_i.host ⊐ r_t then
7  |  |  |  o_i.host ←^{r_t} (r_t ∨ μr)                 /* Add μr as a host */
8  |  foreach (o_i ∈ 𝕆_s^+) do              /* Find operation with the host r_s */
      // Request mediation
9  |  |  if o_i.type = "response" ∧ o_i.host ⊐ μr then
10 |  |  |  If (o_i.out ≠ null) then
11 |  |  |  |  foreach l_k ⊐ o_i.out do
               // Create a new mediated operation μo
12 |  |  |  |  |  μo.host=μr ; μo.type="mediation"
               // Find a similar output relation into L_t
13 |  |  |  |  |  l* = findSimilarRelation(l_k, 𝕃_t^+)
14 |  |  |  |  |  μo.in = l* ; μo.out = l_k
15 |  |  |  |  |  μ𝕆_st = 𝕆_st ∪ {μo}
               // The relation l* need to be requested
16 |  |  |  |  |  o* = findOperation(type = "request", l*, 𝕆_t^+)
17 |  |  |  |  |  o*.call ←^{o*.call} (o*.call) ∨ μo
18 |  |  |  |  |  o_i.call ←^{o_i.call} (o_i.call) ∨ o*
      // Update mediation
19 |  |  |  foreach o_k ⊐ o_i.call do
20 |  |  |  |  if o_k.type = "refresh" ∨ o_k.type = "boostrap" then
21 |  |  |  |  |  foreach l_p ⊐ o_k.in do
22 |  |  |  |  |  |  μo.host=μr ; μo.type="mediation"
23 |  |  |  |  |  |  l* = findSimilarRelation(l_p, 𝕃_t^+)
24 |  |  |  |  |  |  μo.in = l_p ; μo.out = l*
25 |  |  |  |  |  |  o* = findOperation(type = o_k.type, l*, 𝕆_t^+)
26 |  |  |  |  |  |  μo.call = o*
27 |  |  |  |  |  |  μ𝕆_st = μ𝕆_st ∪ {μo}
28 |  |  |  |  |  |  o_i.call ←^{o_i.call} (o_i.call) ∨ μo
29 end
```

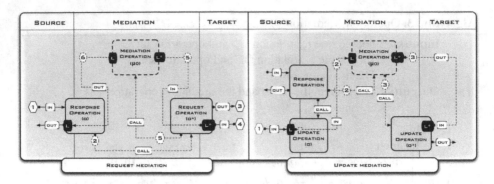

Fig. 4. Operation mediation process

Table 5. TM_C and TM_D Composition: Operation set

Operation set $\bigcirc$
o_0 = <name="getManagerTrustworthiness", host=$((r_S \vee \mu r) \vee r_B)$, type=request, in=$l_0$, out=$l_0$ >
o_1 = <name="assessSellerTrustworthiness", host=$(r_S \vee \mu r)$, type=concatenation, type="product", in=$(l_0 \wedge l_3)$, out=l_1 >
o_2 = <name="assessBuyerFeedback", host=$(r_S \vee \mu r)$, type=update, type="rating", in=l_2, out=l_2, call=o_8 >
o_3 = <name="setSellerReputation", host=r_M, type=aggregation, in=l_2, out=l_3 >
o_4 = <name="getSellerTrustworthiness", host=r_S,type=request, via=l_0, out=l_1, in=l_3, call=$o_1 \vee \mu o_1$ >
o_5 = <name="getSellerReputation", host=r_M,type=response, in=l_3, out=l_3 >
o_6 = <name="sendSellerReputation", host=r_M,type=response, via=l_0, in=l_1, out=l_3, call=o_5 >
o_7 = <name="getBuyerFeedback", host=$(r_S \vee \mu r)$,type=request, in=l_2, out=l_2, call=μo_2 >
o_8 = <name="sendBuyerFeedback", host=$(r_S \vee \mu r)$,type=request, via=l_0, out=l_2 >
o_9 = <name="updateSellerReputation", host=r_M,type=response, via=l_0, in=l_2, call=o_3 >
o_a = <name="getLocalCustomerTrustworthiness", host=r_C, type=request, in=l_a, out=l_a >
o_b = <name="assessCustomerTrustworthiness1", host=$(r_C \vee \mu r)$, type=concatenation, in=$(l_a \wedge (l_a \vee l_b))$, out=l_b, call=o_c >
o_c = <name="assessCustomerTrustworthiness2", host=$(r_C \vee \mu r)$, type=aggregation, , in=l_b , out=l_b >
o_d = <name="getRemoteCustomerTrustworthiness", host=r_C,type=request, via=l_a, out=l_b, in=$(l_a \vee l_b)$, call=o_b >
o_e = <name="sendCustomerTrustworthiness", host=$(r_C \vee \mu r)$,type=response, via=l_a, in=l_b, out=$(l_a \vee l_b)$, call=$(o_a \vee o_d) \vee o_4 \vee o_7$ >
o_f = <name="sendCustomerFeedback", host=r_C,type=request, via=l_a, out=l_a >
o_g = <name="setCustomerTrustworthiness", host=$(r_C \vee \mu r)$,type=update, out=l_a, call=o_f >
o_h = <name="updateCustomerTrustworthiness", host=$(r_C \vee \mu r)$,type=response, via=l_a, in=l_a, call= $o_g \vee \mu o_3$ >
μo_1 = <name="Translate$l_1 l_b$", host=μr,type=mediation, in=l_1, out=l_b >
μo_2 = <name="Translate$l_2 l_a$", host=μr,type=mediation, in=l_2, out=l_a >

operation) to retrieve similar o_e output relations in TM_C, i.e., the relations l_a and l_b that are respectively similar to l_1 and l_2. The operation o_e can hence call o_4 or o_7 to search for l_1 or l_2. Then, as for o_e, the called operations are extended as well, by calling the mediation operations μo_1 and μo_2 to translate respectively l_1 and l_2 into l_b and l_a. Thus, o_e is able to reply the appropriate trust relationships which are interpretable by *Customers*. Moreover, Algorithm 3 (see lines 19-28) enables *Customers* feedback to be propagated to the *Manager* of the target model TM_C, so that the reputation of *Sellers* can be refreshed with the source model feedback. According to the resulting operation set (see Table 5), when the mediator role μr performs the response operation o_h, it calls μo_3 to translate the feedback denoted by the relation l_a into *Buyer* feedback, I.e., l_2. Then, μo_3 is able to call o_2 with the l_2 to advertise its feedback to TM_C *Manager*.

5 Conclusion

In this paper, we have introduced a trust meta-model as the basis to express and to compose a wide range of trust models. The composition of trust models enables assessing the trustworthiness of stakeholders across heterogeneous trust management systems. Such a composition is specified in terms of mapping rules between roles. Rules are then processed by a set of mediation algorithms to overcome the heterogeneity between the trust metrics, relations and operations associated with the composed trust models. We are currently implementing our approach as part of the *Connect* project[3] where we have defined an XML-based description of the trust meta-model, which we call TMDL (i.e., Trust Model Description Language). Thus, mediators are synthesized on-the-fly given the TMDL description of Trust models.

As future work, we are also considering the implementation of a simulator to a priori assess the behavior of trust composition of given trust models and thus allows fine tuning of the mapping rules. We are also investigating the use of ontologies to specify the semantics of trust model elements and thus possibly infer the mapping rules as well as infer the similarity of trust relations from the semantics.

References

1. Abdul-Rahman, A., Hailes, S.: A distributed trust model. In: NSPW: New Security Paradigms Workshop, pp. 48–60. ACM Press, New York (1997)
2. Ahamed, S., Monjur, M., Islam, M.: CCTB: Context correlation for trust bootstrapping in pervasive environment. In: 2008 IET 4th International Conference on Intelligent Environments, pp. 1–8 (2008)
3. Ferraiolo, D.F., Sandhu, R., Gavrila, S., Kuhn, D.R., Chandramouli, R.: Proposed nist standard for role-based access control. ACM Transactions on Information and System Security 4(3), 224–274 (2001)
4. Fullam, K., Klos, T., Muller, G., Sabater, J., Schlosser, A., Topol, Z., Barber, K., Rosenschein, J., Vercouter, L., Voss, M.: A specification of the Agent Reputation and Trust (ART) testbed. In: Conference on Autonomous Agents and Multiagent Systems, pp. 512–518. ACM, New York (2005)
5. Grandison, T., Sloman, M.: A survey of trust in internet applications. IEEE Communications Surveys & Tutorials 3(4), 2–16 (2009)
6. Haque, M., Ahamed, S.: An omnipresent formal trust model (FTM) for pervasive computing environment. In: 31st Annual International Computer Software and Applications Conference, COMPSAC 2007, vol. 1 (2007)
7. Jøsang, A., Pope, S.: Semantic constraints for trust transitivity. In: APCCM: 2nd Asia-Pacific Conference on Conceptual Modelling, pp. 59–68. Australian Computer Society, Inc., Newcastle (2005)
8. Jsang, A., Ismail, R.: The beta reputation system. In: Proceedings of the 15th Bled Electronic Commerce Conference, pp. 17–19 (2002)
9. Kaffille, S., Wirtz, G.: Engineering Autonomous Trust-Management Requirements for Software Agents: Requirements and Concepts. Innovations and Advances in Computer Sciences and Engineering, 483–489 (2010)
10. Kautz, H., Selman, B., Shah, M.: Referral Web: combining social networks and collaborative filtering. Communications of the ACM 40(3), 63–65 (1997)

---

[3] http://connect-forever.eu/

11. Kim, Y., Doh, K.: Trust Type based Semantic Web Services Assessment and Selection. In: Proceedings of ICACT, IEEE Computer, pp. 2048–2053 (2008)
12. Marsh, S.: Formalising Trust as a Computational Concept. PhD thesis, University of Stirling, Scotland (1994)
13. Mui, L., Mohtashemi, M., Ang, C., Szolovits, P., Halberstadt, A.: Ratings in distributed systems: A bayesian approach. In: Proceedings of the Workshop on Information Technologies and Systems (WITS), pp. 1–7. Citeseer (2001)
14. Nurmi, P.: A bayesian framework for online reputation systems. In: International Conference on Internet and Web Applications and Services/Advanced International Conference on AICT-ICIW 2006, p. 121 (February 2006)
15. Paradesi, S., Doshi, P., Swaika, S.: Integrating Behavioral Trust in Web Service Compositions. In: Proceedings of the 2009 IEEE International Conference on Web Services, pp. 453–460. IEEE Computer Society, Los Alamitos (2009)
16. Quercia, D., Hailes, S., Capra, L.: TRULLO-local trust bootstrapping for ubiquitous devices. In: Proc. of IEEE Mobiquitous (2007)
17. Rahman, A., Hailes, S.: Supporting trust in virtual communities. In: IEEE Hawaii International Conference on System Sciences, p. 6007 (2000)
18. Saadi, R., Pierson, J.M., Brunie, L.: Establishing trust beliefs based on a uniform disposition to trust. In: ACM SAC: Trust, Reputation, Evidence and other Collaboration Know-how track. ACM Press, New York (2010)
19. Suryanarayana, G., Erenkrantz, J., Hendrickson, S., Taylor, R.: PACE: an architectural style for trust management in decentralized applications. In: Software Architecture, WICSA 2004, pp. 221–230. IEEE, Los Alamitos (2004)
20. Suryanarayana, G., Taylor, R.: SIFT: A Simulation Framework for Analyzing Decentralized Reputation-based Trust Models. Technical Report UCI-ISR-07-5 (2007)
21. Vercouter, L., Casare, S., Sichman, J., Brandao, A.: An experience on reputation models interoperability based on a functional ontology. In: Proceedings of 20th International Joint Conference on Artificial Intelligence, IJCAI 2007 (2007)
22. Wiederhold, G.: Mediators in the architecture of future information systems. Computer 25(3), 38–49 (2002)
23. Zhou, R., Hwang, K., Cai, M.: Gossiptrust for fast reputation aggregation in peer-to-peer networks. IEEE Transactions on Knowledge and Data Engineering, 1282–1295 (2008)
24. Zimmermann, P.R.: The official PGP user's guide. MIT Press, Cambridge (1995)

Identifying Knots of Trust in Virtual Communities

Nurit Gal-Oz, Ran Yahalom, and Ehud Gudes

Deutsche Telekom Laboratories at Ben-Gurion University, Beer-Sheva, 84105, Israel
{galoz,yahalomr,ehud}cs.bgu.ac.il

Abstract. Knots of trust are groups of community members having overall "strong" trust relations between them. In previous work we introduced the knot aware trust based reputation model. According to this model, in order to provide a member with reputation information relative to her viewpoint, the system must identify the knot to which that member belongs and interpret its reputation data correctly. In the current paper we present the problem of identifying knots which is modeled as a graph clustering problem, where vertices correspond to individuals and edges describe trust relationships between them. We propose a new perspective for clustering that reflects the subjective idea of trust and the nature of the community. A class of weight functions is suggested for assigning edge weights and their impact on the stability and strength of knots is demonstrated. Finally we show the efficiency of knots of high quality for providing their members with relevant reputation information.

1   Introduction

Trust is itself a term for clustering of perceptions. (White, 1992)

Trust and reputation systems are considered key enablers of virtual communities, especially communities of strangers, where users are not required to reveal their real identities and use pseudonyms instead. These systems support the accumulation of member reputation information and leverage this information to increase the likelihood of successful member interactions and to better protect the community from fraudulent members.

As the scale of virtual communities continues to increase, they become more and more heterogeneous. This implies that, rather than being a single, homogeneous community, they become a collection of loosely-coupled *knots* (i.e. sub-communities) of users. A *knot* is defined as a group of community members having overall "strong" trust relations between themselves. Typically, members belonging to the same knot are more likely to have similar viewpoints and preferences as compared to members that belong to different knots.

The knot-aware trust-based reputation model, introduced in previous work [12], models virtual communities of strangers where members seek services or expert advice from other members. Two key examples of such communities are eBay [1] and Experts-Exchange [2]. The assumption underlying our knot-aware model is that "less is more": the use of relatively small, but carefully selected, subsets of the overall community's reputation data yields better results than those represented by the full data set.

I. Wakeman et al. (Eds.): IFIPTM 2011, IFIP AICT 358, pp. 67–81, 2011.

Since members are primarily influenced by members that shared their preferences in the past, a useful feature of the knot model is that it naturally prevents malicious attempts to bias community members' decisions. Another advantage is that smaller sub-communities, whose viewpoints differ from the overall community average, can maintain their distinctive preferences without having their opinions "diluted' by those of the majority of users outside their knot.

In this paper we focus on the task of partitioning the community into knots. We model the community as a graph where vertices correspond to members and edges describe direct trust relations between them and refer to this task as graph clustering. Specifically, we find the knot clustering task very close to the optimization problem known as correlation clustering [5] which aims at obtaining clusters based on pairwise node relations without specifying the number of clusters in advance. However, unlike the general problem of graph clustering, knot clustering is also motivated by several objectives which arise from the domain of virtual communities and the essence of trust knots.

First, a desirable goal is to group together vertices that are connected with high weighted edges while simultaneously avoiding the inclusion of low weighted edges within the same group. The inherent difficulty we have with this goal is that edge weights are derived from trust relations and are not a distance metric; therefore a person may have a great deal of trust in two other members who have very little trust between themselves.

Second, the length of the path between each pair of vertices should be restricted. A path length greater than one indicates a transitive trust chain that represents an indirect trust relation. The longer a chain is, the lower is the trust between its endpoint vertices. Transitive trust chains [15] are a means to overcome the sparsity problem from which community graphs representing trust relations may suffer. However, allowing a long trust chain may result in very large knots. As such, we may prefer to divide a big cluster into several smaller clusters (i.e., "less is more") in which the path between each pair of vertices is shorter.

Third, clusters should be stable. Intuitively a cluster is considered to be more stable as more modifications to its edges' weights are required to justify splitting it. Weight functions that were mentioned in the literature [11] refer to the same notion of correlation for all input graphs. Our research regards trust as correlation and we assert that the extent to which two individuals are correlated is relative to a required level of mutual trust and subject to its existence in the community. Thus we support different notions of correlation by using different weight functions for different community graphs.

Finally although clustering is a common technique in AI and data mining, in most clustering applications, the graph representation of the problem is an obvious step. In knot clustering this step is very significant. The graph representation, the weights on the edges and the distance functions all reflect the subjective idea of trust and the nature of the community to which our clustering is sensitive. This is shown in our experimental evaluation and is a major contribution of our paper.

The rest of the paper is organized as follows. Section 2 provides an overview of the related work. In section 3, we describe the knots-aware clustering problem and in section 4 we provide the knot clustering algorithm. Evaluation results are presented in Section 5. We conclude by discussing future research directions in Section 6.

2   Related Work

One of the basic properties of trust is directness [17]. Direct trust refers to trust based on first hand experience. Indirect trust is based on the opinion of one's trustees by transitivity. Several studies use transitive trust-chains to propagate trust. Instead of using trust propagation as in [6,16,14] we use clustering that leans on the transitivity property to make sure there exists a predefined level of propagated trust among a knot's members.

Given a data set in the form of a graph, the goal of graph clustering is to divide the set of vertices into clusters such that the vertices assigned to a particular cluster are similar or connected in some predefined sense. Commonly used clustering algorithms such as k-means, k-sum and k-center require prior knowledge of the number of clusters that we wish to divide the data into. However in some applications this information is unknown. The Correlation Clustering (CC) problem introduced by Bansal et al. [5] is a method for clustering a graph into the optimal number of clusters without knowing that number in advance. This problem is defined on a complete graph of n vertices (items), where each edge is labeled $< + >$ if its end vertices are considered similar or $< - >$ if they are considered different. The objective of CC is to produce a clustering that agrees as much as possible with the edge labels. This corresponds to the optimization problem of maximizing agreements or to its equivalent problem of minimizing the number of disagreements. The solution of the CC optimization problem is known to be NP-hard [5]. Integer linear programming (ILP) can be used to solve the general problem optimally, for a relatively small number of vertices. According to [11], beyond a few hundred vertices, the only available solutions are heuristic or approximate. Several effective approximation algorithms were proposed for CC with worst-case theoretical guarantees (e.g. [5,9,7]). Bansal et al. [5] provide an approximation algorithm for clustering by minimizing disagreements in complete graphs. They show that the number of disagreements in the solution found by the algorithm is bounded by a constant factor of the optimal solution. Demaine et al. [9] present an $O(logn)$ approximation algorithm for minimizing disagreements in general weighted graphs. This algorithm first solves a linear program and then uses the resulting fractional values to determine the distance between two vertices. They use a region-growing technique to group close vertices together and round the fractional values. Swamy [23] shows that the maximization problem is solvable within a factor of 0.7666 approximation. Correlation Clustering has applications in data mining and natural language processing [8], consensus clustering [13], co-reference resolution [22,21,8]. Elsner and Schudy [11] have examined four greedy algorithms First [22], Best [21] Vote and Pivot [4]. They used an implementation of the semidefinite programming (SDP) relaxation to provide lower bounds on the optimal solution and show that the heuristic algorithms are quite close to optimal.

The goal of limiting the cluster diameters is discussed in [10]. The authors present a heuristic algorithm for graph clustering using distance-k cliques. A sub-graph is a distance-k clique if any two vertices in it are connected by a path of length k or less.

This study also considers the goal of limiting the clusters' diameter as well as other goals which involve using the edge weights as additional criteria for assigning vertices to clusters.

3   Applying Clustering for Identifying Knots

A *knot* [12] is a subset of community members identified as having overall strong trust relations among them. A trust member i has in member j is derived from a trust computation model(e.g., the knot model [12]) or from directly assigned trust values [18]. Two members i and j should belong to the same knot if i has high enough direct trust in j denoted $TM(i,j)$, or if i has high enough transitive trust in j (e.g., if i trusts k and k trusts j we conclude that i trusts j), and vice versa. Knots are groups of members that can rely on each other's recommendations even if they did not rate the same experts. Different knots typically represent different view points and preferences. It is therefore plausible that the reputation of the same expert may differ significantly between different knots. Using the knot-aware approach, we can deal with heterogeneous communities where an experts reputation may be distributed in a multi-modal manner. As discussed in [12], knots have the ability of reducing the risk of relying on dishonest or biased recommendations, since the members that provide them can be identified and excluded from the knot.

A community is modeled as a directed graph $G = (V, E)$ (called the community graph), in which vertices represent members and edges represent the trust relations between the members at their end-point vertices. The weight on a directed edge from vertex i to vertex j is the level of direct trust i has in j at time t and is computed by $TM^t(i, j)$. Since we deal with the state of the graph at time t, for simplicity, we omit the time indicator.

We refer to the task of identifying knots as graph clustering. More specifically, we aim to find a partition of the community graph based on the direct trust between pairs of members. For this purpose, we replace the trust relations between any two members $TM(i, j)$ and $TM(j, i)$ with a weaker relation named Mutual Trust in Member (MTM). Thus, the directed edges (i, j) and (j, i), whose weights were $TM(i, j)$ and $TM(j, i)$, are replaced by a single, undirected edge whose weight is $MTM(i, j) = MTM(j, i) = min\{TM(i, j), TM(j, i)\}$. This way we can use the edge relation as the input for the clustering algorithm, which must decide if its two end-vertices should reside in the same cluster or not. Intuitively, the new relation is more stringent in the sense that it takes into account the minimum level of mutual trust between any two members as the representing value of trust between them.

3.1   Correlation Clustering

We consider the problem of clustering a community of members based on the mutual trust they have in each other. Each cluster in the resulting clustering will constitute a different knot. For this purpose, we adopt the correlation clustering (CC) approach defined by [5]. Given a graph $G_{CC} = <V, E_{CC}>$, each edge $e_{ij} \in E_{CC}$ is either labeled $< + >$ if we believe that i and j should belong to the same cluster or $< - >$ if we believe that they should not. In addition, the edge is assigned a weight w_{ij} that quantifies our belief. The process of assigning of the label and weight to e_{ij} is based on $MTM(i, j)$ and controlled by the weight function discussed in the next sections.

A partition of V is defined by a set of variables $x_{ij} \in \{0, 1\}$ corresponding to the set of edges $e_{ij} \in E_{CC}$. The assignment of vertices i and j to the same cluster is expressed by assigning $x_{ij} = 1$, and assigning them to different clusters is expressed by assigning $x_{ij} = 0$.

We search for a partition that agrees as much as possible with the edge labels. An agreement with a label refers to either assigning a positive edge within a cluster or assigning a negative edge between clusters. Our goal is therefore to maximize the amount of agreement (known as the maximization version of CC in incomplete graphs). Following [7], we thus define the objective function as follows:

$$Maximize(\sum_{e_{ij} \in E+} w_{ij} \cdot x_{ij} + \sum_{e_{ij} \in E-} w_{ij} \cdot (1 - x_{ij})) \tag{1}$$

where $E+$ and $E-$ denote all positive and negative labeled edges, respectively, and subject to: $x_{ij} \in \{0, 1\}$; $x_{ij} = x_{ji}$; $x_{ii} = 1$ and $x_{ij} = x_{jk} = 1$ implies $x_{ik} = 1$. This objective function is referred to as the MaxAgree objective.

3.2 Clustering Criteria

A clustering algorithm aimed at achieving the MaxAgree objective attempts to assign edges with high values of MTM within knots while keeping edges with low MTM values outside knots. However, we also require our clustering to meet three other objectives related to the essence of knots, which we to address by fine tuning the weight function and clustering algorithm. The first objective is to create strong knots, or in other words, to construct clusters having a large aggregated amount of MTM. Although this may seem to derive from the MaxAgree objective, it emphasizes the need to have as many high MTM edges and as few low MTM edges within knots as possible. Our second objective is ensuring that the indirect trust relations between any two members in any knot meets some minimal level of reliability, thereby increasing knot efficiency. This reliability depends highly on the trust chain of the clustering (definition 1). The longest trust chain that exists between any two vertices in a knot, known as the diameter of the subgraph denoted by the knot, characterizes the connectivity of the knot.

Definition 1. *A Trust Chain Length (TCL) of a clustering C, denoted by κ, is the length of the longest trust chain connecting any two vertices within any knot in the clustering. Formally:*

$$\kappa = \max_{K \in C} \max_{i, j \in V_K} TC_K(i, j) \tag{2}$$

where $|TC_K(i, j)|$ is the length of the trust chain between nodes i and j in knot K.

A path of length greater than one is a transitive trust chain which represents an indirect trust relation. The longer a chain is, the lower we rely on the trust between its endpoint vertices, regardless of the actual trust level assigned to each edge on the path. Assuming that the reliability of indirect trust between members in the same knot decreases as the trust chain between them becomes longer, limiting the TCL of a clustering can be used as a mechanism of ensuring that the indirect trust relations between any two members in any knot will meet some minimal level of reliability.

Finally, we want to generate stable knots. Since trust relations are constantly updated, we need the clustering to be firm enough so that no single trust modification will turn it incorrect, which is important for practically maintaining knots. Next we formally define trust chain length and the measures of strength and stability.

The strength of a clustering is defined in terms of the strength of its clusters (see definition 2 for knot strength). For consistency with the clustering graph, instead of using $TM(i,j) + TM(j,i)$ as in definition 2, we use $2 \cdot MTM(i,j)$.

Definition 2. Strength *of a clustering C is the sum of the strength of all the knots in the clustering,* $K = < V_K, E_K > \in C$.

$$Strength(C) = \sum_{K \in C} \frac{\sum_{i \in V_K} deg_i}{|V_K|} = \sum_{K \in C} \frac{2 \cdot \sum_{e_{ij} \in E_K} MTM(i,j)}{|V_K|} \qquad (3)$$

Intuitively, as the average node degree increases and the knot becomes stronger, it has a better edges-to-vertices ratio and more paths between vertices. This indicates that the members of the knot have a lot of mutual "trustees," and therefore, they are more likely to trust each other.

Stability of a clustering C is calculated as the average stability of its knots. The stability of a knot $K = < V_K, E_K >$ represents the minimal amount of trust loss that would justify splitting the knot into two sub-knots. More specifically, we search for a minimum cut (*MinCut*) of the knot, i.e., the cut having the smallest sum of MTM values of edges. Intuitively, if the *MinCut* value of a knot is high, many changes (e.g., decrease of intra-knot or increase of inter-knot edge MTM values) must occur to justify a split. Furthermore, we require that knot stability indicate the consequence of the *MinCut* split. The closer the sizes of the two sub-knots, the greater the affect on the knot's structure, and therefore, the knot is considered less stable. Thus we define stability as follows:

Definition 3. Stability *of a knot is the weight of the minimum cut on edges relative to the ratio between the size of the sub-knots derived from this cut.*

$$Stability(K) = \frac{MinCut_K \cdot \frac{|K'|}{|K''|}}{|V_K| - 1} \qquad (4)$$

where K' and K'' are the two sub-knots induced by the removal of the minimum cut edges and $|V_{K'}| \geq |V_{K''}|$.

Stability of a clustering is calculated accordingly:

$$Stability(C) = \frac{\sum_{K \in C} Stability(K)}{|C|} \qquad (5)$$

3.3   Different Weight Functions

An integral element of the CC graph generation is the weight function (WF). The WF provides a pairwise decision of whether or not two members should be assigned to the same knot. If the sign of the WF output is positive it means the two members should be assigned to the same knot, otherwise they should not. The WF also provides the extent to which the decision is believed to be true (the confidence in the decision), and corresponds to the weight of the edge in the CC graph. The WF output is calculated from the MTM between the two members while taking into consideration a community dependent trust threshold level (definition 4):

Definition 4. Trust Threshold Level *(TTL) is a value in $[0.5, 1]$, denoted by α, which represents the minimum level of MTM required for an edge to be labeled $< + >$. The TTL is a community dependent parameter. It is defined in the range of $[0.5, 1]$ since trust in our model ranges in $[0, 1]$ where complete trust is set to 1, and complete distrust is set to 0.*

The WF is formally defined in definition 5:

Definition 5. $WF : [0, 1] \times [0.5, 1] \rightarrow \Re$ *is a function that assigns the weight $w_{ij} = |WF(MTM(i, j), \alpha)|$ for edge e_{ij} and labels it with $sign(WF(MTM(i, j), \alpha))$.*

A WF is required to have the following two properties:

1. It must be be monotonically non-decreasing to give higher MTM valued pairs a higher tendency of being assigned to the same knot.
2. The MTM value for which the WF switches its sign, denoted as $MTM_{boundary}$, must be in the range $[0.5, \alpha]$, where $\alpha > 0.5$. This is necessary to reflect our assumptions that, for any given pair of members, if $MTM < 0.5$, they **do not** trust each other enough to be assigned to the same knot whereas if $MTM > \alpha$, they **do**.

A key aspect of the WF is its slope, which controls controlling how sensitive its labeling is to changes in MTM values. Defining different slopes for different intervals of MTM results in different levels of labeling sensitivity between those intervals. Another key aspect is whether its output weight values are symmetric with respect to $MTM_{boundary}$. One may choose to define a symmetric WF for which the MTM values at equal distances from $MTM_{boundary}$ derive the same weight but with opposite signs. However, if the WF is asymmetric, a value of $MTM = MTM_{boundary} + \varepsilon$ corresponds to a positive output whose magnitude differs from the negative output corresponding to a value of $MTM = MTM_{boundary} - \varepsilon$. An asymmetric WF allows us to distinguish between the significance of positive and negative edges (and therefore, to detect the effect that they have on the clustering algorithm). For example, by defining the slope after $MTM_{boundary}$ to be steeper than the slope before it, one can express that $MTM = MTM_{boundary} + \varepsilon$ corresponds to a heavier positive edge when compared to the weight of the negative edge corresponding to $MTM = MTM_{boundary} - \varepsilon$. A basic weight function simply considers the difference between an edge's MTM value and α:

$$WF_{basic}(MTM(i, j), \alpha) = MTM(i, j) - \alpha \tag{6}$$

This WF is symmetric and satisfies $MTM_{boundary} = \alpha$: an MTM value of $\alpha + \varepsilon$ for $0 < \varepsilon < min(\alpha, 1 - \alpha)$ is "good" to the same extent that an MTM value of $\alpha - \varepsilon$ is considered "bad". An asymmetric growth WF involves a parameter $\lambda \geq 0$ which allows us to regulate both the value of $MTM_{boundary}$ and the slope:

$$WF_{asymGrowth}(MTM(i,j),\alpha) = \frac{\lambda}{1 + e^{(\alpha - MTM(i,j)) \cdot 10}} - (\alpha - MTM(i,j)) \qquad (7)$$

This WF is identical to WF_{basic} for $\lambda = 0$. Notice that $0 \leq MTM_{boundary} \leq \alpha$. As λ increases, $MTM_{boundary}$ becomes smaller and positive edges receive much higher weights than negative ones.

The ability to use different values of TTL and/or different WFs is cardinal for knot identification. This ability is essential for accommodating different views of how it is best to determine whether or not two members should be in the same knot. This is important not only for working with different communities but also for dynamic communities where the perception of trust may change over time as more rating data is accumulated.

Figure 1 presents an example for this. The central graph represents a toy community of whose knots were identified using WF_{basic} with $\alpha = 0.7$, representing the perceived TTL at time t_0. The strength of this clustering is 4 and its stability is 2. Now assume that a maintenance reclustering is done every T days. Consider a scenario s_1 in which members 3 and 4 rated the same experts similarly during the T days after t_0 causing $MTM(3,4)$ to increase by 0.3 (upper part of Figure 1). Reclustering the community with the same WF and α, results in a weaker (strength = 2.27) and less stable (stability = 0.16) clustering (upper-left clustering). However, if we realize that the community has changed in a way that requires us to raise the TTL (e.g. there is no point in having a TTL that is lower than all MTM values in the community), we could recluster using WF_{basic}, with say $\alpha = 0.9$, and get the stronger and more stable clustering we had at t_0. In a different scenario s_2, members 1 and 2 rated the same experts as member 3 only differently (again, between t_0 and $t_0 + T$), causing both $MTM(1,3)$ and $MTM(2,3)$ to decrease by 0.31 (lower part of Figure 1). Reclustering the community with the same WF and α will result in a weaker (strength = 3) and less stable (stability = 1) clustering (lower-left clustering). This may be acceptable in communities where we would be willing to sacrifice stability on account of gaining accuracy. However, if 0.7 adequately represents the TTL and the community is more interested in stability, we could make this threshold tolerant to MTM values in its vicinity. One way to do this is by switching to an appropriate $WF_{asymGrowth}$. Reclustering would then result in a stronger (strength = 3.59) and more stable (stability = 1.69) clustering (lower-right clustering).

4   The Knot Clustering Algorithm

The knot clustering algorithm uses the hierarchical approach [24] as a feasible solution to the CC problem defined in section 3. First, the CC graph $G_{CC} = <V, E_{CC}>$ is derived from the community graph G using the given WF and TTL. Next, we calculate the connectivity components of the graph induced by the positive edges, denoted by G_C^+, instead of G_C. For each connectivity component with n vertices, we initialize its clustering to n singleton clusters, and iteratively merge pairs of clusters until a stopping criterion is met, and the clustering is final. The stopping criterion is derived from the

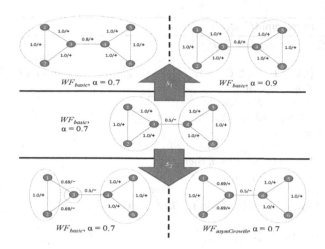

Fig. 1. Motivation for TTL/WF adjustment in dynamic communities. All graphs represent the same toy community where the central graph represents the community at time t_0 and all other graphs at time $t_0 + T$. The upper two graphs depict the changes in the graph due to new ratings that were introduced according to scenario s_1 and the lower two due to a different scenario, s_2.

TCL requirement and the MaxAgree objective, the latter of which is used to guide the merging process. More specifically, at each step, the pair of clusters whose merging leads to the highest increase in the value of the MaxAgree objective function, without violating the TCL requirement, are merged.

A clustering C can be defined by its corresponding clustering matrix $M^C = \{x_{ij} | i, j = 1, \ldots, |V|\}$, where $x_{ij} = 1$ if vertices v_i and v_j belong to the same cluster or $x_{ij} = 0$ if they are in different clusters. For a given clustering C, the assignment of its clustering matrix in the MaxAgree objective function (eq. 1) can be written as:

$$Agreement(C) = \sum_{e_{ij} \in E^+, x_{ij}=1} w_{ij} + \sum_{e_{ij} \in E^-, x_{ij}=0} w_{ij} \qquad (8)$$

where $x_{ij} \in M^C$. The Agreement function expresses the amount of weighted agreement associated with a clustering by summing the weights of all positive intra-cluster edges and negative inter-cluster (bridge) edges.

To quantify the contribution of merging clusters c_1 and c_2, we define the utility of merging as the increase in the Agreement function resulting from the merging denoted $MergeUtil$: $MergeUtil(c_1, c_2) = Agreement(C') - Agreement(C)$, where C' is the clustering derived from clustering C by merging clusters $c_1, c_2 \in C$ into a single new cluster $c'_{12} \in C'$. Inserting equation 8 into this definition gives:

$$MergeUtil(c_1, c_2) = \sum_{e_{ij} \in Bridge^+_{c_1,c_2}} w_{ij} - \sum_{e_{ij} \in Bridge^-_{c_1,c_2}} w_{ij} \qquad (9)$$

where $Bridge^+_{c_1,c_2}$ and $Bridge^-_{c_1,c_2}$ are respectively the sets of positive and negative bridge edges between clusters c_1 and c_2. Intuitively, the only edges that can affect the value of the Agreement function due to a merging of c_1 and c_2 are the bridge edges

---

Algorithm 1. ClusterGraph(G, κ, WF, α)

1: $G_{CC} \leftarrow <V, E_{CC}>$ s.t. $E_{CC} = WF(E, \alpha)$;
2: $C \leftarrow \emptyset$
3: $ConComps \leftarrow \{C_{comp} | C_{comp} \subset G_{cc} \wedge \forall e_{ij} \text{ s.t. } i \in C_{comp}, j \notin C_{comp} \rightarrow e_{ij} \in E_{CC}^-\}$;
4: **for all** $comp \in ConComps$ **do**
5:      $C_{comp} \leftarrow \{c_i | c_i = \{i\}, \forall i \in V_{comp}\}$;
6:      $S \leftarrow \{(c_i, c_j) | MergeUtil(c_i, c_j) > 0; c_i, c_j \in C_{comp}\}$;
7:      **while** $S \neq \emptyset$ **do**
8:          $c_{ij} \leftarrow c_i \cup c_j$ s.t. $Max_{(c_i,c_j)\in S}MergeUtil(c_i, c_j)$;
9:          **if** $\forall u, v \in V_{c_{ij}} : |TC_{c_{ij}}(u, v)| \leq \kappa$ **then**
10:             $C_{comp} \leftarrow C_{comp} - \{c_i, c_j\}$;
11:             $C_{comp} \leftarrow C_{comp} \cup c_{ij}$;
12:             $S \leftarrow \{(c_r, c_s) | MergeUtil(c_r, c_s) > 0; c_r, c_s \in C_{comp}\}$;
13:         **else**
14:             $S \leftarrow S - \{(c_i, c_j)\}$;
15:         **end if**
16:     **end while**
17:     $C \leftarrow C \cup C_{comp}$
18: **end for**

---

between them, which become intra-cluster edges in c_1'. Any such positive edge adds to the overall agreement in the clustering, and therefore increases the value of the Agreement function. On the other hand, any such negative edge no longer contributes what it contributed when it was a bridge edge, thereby decreasing the value of the Agreement function. Thus, the MergeUtil can be computed by iterating over all bridge edges between c_1 and c_2 while adding the weights of the positive ones and subtracting the weights of negative ones.

Algorithm 1 outlines the knot clustering algorithm. Lines 1-3 construct the clustering graph with the appropriate weights and separate this graph into connectivity components. Lines 5-14 perform the clustering for each connectivity component. In line 5, we initialize the clustering for the current connectivity component by creating a singleton cluster for each vertex in the graph. In line 6, we calculate the MergeUtil values of all cluster pairs and generate the list S. This list contains references to the cluster pairs (c_i, c_j) whose merging into cluster c_{ij} can increase the value of the Agreement function, i.e., the MergeUtil value of this pair is positive. In lines 8-9, the best candidate pair of clusters is checked for TCL-compliance. If found compliant, then each of the clusters in the pair is removed from the clustering and the candidate merged cluster is added to the clustering in lines 10-11. Any MergeUtil values that may have consequently changed are recalculated and S is repopulated with the positive MergeUtil valued cluster pairs. If the candidate pair for merge is not TCL-compliant, the pair is removed from the list S (line14). The algorithm terminates when the list S is empty. Termination is guaranteed since the size of S is reduced in each step of the loop.

5   Clustering Evaluation

We evaluate the knot clustering in light of the objectives discussed in section 3. The evaluation is divided into two parts. First, we evaluate the quality of the clustering on a synthetic dataset produced by a simulation program in different settings. Then we evaluate the quality of the knot as a group of trustees by testing the reputation computation based on the knots we identify in the MovieLens [3] community.

The evaluation of the clustering requires a set of community graphs as input. The structure of a community graph depends on the existence of trust relations between the members and the level of trust they represent. In the early days of a community, its graph is necessarily very sparse, increasing in density as more experience is gained within the community. Moreover, the extent of member nodes partitioning in a graph may vary from a clearly structured graph to a completely uniform one with the edges evenly distributed over the set of vertices. In the latter case, the clustering computed by any algorithm will be rather arbitrary. If the graph is clearly structured and a clear clustering based on the trust levels exists, our task is to identify it. We may further divide this structure by restricting the TCL if the graph is highly connected. However, a more challenging task is to identify the best set of knots, when the data set is noisy. We refer to two types of noise – graph sparsity and a lack of a clear structure of groups of members that trust each other. We constructed graphs that simulate communities with different levels of density and cluster-structure clarity. Assuming that each community is characterized by some TTL value, referred to as the characteristic TTL and denoted by $\widehat{\alpha}$, we also generate graphs with different values of $\widehat{\alpha}$. The cluster-structure was created by first defining groups of members that correspond to knots and then generating their MTM values accordingly, with respect to $\widehat{\alpha}$. Different levels of cluster-structure clarity were introduced by generating MTM values that agree with the pre-defined knots with different values of probability p (i.e. there is a $p\%$ chance that the MTM will be $\geq \widehat{\alpha}$). The purpose of this experiment is to demonstrate how we overcome the two types of noise by using our approach. The second measure is the Mathews Correlation Coefficient [19] which is generally regarded as a balanced measure that can be used for comparing clusterings of very different sizes. The third measure we used is variation of information (VI), suggested by Meila [20], which is based on using entropy and measures the amount of information lost and gained in changing from one clustering to another.

5.1 Evaluation Results

Our experiment includes 1200 tests in which we tested values of TTL ranging from 0.5 to 0.95 (with a 0.05 increment); TCL values ranging from 1 to 6; density levels of $5 - 15\%, 16 - 25\%$, and $26 - 35\%$; levels of cluster-structure clarity represented by probabilities ranging from 0.6 to 1 (with increments of 0.1); and $\widehat{\alpha}$ values of 0.6, 0.7, 0.8, and 0.9.

As expected, the best results were obtained when we used a weight function with $\widehat{\alpha}$. This was right even when the probability for a clear structure was decreased to 0.6 and as the graph density was as low as 9%. Table 1 shows the average improvement in clustering gained by using WF_{basic} with $TTL = \widehat{\alpha}$ in our algorithm instead of using other TTL values. The first column represents the $\widehat{\alpha}$ examined and each of the other three columns depicts the average improvement (in percents) according to one of the three measures F-score, Matthews-CC, or VI, respectively, when using the $\widehat{\alpha}$ as the TTL instead of the rest 3 TTL values.

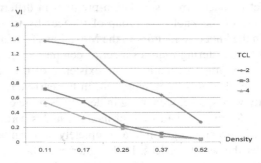

Fig. 2. Quality of clustering measured by VI in different levels of sparsity of the same graph

We show that in dense communities, different values of TCL have little benefit on the quality of clustering whereas in sparse communities the difference is significant and a higher TCL is required to overcome sparsity. Figure 2 demonstrates that a TCL of 4 significantly improves the quality of clustering when the density of the community is low compared to lower TCL values. As the density increases, the improvement becomes less significant. The clustering quality is measured here by VI (VI is best as it tends to 0) but similar results were also obtained for the F-score and Mathews Correlation Coefficient measures.

Table 1. Clustering improvement (%) when using $\widehat{\alpha}$, as measured by F-score, Matthews-CC or VI.

$\widehat{\alpha}$	F-Score	Matthews-CC	VI
0.6	75.6	55.1	3.3
0.7	49.2	49.0	2.6
0.8	25.5	40.9	3.5
0.9	11.3	40.8	4.9

Next we show the tradeoff between strength and stability. We compared the results from using $WF_{AsymGrowth}$ with $\lambda = 1$ to using WF_{Basic} to demonstrate their impact on stability and strength. When comparing different levels of TTL (Figure 3(a) and (b)) we can see that $WF_{AsymGrowth}$ yields better stability for all levels of TTL. However, this advantage is significantly reduced for high levels of TTL where the knots obtained where relatively small for both WFs and the clustering tends to contain many singleton clusters. WF_{Basic} yields better strength in general with the exception of high levels of TTL in which the clusters obtained by the $WF_{AsymGrowth}$ consisted of more edges whose MTM was less than the TTL. Figure 3(c), shows that the $WF_{AsymGrowth}$ yields better stability for all values of TCL, although for low TCL values the difference between the two WFs is relatively minor due to high connectivity of the knots. WF_{Basic} yields better strength in general but for a TCL value of 1, which assigns only connected members to the same knot, the $WF_{AsymGrowth}$ is stronger. This is because $WF_{AsymGrowth}$ is more tolerant to edges with an MTM value lower than α [Figure 3(d)].

In the second experiment we used a MovieLens [3] dataset to evaluate the quality of the knots. This dataset consists of 100,000 movie ratings submitted from 943 users on

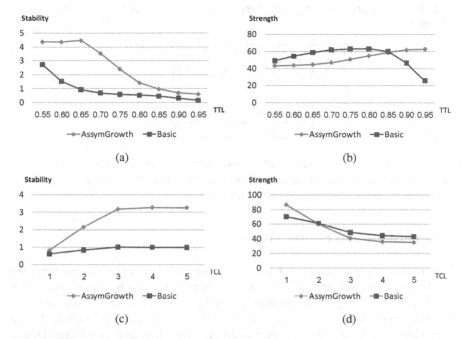

Fig. 3. Average Strength and Stability for different WFs: (a) Stability by TTL, (b) Strength by TTL, (c) Stability by TCL, (d) Strength by TCL.

1682 movies. Movies play the role of experts and the reputation of an expert is replaced by a movie score. In this case our criteria was how well a movie's reputation within a knot represents what knot members may think of it (in terms of predicting how they may rate the movie).

We divided the complete set of ratings into a training set, from which MTM values were derived and the community graph was constructed, and a test set which we kept aside for later evaluation. In this experiment we used a 4-fold cross validation. After identifying the knots in the community graph, we calculated the mean absolute error (MAE) between the knot based reputation scores and their corresponding test set rating scores. The majority of ratings in the MovieLens (over 60%) are of ratings 3 and 4 and therefore predicting these ratings according to any popularity measure such as average, will produce good results. Since low ratings (1,2) and high rating (5) are relatively rare in the dataset, our goal was to show that by using the knots as a group of trustees we can provide a good prediction for these ratings where using the popularity measure would be less precise. We compared two different configurations of the knot clustering algorithm, both conducted with the $WF_{AsymGrowth}$ which is more suitable for a movies rating community. We used a TTL value of 0.9 and TCL values of 2 and 5 respectively. The results showed that in general the reputation scores provided to members by their knots were better than the global reputation [12] computed based on all knots which are not singletons. Table 2 presents the advantage of using knot based reputation over the global reputation for each score separately. It presents the improvement in percentage of the MAE of the global reputation. As shown, the improvement was stressed for

Table 2. The improvement (%) in MAE of reputation scores provided by knots compared to global reputation

Rating	TCL=2 TTL=0.9	TCL=5 TTL=0.9
1	5.16	4.46
2	3.1	3.12
3	-0.32	0.74
4	-1.13	-0.89
5	2.17	1.7

the extreme scores while for values of 3 and 4 knots had no advantage. This can be attributed to the distribution of ratings as noted above. Clustering with TCL of 2 and 5 showed no significant advantage of one over the other.

6 Conclusions and Future Work

The community graph represents a dynamic trust network that changes all the time. We define the problem of identifying knots of members in the graph and propose a new perspective for clustering the community graph that refers to the underlying levels of trust existing in the community at a given time. The knot clustering problem is close to the correlation clustering problem with an additional limitation on the trust chain length. We suggest a heuristic algorithm related to the agglomerative hierarchical clustering that uses different weight functions to cluster different graphs. We show that the best solution that can be achieved with our approach, strongly depends on understanding the state of the community. This understanding allows us to adjust the TTL and weight function to meet the required objectives such as strength and stability of knots.

In future work we intend to further explore the subject of knot stability for the purpose of maintaining knots. *Knots Maintenance* is an action taken in order to refine the clustering upon changes in the community. Refinement corresponds to either restoring the quality of a clustering which has decreased or improving the quality of a clustering when possible. Our goal is to carry out maintenance actions only when there is high probability that a better clustering exists and/or in accordance with a community policy.

References

1. eBay, http://www.ebay.com/
2. Experts-exchange, http://www.experts-exchange.com/
3. Grouplens, http://www.grouplens.org/
4. Ailon, N., Charikar, M., Newman, A.: Aggregating inconsistent information: ranking and clustering. Journal of the ACM (JACM) 55(5), 1–27 (2008)
5. Bansal, N., Blum, A., Chawla, S.: Correlation clustering. In: Proceedings of the 43rd Symposium on Foundations of Computer Science (FOCS 2002), pp. 238–247. IEEE Computer Society, Washington, DC, USA (2002)
6. Chakraborty, S., Ray, I.: Trustbac: integrating trust relationships into the rbac model for access control in open systems. In: Proceedings of the 11th ACM Symposium on Access Control Models and Technologies (SACMAT 2006), pp. 49–58. ACM, New York (2006)

7. Charikar, M., Guruswami, V., Wirth, A.: Clustering with qualitative information. Journal of Computer and System Sciences 71(3), 360–383 (2005)
8. Cohen, W.W., Richman, J.: Learning to match and cluster large high-dimensional data sets for data integration. In: Proceedings of the Eighth ACM SIGKDD International Conference on Knowledge Discovery and Data Mining, pp. 475–480 (2002)
9. Demaine, E.D., Emanuel, D., Fiat, A., Immorlica, N.: Correlation clustering in general weighted graphs. Theoretical Computer Science 361(2-3), 172–187 (2006), Special issue on approximation and online algorithms
10. Edachery, J., Sen, A., Brandenburg, F.J.: Graph clustering using distance-k cliques. Graph Drawing, 98–106 (1999)
11. Elsner, M., Schudy, W.: Bounding and comparing methods for correlation clustering beyond ilp. In: NAACL-HLT Workshop on Integer Linear Programming for Natural Language Processing (ILPNLP 2009), pp. 19–27 (2009)
12. Gal-Oz, N., Gudes, E., Hendler, D.: A robust and knot-aware trust-based reputation model. In: Proceedings of the 2nd Joint iTrust and PST Conferences on Privacy, Trust Management and Security (IFIPTM 2008), Trondheim, Norway, pp. 167–182 (June 2008)
13. Gionis, A., Mannila, H., Tsaparas, P.: Clustering aggregation. ACM Transactions on Knowledge Discovery from Data (TKDD) 1(1), 4 (2007)
14. Guha, R., Kumar, R., Raghavan, P., Tomkins, A.: Propagation of trust and distrust. In: Proceedings of the 13th International Conference on World Wide Web (WWW 2004), pp. 403–412. ACM, New York (2004)
15. Jøsang, A., Gray, E., Kinateder, M.: Analysing topologies of transitive trust. In: Proceedings of the 1st International Workshop on Formal Aspects in Security and Trust (FAST 2003), pp. 9–22 (2003)
16. Kamvar, S.D., Schlosser, M.T., Garcia-Molina, H.: The eigentrust algorithm for reputation management in p2p networks. In: Proceedings of the 12th International Conference on World Wide Web (WWW 2003), pp. 640–651. ACM, New York (2003)
17. Kinateder, M., Baschny, E., Rothermel, K.: Towards a generic trust model – comparison of various trust update algorithms. In: Herrmann, P., Issarny, V., Shiu, S.C.K. (eds.) iTrust 2005. LNCS, vol. 3477, pp. 177–192. Springer, Heidelberg (2005)
18. Massa, P., Avesani, P.: Avesani. Controversial users demand local trust metrics: An experimental study on epinions. com community. In: Proceedings of the National Conference on Artificial Intelligence (AAAI 2005), vol. 20, p. 121 (2005)
19. Matthews, B.W.: Comparison of the predicted and observed secondary structure of T4 phage lysozyme. Biochimica et Biophysica Acta (BBA)-Protein Structure 405(2), 442–451 (1975)
20. Meilă, M.: Comparing clusterings–an information based distance. Journal of Multivariate Analysis 98(5), 873–895 (2007)
21. Ng, V., Gardent, C.: Improving machine learning approaches to coreference resolution. In: ACL, pp. 104–111 (2002)
22. Soon, W.M., Ng, H.T., Lim, D.C.Y.: A machine learning approach to coreference resolution of noun phrases. Computational Linguistics 27(4), 521–544 (2001)
23. Swamy, C.: Correlation clustering: maximizing agreements via semidefinite programming. In: Proceedings of the Fifteenth Annual ACM-SIAM Symposium on Discrete Algorithms, pp. 526–527. Society for Industrial and Applied Mathematics, Philadelphia (2004)
24. Ward, J.H., Hook, M.E.: Application of an Hierarchical Grouping Procedure to a Problem of Grouping Profiles, vol. 23(1), pp. 69–82 (1963)

Clustering Recommenders in Collaborative Filtering Using Explicit Trust Information

Georgios Pitsilis[1,*], Xiangliang Zhang[2], and Wei Wang[3]

[1] Faculty of Science, Technology and Communication
Université du Luxembourg, Luxembourg
georgios.pitsilis@uni.lu
[2] Division of MCSE,
King Abdullah University of Science and Technology (KAUST), Saudi Arabia
xiangliang.zhang@kaust.edu.sa
[3] Interdisciplinary Centre for Security, Reliability and Trust (SnT Centre),
Université du Luxembourg, Luxembourg
wwangemail@gmail.com

Abstract. In this work, we explore the benefits of combining clustering and social trust information for Recommender Systems. We demonstrate the performance advantages of traditional clustering algorithms like *k-Means* and we explore the use of new ones like *Affinity Propagation* (AP). Contrary to what has been used before, we investigate possible ways that social-oriented information like explicit trust could be exploited with AP for forming clusters of high quality. We conducted a series of evaluation tests using data from a real Recommender system *Epinions.com* from which we derived conclusions about the usefulness of trust information in forming clusters of Recommenders. Moreover, from our results we conclude that the potential advantages in using clustering can be enlarged by making use of the information that Social Networks can provide.

Keywords: Social Trust, Clustering, Recommender Systems, Epinions.com, Affinity Propagation.

1 Introduction

Recommender systems are widely used nowadays and in simple terms they are services used for suggesting products to people who might be interested in them. Recommender systems became popular because they were able to provide personalized recommendations using as input the rating profiles of users. Despite their success and adoption in user communities, they have not shown their full potential yet. Various techniques such as *Nearest Neighborhood*, *Trust* and *Clustering* have been employed in Recommender Systems. Collaborative Filtering (CF), the best known type of Nearest-Neighborhood, has as fundamental idea the agreement on taste of people for predicting their future liking on new items.

---

* The author carried out this work during the tenure of an ERCIM "Alain Bensoussan" Fellowship program.

I. Wakeman et al. (Eds.): IFIPTM 2011, IFIP AICT 358, pp. 82–97, 2011.

Information overloading and *Data sparsity* are two known issues [15][4] in information retrieval that Recommender Systems come to address. Being contrary to each other, the former is referred to the presence of too much information for making a choice, while the latter is caused by the lack of sufficient information during start-up. Information overload has serious implications on performance as it affects the scalability and responsiveness of a system due to the intensive processing power that is needed to correlate the increased amounts of data. Sparsity on the other hand, also known as *cold start problem*, is responsible for the poor performance of traditional Recommender Systems and appears when there is no sufficient information to correlate.

Clustering has been widely investigated in computer science as an unsupervised learning method [9,11,12]. In general, the idea of dividing the big communities of users into smaller sets (clusters) has seemed to offer advantages, such as scalability, which as a result improves the response time, due to the smaller set of data that algorithms operate on. On the other hand, the loss of prediction accuracy is not compensated at a sufficient level to render the use of clusters an attractive solution.

Trust has also been used to mitigate the problem of information overload [18], incorporating the idea of filtering out the available options to the trustworthy ones. Various models for trust propagation [21,20] have been proposed for filtering the selection of neighbors. Despite the benefits offered by employing trust in the production of recommendations, the additional computation effort for trust derivation incurs a penalty in performance, which can limit scalability.

Even though clustering and trust can both individually offer some distinguishable advantages over not using them, there is no previous work to investigate the benefits when used together. In our opinion a more systematic investigation is necessary in how trust expressed by people could be utilized for building neighborhoods, in which recommendations' performance will be enhanced by clustering those neighborhoods. The contribution of this paper is two fold. First, we demonstrate the advantages that a new clustering algorithm *Affinity Propagation* (AP) offers over the use of widely known *k-Means* approach. Second, we explore the potential benefits of using the combination of Explicit trust information with two different clustering algorithms.

The rest of the paper is organized as follows. In section 2 we refer to related work in the area. In section 3 we describe our motivation and essential knowledge about the clustering algorithms we used. Next, in section 4 we describe in more detail the setting used in our evaluation and finally our results and discussion follows in sections 5 and 6 respectively.

2   Related Work

Clustering has been the subject of research in the area of Recommender systems, but it has not been widely studied yet. We mention the research done by Sarwar et al. in [7] as the pioneer work in the field. The main idea behind clustering is to permanently partition choices into smaller sets so that making easier a future choice for a neighbor. This is an idea very much adopted in Social Networking where information can be overwhelming. Truong et al. in [13] introduce an algorithm for producing uniform clusters of items by minimizing the variance between the items within the same clusters. Even though this work is useful, its applicability is still limited to a special algorithm of collaborative filtering (item-based), in which correlations are performed over items rather than users.

Despite a selection of neighbors that is based on trust alone does improve the quality of predictions, as quite many researches have shown [8,2], it is yet not enough to overcome the problem of information overload.

Implying trust from existing properties is an idea that has been employed in quite many schemes. In order to alleviate the sparsity problem, the authors in [22] proposed to build an implicit web-of-trust using information like the personal interactions between users. Massa et al. in [19] try to address the problem of information overload by utilizing the explicitly provided trust links of users. Different from ours, in their work they proposed a mechanism that used the trust values in the computation of predictions. Lathia et al. [8] used an algorithm for deriving how much users should trust each other based on their past ratings.

In recent work in [5], it has been attempted Clustering and Trust models to combine together, which at some point did improve the quality of recommendations. The same authors in [6] are driven by the idea that trust networks can be treated as random graphs, and they proposed a trust inference algorithm in which trust is derived from the connection distance in the graph. Even though there is still wide space for development into clustered networks, it so far remains unexplored how much helpful clustering can be for producing recommendations of good quality.

The development of new Clustering algorithms [3] highlights the need for a more systematic approach of Clustering in Recommender systems, similarly to other areas like intrusion detection for security systems [16] or data streaming [10].

Moreover, the emergence of social networking has given access to much more information than before, such as the explicitly expressed trustworthiness of users, and thus it has increased the potential for existing approaches to develop further. This combined with the fact that new clustering algorithms have not been explored adequately should mean that clustering trust information can be promising for further improving the performance of Recommender Systems.

3   Motivation

In traditional classic CF, only inputs from relevant users referred to as 'neighbors' or 'predictors' are employed in predictions to provide accurate recommendations. Contrary to traditional nearest neighborhood based approaches for CF, which require data to be globally available for being able to compute predictions for all users, in Clustering, user neighborhoods have more static sense. With clustering, neighbors should be pre-selected and be used the same for all predictions made thereafter. A widely adopted CF technique called k-Nearest

Neighborhood (*k-NN*) scheme, identifies the k most similar neighbors to use as inputs in the predicted recommendations. The pure *k-NN*, due to the requirement for neighbors to be selected dynamically from the whole set of users, still fails to overcome the problem of information overload. On the other hand, grouping users along with the information they carry into independent sets has the risk of deteriorating the performance. This necessitates that clustering should be done in a careful manner. A possible solution that we come to investigate in this paper is to utilize other sources of information which normally do not take part in the process of recommendation production. An interesting challenge we come to explore in this paper is to exploit the information provided by users in such a way that clusters of high quality can be built. With quality in clustering we refer to how suitable neighbors have been grouped together for computing predictions of high accuracy.

In total we attempted to test two different clustering schemes, an easily applicable, but established one, and another one which uses a newly developed algorithm. More particularly, our objective is to improve the quality of clustering and to quantify how extraneous information like social data could contribute to the performance of Recommendations. Contrary to using infered trust, as other researchers have attempted in the past [5], we used the trust information expressed by the users, as input to clustering. Furthermore, in order to quantify the contribution of either part in the performance gain, we attempted a comparison between using various sources of information over different clustering algorithms.

3.1   Clustering Algorithms

K-Means. Clustering analysis with k-means regards the partition of a number of n observations $S = \{x_1, x_2, ..., x_n\}$, into a predefined number of k clusters ($k < n$). The main idea is to define k centroids, one for each cluster, as much as possible far away from each other. Next, points that belong to a given data set are associated with the nearest centroids. The allocation of each observation into a cluster is done on the basis of choosing the one which has the nearest mean. The aim is to minimize the within cluster sum of squares given by:

$$\arg\min \sum_{i=1}^{k} \sum_{x_j \in S_i} \| x_j - m_i \|^2 \tag{1}$$

where m_i is the mean of points in the cluster S_i. The last step of binding the data points to clusters is repeated for a number of iterations where a new centroid is re-calculated for each cluster until the centroids have not changed their location any more.

Two key features of *k-Means* include the use of the *Euclidean distance* as a metric for measuring the distances between the points, and the number of clusters k, which is given as an input parameter to the algorithm. The latter is known as a weakness, as not well-defined values can lead to poor results.

Obviously the cluster centroids generated by *k-Means* do not necessarily represent real existing points from the cluster. Fig.1 shows an example of clustering

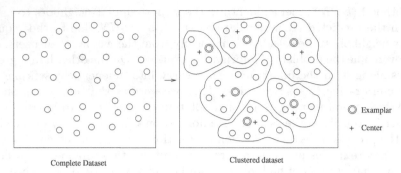

Fig. 1. Neighborhood formation with Clustering. The center of a cluster is normally generated by averaging all the data inside of the cluster, while the exemplar of the cluster is a real data point that best represents the cluster.

a number of points into 6 clusters, with the cross symbol (+) denoting the cluster center generated by *k-Means*.

Affinity Propagation. Affinity Propagation (AP) is a newly developed clustering algorithm proposed by Frey et al. [3]. AP takes as input negative similarities between data points which exchange two types of messages called *Responsibility* and *Availability*. These two messages are communicated between the candidate exemplar points.

An *Availability* message from a candidate k to another point i regards the supporting evidence that k has collected from other points for being an exemplar and is announced to i. The point i in response to the candidate k replies his opinion for this candidature taking into account other candidate exemplars. This type of message is called *Responsibility* and reflects to how well-suited point k is to serve as exemplar for i.

Finally after a few iterations of message exchanges, a set of exemplars emerges from the data points. An exemplar is a selected point of a cluster used as the center. Opposite to what happens in *k-Means*, in AP the exemplars are real data points (See exemplars in Fig.1).

Given a fitness function:

$$E(c) = \sum_{i=1}^{n} S(x_i, x_{c(i)}) \tag{2}$$

where $c(i)$ is the index of the exemplar that represents the point x_i in the cluster of n points, AP finds the mapping c that maximizes the fitness function $E(c)$. $S(x_i, x_j)$ is set to $-d(x_i, x_j)^2$ if $i \neq j$, and otherwise is set to a small constant $-s^*$ ($s^* \geq 0$). $-s^*$ represents a preference that x_i itself be chosen as an exemplar.

Rather than requiring a predefined number of clusters (e.g., *k-Means*), in AP the number of exemplars will emerge from the procedure of message passing. In detail, AP specifies the preference s^* for allowing a data point to become an exemplar. Note that for $s^* = 0$, the best solution is the trivial one, selecting every item as an exemplar.

4 Experimental Setting

Since the observations we intended to use from Recommender Systems could not be represented as points in n-space, we used derived quantities instead to map into the necessary attributes that clustering algorithms required. For the k-Means we mapped each pair of Correlation Coefficient ($w_{a,b}$) value between each two users a and b into distances from the hypothetical mean. In Collaborative Filtering the $w_{a,b}$ values are derived by applying the user's liking (ratings) for products to Pearson's formula:

$$w_{a,b} = \frac{\sum (r_{a,k} - \bar{r}_a)(r_{b,k} - \bar{r}_b)}{\sqrt{\sum (r_{a,k} - \bar{r}_a)^2 \sum (r_{b,k} - \bar{r}_b)^2}} \tag{3}$$

where $\bar{r}_a$ and $\bar{r}_b$ denote as the average of all ratings of user a and b respectively while $r_{a,k}$ and $r_{b,k}$ are the ratings for item k given by users a and b.

Finally, the derived values $w_{a,b}$ are then used in Resnick's prediction formula [17] along with the ratings of the selected predictors $r_{i,j}$ for the item of interest i to provide a prediction of likeness for user a.

$$p_{a,i} = \bar{r}_a + \frac{\sum [w_{a,j}(r_{j,i} - \bar{r}_j)]}{\sum |w_{a,j}|} \tag{4}$$

where $\bar{r}_j$ denote as the average value of the ratings given by a predictor.

Eqns. (3) and (4) describe the traditional CF approach which we use as baseline for our comparison.

Since k-Means algorithm does not necessarily find the most optimal configuration, as far as to minimize the objective function (1), we applied k-Means++ algorithm [1], an algorithm proposed for optimized selection of the cluster centers. Rather than arbitrarily selecting the initial centers of clusters, k-Means++ can be used to seed k-Means with a series of suitable candidate centers. More specifically, with k-Means++ the first cluster center is chosen uniformly at random among the data points. The remaining centers are chosen from the remaining points with probability proportional to the distance $D(x)^2$ of this point x from the nearest cluster center. Once all new cluster centers have been determined, the standard k-Means is applied. As a result, the speed and accuracy is improved over the random selection, as the k-Means converges quite faster after this seeding.

For *Affinity Propagation* we considered employing properties used to study the structural characteristics of Social Networks. The explicit trust information that is available in *Epinions.com* makes easier to derive properties from the structural characteristic of the network of users. The information that was provided as explicit trust of a user for another user is given in binary form, with a value of 1 denoting trust, or it is unknown if no value exists.

Vertex Similarity is an important concept used in social network analysis and data mining. The need for quantifying the similarity between vertices in a network can be approached from various perspectives. Consequently, it is reasonable to consider the structure of the network as a way to capture this.

Similarities between the vertices in a social network graph can possibly be identified by analyzing the patterns of edges between the vertices. A common heuristic that can be used for deciding whether two vertices (or users in the case of a social network) are similar with each other is to assume their similarity to be proportional to the number of neighbors they share.

The idea of transforming the process of community detection in social networks into clustering is a concept which has also been studied by other researchers [23]. Nevertheless, here we attempt to study it within a particular application domain.

We used a function proposed by *Jaccard* [25] to express the similarity between entities based on their connectivities with their neighbors. The formula is given by Eqn. 5. It was chosen as a simple and straightforward way to start our experimentation on transforming social behavioral information into similarity.

$$S_{jaccard}(i,j) = \frac{\mid N_i \cap N_j \mid}{\mid N_i \cup N_j \mid} \tag{5}$$

where N_i and N_j denote as the sets of users trusted by i and j respectively. The $S_{jaccard}$ similarity metric has a value range in the interval [0,1], and maximizes when $N_i = N_j$. $\mid$ $\mid$ indicates the cardinality (i.e., the number of elements in the set). *Jaccard* metric is typically used in the field of data mining to measure the diversity or similarity of sample sets. In our particular case with *Jaccard* metric is meant the level of potential direct trust that might exist between two entities a and b, given their explicit trust to third parties whom they trust in common. The intuition behind this formula can be phrased as: *Two users i and j are more similar in taste as the more users they trust in common.*

$$w_{new(a,b)} = w_{a,b}(1 + \frac{S_{jaccard(a,b)}}{2}) \tag{6}$$

Finally, the value of $S_{jaccard(a,b)}$ is reduced by the Correlation Coefficient $w_{a,b}$ to weighted similarity $w_{new(a,b)}$, which is then applied on Resnick's Eqn. 4 to predict ratings.

We consider the computation of N_i and N_j feasible in a social networking environment for the reason that, even though in many cases social links are meant strictly private, they can still be computable by a third trusted party such as the social networking service provider itself.

4.1   Test Schemes - Dataset

In performing our experimental validation we used data taken from a real Recommender System *Epinions.com*. We chose this particular Recommender system because it provides both ratings of users for products as well as trust information for users. In that system people can rate and write reviews for products. Ratings regard the evaluation of experiences of products by users and are expressed in a five star scale. Also, the members of *Epinions.com* can rate each other based on the reviews they have written for products, forming in this way a web-of-trusted recommenders. The trust information relates to the level of confidence expressed by users for other users based on the reviews they have written for products, and it is provided in binary form. Yet, in the current form of *Epinions* the trust information is not used for computing personalized recommendations. Instead, users are expected to digest manually the reviews coming from sources trusted by users.

The special set we used was collected by Paolo Massa [14] in Nov-Dec 2003. This data set contained 664K ratings, 49K users and 139K products and thus being very sparse (99.025 %). To avoid poor performance due to the noisy behavior of Correlation Coefficient in sparse data sets, we selected a subset of the 1500 most experienced users on the basis of number of ratings given by each other (no matter how many outward and inward trust links they have). This was also done to ensure that the Pearson similarity value between the users is computable as long as there is adequate number of commonly trusted items.

In order to be able to compare in a fair way the results produced between the tested schemes and the baseline *k-NN* approach, we selected predictors for *k-NN* equal in number with those actually selected for the contrasted clustered method. In this way, both clustered and CF techniques used almost the same amount of information from the available knowledge that is expressed as ratings. As far as comparing with classic CF technique, we used all the available information for computing predictions by selecting all the available predictors (i.e., all users which have rated the item in question and the $w_{a,b}$ value with the querying user is computable).

In our experiments, we assumed random selection of predictors for the baseline technique. Since the traditional CF requires no trust information, we made no use of the trust values for the *k-NN* and the classic CF. We neither used the trust as input to the original *k-Means* scheme, which used only the traditional Pearson's similarity ($w_{a,b}$). In addition, for being able to investigate the contribution of social trust data in the performance we attempted to use the social data on both the traditional Clustering *k-Means* scheme as well as the new one which employs the AP algorithm. We called *Jaccard-AP* and *Jaccard-k-Means* the additional two test schemes which used the w_{new} quantity as input information in the clustering.

The static dataset we used limited our options of simulating the prediction creation process and the submission of feedback, as would normally happen in a real environment. Therefore, we tried a 'cross validation' scheme for being able to know how good our predictive model would be in estimating some rating that a user would give for an item before he had experienced that item. More specifically we applied a technique called *leave-one-out*. That is, each rating that was already provided in the dataset by some users was kept hidden and its value was predicted using the rest of the data. This method produces results of acceptable accuracy with that achieved by *k*-fold cross validation scheme. The reason for not using *k*-fold was mainly due to the small data samples we had available and which would lead to poor results with clustering.

4.2   Evaluation Metrics

As far as evaluating accuracy we considered both *Predictive* and *Classification Accuracy* as being important to be shown. *Predictive Accuracy* demonstrates the efficiency of the system to predict accurately the liking of users to products. Two metrics, the first called *Mean Absolute Error* (MAE), and the second *Root Mean Squared Error* (RMSE) are used to demonstrate this. RMSE is useful for quantifying undesirably large errors. *Classification Accuracy* measures the ability for a Recommender system in creating personalized lists of suggested products to users. In other words, it means the frequency at which the system decides correctly or not about if a product would be a good choice for a user. *F-Score* (*f*) is a metric, known also as *Harmonic Mean*, for measuring the efficiency of retrieval with respect to the cost of retrieval. *F-Score* became popular in measuring Recommender systems performance because it reflects the ability of the studied system to produce personalized top-*k* lists of liking products for users.

$$p = \frac{tp}{tp + fp}, \quad r = \frac{tp}{tp + fn}, \quad f = \frac{2pr}{p + r} \tag{7}$$

True Positive (*tp*) or a *hit* denotes the case that a product is of user's liking and the Recommender system has predicted as such. Similarly, False Positive (*fp*) denotes the case of an item that has wrongly been predicted to be of liking of a user. False Negative (*fn*) is when an item has been predicted of not being of user's liking, but in reality it was. We used the value of 4 stars in a 5 star scale of our data as the threshold for classifying a bad experience from a good one (values 4 and 5 considered as Positive *p*). We considered as such, since rate 3 may even be used by users who are not happy enough with their choice.

F-score (*f*) requires another two metrics, *Precision* (*p*), which is the success in retrieving items that is of users interest, and *Recall* (*r*), which is the success in retrieving items that are truly of interest in relation to the number of all items that claim to be of interest.

To capture the implication on the number of items that can be predicted, we used the metric of *Coverage*. This metric (shown as C_a in Eqn.8) is specific to a particular user *a* who has in total rated a set of items I_a. I_b is referred to the items rated by some neighbor *b* and for which predictions can be made by *a*.

$$C_a = \frac{1}{|I_a|} \; | \, I_a \cap \{\cup_{b \in K} I_b\} \, | \tag{8}$$

5   Test Results

We present the most interesting results from our experimentation. In AP, it was not possible to directly generate any exact user-specified number of clusters for the set of data provided. Therefore we were able to experiment only with numbers of clusters that were possible to produce for our data. Conversely, for *k-Means* we provide results for all sizes of cluster communities, as it was possible to make

Table 1. Comparative Results of Prediction Accuracy

k	k-NN			k-Means			Jaccard K-means			Jaccard AP		
	MAE	RMSE	F-Score	MAE	RMSE	F-Score	MAE	RMSE	F-Score	MAE	RMSE	F-Score
5	0.1756	1.236	0.7256	0.1747	1.223	0.7348	0.1734	1.216	0.7372	-	-	-
10	0.1709	1.233	0.7237	0.1705	1.190	0.7383	0.1699	1.126	0.7417	-	-	-
15	0.1691	1.228	0.7217	0.1668	1.163	0.7456	0.1674	1.166	0.7447	-	-	-
16	-	-	-	-	-	-	-	-	-	0.1641	1.133	0.7481
20	0.1665	1.228	0.7173	0.1634	1.137	0.7492	0.1647	1.147	0.7556	-	-	-
25	0.1615	1.211	0.7309	0.1587	1.118	0.7652	0.1616	1.128	0.7599	-	-	-
26	-	-	-	-	-	-	-	-	-	0.1632	1.128	0.7578
29	-	-	-	-	-	-	-	-	-	0.1549	1.077	0.7682
30	0.1612	1.217	0.7315	0.1581	1.111	0.7696	0.1628	1.140	0.7603	0.1530	1.067	0.7717
40	0.1594	1.206	0.7382	0.1545	1.087	0.7742	0.1573	1.106	0.7717	0.1479	1.024	0.7798
44	-	-	-	-	-	-	-	-	-	0.1471	1.020	0.7891
45	0.1596	1.206	0.7357	0.1547	1.084	0.7764	0.1556	1.096	0.7778	0.1459	1.015	0.7889
47	-	-	-	-	-	-	-	-	-	0.1480	1.027	0.7869

the appropriate adjustments to the algorithm so as to generate the number of clusters we preferred.

Detailed results for prediction accuracy are provided in Table 1, with k denoting as the number of clusters. MAE is expressed in percentage as a fraction of 1.

In the comparison diagram in Fig. 2 for all schemes tested, we observe for MAE the following: first, it follows a decreasing trend for all figures as the number of clusters increases, and second, the error measured in the original *k-Means* clustering has lower figure (with a small exception at 5 clusters) than in both *k-NN* and *Jaccard-k-Means*. The former can be likely due to the way

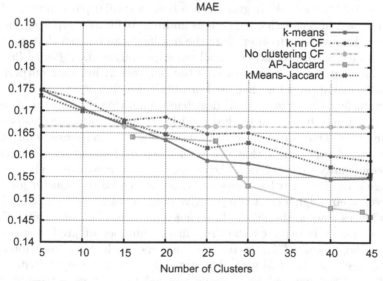

Fig. 2. Comparative diagram for Mean Absolute Error

that clustering works. Increasing the number of clusters while keeping the whole population constant has as a result clusters produced of smaller number of users, but still highly similar with each other. The high similarity of users within the same clusters is the reason of the improvement of the quality in predictions. Besides, selecting the most influential users has been the fundamental idea of k-NN filtering in Recommender Systems [24]. For instance we mention that the Intra-cluster distance for clusters generated with AP ranged between 0.75 to 0.82 for the whole range of Cluster sizes we experimented with. For the CF field as Intra-cluster distance is meant the average squared similarity between the members of the same cluster. For K-means clustering respectively Intra-cluster distance remained significantly lower between 0.35 and 0.60.

In the same diagram, it is also depicted the case of using all available predictors for each rating prediction (no-clustering) which roughly considers all users in a unique cluster. As can be seen, the no-clustering approach outperforms all the other techniques for small number of clusters (less or equal to 15). However, the distinctive difference with the no-clustering is on the higher computational cost needed, due to the larger quantities of data used to achieve the same result (Information Overload problem).

Our findings regarding the prediction accuracy of k-Means are in line with those reported by pioneer researchers in the field, like Sarwar et al. in [7]. More specifically, in our figures for MAE, it is shown a decreasing trend for accuracy as the number of clusters increases. We identify the reason why in our results k-Means clustering seems to outperform the baseline k-NN approach on the fact that in our case we assumed the standard CF algorithm as the baseline rather the no-Clustering approach. Also in the latter scheme, no filtering has been applied on the less similar predictors. We considered that option because neighbors who might have bad influence on prediction quality can still be potential candidates.

We omitted the RMSE diagram as it follows a similar pattern with MAE and hence it is still in line with our previous finding. As far as comparing the clustering algorithms with each other, from the results it can be seen that, for both the MAE and RMSE of predictions, in all our experiments the *Affinity Propagation* algorithm, that used explicit trust, is the only algorithm that outperforms all the traditional approaches that used or didn't use clustering.

Nevertheless, clustering has the drawback of limiting the number of predictors that can actually be chosen to those which belong to the same cluster with the querying user. That appears as reduced coverage, and responsible for this is the smaller set of experiences that can be utilized by making them shared into a small community rather than a bigger one. For *AP* responsible also for the low coverage is the fact that less users finally get allocated to a cluster for receiving help from their neighbors. A comparative diagram of the Coverage for k-Means, AP, k-NN as well as the other clustering approaches can be seen in Fig. 3. In this diagram, it is depicted the drop in the number of predictions for items that can be computed for increasing numbers of clusters. Very interestingly, coverage decreases fourfold with clustering when the number of clusters is large, regardless of the particular clustering method used. It is worth noticing that

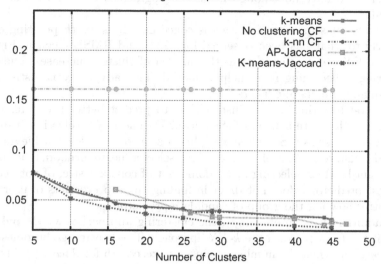

Fig. 3. Coverage in % of predictions

Coverage does not decrease sharply over 15 clusters and it is maintained at a constant level further on.

Concerning a comparison between *Affinity Propagation* clustering and the traditional *k-Means*, it can be seen from Figure 3 that the penalty paid for clustering remains at the same level, no matter if the social trust information is actually used or not. Apparently though, the AP approach is undoubtedly better, given the significant weakness of *k-Means* over AP, as far as the prediction accuracy. A comparison between the two schemes which used social trust information (AP and Jaccard *k-Means*) shows that the better quality of clusters achieved with AP finally does have an impact on the number of experiences that users can finally find useful within the clusters. This can be interpreted as saying: *A user clustered with AP is more likely to be allocated to a cluster whose members can contribute most useful experiences for him/her.* In that respect Affinity Propagation is the winner.

The general observation is that the use of explicit trust information in fact does not help Coverage to improve, as in the best case it remains at the same levels achieved with *k-Means*. The use of sparse trust data is mainly responsible for this. As a consequence, it becomes less likely for the distance between two users (expressed as w_{new} in Eqn. (6)) to be computed. That means the ratio of useful neighbors over all neighbors remains almost constant for 15 clusters and above. *Jaccard k-Means* fails to compensate the loss of useful neighbors, whereas *Jaccard AP*, by clustering together users which are more useful to each other, has been more successful. Using other sources of information, such as: implicit trust derived from trust propagation, might be a solution to overcome this weakness. Abstracting clusters and using representative values of rates across clusters for users who have not enough neighbors might also be way to overcome the problem.

As far as classification accuracy is concerned, it is worth pointing out that similarly to what has been observed for MAE and RMSE (seen in Fig. 2 and table 1), F-Score does improve as the number of clusters increases. That means, clustering is becoming more helpful indeed. This advantage is distinguishable from small numbers of clusters.

The no-Clustering scheme instead fails to predict better the items of user's liking, and therefore achieves F-Score=0.752. The *k-NN* selection instead performs even worse as F-Score remains almost at a constant level, achieving a score around 0.725, regardless of the size of the selected neighborhood. The reason for this might be that: selecting at random a set of constant size, of not necessarily the best predictors, does not differ in finding the top products of user's liking, no matter how big the group of candidate predictors is.

In addition, very interestingly, the clustering approaches which make use of explicit trust, outperform the *k-NN* approach. This advantage becomes obvious from early on when the number of clusters exceeds 15 for *Jaccard* k-Means. For *Jaccard AP*, similarly as observed for MAE and RMSE, the accuracy improves dramatically beyond the 26 clusters. The reason for this performance improvement is the same as for predictive accuracy.

In conclusion, clustering can clearly give predictions of higher precision than the conventional method can achieve. This advantage is enhanced when the explicit trust information is used for forming the clusters. Moreover, the successful selection of neighbors that novel clustering schemes, like AP, can achieve is found more beneficial when applied to small clusters rather than large ones.

6   Concluding Remarks

Trust and Data Clustering have been the subject of investigation in the research community in recent years, as a solution to improving the accuracy of Recommender Systems and to overcoming the sparsity and information overload problem. Nevertheless, little effort has been put on exploring the potential of new clustering algorithms and exploiting the information that users provide explicitly for the people they trust.

We performed a series of experiments in the context of Recommender Systems with the purpose to investigate our central question of whether clustering can be benefited by the use of trust information that users provide explicitly. We tested two clustering schemes, *k-Means* and *Affinity Propagation* and contrasted with the baseline Collaborative Filtering and *k-NN* approaches which make no-use of clusters. To the best of our knowledge, this is the first time that *Affinity Propagation* algorithm has been tested in Recommender Systems. Since it is known that clustering has potential advantages in Recommender Systems, in this work we also came to answer the question if the use of social trust can provide benefits to clustered users.

Apparently, our experimentation with the clustering algorithms showed that the trust information which people express explicitly for the people they know can undoubtedly be useful for improving the accuracy of their recommendations. At the same time, with clustering the problem of information overload is overcome. The fact that such trust data we used as input to the clustering algorithm is already provided in social networks as core information, makes profound what the benefit from social networking can be. We should note though that there is a drawback of clustering in general, which reflects the number of predictions that can be produced for the clustered users.

An interesting motivation for justifying the behavior of the results we received for Affinity Propagation algorithm could be useful to further investigate possible correlations between the principal objectives of the clustering algorithms we tried and the prediction algorithm used in CF. However, it is equally interesting to further investigate the reasons why particularly clusters formed up by using explicit trust information can be more useful than when the traditional Pearson's similarity is used.

Our choice of trying different sources of information into conventional clustering algorithms helped our understanding on the key factors for achieving good performance when applying clustering in Recommender Systems.

As far as the drawbacks of clustering which came up by the use of explicit trust and which sparsity of the social network is mainly responsible for, there is much hope to overcoming this with the application of cluster abstraction techniques. There is also much to learn from other disciplines related to Social Networking including Behavioral Science.

References

1. Arthur, D., Vassilvitskii, S.: k-means++: The Advantages of Careful Seeding. In: Proc. of Eighteenth Annual ACM-SIAM Symposium on Discrete Algorithms (SODA 2007), pp. 1027–1035. Society for Industrial and Applied Mathematics, Philadelphia (2007)
2. O'Donovan, J., Smyth, B.: Trust in recommender systems. In: Proc. of 10th International Conference on Intelligent User Interfaces (IUI 2005), pp. 167–174. ACM, New York (2005)
3. Frey, B., Dueck, D.: Clustering by Passing Messages Between Data Points. Science 315, 972–976 (2007)
4. Sarwar, B., Karypis, G., Konstan, J., Riedl, J.: Analysis of recommendation algorithms for e-commerce. In: Proceedings of the 2nd ACM conference on Electronic commerce (EC 2000), pp. 158–167. ACM, New York (2000)
5. DuBois, T., Golbeck, J., Kleint, J., Srinivasan, A.: Improving Recommendation Accuracy by Clustering Social Networks with Trust. In: ACM RecSys 2009 Workshop on Recommender Systems & the Social Web, New York (2009)
6. DuBois, T., Golbeck, J., Srinivasan, A.: Rigorous Probabilistic Trust-Inference with Applications to Clustering. In: Proc. of 2009 IEEE/WIC/ACM International Joint Conference on Web Intelligence and Intelligent Agent Technology (WI-IAT 2009), vol. 01, pp. 655–658. IEEE Computer Society, Washington, DC, USA (2009)

7. Sarwar, B.M., Karypis, G., Konstan, J.A., Riedl, J.: Recommender Systems for Large-Scale E-Commerce: Scalable Neighborhood Formation Using Clustering. In: The Fifth International Conference on Computer and Information Technology, ICCIT 2002 (2002)

8. Lathia, N., Hailes, S., Capra, L.: Trust-Based Collaborative Filtering in Trust Management II. In: IFIP International Federation for Information Processing, vol. 263, pp. 119–134. Springer, Boston (2008)

9. Ester, M., Kriegel, H.P., Sander, J., Xu, X.: A Density-Based Algorithm for Discovering Clusters in Large Spatial Databases with Noise. In: Simoudis, E., Han, J., Fayyad, U. (eds.) Proc Second International Conference on Knowledge Discovery and Data Mining, pp. 226–231. AAAI Press, Menlo Park (1996)

10. Zhang, X., Furtlehner, C., Sebag, M.: Data streaming with affinity propagation. In: Daelemans, W., Goethals, B., Morik, K. (eds.) ECML PKDD 2008, Part II. LNCS (LNAI), vol. 5212, pp. 628–643. Springer, Heidelberg (2008)

11. Kaufman, J., Rousseeuw, P.J.: Clustering by means of medoids. In: Dodge, Y. (ed.) Statistical Data Analysis Based on the L Norm. Elsevier, Amsterdam (1987)

12. MacQueen, J.B.: Some Methods for Classification and Analysis of MultiVariate Observations. In: Proc. of the Fifth Berkeley Symposium on Mathematical Statistics and Probability, vol. 1, pp. 281–297. University of California Press (1967)

13. Truong, K., Ishikawa, F., Honiden, S.: Improving Accuracy of Recommender System by Item Clustering. IEICE - Trans. Inf. Syst. E90-D 9, 1363–1373 (2007)

14. A cooperative environment for the scientific research of trust metrics on social networks, http://www.trustlet.org/ (retrieved May 2009)

15. Bollen, D., Knijnenburg, P.B., Willemsen, M.C., Graus, M.: Understanding choice overload in recommender systems. In: Proc. of fourth ACM conference on Recommender systems (RecSys 2010), pp. 63–70. ACM, New York (2010)

16. Wang, W., Zhang, X., Pitsilis, G.: Abstracting audit data for lightweight intrusion detection. In: Jha, S., Mathuria, A. (eds.) ICISS 2010. LNCS, vol. 6503, pp. 201–215. Springer, Heidelberg (2010)

17. Melville, P., Mooney, R.J., Nagarajan, R.: Content-boosted collaborative filtering for improved recommendations. In: Dechter, R., Kearns, M., Sutton, R. (eds.) Proc. 18th National Conference on Artificial Intelligence, pp. 187–192. American Association for Artificial Intelligence, Menlo Park (2002)

18. Walter, F., Battiston, S., Schweitzer, F.: Coping with Information Overload through Trust-Based Networks. In: Helbing, D. (ed.) Managing Complexity: Insights, Concepts, Applications, vol. 32, pp. 273–300. Springer, Heidelberg (2008)

19. Massa, P., Avesani, P.: Trust-aware recommender systems. In: Proceedings of the 2007 ACM conference on Recommender systems (RecSys 2007), pp. 17–24. ACM, New York (2007)

20. Josang, A.: A logic for uncertain probabilities. Int. J. Uncertain. Fuzziness Knowl.-Based Syst. 9(3), 279–311 (2001)

21. Avesani, P., Massa, P., Tiella, R.: A trust-enhanced recommender system application: Moleskiing. In: Liebrock, L.M. (ed.) Proc. of 2005 ACM symposium on Applied computing (SAC 2005), pp. 1589–1593. ACM, New York (2005)

22. Liu, H., Lim, E., Lauw, H.W., Le, M.-T., Sun, A., Srivastava, J., Kim, Y.A.: Predicting trusts among users of online communities: an epinions case study. In: Proc. of 9th ACM conference on Electronic commerce (EC 2008), pp. 310–319. ACM, New York (2008)

23. Liu, Z., Li, P., Zheng, Y., Sun, M.: Community Detection by Affinity Propagation, Technical Reports No. 001, 200, Dept. of Computer Science and Technology, Tsinghua University,Beijing,China (2008)
24. Herlocker, J., Konstan, J., Borchers, A., Riedl, J.: An algorithmic framework for performing collaborative filtering. In: Proc. of the 22nd annual international ACM SIGIR conference on Research and development in information retrieval (SIGIR 1999), pp. 230–237. ACM, New York (1999)
25. Jaccard, P.: Bulletin de la Société Vaudoise des Sciences Naturelles. Distribution de la flore alpine dans le bassin des Dranses et dans quelques régions voisines 37, 241–272 (1901)

From Reputation Models and Systems to Reputation Ontologies

Rehab Alnemr and Christoph Meinel

Hasso Plattner Institute, Potsdam University, Germany
rehab.alnemr@hpi.uni-potsdam.de

Abstract. Reputation has been explored in diverse disciplines such as artificial intelligence, electronic commerce, peer-to-peer network, and multi-agent systems. Recently it has been a vital component for ensuring trust in web services and service oriented architectures domains. Although there are several studies on reputation systems as well as reputation models, there is no study that covers reputation ontologies especially the ones implemented using standardized frameworks like semantic technologies. In this paper, we show the evolution towards reputation ontologies and investigate existing ones in the domains of multi-agent systems, web services, and online markets. We define the requirements for developing a reputation ontology and use them to analyze some of the existing ontologies. The components and functionalities of reputation models and systems are described briefly and the importance of developing and using reputation ontologies is highlighted within the emergence of the Semantic Web and Semantic Web services.

Keywords: Reputation, Reputation Models and Systems, Ontology, Reputation Ontologies, Semantic Web.

1 Introduction

Reputation is a social control artifact that has been studied in psychology, sociology, economics, and computer systems. Reputation systems are used as a way of establishing trust between unrelated parties, especially if enforcement methods like institutional policies are not implemented. They may help lower the risks of online interactions, increasing the robustness and efficiency of internet-based applications. A *reputation model* describes all of the reputation statements, events, and processes for a particular context. This *context* is the relevant category for a specific reputation. The way such systems query, collect, and represent reputation varies. Some systems use stars or scaling bars as the visual format of reputation while others use numbers and percentages such as rating an e-market participant. Online reputation systems are the biggest and most obvious examples of these systems. It can be categorized based on the common features and properties of the web communities such as e-markets, activity sharing, social and entertainment sites, news sites, P2P systems and systems build upon the Semantic Web.[6] In service-oriented systems, quality attributes and ratings given by other services or service consumers are used to represent *service reputation*.

I. Wakeman et al. (Eds.): IFIPTM 2011, IFIP AICT 358, pp. 98–116, 2011.

There are extensive studies about reputation systems that discuss not only the current commercial ones but also proposed approaches from academia. For example, studies done by Jøsang in [18] and Sabater in [34] provide an exhaustive view of the status of the reputation community. However, there is still a confusion on the definitions and use of the associated terminologies between researchers and developers. Some describe their work to be a reputation system or a framework, others describe it as a model or a mechanism and few as an ontology. Moreover, there is still no explicit and standard theory of the cognitive components and processes which reputation is made of, despite the rapid advances in cooperation networks studies. According to [18], several algorithms for computing reputation were proposed in the past decade. However, commercial applications implementing trust and reputation mechanisms use relatively simple schemes than those proposed by research papers. In this paper, first we distinguish between the used terminologies then we focus on analyzing existing and proposed reputation ontologies and briefly show the difference between reputation mechanisms, models, frameworks, systems on one hand and ontologies on the other hand.

Lack of common terminology, proper definition, and means to exchange understandable reputation information, led to attempts to define reputation ontologies that can be used across several domains. In information systems, ontologies promote and facilitate interoperability as well as intelligent processing. They are developed to enhance knowledge reuse by sharing a common understanding of a domain that can be communicated between people, and heterogeneous and widely spread application systems. Usually, they are composed of a set of terms representing concepts (hierarchically organized) and some specification of their meaning. In this paper, we study the importance of developing such ontologies for reputation systems. We investigate existing reputation ontologies developed in multi-agent systems (MAS), web services and service-oriented environments (SOA), and online markets. Using a methodology for developing proper ontology, we define a set of questions that is later used in the analysis of these ontologies. The paper is organized as follows: in section 2 we briefly describe reputation systems and models and distinguish between the used terms. Section 3 explains the importance of ontologies followed by the requirements to develop one. In section 4 we investigate current reputation ontologies. Based on the requirements, we analyze these ontologies in section 5.

2   Reputation Models, Frameworks, and Systems

Since there is a vast literature showing reputation systems from different perspectives (i.e.[24], [18], threats in [1], mechanisms in [13]), here we will briefly point out several definitions to distinguish between some terminologies. Resnick [30] defines a **reputation system** as: *"a system that collects, distributes, and aggregates feedback about participants' past behavior"*. It must have three properties to operate: long lived entities with an expectation for future interactions, ratings that can be captured and distributed, and past interactions' ratings used to guide the decision making. Conte and Paolucci [29] defines reputation-based systems as: *"a spontaneous and implicit norm-based system for social control"*. Jøsang [18] defines **reputation architecture** as a network architecture which determines how ratings and reputation scores are communicated between participants in a reputation system. He identifies two main types for the networks: *centralized* and *distributed* architectures. Both architectures have a reputation computation engine, but each has a different communication protocol (i.e. centralized protocol for centralized architecture). A **reputation computation engine** computes the reputation value based on plenty of factors (according to the model used) such as one's own experience, others referrals, a combination of both, etc. Some of the used algorithms or computation functions are: summation, average [31], bayesian systems [23][39], discrete trust models [2][9], belief models [17][40], fuzzy models [33][36], cognitive as [14], etc.. A **reputation model** describes all of the reputation statements (i.e. a source rating a target), events, and processes for a particular context. They were developed using different approaches and different semantics. A **reputation context** is the relevant category for a specific reputation. A reputation system should describe therefore:

- Computation functions/mechanisms i.e. how to calculate reputation?
- Communication model i.e. how to collect and disseminate reputation?
- Participants i.e. who use and/or is affected by reputation?
- Resources i.e. what is the information used to calculate reputation?
- Representation model i.e. how to represent, view, or visualize reputation?
- Storage i.e. where and how reputation is stored?
- Functionalities and applications i.e. what are the benefits of using reputation in the domain of its creation

It should also describe how these components are integrated into a given system. Here, we distinguish between: reputation ontology, reputation system, model, or framework, reputation engine or mechanism, and reputation architecture. A **reputation ontology** describes the notion of reputation and the relations to the concepts that compose it, while a *reputation system, model, or framework* describes the collection, distribution, and aggregation of reputation information. A *reputation computation engine or mechanism* is one of the modules in a reputation system which shows how reputation value(s) are calculated. A *reputation architecture* is a set of protocols that determines how reputation values are communicated between the participants in a reputation system.

3   Why Ontologies

In [19], an ontology is defined as: *"A set of terms of interest in a particular information domain and the relationship among them"*. Ontologies describe domain-dependent as well as domain-independent knowledge. An Ontology defines common vocabulary for researchers who need to share information in a domain. In [22], the authors explain the reasons why anyone wants to develop an ontology. Some of them are [22]:

- sharing common understanding of the structure of information
- enabling information reuse
- making domain assumptions explicit and clear
- separating domain knowledge from operational knowledge
- analyzing the domain knowledge
- ability to integrate existing ontologies describing portions of the large domain

Within the same community, ontologies enable mutual understanding among peers by providing precise semantics to concepts and relationships between these concepts. Our domain of focus in this case is reputation. According to Jøsang in [18], most reputation systems proposals from the academic communities lack coherence and are usually designed from scratch. Mostly, researchers do not build upon other researchers work. Usually because these proposals do not clearly define the involved concepts (i.e. reputation) and the knowledge in a standardized or formal manner. The lack of semantics of the concepts as well as of the elements included in reputation systems prevent others from reusing or extending -sometimes even *understanding*- the proposed work.

In order to define a standard notion of reputation, a *general* reputation ontology must be developed. However, it is important to separate, for instance, *what is a reputation computation function* from *how it is computed*. The former is domain knowledge while the latter is operational knowledge. Therefore, formalizing reputation concepts into ontologies has several advantages such as:

- creates a common understanding for reputation
- specifies the factors involved in computing reputation and the semantics of these factors
- separates the definition of reputation from how it is calculated
- enables the mapping between reputation concepts, in the current variety of reputation models
- facilitates the use of existing mapping and integration techniques in information systems for reusing reputation information
- increases the possibility of reputation interoperability and cross community sharing of reputation information

The semantic characteristics of reputation values are essential so that the participants are able to interpret them. These characteristics may differ from one domain/discipline to the other but the general description- as factors affecting the notion of reputation- is the same. For example, "service availability" is a factor that affects a web service provider's reputation in SOA while an agent's "trustworthiness" in MAS is a factor in calculating his rating for another agent. Both can be considered as quality attributes or reputation contexts.

The authors in [27] describe an ontology life cycle as: *specification* (why building an ontology) , *conceptualization* (describing a conceptual model of the ontology), *formalization* (transform into formal model), *implementation* (implement in knowledge representation language), *maintenance* (update and correct), *knowledge acquisition* (of the subject by using elicitation techniques), *evaluation* (by judging technically the quality of the ontology), and *documentation* (report what was done, how, and why). Creating a general ontology that describes reputation involves separating clearly the closely related social artifacts like image [29] and reputation. In this paper, we discuss work that attempts to define and separate between reputation and trust concepts as well as analyzing those few ontologies that reached the implementation phase (not necessarily going through the preceding steps of conceptualization and formalization).

3.1   Ontology Standards

Developing such interoperable reputation ontologies requires a technology that can provide means of *integrating data sources* and methods to *relate the data to its semantics*. Semantic Web technologies were developed with the goal of providing common data representation framework in order to facilitate the integration of multiple sources to draw new conclusions, increasing the utility of information by connecting it to its definitions and to its context, and providing more efficient information access and analysis [8]. The Semantic Web organization [1] considers ontologies as one of the pillars of the Semantic Web. To achieve the main goal of Semantic Web, shared ontologies have to be established, which specify the fundamental objects and relations important to particular communities. Since these ontologies describe a concept in a certain domain, domain experts are often the ones who craft them. The representation languages includes XML Schema, RDF Schema [2], the Web Ontology Language (OWL)[3], and the Web Services Modeling Language (WSML)[4]. The advantage of defining an ontology using these technologies are: focusing on the representation of the semantics of the information, expressiveness, information reuse, easy discovery, and integration of information. Further information can be found in the references.

3.2   Ontology Requirements

Following the methodology of Grüninger [16] for ontology development, a reputation ontology should describe: the notion, the relation between the involved concepts, what computation function used to calculate the reputation value, in what domain it was collected, and the context of the computed reputation. The methodology involves defining a set of competency questions in the process of ontology development. These questions act as requirements in the form of queries that an ontology should be able to answer. Based on analysis and learning from others' experience, we define the following informal competency questions in the context of using and processing reputation in several domains:

Q1. *Reputation definition*: can we clearly define the notion of reputation within the domain?

---

[1] http://semanticweb.org/
[2] RDF Schema: http://www.w3.org/TR/rdf-schema/
[3] OWL-2: http://www.w3.org/TR/owl2-overview/
[4] WSML Working group:http://www.wsmo.org/wsml/

Q2. *Reputation Identity*: in a specific context, can we define entities that can have reputation? can we define reputation roles such as source, target, evaluator, etc.?

Q3. *Reputation representation*: in a specific context, is the reputation value represented in a single format? if so, is it enough to express its meaning? how reputation will be represented, communicated, and visualized if necessary?

Q4. *Reputation statement*: what constitute as a reputation statement? what information does a reputation transaction hold?

Q5. *Reputation computation mechanism*: in a specific context, is there a property that defines and describes the mechanism by which reputation is computed?

Q6. *Reputation context*: is reputation related to its context? is there a property that expresses the relation between a reputation value and the context of its creation? and for a given entity, can we combine its reputation in different contexts?

Q7. *Reputation factors*: in a specific domain, can we define and describe the factors affecting reputation? does the reputation of the source (reputee) affect the calculation of reputation?

Q8. *Reputation dynamics and temporal effect*: does reputation change through time? if so, can we reflect this in the ontology? are there properties that reflect the change in reputation values? for example, is there a time validity property to reputation? for every new transaction, is the new value timestamped?

Q9. *Reputation history*: for a given entity, can we maintain the history of reputation values that said entity owned?

Q10. *Reputation expressiveness*: can we define and describe the semantics of the involved factors, contexts, relations, and concepts? is there a way to define as well as communicate the semantics of a reputation context?

This set of questions is not complete, it is rather an attempt to guide our analysis and discussion of the existing ontologies. According to [16], they should be used to evaluate the ontological commitment that has been made and evaluate the expressiveness of the ontology.

3.3   A Literature of Defining Reputation Concepts

Developing an ontology does not have to be from scratch. On the contrary, it is preferable to use the existing literature -if not extending an existing ontology- to define reputation concepts, form competency questions, and reach a formal model that leads to proper implementation. In the literature, reputation is defined as an expectation about an entity's behavior based on information about or observations of its past behavior [2]. In the business world, Balmer [7] defines two characteristics for *corporate reputation*: it evolves through time and is based on what the organization has done and how it has behaved. It deals with the cause of a problem, offers solutions, sets processes in motion, and monitors progress towards these solutions. Reputation definition evolves through the introduction of more complicated models. For example, Paolucci and Conte in [29] introduce a cognitive theory that clearly distinguish between two concepts- *image* and *reputation*. The computation algorithm was defined in [32] as the Repage model. One of the major efforts that has been done to define a set of terms about reputation concepts can be seen in the European project eRep [5]. Based on the model described by [29], the project explains in details the elements of social evaluations, the process of transmitting them, and agent decisions regarding reputation. The model distinguishs between two social artifacts that pertain to the evaluation of a target: *image* and *reputation*. *Image* is the the output of the evaluation process of other agents and assumed to be true by the agent who holds it. *Reputation* is the voice the agent is spreading which is not necessarily the truth. One should make use of the literature on the subject before re-defining the concepts or the terminologies when developing a reputation ontology. However, sometimes it is essential to clearly distinguish one's perspective of a concept than other's vantage point by creating different terminologies.

4   Existing Approaches to Reputation Ontologies

In this section we describe some of the existing reputation ontologies developed and/or implemented with standardization in mind. We show how these ontologies were used as well as their limitations. They are categorized based on the domain they were created for. Some of these ontologies were created to define not only reputation but the associated concepts that will affect it. Others like [12] defines a reputation ontology in terms of its computation mechanism; that is; they define reputation as the mechanism used to compute it. We chose to show the graphical representation for each ontology to better illustrate the relation between its classes and their taxonomy. Finally we discuss these ontologies as opposed to the previously mentioned competency questions.

4.1   For Multi Agents Systems

Functional ontology for reputation (FORe) [11]. The goal of this ontology is to represent the knowledge about reputation in psychology and AI in a structured form. The Ontology follows the categorization of reputation in law; following the work of [37]. It extends the concept in the legal world to the social norm with different penalty of rule violation. While the legal penalty is a legal punishment, in the social world the penalty is having a bad reputation. The authors define reputation as a social product (an opinion or agreement) and a social process (contains a flow of information and influence on the social network). They present a functional ontology of reputation that contains four categories: *Reputative Knowledge* (deals with the agent's reward or penalty and models the products as well as the processes involved in the reputation notion), *Responsibility Knowledge* (associates a cause, whether it is intentional or based

---

[5] eRep project: http://megatron.iiia.csic.es/eRep/?q=node/93

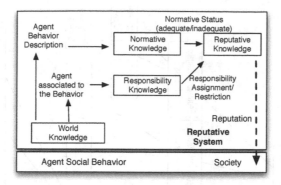

Fig. 1. Reputation Functional Ontology [11]

on circumstances, to a specific agent behavior), *Normative Knowledge and World Knowledge* (classifying the agent behavior and providing a model of social behavior). The distinction between these categories is based on the function that each component in the system performs. Since the ontology is complicated and there are plenty of classes involved, we show their detailed structure in figure 2 and the relation between the four categories in figure 1. Refer to [11] for the details of these components.

The authors in [38] used this ontology to examine different technologies in order to allow reputation interoperability between agents. This is done by asking the contributing agents to map their own ontology concepts to the functional ontology [11] and send the mapped information to the other agents that can in return convert it to their own model. The experiments were done using ART Testbed [15] which is a testbed to compare and evaluate between different heterogeneous reputation models or functions. They modified the testbed so that the mapping to a common ontology is no longer simple (which was a numerical value between 0 and 1) but rather sending interaction messages that are strings that hold queries and answers. The general architecture includes: the interaction module (receives a reputation message), mapping module (analyzes its contents), translated message (from the mapping module to the reasoning module) and the resulting query (the translated result sent to the interaction module). The work was extended in [25] to propose a separate mapping service that maps a reputation ontology to the functional ontology. The service was implemented so that agents do not have to map the ontologies themselves thus removing the mapping function from the agent architecture. Interoperability is achieved byt implementing two functions: *mapping* (assigning concepts and relations from one ontology to the other) and *translating* (application of the mapping function to translate sentences from one ontology to the other). Figure 3 illustrates the proposed service-oriented architecture (SOA) wherein mapping service was implemented as a web service using Protégé plugins.

Notes and comments. This ontology though gathering most of the notions associated with or relevant to reputation, do not provide a concrete way to represent

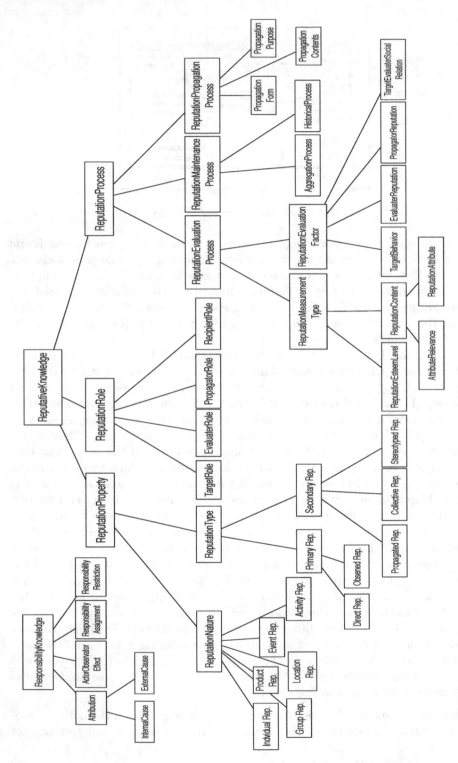

Fig. 2. Reputative Knowledge and Responsibility Knowledge [11]

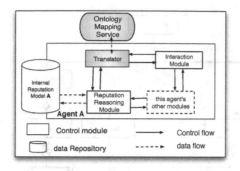

Fig. 3. SOARI Architecture [25]

and communicate this reputation; that is, a reputation representation. It is rather a meta-level description of the notions the surrounds reputation. Also, as illustrated in the figures, the functional ontology is complex and not all of its components are related to reputation transactions. Therefore, in order to adapt the approach used in [38] each agent must fully [understand] the ontology in order to: a] map his ontology- correctly- to it, b] answer any query sent from another agent. The ontology mapping service though beneficial but it still strictly requires that the involved reputation models are described using ontologies and specifically; OWL[6]. Moreover, the results showed that the binary mapping to FORe can not always be done and causes sometimes loss of information (e.g. mapping from Repage [32] to FORe, the concepts `AgentReputation` and `AgentImage` are mapped to `ReputationNature` concept in FORe).

Social evaluation and voice ontology [28]. Pinyol and Sabater use the concepts presented in the eRep project[7] and propose a common ontology in [28] for reputation (as a subset of the defined concepts in the project). They claim that the ontology allows the communication of social evaluations -reputation in this case- among agents using different reputation models. They argue that each agent use its own representation of the evaluations and interaction, therefore preventing communication between two agents using different reputation models. Even if the source knew which model the recipient is using, there is no reason to think that it will know the internal functionalities of other participants. They focus on the concepts concerning agents beliefs that deal with social evaluations and on the implementation with emphasis on the representation of the social evaluation values. The elements of the ontology are: an `Entity` is any object of the society being evaluated or having an active role in the evaluation (as `Target`, `Source`, `Gossiper`, `Recipient`), `Focus` is the context of the `Evaluation`, and `Value` describes the goodness or badness of this evaluation weighed by `Strength` to indicate how reliable the evaluation is. This measure of reliability is subjective and belongs to the interval $[0, 1]$ with 1 being the maximum reliability and is

---

[6] OWL Web Ontology:http://www.w3.org/TR/owl-features/
[7] eRep project: http://megatron.iiia.csic.es/eRep/?q=node/93

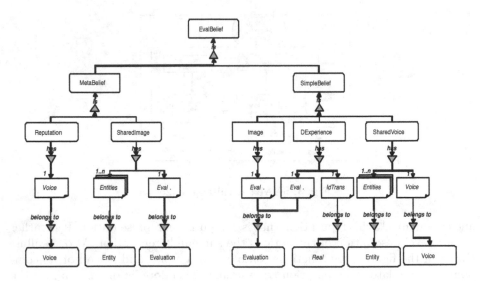

Fig. 4. Social evaluation and voice Ontology [28]

strongly related to an uncertainty factor called `UncertaintyConversion` (CU). It is the decision of an agent to use or ignore these factors. `Evaluation` encloses all the concepts involved in the social evaluation, while `Voice` is what actually being reported about the target's reputation. The ontology also presents a concept of evaluative belief `EvalBelief` which means what the agent holds in its belief system; `SimpleBelief`, a belief that the holding agent considers as true (that is not necessarily the voice being reported, hence, `image` belongs to this class), and `MetaBelief`, a belief about what others belief (the one being transmitted, hence, `reputation` belongs to this class). (See figure 4)

This work further discusses how the evaluation or these believes is represented because when developing a common ontology it is important to have a common understable representation of the evaluations. Therefore, the authors show a set of transformation functions between *Boolean, Real, Discrete Set* and *Probability Distribution* representations since they are the most common ones. They implemented an API interface of a set of common operations whose inputs and outputs are elements of the ontology, and must be implemented for each particular model. They show some implementation examples for famous models such as eBay [8] and Repage [32] by implementing its mapping to the ontology (only the first level of the API hierarchy of each model).

Notes and comments. The presented ontology though not as complicated as the functional ontology but also presents a level of complexity that can not be handled outside the multi-agent based community. However, it also covers all the factors affecting reputation and the process of decision making. Note also

---

[8] eBay: http://www.ebay.com

that it is a static ontology- a fact addressed by the authors- meaning that for every new reputation model a new API must be implemented. Dynamic ontology alignment is addressed by the ontology presented in 4.4.

4.2   For Web Services

Service reputation ontology [21]. Maximilien and Singh presented a service reputation ontology in [21] to organize ratings (aggregated to reputation) to be used in service selection. They address the problem that trust criteria- that are involved in service selection- are not usually available in the service descriptions. The idea is that a service reputation is the aggregation of the ratings of the given service by other principals and is a vector of attribute values. The ontology includes domain independent as well as domain specific attributes and is described using DAML [9](which formalizes models to express service capabilities through service descriptions).

In their architecture, the parties involved are called `principals`. `Agencies` are gathering and disseminating reputations and endorsements, and for each service used by the service consumer a *proxy software agent* is established. A `ProxyAgent` is responsible for: consulting outside registries and reputation and endorsement agencies, finding appropriate providers, recording feedbacks, learning from the experience, and finally sharing its knowledge. The ontology defines: a `Service` that has one `Reputation` which has one or more `Ratings` and is affected by `History`. A `ReputationAlgorithm` aggregates various `attributes`. A `Principal` rates a service and a `RatingAlgorithm` calculates the rating. Figure 5 illustrates the ontology and shows that a service reputation is a function of attributes that matter to a specific agent by adding a `weight` to the rating. This is the authors' interpretation of the real-world fact that reputation is subjective and depends on the domain of its creation. They also includes other factors affect service reputation such as attribute aggregation algorithm, the set of endorsers, and the damping factors for the ratings.

Notes and comments. So far, this ontology is the most expressive and practical ontology for service reputation. It is expressive because it captures most of the aspects that affect reputation and also because it addresses the effect of the domain on the attributes contributing to construct this reputation. Most of the systems addressing service reputation represent it as a single value such as [20] and [10] whereas in this ontology it is a vector of values. However, this vector of values does not have the semantics of the attribute embedded in the representation which makes it difficult for the destination (or the recipient of the transmitted reputation) to understand the source's interpretation of the attribute meaning.

4.3   For e-Markets and Service-oriented Architecture

e-Market and SOA ontology [12]. Chang et. al. describe an ontology for product, service, and agent reputation in the domain of e-markets. This was

---

[9] The DARPA Agent Markup Language (DAML): http://www.daml.org

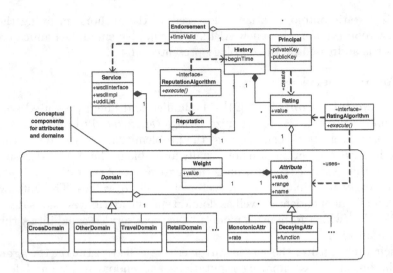

Fig. 5. Maximillian and Singh Service Reputation Ontology [21]

extended later to the domain of service-oriented architectures (SOA). They propose two definitions for reputation: a *basic* one and an *advanced* one. Basic Reputation ontology defines the reputation of a *trusted agent* as the aggregation of all the recommendations from all of the *Third Party Recommendation Agents*. Since this simple view do not address the dynamic nature of reputation (change over time) nor it ensures the depth of the context or the accuracy of the distribution, an *advanced reputation* was defined as the aggregation of all the recommendations from all of the *Third Party Recommendation Agents* weighed by the trustworthiness of the recommendation agents and the trustworthiness of the opinion. Figure 6 shows their ontology of advanced reputation and the following equations represent basic and advanced reputation ontologies respectively:

- *Basic Reputation* $= \cup(RecommendationValue)$
- *Advanced Reputation* $= \cup(RecommendationValue \times TrustworthinessOf$
  $Opinion \times Perceived1^{st}, 2^{nd}, and 3^{rd} opinion \times TimeElapsedFactor)$

Notes and comments. The presented ontology depends on the definition that reputation:*"... developing the measure of trustworthiness from Third Party Agents recommendations, not by the Trusting Agents themselves"*[12]. This greatly limits the view of reputation and the generic sense of reputation notion as well as over-simplifying its real nature. Hence, it is not generic enough to address several domains, especially an open one like SOA. Also, there is no definition of relevant concepts and ontology matching. Moreover, reputation at the end is a simple representation value which rather oversimplify the meaning of it.

4.4   Generic Reputation Ontology

Reputation Object ontology [5]. Most of the existing work on reputation systems focuses on improving the calculation of reputation values, preventing

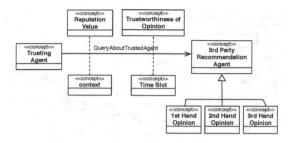

Fig. 6. Chang et. al. Reputation Ontology of the Trusted Agent [12]

malicious actions, and the deployment into the business world where reputation is mostly represented in a singular value form. This work focuses on how to represent reputation to reflect its real-world concept (i.e. non-general, context specific, and dynamic). The argument is that in most reputation systems the context of a reputation value is not embedded within the given reputation information. Mostly because it has the single value format. Since reputation changes with time and is used within a context and every domain has its own information sources as well as its own requirements, the representation -not the calculation- of reputation should be unified between communities in order to facilitate knowledge exchange. In this ontology reputation is represented as a new form of reputation value: *Reputation Object (RO)*. This object holds information on the reputation of an entity in multiple contexts. The ontology's components are: a `ReputationObject hasCriteria` of one or multiple instances of class `Criterion` or `QualityAttribute` (for a service, the criterion describing service reputation is referred to as a quality attribute). The criterion is collected using a `CollectingAlgorithm` and `hasValue ReputationValue`. Each criterion instance has a `ReputationValue` (which includes the `currentValue`, its time stamp, and a simple list of its previous values called `historyList`) that in turn has the range of values defined in `PossibleValues`. It describes the data type that the criterion can have or a specific set of values (literals or resources URI) evaluating this criterion (e.g. a set of integers $\{1, 2, 3, 4\}$ describing 4 trust levels or a set of Strings $\{"good","bad","excellent"\}$ describing a user opinion). Each time a criterion is being evaluated (i.e. a new entry value for this criterion), a new `currentValue` is calculated using the `ComputationAlgorithm` which is the reputation computation function/engine used with this criterion such as *sum, avg, etc.*.

Since it is not always easy to identify intuitively what the highest reputation value is - among the defined possible value set -, the `PossibleValues` class has an `orderedList` that is ordered from the relatively highest reputation value to the lowest (e.g.$\{"excellent","good","bad"\}$). It also has the possibility to define a comparison and ordering function; `OrderFunction` to compare between values within each criterion and to be used by the reasoning engine. A RO is constructed either offline or during negotiation process. It's a generic object that changes according to the domain and the user preference but in general it holds

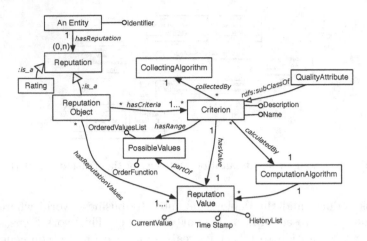

Fig. 7. Reputation Object Ontology [5]

a profile (functionality, quality, ratings, etc.) about an entity (service or agent) which is collected from heterogeneous information sources. The ontology is implemented using Protégé-OWL [10]. A java library was also developed to facilitate the integration of the ontology within any system on the implementation layer. The implementation for processing an RO was developed using Jena-API [11]. This ontology was used to represent an entity's reputation in several domains such as multi-agent based system (in [26], as the reputation of an agent and a way for decision making), for usage control in Internet-of-services (IoS) [4], and as an underlying ontology for a SOA reputation service in [3] that was later used in [35] for cloud service provider selection.

Notes and comments. This ontology was designed mainly to facilitate reputation information exchange or reputation interoperability in any domain. Using this ontology, a dynamic ontology alignment is possible between two entities since reputation information (that helps in the alignment specially during runtime) are embedded in the reputation object. However, since the ontology focuses on representation, it does not address factors like transformation functions. Though one can still use the functions presented in [28] (section 4.1) to enhance the use of the ontology.

5   Discussion

Despite that the aforementioned ontologies provide broad knowledge about reputation, most of them still represent reputation as a single value. Maximillian &Sangh approach (section 4.2) perceives it as a single quality-attributes vector which increases the comprehensiveness of service reputation. The complexity

---

[10] Protege OWL: http://protege.stanford.edu/overview/protege-owl.html
[11] Jena framework: http://jena.sourceforge.net/

Table 1. Analysis based on competency questions

Reputation	FORe	Pinyol & Sabater	Maximillian & Sangh	Chang	Reputation Object
Definition	clearly define reputation in the domain of its creation	clearly define reputation in the domain of its creation	clearly define reputation in the domain of its creation	lacks proper definition, definition in terms of computation functions	clearly define reputation in the domain of its creation
Identity	distinguished using roles (i.e. source, target, evaluator, gossiper)	distinguished using roles (i.e. source, target, evaluator, gossiper)	defines the roles of the agents who collect and deliver the reputation	not defined	links to a separate identity ontology
Representation	single value	single value	vector of values	single value	represented as an *object* that holds relevant reputation information
Computation mechanism	implicit description	implicit description	implicit description	implicit description	described explicitly as ComputationAlgorithm
Context	not represented	not represented	as an attribute Domain	as a single context (but not communicated through the community)	as multiple Criterion that can aggregates to a Context. Only in this ontology, a reputation of an entity in multiple context can be combined.
Factors	includes broad view on factors affecting reputation	reputation of the source affects the calculation of reputation by the elements Trustworthiness-of-opinion and Strength	an attribute is weighed by Weight to represent the importance of the attribute to the agent	reputation of the source affects the calculation	reputation elements such as context, collectionAlgorithm, PossibleValues
Dynamics & temporal effect	no explicit description or attribute	no explicit description or attribute	addressed as timeValid & as decaying effect to some of the attributes categorized as DecayingAttr	reflected by the property TimeSlot	reflected as multiple of timeStamp
History	represented as ReputationMaintenance-Process	not explicitly represented	represented as History	not represented	represented as historyList
Expressiveness	expressiveness rather scales to high *complexity*	how they explicitly distinguish between what the agent believes to be true and what the others believe	shows in the process of relating reputation to multiple quality attributes	not expressive and over-simplified	context's semantics is explained by the property Description and the ReputationValue is connected to its set of PossibleValues & its explained order through OrderedValuesList

of the functional ontology FORe (section 4.1) prevents it from being adapted despite of the presented mapping service in SOARI. While the ontology presented by Chang (section 4.3) reflects the existing approaches in online markets, it inherits their problems of over-simplifying the meaning of reputation, hence alienating factors that affect reputation calculation. The discussed ontologies are implemented using standardized technologies such as OWL and DAML-S. Pinyol &Sabater present the elements of their ontology as an API interface which can be reused and the RO ontology provides a Java library and is described in OWL. Back to the competency questions in section 3.2, we find that some of these ontologies answer most of said questions as explained in table 1. Note that each one was created from a different point of view and for different purposes. However, when one intends to use an ontology, it is important to know its features.

6   Conclusion and Future Wrok

Reputation ontologies create a common understanding of the notion as well as facilitate reputation exchange. While there is a vast body of reputation systems studies, there is no study that covers reputation ontologies. In this paper we distinguish between reputation models, mechanisms, systems and reputation ontologies. We show why developing ontologies is important and construct a set of competency questions to guide the analysis of the existing reputation ontologies. Furthermore, some of these ontologies are described in this study and are analyzed based on the aforementioned competency questions. Until now, reputation systems do not use or even share one common ontology to facilitate reputation exchange. The initiative by the ORMS[12] is trying to achieve that though it is still in its early stages. In order to use the resulting reputation ontology on a web scale, it should be compliant with current semantic web or web services standards and deployable on available Semantic Web infrastructure. It is encouraged to use standardized technologies to describe and exchange reputation information in a format that can be understandable to both humans and machines. This will greatly affect the decision making process in open environments such as service oriented architectures. We developed the ontology described in 4.4 with these goals in mind and we plan to continue to enhance the ontology as well as extending the competency questions to act as a guide reference for future ontology development or integration.

References

1. Reputation-based Systems: a security analysis (2007)
2. Abdul-Rahman, A., Hailes, S.: Supporting trust in virtual communities. In: Proceedings of the 33rd Hawaii International Conference on System Sciences, vol. 6. IEEE Computer Society, Los Alamitos (2000)

---

[12] Open Reputation Management Systems:
http://www.oasis-open.org/committees/tc_home.php?wg_abbrev=orms

3. Alnemr, R., Bross, J., Meinel, C.: Constructing a context-aware service-oriented reputation model using attention allocation points. In: Proceedings of the IEEE International Conference on Service Computing (2009)
4. Alnemr, R., König, S., Eymann, T., Meinel, C.: Enabling usage control through reputation objects: A discussion on e-commerce and the internet of services environments. Special issue of Trust and Trust Management, Journal of Theoretical and Applied Electronic Commerce Research (2010)
5. Alnemr, R., Paschke, A., Meinel, C.: Enabling reputation interoperability through semantic technologies. In: ACM International Conference on Semantic Systems. ACM, New York (2010)
6. Alnemr, R., Quasthoff, M., Meinel, C.: Taking Trust Management to the Next Level. Handbook of Research on P2P and Grid Systems for Service-Oriented Computing: Models, Methodologies and Applications
7. Balmer, J.M.T., Greyser, S.A. (eds.): Revealing the corporation. Routledge, New York (2003) ISBN:0415284201,
   http://gso.gbv.de/DB=2.1/
   CMDACT=SRCHA&SRT=YOP&IKT=1016&TRM=ppn+349820163&sourceid=fbw_bibsonomy
8. Berners-Lee, T., Hendler, J., Lassila, O.: The semantic web. Scientific American Magazine (May 17, 2001)
9. Carbone, M., Nielsen, M., Sassone, V.: A formal model for trust in dynamic networks. In: Proc. of International Conference on Software Engineering and Formal Methods, pp. 54–63 (2003)
10. Cardoso, J., Sheth, A.P., Miller, J.A., Arnold, J., Kochut, K.: Quality of service for workflows and web service processes. J. Web Sem (2004)
11. Casare, S., Sichman, J.: Towards a functional ontology of reputation. In: Proceedings of the Fourth International Joint Conference on Autonomous Agents and Multiagent Systems, p. 505 (2005)
12. Chang, E., Hussain, F.K., Dillon, T.: Reputation ontology for reputation systems. In: Meersman, R., Tari, Z., Herrero, P. (eds.) OTM 2006 Workshops. LNCS, vol. 4278, pp. 1724–1733. Springer, Heidelberg (2006)
13. Dellarocas, C.: Reputation mechanisms (2005)
14. Esfandiari, B., Chandrasekharan, S.: On how agents make friends: Mechanisms for trust acquisition (2001)
15. Fullam, K.K., Klos, T.B., Muller, G., Sabater, J., Schlosser, A., Topol, Z., Barber, K.S., Rosenschein, J.S., Vercouter, L., Voss, M.: A specification of the agent reputation and trust (ART) testbed: Experimentation and competition for trust in agent societies. In: The 4th International Joint Conference on Autonomous Agents and Multiagent Systems (2005)
16. Grÿninger, M., Fox, M.S.: Methodology for the design and evaluation of ontologies. Basic Ontological Issues in Knowledge Sharing (1995)
17. Jøsang, A.: A logic for uncertain probabilities. Int. J. Uncertain. Fuzziness Knowl.-Based Syst. 9, 279–311 (2001)
18. Jøsang, A., Ismail, R., Boyd, C.: A survey of trust and reputation systems for online service provision. Decision Support Systems, 618–644 (2007)
19. Kashyap, V., Bussler, C., Moran, M.: The Semantic Web, Semantics for Data and Services on the Web. Springer, Heidelberg (2008)
20. Liu, Y., Ngu, A.H., Zeng, L.Z.: Qos computation and policing in dynamic web service selection. In: Proceedings of the 13th international World Wide Web conference, pp. 66–73. ACM, New York (2004)
21. Maximilien, E.M., Singh, M.P.: An ontology for web service ratings and reputations (2003)

22. McGuinness, D.L.: Ontologies come of age. In: Spinning the Semantic Web: Bringing the World Wide Web to Its Full Potential. MIT Press, Cambridge (2003)
23. Mui, L., Mohtashemi, M., Halberstadt, A.: A computational model of trust and reputation for e-businesses. In: Proceedings of the 35th Annual Hawaii International Conference on System Sciences, HICSS 2002. IEEE Computer Society, Los Alamitos (2002)
24. Mui, L., Halberstadt, A., Mohtashemi, M.: Evaluating reputation in multi-agents systems. In: Falcone, R., Barber, S.K., Korba, L., Singh, M.P. (eds.) AAMAS 2002. LNCS (LNAI), vol. 2631, pp. 123–137. Springer, Heidelberg (2003)
25. Nardin, L.G., Brandao, A.A.F., Sichman, J.S., Vercouter, L.: An ontology mapping service to support agent reputation models interoperability. In: 11th Workshop on Trust in Agent Societies, Estoril, Portugal (2008)
26. Paschke, A., Alnemr, R., Meinel, C.: The rule responder distributed reputation management system for the semantic web. In: RuleML-2010 Challenge, Washington DC, USA. ACM, New York (2010)
27. Pinto, H.S., Martins: Ontologies: How can they be built? Knowl. Inf. Syst. 6, 441–464 (2004)
28. Pinyol, I., Sabater-Mir, J., Cuni, G.: How to talk about reputation using a common ontology: From definition to implementation. In: Proceedings of the Ninth Workshop on Trust in Agent Societies, Hawaii, USA, pp. 90–101 (2007)
29. Conte, R., Paolucci, M.: Reputation in Artificial Societies. Social Beliefs for Social Order (2002)
30. Resnick, P., Kuwabara, K., Zeckhauser, R., Friedman, E.: Reputation systems. Commun. ACM, 45–48 (2000)
31. Resnick, P., Zeckhauser, R.: Trust among strangers in Internet transactions: Empirical analysis of eBay's reputation system. In: The Economics of the Internet and E-Commerce, pp. 127–157 (2002)
32. Sabater, J., Paolucci, M., Conte, R.: REPAGE: REPutation & imAGE among limited autonomous partners. Artificial Societies & Social Simulation Jour. (2006)
33. Sabater, J., Sierra, C.: Regret: reputation in gregarious societies. In: Proceedings of the Fifth International Conference on Autonomous Agents, AGENTS 2001, pp. 194–195. ACM, New York (2001)
34. Sabater, J., Sierra, C.: Review on computational trust and reputation models. Artif. Intell. Rev. 24, 33–60 (2005)
35. Schnjakin, M., Alnemr, R., Meinel, C.: A security and high-availability layer for cloud storage. In: The 2nd Int. Workshop on Cloud Information System Engineering (Springer CISE 2010) (2010)
36. Sen, S., Sajja, N.: Robustness of reputation-based trust: boolean case. In: Proceedings of the First International Joint Conference On Autonomous Agents and Multiagent Systems, AAMAS 2002, pp. 288–293. ACM, New York (2002)
37. Valente, A.: Legal Knowledge Engineering- A modeling Approach (1995)
38. Vercouter, L., Casare, S.J., Sichman, J.S., Brandão, A.A.F.: An experience on reputation models interoperability based on a functional ontology. In: Proceedings of the 20th International Joint Conference on Artifical Intelligence, San Francisco, CA, USA, pp. 617–622 (2007)
39. Whitby, A., Jøsang, A., Indulska, J.: Filtering out unfair ratings in bayesian reputation systems (2004)
40. Yu, B., Singh, M.P.: An evidential model of distributed reputation management. In: Proceedings of the First International Joint Conference on Autonomous Agents and Multiagent Systems, AAMAS 2002, pp. 294–301. ACM, USA (2002)

Enhancing Data Privacy in the Cloud

Yanbin Lu and Gene Tsudik

University of California, Irvine
{yanbinl,gts}@uci.edu

Abstract. Due to its low cost, robustness, flexibility and ubiquitous nature, cloud computing is changing the way entities manage their data. However, various privacy concerns arise whenever potentially sensitive data is outsourced to the cloud.

This paper presents a novel approach for coping with such privacy concerns. The proposed scheme prevents the cloud server from learning any possibly sensitive plaintext in the outsourced databases. It also allows the database owner to delegate users to conducting content-level fine-grained private search and decryption. Moreover, our scheme supports private querying whereby neither the database owner nor the cloud server learns query details. Additional requirement that user's input be authorized by CA can also be supported.

1 Introduction

Cloud computing involves highly available massive compute and storage platforms offering a wide range of services. One of the most popular and basic cloud computing services is storage-as-a-service (SAAS). It provides companies with affordable storage, professional maintenance and adjustable space.

On one hand, due to above-mentioned benefits, companies are excited by the public debut of SAAS. On the other hand, companies are reticent about adopting SAAS. One of the major concerns is the privacy as cloud service is generally provided by the third party. In the following, we call the company, who uses SAAS, the *database owner*. We call anyone who queries the company's database, the database *user*. And we call the cloud servers, which store the database, *the cloud server*. Now we start to clarify different types of privacy challenges during the deployment of cloud service.

From the perspective of the database owner, three challenges arise.

- *Challenge 1:* how to protect outsourced data from theft by hackers or malware infiltrating the cloud server? Encryption by the cloud server and authenticated access by users seems to be a straightforward solution. However, careful consideration should be given to both encryption method and its granularity.
- *Challenge 2:* how to protect outsourced data from abuse by the cloud server? A trivial solution is for the owner to encrypt the database prior to outsourcing. Subsequently, users (armed with the decryption key(s)) can download the entire encrypted database, decrypt it and perform querying *in situ*. Clearly, this negates most benefits of using the cloud. A more elegant approach is to use searchable encryption. Unfortunately, current searchable encryption techniques only support simple search (attribute=value), as opposed to complicated SQL, queries.

I. Wakeman et al. (Eds.): IFIPTM 2011, IFIP AICT 358, pp. 117–132, 2011.

– *Challenge 3:* how to realize content-level fine-grained access control for users? This challenge is even harder to solve as it requires variable decryption capabilities for different users. Even trivial solution to the second challenge does not solve this challenge as it gives each user equal decryption capability (same decryption key). An ideal solution would entail the database owner issuing a given user a key that only allows the user to search and decrypt certain records.

From user's perspective, three more challenges arise.

– *Challenge 4:* how to query the cloud server without revealing query details? Learning user's query details means learning user's possibly sensitive search interest. In addition, by learning user queries, the cloud server gradually learns the information in the encrypted database.

– *Challenge 5:* how to hide query contents (e.g., values used in "attribute=value" queries) from the database owner. For the database owner to exercise access control over its outsourced data, a user should first obtain an approval from the database owner over its query contents. However, in some cases, the user may want to get the approval without revealing its query contents even to the database owner. This is the case when the user happens to be a high-level executive who is automatically qualified to search any value and is not willing to reveal query to anyone.

– *Challenge 6:* how to hide query contents while assuring database owner the hiden contents are authorized by some certificate authority (CA). Such challenge surfaces, for example, when the user is FBI who does not want to reveal the person it is investigating while database owner wants to get some confidence by making sure FBI is authorized by the court to do this investigation.

To address the above challenges, we need a scheme for the scenario shown in Fig. 1. In the initial deployment phase, the owner encrypts its database and transfers it to the cloud server. The encryption scheme should guarantee that no plaintext is leaked in the encrypted database, thereby addressing challenges 1–2. When user poses an SQL query, such as:

"select from sample where ((last_name='Lobb' AND birth_date='3/26/1983') OR blood_type='B')"

it first obtains a search token and decryption key from the database owner. Then, the user supplies the search token to the cloud server who uses the token to search the encrypted database. Matching encrypted records are returned to the user who finally decrypts them. The search token and the decryption key should only allow user to search and decrypt records meeting the conditional expression in the specific query, therefore addressing challenge 3. The search token should not reveal the conditional expression specified by user, therefore solving challenge 4. Further, user should be able to get the search token and decryption key without letting database owner know the query contents in order to solve challenge 5. Finally, to solve challenge 6, database owner, even though not knowing the query contents, should be able to verify if these contents are authorized by a CA.

In this paper, we present a new scheme that addresses aforementioned requirements. It relies on attribute-based encryption [1] and blind Boneh-Boyen weak signature scheme [2]. In fact, we amend the standard attribute-based encryption to make it privately searchable in the cloud computing scenario. Furthermore, we use the blind Boneh-Boyen signature scheme to let user obliviously retrieve a search token and decryption key. Moreover, blind search token and decryption key extraction procedure can be coupled with CA authorization on user's input.

This paper aims to make four contributions: First, we define the adversary and security model for an encryption scheme aimed at the cloud database system. Second, we construct an encryption scheme that protects data privacy and allows access control. Third, we develop techniques for a user to retrieve search token and decryption key from database owner without revealing query contents. Fourth, we make it possible that the database owner, without knowing query contents, can make sure these contents are authorized by CA.

The rest of the paper is organized as follows. Sec. 2 overviews related work. Next, Sec. 3 defines the function and security model. Then, Sec. 4 discusses some background issues. The new scheme is presented in Sec. 5, followed by Sec. 6 that analyzes its performance. An in-depth performance evaluation is shown in Sec. 7. Limitations of our scheme are discussed in Sec. 8. Finally, Sec. 9 concludes this paper. A complete security proof is provided in the full version [3].

2   Related Work

Private Information Retrieval and Oblivious Transfer: Private Information Retrieval (PIR) [4] allows a user to retrieve an item from a server's (public) database without the latter learning which item is being retrieved. While PIR is not concerned with privacy of the server database, Oblivious Transfer (OT) [5] adds an additional requirement that the user should not receive records beyond those requested. Several results [6, 7] apply PIR/OT concepts to relational databases in order to hide user SQL queries from the database server.

There are significant differences between these approaches and our work. First these approaches target a user/server scenario and it is unclear how to extend them to the cloud setting with the additional requirement of protecting data from untrusted cloud server. Second user can query any items inside the database and there is no way to enforce access control in these approaches.

Search on encrypted database: Searching on encrypted data (SoE), also known as privacy preserving keyword-based retrieval over encrypted data, was introduced in the symmetric key setting by Song, et al. [8]. This scheme allows a user to store its symmetrically encrypted data on an untrusted server and later search for a specific keyword by giving the server a search capability, that does not reveal the keyword or any plaintext. Its security and efficiency was later improved in [9] and [10]. Golle, et al. [11] developed a symmetric-key version of SoE that supports conjunctive keyword search. Boneh, et al. [12] later proposed a public-key version of encryption with keyword search

(PEKS), where any party in possession of the public key can encrypt and send encryption to an untrusted server, while only the owner of the corresponding private key can generate keyword search capabilities. The server can identify all messages containing the searching keyword, but learn nothing else.

Our work is different from SoE and PEKS since it supports flexible access control (any monotonic access structure) on encrypted data, i.e. the database owner can issue a user a decryption key that only decrypts data meeting a certain conditional expression. Also, our scheme supports oblivious (search token/decryption key) retrieval.

Attribute-based encryption: Sahai and Waters [13] introduced the concept of Attribute-Based Encryption (ABE) where a user's keys and ciphertexts are labeled with sets of descriptive attributes and a particular key can decrypt a particular ciphertext only if the cardinality of the intersection of their labeled attributes exceeds a certain threshold. Later, Goyal, et al. [1] developed a Key-Policy Attribute-Based Encryption (KP-ABE) where the trusted authority (master key owner) can generate user private keys associated with any monotonic access structures consisting of **AND, OR** or threshold gates. Only ciphertexts that satisfy the private key's access structure can be decrypted. Bethencourt, et al. [14] explore the concept of Ciphertext-Policy Attribute-Based Encryption where each ciphertext is associated with an access structure that specifies which type of secret keys can decrypt it. Ostrovsky, et al. [15] extended [1] by allowing negative constraints in a key access structure.

Our scheme is derived from that in [1]. However, compared to traditional ABE, there are several notable differences. First, ABE only achieves payload hiding, i.e., attributes are revealed in plaintext, while our scheme hides the attributes. Second, ABE does not support private search on encrypted data, while our scheme does. Third, ABE does not support oblivious private key retrieval from the authority, while our scheme does.

Predicate encryption: Predicate encryption can be considered as attribute-based encryption supporting attribute-hiding. Ciphertexts are associate with a set of hidden attributes I. The master secret key owner has the fine-grained control over access to encrypted data by generating a secret key sk_f corresponding to predicate f; sk_f can be used to decrypt a ciphertext associated with attribute I if and only if $f(I) = 1$.

Several results have yielded predicate encryption schemes for different predicates. Waters, et al. constructed an equality tests predicate encryption scheme [16]. Shi and Waters [17] constructed a conjunction predicate encryption scheme. In [18], Shi, et al. proposed a scheme for range queries. Boneh and Waters [19] developed a scheme that handles conjunctions and range queries while satisfying a stronger notion of attribute hiding. Katz, et al. [20] move a step further by making predicate encryption support inner products, therefore supporting disjunction and polynomial evaluation.

Our approach is different in several respects. First, no concrete private search scheme exists in predicate encryption. Although a predicate-only version is enough for private search [20], requiring private search on a cloud server and access control for users probably means that two separate implementations of predicate encryption are needed. Second, our scheme supports more flexible access control; although, range queries are not covered. Finally, no oblivious retrieval of decryption key for predicate encryption exists so far.

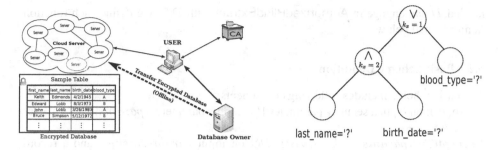

Fig. 1. Cloud storage architecture   **Fig. 2.** Access tree example

3 Definition

3.1 Problem Description

Fig. 1 shows the architecture of the envisaged cloud storage scenario. There are four entities: the cloud server ($\mathcal{S}$), the database owner ($\mathcal{DO}$), the database user ($\mathcal{U}$) and the CA ($\mathcal{CA}$). $\mathcal{DO}$'s database table consists of w attributes $\{\alpha_1, \alpha_2, \ldots, \alpha_w\}$. Let $\Omega = \{1, \cdots, w\}$. For ease of description, we assume that every attribute is searchable. Each record m includes w values: $\{v_i\}_{1 \leq i \leq w}$ with each v_i corresponding to attribute α_i. Fig. 1 also illustrates a sample database. The first row describes attribute names and each subsequent row denotes a record.

$\mathcal{U}$ may issue $\mathcal{S}$ any SQL query with monotonic access structure. By monotonic access structure, we mean a boolean formula only involving 'AND/OR' combinations. We use an **access tree** (see Sec. 4.2 for details) to describe any monotonic access structure. In our context, the access tree describes a combination of 'AND/OR' of attribute names, without specifying their values. For example, Fig. 2 depicts one type of access tree corresponding to a conditional expression ((last_name=? AND birth_date=?) OR blood_type=?). If concrete values are supplied together with an access tree, a complete conditional expression can be defined. For example, if a value set (Lobb, 3/26/1983, B) is specified, the expression will be ((last_name='Lobb' AND birth_date='3/26/1983') OR blood_type='B'). We use $\mathcal{T}_\gamma$ to denote an access tree constructed over a subset γ of Ω and use $\mathbf{v}_\gamma$ to describe a set of values for $\mathcal{T}_\gamma$ to completely define a conditional expression. A complete record can be viewed as $\mathbf{v}_\Omega$. We use $\mathcal{T}_\gamma(\mathbf{v}_\gamma, \mathbf{v}_{\gamma'})$ to test whether a set of values $\mathbf{v}_{\gamma'}$ satisfies the conditional expression defined by $\mathcal{T}_\gamma$ and $\mathbf{v}_\gamma$.

Our basic encryption scheme is a set of components: Setup, Encrypt, Extract, Test, Decrypt. Before starting, the CA runs Setup to initialize some parameters. Then $\mathcal{DO}$ runs Encrypt over each record in its table to form an encrypted database. The encrypted database is exported to $\mathcal{S}$ (off-line) and $\mathcal{DO}$ can insert new encrypted items later. Whenever $\mathcal{U}$ forms an SQL query, it runs Extract with $\mathcal{DO}$ to extract a search token and decryption key. Then, $\mathcal{U}$ hands the search token to $\mathcal{S}$ and the latter runs Test over each encrypted record, in order to find matching records. After that, $\mathcal{S}$ sends matching records back and $\mathcal{U}$ runs Decrypt to recover plaintext records. If additional requirement that $\mathcal{DO}$ learns nothing about query content is needed, $\mathcal{U}$ can run BlindExtract instead of Extract with $\mathcal{DO}$. If further requirement that $\mathcal{U}$'s query should be Authorized by CA is needed, $\mathcal{U}$ can engage in AuthorizedBlindExtract with $\mathcal{DO}$. We define each function in more detail below.

3.2   Basic Scheme Definition

The basic scheme includes following components:

Setup(1^k): on input a security parameter 1^k, outputs parameters $params$, $\mathcal{DO}$'s master key $msk_{\mathcal{DO}}$.

Encrypt($\mathcal{DO}(params, msk_{\mathcal{DO}}, \mathbf{v}_\Omega)$): $\mathcal{DO}$ on input $params, msk_{\mathcal{DO}}$ and a record $\mathbf{v}_\Omega$, outputs a ciphertext.

Extract($\mathcal{U}(params, \mathcal{T}_\gamma, \mathbf{v}_\gamma), \mathcal{DO}(params, msk_{\mathcal{DO}})$): $\mathcal{U}$ on input $(params, \mathcal{T}_\gamma, \mathbf{v}_\gamma)$ and $\mathcal{DO}$ on input $(params, msk_{\mathcal{DO}})$ engage in an interactive protocol. At the end, $\mathcal{U}$ outputs a search token $tk_{(\mathcal{T}_\gamma, \mathbf{v}_\gamma)}$ and a decryption key $sk_{(\mathcal{T}_\gamma, \mathbf{v}_\gamma)}$, and $\mathcal{DO}$ outputs $(\mathcal{T}_\gamma, \mathbf{v}_\gamma)$.

Test($\mathcal{S}(params, tk_{(\mathcal{T}_\gamma, \mathbf{v}_\gamma)}, C)$): $\mathcal{S}$ on input parameters $params$, a search token $tk_{(\mathcal{T}_\gamma, \mathbf{v}_\gamma)}$ and a ciphertext $C =$ Encrypt($msk_{\mathcal{DO}}, \mathbf{v}'_\Omega$), outputs "yes" if $\mathcal{T}_\gamma(\mathbf{v}_\gamma, \mathbf{v}'_\Omega) = 1$ and "no" otherwise.

Decrypt($\mathcal{U}(params, tk_{(\mathcal{T}_\gamma, \mathbf{v}_\gamma)} sk_{(\mathcal{T}_\gamma, \mathbf{v}_\gamma)}, C)$): $\mathcal{U}$ on input $params$, a search token $tk_{(\mathcal{T}_\gamma, \mathbf{v}_\gamma)}$, a decryption key $sk_{(\mathcal{T}_\gamma, \mathbf{v}_\gamma)}$ and a ciphertext $C =$ Encrypt($msk_{\mathcal{DO}}, \mathbf{v}'_\Omega$), outputs $\mathbf{v}'_\Omega$ if $\mathcal{T}_\gamma(\mathbf{v}_\gamma, \mathbf{v}'_\Omega) = 1$ and $\perp$ otherwise.

3.3   Blind Extraction Definition

In order to protect $\mathcal{U}$'s query from $\mathcal{DO}$, we need to replace Extract with a blinded version, called BlindExtract.

BlindExtract($\mathcal{U}(params, \mathcal{T}_\gamma, \mathbf{v}_\gamma), \mathcal{DO}(params, msk_{\mathcal{DO}})$): $\mathcal{U}$ on input $(params, \mathcal{T}_\gamma, \mathbf{v}_\gamma)$ and $\mathcal{DO}$ on input $(params, msk_{\mathcal{DO}}, \mathcal{T}_\gamma)$ engage in an interactive protocol. $\mathcal{U}$'s output is a search token $tk_{(\mathcal{T}_\gamma, \mathbf{v}_\gamma)}$ and a decryption key $sk_{(\mathcal{T}_\gamma, \mathbf{v}_\gamma)}$, and $\mathcal{DO}$'s output is $\mathcal{T}_\gamma$.

Sometimes, it makes more sense to require $\mathcal{U}$ to prove that its input in BlindExtract is authorized by a CA before $\mathcal{U}$ can get anything useful. In order to realize that, we introduce two other functions Authorize and AuthorizedBlindExtract. Authorize helps a $\mathcal{U}$ get a commitment ψ and a signature σ from a CA. In AuthorizedBlindExtract, $\mathcal{DO}$ is provided with $\mathcal{T}_\gamma, \psi, \sigma$ while $\mathcal{U}$ can prove statements about commitment ψ using zero-knowledge proof.

Authoriz($\mathcal{U}(params, \mathcal{T}_\gamma, \mathbf{v}_\gamma), \mathcal{CA}(params, msk_{\mathcal{CA}})$): $\mathcal{CA}$ generates a commitment ψ over $\mathcal{U}$'s input $(\mathcal{T}_\gamma, \mathbf{v}_\gamma)$, the randomness $open$ used to compute ψ and a signature σ over ψ. $\mathcal{CA}$'s output is $(\mathcal{T}_\gamma, \mathbf{v}_\gamma, \psi, open, \sigma)$. $\mathcal{U}$'s output is $(\psi, open, \sigma)$.

AuthorizedBlindExtract($\mathcal{U}(params, \mathcal{T}_\gamma, \mathbf{v}_\gamma, \psi, open, \sigma), \mathcal{DO}(params, msk_{\mathcal{DO}})$): $\mathcal{U}$ on input $(params, \mathcal{T}_\gamma, \mathbf{v}_\gamma, \psi, open, \sigma)$ and $\mathcal{DO}$ on input $(params, msk_{\mathcal{DO}})$ engage in an interactive protocol. $\mathcal{DO}$'s output is $(\mathcal{T}_\gamma, \psi, \sigma)$. If $\psi =$ Commit($(\mathcal{T}_\gamma, \mathbf{v}_\gamma)$, $open$) and Vrfy$_{pk_{\mathcal{CA}}}(\psi, \sigma) = 1$, $\mathcal{U}$'s output is a search token $tk_{(\mathcal{T}_\gamma, \mathbf{v}_\gamma)}$ and a decryption key $sk_{(\mathcal{T}_\gamma, \mathbf{v}_\gamma)}$, and otherwise, $\mathcal{U}$ outputs $\perp$.

3.4 Adversary Model and Security Requirement

In this paper, we assume the malicious adversary model (as opposed to semi-honest, aka "honest-but-curious"). A malicious adversary can arbitrarily deviate from the prescribed protocols. We also assume that $\mathcal{U}$ may collude with $\mathcal{S}$. However, $\mathcal{DO}$ does not collude with any party. In the full version of this paper [3], we will prove our scheme is secure against malicious adversary according to Def. 1, 2 and 3.

For the basic scheme, we define adversary's advantage by defining a security game under chosen plaintext attack in a selective set model, similar to [1].

Definition 1. (Selective-Set Secure (IND-SS-CPA)). *Let k be a security parameter. Above scheme is IND-SS-CPA-secure if every p.p.t. adversary $\mathcal{A}$ has an advantage negligible in k for the following game: (1) Run* $\mathsf{Setup}(1^k)$ *to obtain* $(params, msk_{\mathcal{DO}})$, *and give params to $\mathcal{A}$. (2) $\mathcal{A}$ outputs two records m_1, m_2 to be challenged on (3) $\mathcal{A}$ may query an oracle* $\mathcal{O}_{\mathsf{Extract}}(params, msk_{\mathcal{DO}}, \mathcal{T}_\gamma, \mathbf{v}_\gamma)$ *such that* $\mathcal{T}_\gamma(\mathbf{v}_\gamma, m_1) \neq 1$ *and* $\mathcal{T}_\gamma(\mathbf{v}_\gamma, m_2) \neq 1$. *(4) Select a random bit b and give $\mathcal{A}$ the challenge $c^* \leftarrow$* $\mathsf{Encrypt}(params, msk_{\mathcal{DO}}, m_b)$. *(5) $\mathcal{A}$ may continue to query oracle* $\mathcal{O}_{\mathsf{Extract}}(\cdot)$ *under the same conditions as before. (6) $\mathcal{A}$ outputs a bit b'. We define $\mathcal{A}$'s advantage in the above game as* $|\Pr[b' = b] - 1/2|$.

$\mathsf{BlindExtract}$ must satisfy two security properties: *Leak-free Extract* [21] and *Selective-failure Blindness* [22]. Informally, the former means that a malicious $\mathcal{U}$ cannot learn more by executing the $\mathsf{BlindExtract}$ with an honest $\mathcal{DO}$ than by executing $\mathsf{Extract}$ with an honest $\mathcal{DO}$. Whereas, $\mathsf{Selective}$-failure Blindness means that a malicious $\mathcal{DO}$ cannot learn anything about $\mathcal{U}$'s choice of $\mathbf{v}_\gamma$ during $\mathsf{BlindExtract}$. Moreover, $\mathcal{DO}$ cannot cause $\mathsf{BlindExtract}$ to fail based on $\mathcal{U}$'s choice. Now we formally define *Leak-free Extract* and *Selective-failure Blindness*:

Definition 2. (Leak-Free Extract). $\mathsf{BlindExtract}$ *protocol is leak free if, for all p.p.t. adversaries $\mathcal{A}$, there exists an efficient simulator such that for every value k, $\mathcal{A}$ cannot determine whether it is playing Game Real or Game Ideal with non-negligible advantage, where*
Game Real: Run $\mathsf{Setup}(1^k)$. *As many times as $\mathcal{A}$ wants, $\mathcal{A}$ chooses its $\mathcal{T}_\gamma$, $\mathbf{v}_\gamma$ and executes* $\mathsf{BlindExtract}(\cdot)$ *with $\mathcal{DO}$.*
Game Ideal: Run $\mathsf{Setup}(1^k)$. *As many times as $\mathcal{A}$ wants, $\mathcal{A}$ chooses its $\mathcal{T}_\gamma$, $\mathbf{v}_\gamma$ and executes* $\mathsf{BlindExtract}(\cdot)$ *with a simulator which does not know $msk_{\mathcal{DO}}$ and only queries a trusted party to obtain $tk_{(\mathcal{T}_\gamma, \mathbf{v}_\gamma)}$ and $sk_{(\mathcal{T}_\gamma, \mathbf{v}_\gamma)}$.*

Definition 3. (Selective-Failure Blindness). $\mathsf{BlindExtract}$ *is selective-failure blind if every p.p.t. adversary $\mathcal{A}$ has a negligible advantage in the following game: First, $\mathcal{A}$ outputs params and a pair of $(\mathcal{T}, \mathbf{v}_1)$, $(\mathcal{T}, \mathbf{v}_2)$. A random bit b is chosen. $\mathcal{A}$ is given blackbox access to two oracles $\mathcal{U}(params, \mathcal{T}, \mathbf{v}_b)$ and $\mathcal{U}(params, \mathcal{T}, \mathbf{v}_{1-b})$. The $\mathcal{U}$ algorithm produces local output $s_b = (tk_{(\mathcal{T}, \mathbf{v}_b)}, sk_{(\mathcal{T}, \mathbf{v}_b)})$ and $s_{1-b} = (tk_{(\mathcal{T}, \mathbf{v}_{1-b})}, sk_{(\mathcal{T}, \mathbf{v}_{1-b})})$ respectively. If $s_b \neq \perp$ and $s_{1-b} \neq \perp$ then $\mathcal{A}$ receives (s_0, s_1). If $s_b = \perp$ and $s_{1-b} \neq \perp$ then $\mathcal{A}$ receives $(\perp, \epsilon)$. If $s_b \neq \perp$ and $s_{1-b} = \perp$, then $\mathcal{A}$ receives $(\epsilon, \perp)$. If $s_b = \perp$ and $s_{1-b} = \perp$, then $\mathcal{A}$ receives $(\perp, \perp)$. Finally, $\mathcal{A}$ outputs its guess bit b'. We define $\mathcal{A}$'s advantage in the above game as* $|\Pr[b' = b] - 1/2|$.

4 Preliminaries

4.1 Notation

Let $\{0,1\}^l$ denote the set of integers of maximum length l, i.e. the set $[0, 2^l - 1]$ of integers. we employ the security parameters $l_\phi, l_\mathcal{H}$ where l_ϕ (80) is the security parameter controlling the statistical zero-knowledge property, $l_\mathcal{H}$ (160) is the output length of the hash function used for the Fiat-Shamir heuristic. $\mathcal{H}(\cdot)$ and $\mathcal{H}'(\cdot)$ denote two distinct hash function. We use Enc_{pk}^{hom} and Dec_{sk}^{hom} to denote homomorphic encryption and decryption (respectively) under public key pk (or secret key sk). We use Enc_k^{sym} and Dec_k^{sym} to denote symmetric encryption and decryption under key k. We define Lagrange Coefficient as $\Delta_{i,S} = \prod_{j \in S, j \neq i} \frac{j}{j-i}$. Let Ω denote attributes index set, i.e. $\Omega = \{1, \cdots, w\}$. $\mathcal{DO}$'s private and public keys are $sk_{\mathcal{DO}}$ and $pk_{\mathcal{DO}}$, respectively. $server$'s master key is $msk_{\mathcal{DO}}$. $\mathcal{CA}$'s private and public keys are $sk_{\mathcal{CA}}$ and $pk_{\mathcal{CA}}$.

4.2 Access Tree

We use $\mathcal{T}$ to denote a tree representing an access structure. $\mathcal{T}$ represents a combination of 'AND/OR' of attribute names without specifying their values, as shown in Fig. 2. An access structure $\mathcal{T}_\gamma$ defined over a set γ of attributes, coupled with a set of values $\mathbf{v}_\gamma$ defined over the same set, completely defines a conditional expression (See Sec. 3.1 for example). We use $\mathcal{T}_\gamma(\mathbf{v}_\gamma, \mathbf{v})$ to test whether another set of values $\mathbf{v}$ satisfies the condition defined by $\mathcal{T}_\gamma$ and $\mathbf{v}_\gamma$. Each non-leaf node represents a threshold gate, described by its children and a threshold value. Let num_x be the number of children of a node x. The threshold value associated with node x is denoted by k_x that is either 1 or num_x, depending on the threshold gate. In case of an OR gate, $k_x = 1$; in case of an AND gate, $k_x = num_x$. Each leaf node x is described by an attribute with a threshold $k_x = 1$. Standard tree data structures can be used to represent and store $\mathcal{T}$. Since $\mathcal{T}_\gamma$ is exposed to $\mathcal{S}$ in Test, to prevent $\mathcal{S}$ from learning database schema, each leaf node can store an attribute index instead of the attribute name.

To facilitate working with the access trees, we define a few functions. We denote the parent of the node x as $parent(x)$. $node(\alpha_i)$ returns the leaf node corresponding to attribute α_i. $attr(x)$ is defined only if x is a leaf node; it returns the attribute index i of α_i associated with x. Access tree $\mathcal{T}$ also defines an ordering between the children of every node, i.e. each child y of a node x are numbered from 1 to num_x. $index(y)$ returns this number associated with the node y. Let S_x denote a set $[1, \ldots, num_x]$. Finally, let $child_i(x)$ return the ith child of node x.

We also define $\Gamma_{\mathcal{T}_\gamma}$ as a set of minimum subsets of γ that satisfies $\mathcal{T}_\gamma$. By "minimum", we mean the subset cannot become smaller while still satisfying $\mathcal{T}_\gamma$. For example, in Fig. 2, $\Gamma_{\mathcal{T}_\gamma} = \{\{1,2\}, \{3\}\}$ where $1, 2, 3$ is the index of attribute $last\_name$, $birth\_date, blood\_type$ respectively. Here $\Gamma_{\mathcal{T}_\gamma}$ means that either $\{last\_name,$ $birth\_date\}$ or $\{blood\_type\}$ can satisfy $\mathcal{T}_\gamma$. We can determine $\Gamma_{\mathcal{T}_\gamma}$ in a down-top manner. For each leaf node, define $S_x = \{attr(x)\}$. For any other node x, $S_x = \cup_{i \in S_x} S_{child_i(x)}$ if $k_x = 1$. Otherwise if $k_x > 1$, $S_x = \{x' : x' = \cup_{1 \leq i \leq k_x} x'_i, \forall x'_i \in S_{child_i(x)}\}$. And the resulting S_r at root node r is $\Gamma_{\mathcal{T}_\gamma}$. For $\gamma' \in \Gamma_{\mathcal{T}_\gamma}$, we define $\mathcal{T}_{\gamma'}$ as a subgraph of $\mathcal{T}_\gamma$ with only attributes in γ' as leaves. For example, in Fig. 2, if $\gamma' = \{1, 2\}$, then $\mathcal{T}_{\gamma'}$ would be the left-hand subtree of the root node. Note in $\mathcal{T}_{\gamma'}$ each non-leaf node x's k_x should be its number of children, i.e., a conjunctive gate, since γ' is a minimum satisfiable subset.

4.3 Homomorphic Encryption

There are several additively homomorphic public key encryption schemes [23, 24]. We elect to use Paillier encryption [24] due to its easy implementation and amenability to proofs of knowledge. Let n denote an RSA modulus, $\mathfrak{h} = n + 1$ and $\mathfrak{g}$ be an element of order $\phi(n) \bmod n^2$. Let $sk = \{\phi(n)\}$ and $pk = \{\mathfrak{g}, n\}$. Encryption is defined as $c = \mathrm{Enc}_{pk}^{hom}(m) = \mathfrak{h}^m \mathfrak{g}^r \bmod n^2$ where $r \in_R \mathbb{Z}_{\phi(n)}$. Corresponding decryption is defined as: $\mathrm{Dec}_{sk}^{hom}(c) = \left\lceil \frac{(c^{\phi(n)} \bmod n^2) - 1}{n} \cdot \phi(n)^{-1} \bmod N \right\rceil$. Note that, to encrypt, we use $\mathfrak{h}^m \mathfrak{g}^r$ instead of standard $\mathfrak{h}^m r^n$. If the order of $\mathfrak{g}$ has no factor of n and is greater than 2, $\mathfrak{g}^r$ is a random element from the same subgroup as r^n. Therefore $\mathfrak{h}^m \mathfrak{g}^r$ has the same distribution as $\mathfrak{h}^m r^n$. The purpose of using the former is to facilitate zero-knowledge proofs.

4.4 Zero-Knowledge Proof

Our scheme uses various protocols to prove knowledge of, and relations among, discrete logarithms. To describe these protocols, we use the notation introduced by Camenisch and Stadler [25]. For instance, $PK\{(a, b, c) : y = g^a h^b \wedge \mathfrak{y} = \mathfrak{g}^a \mathfrak{h}^c \wedge s \leq b \leq t\}$ denotes a zero-knowledge proof of knowledge of integers a, b, c such that $y = g^a h^b$ and $\mathfrak{y} = \mathfrak{g}^a \mathfrak{h}^c$ holds and $s \leq b \leq t$. The convention is that everything inside parentheses is only known to the prover, while all other parameters are known to both prover and verifier.

The technique for a proof of knowledge of a representation of an element $y \in G$ with respect to several bases $z_1, \ldots, z_v \in G$, i.e., $PK\{(a_1, \cdots, a_v) : y = z_1^{a_1} \cdots z_v^{a_v}\}$, is presented in [26]. A proof of equality of discrete logarithms of two group elements $y_1, y_2 \in G$ to bases $g \in G$ and $h \in G$, respectively, i.e., $PK\{(a) : y_1 = g^a \wedge y_2 = h^a\}$, is given in [27]. Generalizations to proving equalities among representations of elements $y_1, \ldots, y_v \in G$ to bases $g_1, \ldots, g_v \in G$ are straightforward [25]. Boudot [28] demonstrates proof of knowledge of a discrete logarithm of $y \in G$ with respect to $g \in G$ such that $\log_g y$ lies in integer interval $[s, t]$, i.e., $PK\{(a) : y = g^a \wedge a \in [s, t]\}$ under the strong RSA assumption and the assumption that the prover does not know the factorization of the RSA modulus.

4.5 Bilinear Map

We now review some general notions about efficiently computable bilinear maps.

Let $\mathbb{G}_1$ and $\mathbb{G}_2$ be two multiplicative cyclic groups of prime order q. Let g be a generator of $\mathbb{G}_1$ and $\hat{e}$ be a bilinear map, $\hat{e} : \mathbb{G}_1 \times \mathbb{G}_1 \to \mathbb{G}_2$. The bilinear map $\hat{e}$ has the following properties:

1. Bilinearity: for all $u, v \in \mathbb{G}_1$ and $a, b \in \mathbb{Z}_p$, we have $\hat{e}(u^a, v^b) = \hat{e}(u, v)^{ab}$
2. Non-degeneracy: $\hat{e}(g, g) \neq 1$.

We say that $\mathbb{G}_1$ is a bilinear group if the group operation in $\mathbb{G}_1$ and the bilinear map $\hat{e} : \mathbb{G}_1 \times \mathbb{G}_1 \rightarrow \mathbb{G}_2$ are both efficiently computable.

4.6   Cryptographic Assumption

Our scheme's security is based on the decisional bilinear Diffie-Hellman (BDH) assumption [29] and Boneh-Boyen Hidden Strong Diffie-Hellman (BB-HSDH) assumption [30].

Assumption 1 (Decisional Bilinear Diffie-Hellman (BDH) assumption). *Let a, b, c, $z \in \mathbb{Z}_q$ be chosen at random and g be a generator of $\mathbb{G}_1$. We say that the BDH problem is hard if for all p.p.t. adversaries $\mathcal{A}$ there exists a negligible function* negl *such that* $|Pr[\mathcal{A}(g^a, g^b, g^c, \hat{e}(g,g)^{abc}) = 1] - Pr[\mathcal{A}(g^a, g^b, g^c, \hat{e}(g,g)^z) = 1]| \leq$ negl(n) *where in each case the probabilities are taken over the random choice of the generator g, the random choice of a, b, c, z in $\mathbb{Z}_q$ and the random bits consumed by $\mathcal{A}$.*

Assumption 2 (Boneh-Boyen Hidden Strong Diffie-Hellman (BB-HSDH)). *Let x, $c_1, \cdots c_t \in_R \mathbb{Z}_q$. On input $g, g^x, u \in \mathbb{G}_1, h, h^x \in \mathbb{G}_2$ and the tuple $\{g^{1/(x+c_l)}, c_l\}_{l=1\ldots t}$, it is computationally infeasible to output a new tuple $(g^{1/(x+c)}, h^c, u^c)$.*

5   Scheme

We present our scheme Π which consists of following algorithms.

Setup(1^k): Run $\mathcal{G}(1^k)$ to obtain $(q, \mathbb{G}_1, \mathbb{G}_2, \hat{e}, \mathsf{n}, \mathsf{g}, \mathfrak{n}, \mathfrak{g}, \mathfrak{h})$. n is an RSA modulus larger than $2^k q^2$ with generator g. Let $sk_{\mathcal{DO}} = \phi(\mathsf{n})$ and $pk_{\mathcal{DO}} = \{\mathsf{g}, \mathsf{n}\}$. In other words, only $\mathcal{DO}$ knows the factors of n. $\mathfrak{n}$ is another RSA modulus with generator $\mathfrak{g}$ and $\mathfrak{h}$. Note neither factors of $\mathfrak{n}$ nor $\log_\mathfrak{g} \mathfrak{h}$ is known to any party. Pick secret parameters t, t', y, y' which are only known to $\mathcal{DO}$. Make $Y = \hat{e}(g,g)^y$, $Y' = \hat{e}(g,g)^{y'}$, $T = g^t, T' = g^{t'}, e_t = \mathsf{Enc}^{hom}_{pk_{\mathcal{DO}}}(t), e_{t'} = \mathsf{Enc}^{hom}_{pk_{\mathcal{DO}}}(t')$, and π^s proving e_t and $e_{t'}$ are well formed. Output $params \leftarrow (Y, Y', T, T', e_t, e_{t'}, \pi^s, pk_{\mathcal{DO}}, pk_{\mathcal{CA}}, \mathfrak{n}, \mathfrak{g}, \mathfrak{h})$, $msk_{\mathcal{DO}} \leftarrow (t, t', y, y', sk_{\mathcal{DO}})$.

Encrypt($\mathcal{DO}(params, msk_{\mathcal{DO}}, m)$): To encrypt a record $m = \mathbf{v}_\Omega = \{v_1, \ldots, v_w\}$, $\mathcal{DO}$ chooses random values $s, s' \in_R \mathbb{Z}_q$ and outputs the ciphertext as:

$$C = (E, E', \{E_i, E'_i\}_{i \in \Omega}).$$

where $E = \mathsf{Enc}^{sym}_{Y^s}(m)$, $E' = Y'^{s'}$, $E_i = g^{s \cdot (t + \mathcal{H}(i, v_i))}$ and $E'_i = g^{s' \cdot (t' + \mathcal{H}'(i, v_i))}$.

Extract($\mathcal{U}(params, \mathcal{T}_\gamma, \mathbf{v}_\gamma), \mathcal{DO}(params, msk_{\mathcal{DO}})$): This is an interactive protocol between $\mathcal{U}$ and $\mathcal{DO}$.

1. $\mathcal{U}$ chooses an attribute set γ and constructs $\mathcal{T}_\gamma$ and $\mathbf{v}_\gamma$ to fully define a conditional expression it wants to query. Then it submits $\mathcal{T}_\gamma$ and $\mathbf{v}_\gamma$ to $\mathcal{DO}$.

2. $\mathcal{DO}$ defines a polynomial $Q_x(\cdot)$ of degree $k_x - 1$ for each node x in $\mathcal{T}_\gamma$ in a top-down manner. For the root node r, it sets $Q_r(0) = y$ and $k_r - 1$ other points of Q_r randomly to fully define $Q_r(\cdot)$. For any other node x, it sets $Q_x(0) = Q_{parent(x)}(index(x))$ and chooses $k_x - 1$ other points randomly to completely define $Q_x(\cdot)$. Then it outputs decryption key $sk_{(\mathcal{T}_\gamma, \mathbf{v}_\gamma)} = \{\{sk_i\}_{i\in\gamma}, \mathcal{T}_\gamma, \mathbf{v}_\gamma\}$ where $sk_i = g^{Q_{node(\alpha_i)}(0)/(t+\mathcal{H}(i,v_i))}$. $\mathcal{DO}$ defines $Q_x'(\cdot)$ in the same way as $Q_x(\cdot)$ except that $Q_r'(0) = y'$. And it outputs search token $tk_{(\mathcal{T}_\gamma, \mathbf{v}_\gamma)} = \{\{tk_i\}_{i\in\gamma}, \mathcal{T}_\gamma\}$ where $tk_i = g^{Q_{node(\alpha_i)}'(0)/(t'+\mathcal{H}'(i,v_i))}$. Last, $\mathcal{DO}$ sends $tk_{(\mathcal{T}_\gamma, \mathbf{v}_\gamma)}$ and $sk_{(\mathcal{T}_\gamma, \mathbf{v}_\gamma)}$ to $\mathcal{U}$.

Test($\mathcal{S}(params, tk_{(\mathcal{T}_\gamma, \mathbf{v}_\gamma)}, C)$): To test whether an encrypted record $C = $ Encrypt$(msk_{\mathcal{DO}}, \mathbf{v}_\Omega')$ matches a search token $tk_{(\mathcal{T}_\gamma, \mathbf{v}_\gamma)} = \{\{tk_i = g^{Q_{node(\alpha_i)}'(0)/(t'+\mathcal{H}'(i,v_i))}\}_{i\in\gamma}, \mathcal{T}_\gamma\}$, it first calculates $\Gamma_{\mathcal{T}_\gamma}$ from $\mathcal{T}_\gamma$. The search operation starts from the first $\gamma' \in \Gamma_{\mathcal{T}_\gamma}$. Let $i = attr(x)$. For each node x in $\mathcal{T}_{\gamma'}$, it computes a value z_x in a down-top manner. For each leaf node x in $\mathcal{T}_{\gamma'}$, $\mathcal{S}$ computes $z_x = \hat{e}(tk_i, E_i')$. We use v_i' to denote the value embedded in E_i'. Note if $v_i = v_i'$, $z_x = \hat{e}(g^{Q_x'(0)/(t'+\mathcal{H}'(i,v_i))}, g^{s'\cdot(t'+\mathcal{H}'(i,v_i'))}) = \hat{e}(g,g)^{s'\cdot Q_x'(0)}$. For each non-leaf node x, it sets $z_x = \prod_{i\in S_x}(z_{child_i(x)})^{\Delta_{i,S_x}}$. Note if $\{v_i = v_i'\}_{i\in\gamma'}$, $z_x = \prod_{i\in S_x}(\hat{e}(g,g))^{s'\cdot Q_{child_i(x)}'(0)\cdot\Delta_{i,S_x}} = \prod_{i\in S_x}(\hat{e}(g,g))^{s'\cdot Q_x'(i)\cdot\Delta_{i,S_x}} = \hat{e}(g,g)^{s'\cdot Q_x'(0)}$. The procedure continues until it reaches the root node r. If $z_r = E'$, $\mathcal{S}$ outputs 'yes'. Otherwise, it continues to test the next γ'. If all γ's do not meet the criteria, it outputs 'no'.

Decrypt($\mathcal{U}(params, tk_{(\mathcal{T}_\gamma, \mathbf{v}_\gamma)}, sk_{(\mathcal{T}_\gamma, \mathbf{v}_\gamma)}, C)$): The decryption algorithm first identifies γ' satisfying $tk_{(\mathcal{T}_\gamma, \mathbf{v}_\gamma)}$ as **Test** algorithm does. Note this step can be omitted if γ' is provided as input after it is identified by **Test**. Then it follows a down-top manner in $\mathcal{T}_{\gamma'}$. Let $i = attr(x)$. Then for each leaf node $x \in \mathcal{T}_{\gamma'}$, it computes $z_x = \hat{e}(sk_i, E_i)$. Note since v_i equals to v_i', $z_x = \hat{e}(g^{Q_x(0)/(t_i+t\cdot v_i)}, g^{s(t_i+t\cdot v_i')}) = \hat{e}(g,g)^{s\cdot Q_x(0)}$. For non-leaf node $x \in \mathcal{T}_{\gamma'}$, it computes $z_x = \prod_{i\in S_x}(z_{child_i(x)})^{\Delta_{i,S_x}} = \prod_{i\in S_x}(\hat{e}(g,g))^{s\cdot Q_{child_i(x)}(0)\cdot\Delta_{i,S_x}} = \prod_{i\in S_x}(\hat{e}(g,g))^{s\cdot Q_x(i)\cdot\Delta_{i,S_x}} = \hat{e}(g,g)^{s\cdot Q_x(0)}$. The procedure continues until it reaches root r and $z_r = \hat{e}(g,g)^{s\cdot Q_r(0)} = \hat{e}(g,g)^{s\cdot y} = Y^s$ is computed. Then user recovers $m = \text{Dec}^{sym}_{\mathcal{H}(Y^s)}(E)$.

BlindExtract($\mathcal{U}(params, \mathcal{T}_\gamma, \mathbf{v}_\gamma), \mathcal{DO}(params, msk_{\mathcal{DO}})$)

1. $\mathcal{U}$ first verifies π^s. If π^s passes verification, then the user chooses $r_{i,1}, r_{i,1}' \in_R \mathbb{Z}_q$ and $r_{i,2}, r_{i,2}' \in_R [0, \ldots, 2^k q]$ and computes

$$e_i = ((e_t \oplus \text{Enc}^{hom}_{pk_s}(\mathcal{H}(i,v_i))) \otimes r_{i,1}) \oplus \text{Enc}^{hom}_{pk_s}(r_{i,2}\cdot q), \forall i \in \gamma$$

$$e_i' = ((e_{t'} \oplus \text{Enc}^{hom}_{pk_s}(\mathcal{H}'(i,v_i))) \otimes r_{i,1}') \oplus \text{Enc}^{hom}_{pk_s}(r_{i,2}'\cdot q), \forall i \in \gamma$$

It also computes a zero-knowledge proof π^c proving e_i, e_i' are well formed and $r_{i,1}, r_{i,2}, r_{i,1}', r_{i,2}'$ are in appropriate interval. Then it sends $\{e_i, e_i'\}_{i\in\gamma}, \mathcal{T}_\gamma, \pi^c$ to $\mathcal{DO}$.

2. $\mathcal{DO}$ verifies π^c to make sure $e_i, e'_i, r_{i,1}, r'_{i,1}, r_{i,2}, r'_{i,2}$ are correctly embedded. Then $\mathcal{DO}$ starts to define a polynomial $Q_x(\cdot)$ of degree $k_x - 1$ for each node x in $\mathcal{T}_\gamma$ in a top-down manner. For the root node r, it sets $Q_r(0) = y$ and $k_r - 1$ other points of Q_r randomly to fully define Q_r. For any other node x, set $Q_x(0) = Q_{parent(x)}(index(x))$ and choose $k_x - 1$ other points randomly to completely define Q_x. $\mathcal{DO}$ defines another polynomial $Q'_x(\cdot)$ in the same way as $Q_x(\cdot)$ except that $Q'_x(0) = y'$. Next, for each $i \in \gamma$, $\mathcal{DO}$ decrypts $d_i = \mathsf{Dec}^{hom}_{sk_{\mathcal{DO}}}(e_i), d'_i = \mathsf{Dec}^{hom}_{sk_{\mathcal{DO}}}(e'_i)$ and sends $a_i = g^{Q_{node(\alpha_i)}(0)/d_i}$ and $a'_i = g^{Q'_{node(\alpha_i)}(0)/d'_i}$ to $\mathcal{U}$.

3. $\mathcal{U}$ computes $sk_i = a_i^{r_{i,1}} = g^{Q_{node(\alpha_i)}(0)/(t+\mathcal{H}(i,v_i))}$ and $tk_i = a_i'^{r'_{i,1}} = g^{Q'_{node(\alpha_i)}(0)/(t'+\mathcal{H}'(i,v_i))}$ for $i \in \gamma$. Then $\mathcal{U}$ checks the validity of sk_is. To do that, it computes $p_i = e(sk_i, T \cdot g^{\mathcal{H}(i,v_i)}) = e(g,g)^{Q_{node(\alpha_i)}(0)}$ for all $i \in \gamma$. After that, it starts to compute a value q_x for each node x in $\mathcal{T}_\gamma$ in a down-top manner starting from leaves. For each leaf node x in $\mathcal{T}_\gamma$, its q_x is set to $p_{attr(x)}$. For a non-leaf node x, q_x is dependent on k_x. If $k_x = 1$, user first verifies that each $q_{child_i(x)}$, for all $i \in S_x$, is the same. Then it sets $q_x = q_{child_i(x)}$, for arbitrary $i \in S_x$. If $k_x > 1$, it sets $q_x = \prod_{i \in S_x}(q_{child_i(x)})^{\Delta_{i,S_x}}$. The procedure continues until it reaches the root node r. Finally, the user checks whether $q_r \overset{?}{=} Y$. If any above verification fails, $\mathcal{U}$ quits. $\mathcal{U}$ checks tk_i in the same way as it does sk_i except that q_r should be equal to Y' this time. $\mathcal{U}$ outputs decryption key $sk_{(\mathcal{T}_\gamma, \mathbf{v}_\gamma)} = \{\{sk_i\}_{i \in \gamma}, \mathcal{T}_\gamma, \mathbf{v}_\gamma\}$ and search token $tk_{(\mathcal{T}_\gamma, \mathbf{v}_\gamma)} = \{\{tk_i\}_{i \in \gamma}, \mathcal{T}_\gamma\}$.

Authorize($\mathcal{U}(params, \mathcal{T}_\gamma, \mathbf{v}_\gamma), \mathcal{CA}(params, sk_{\mathcal{CA}})$): $\mathcal{U}$ submits $\mathcal{T}_\gamma, \mathbf{v}_\gamma$ to $\mathcal{CA}$. $\mathcal{CA}$ verifies that $\mathcal{U}$ has the right to search for the conditional expression defined by $(\mathcal{T}_\gamma, \mathbf{v}_\gamma)$. If it approves user request, then $\mathcal{CA}$, on $\mathcal{U}$'s behalf, makes pedersen commitments c_{v_i}, c'_{v_i} on each $v_i \in \mathbf{v}_\gamma$, i.e. $c_{v_i} = \mathfrak{g}^{\mathcal{H}(i,v_i)}\mathfrak{h}^{r_{v_i}}$ and $c'_{v_i} = \mathfrak{g}^{\mathcal{H}'(i,v_i)}\mathfrak{h}^{r'_{v_i}}$. Next, $\mathcal{CA}$ maps $\mathcal{T}_\gamma$ to a Merkle hash tree. Specifically, it computes a hash value for each node x in $\mathcal{T}_\gamma$. For each leaf node x, its hash value is $h_x = \mathcal{H}(k_x)$. For non-leaf node, its hash value is defined as the hash of concatenations of its k_x and its children's hash values, i.e. $h_x = \mathcal{H}(k_x||h_{child_1(x)}|| \cdots ||h_{child_{num_x}(x)})$. Let h_r denote the hash value for the root node r. CA issues a signature σ on h_r and $\{c_{v_i}, c'_{v_i}\}_{i \in \gamma}$, i.e. $\sigma = \mathsf{Sign}_{sk_{\mathcal{CA}}}(h_r, \{c_{v_i}, c'_{v_i}\}_{i \in \gamma})$, and send $\{\{r_{v_i}, c_{v_i}, r'_{v_i}, c'_{v_i}\}_{i \in \gamma}, \sigma\}$ back to $\mathcal{U}$.

AuthorizedBlindExtract ($\mathcal{U}(params, \mathcal{T}_\gamma, \mathbf{v}_\gamma, \psi, open, \sigma), \mathcal{DO}(params, msk_{\mathcal{DO}})$) : This protocol is detailed in [3]. Here $\psi = \{c_{v_i}, c'_{v_i}\}_{i \in \gamma}$ and $open = \{r_{v_i}, r'_{v_i}\}_{i \in \gamma}$. The protocol basically follows the **BlindExtract** protocol except that $\mathcal{U}$ needs to prove statements about commitments using zero-knowledge proof.

6   Performance Analysis

Before presenting performance analysis, we point out two possible improvements to the scheme. First, in Test algorithm, if the identified matching set γ' is sent to $\mathcal{U}$, then Decrypt algorithm does not need search token to seek γ' again. Second, as pointed out in [1], instead of exponentiating at each level during the computation of z_x in Decrypt, for each leaf node in γ', we can keep track of which Lagrange coefficient is multiplied with each other. Using this, we can compute the final exponent f_x for each leaf node

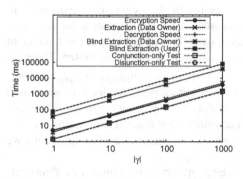

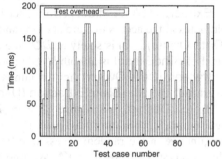

Fig. 3. Performance of Encryp, Extract, Decrypt vs. number of attributes

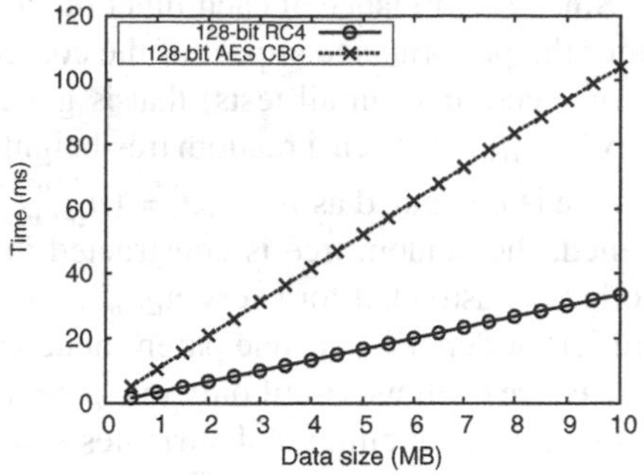

Fig. 4. Symmetric encryption overhead

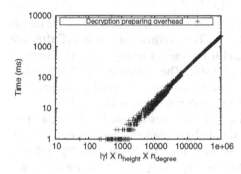

Fig. 5. Decryption preparing time

Fig. 6. Performance of Test when $|\gamma| = 10$

$x \in \mathcal{T}_{\gamma'}$ by doing multiplication in $\mathbb{Z}_q$. Now z_r is simply $\prod_{i \in \gamma'} \hat{e}(sk_i, E_i)^{f_{node}(\alpha_i)}$. The same optimization applies to Test algorithm.

We now consider the efficiency of the scheme. The Encrypt algorithm takes $2n$ group exponentiations in $\mathbb{G}_1$. The Extract algorithm takes $2 \cdot |\gamma|$ group exponentiations in $\mathbb{G}_1$. In BlindExtract algorithm, $\mathcal{DO}$ spends $20 \cdot |\gamma|$ group exponentiations in $\mathbb{G}_1$. $\mathcal{U}$ spends $28 \cdot |\gamma|$ group exponentiations in $\mathbb{G}_1$ plus some verification time dependent on access tree. The Test algorithm's performance depends on the access tree $\mathcal{T}_\gamma$. In conjunction-only case, it involves 1 test of $|\gamma|$ pairing and $|\gamma|$ exponentiation in $\mathbb{G}_2$. In disjunction-only case, it involves $|\gamma|$ tests of 1 pairing operation. Compared to $|\gamma|$ pairing overhead in [17,19,20], our scheme has similar overhead while supporting more flexible queries. The optimized Decrypt algorithm takes $|\gamma'|$ pairing and $|\gamma'|$ group exponentiations in $\mathbb{G}_2$.

7 Performance Evaluation

We implemented the proposed scheme in C++ using PBC (ver. 0.57) [31] and OpenSSL (ver. 1.0.0) [32] library. This section discusses the performance of each function in our scheme. All benchmarks were performed on a Ubuntu 9.10 desktop platform with Intel Core i7-920 (2.66GHz and 8MB cache) and 6GB RAM.

Since performance of each function only depends on the access tree, we do not consider the performance impact of the contents associated with leaf nodes. We use a random access tree (in all tests) that is generated as follows. First we fix the number of leaves, n_{leaves}. Then a random tree height n_{height} between 1 and 5 is chosen. The node degree is computed as $n_{degree} = \lceil n_{leaves}^{1/n_{leaves}} \rceil$. After $n_{leaves}, n_{height}, n_{degree}$ is determined, the random tree is constructed in a down-top manner. At depth l, one parent node is constructed for every n_{degree} nodes at depth $l + 1$. If less than n_{degree} nodes are left at depth $l + 1$, one parent node is constructed for these remaining nodes. The procedure continues until only one parent (root) can be constructed. For simplicity, we assume the total number of attributes $w = |\gamma| = n_{leaves}$.

First we test the speed of Encrypt. Fig. 3 (Encryption Speed line) shows the overhead to compute $Y^s, E', \{E_i, E'_i\}_{i \in \Omega}$ versus the number of attributes $|\gamma|$. As we can see, its overhead increases linearly with $|\gamma|$. Fig. 4 shows the performance of symmetric encryption, which is needed to compute $E = \text{Enc}_{\mathcal{H}(Y^s)}^{sym}(m)$.

Extract and BlindExtract performance is also shown in Fig. 3. In this test, the threshold gates in the access tree are chosen randomly. The overhead of Extract (Extraction (Data Owner) line) is solely at $\mathcal{DO}$ side and it increases linearly with $|\gamma|$. The overhead of BlindExtract is at both $\mathcal{U}$ side and $\mathcal{DO}$ side. The overhead at $\mathcal{DO}$ side (Blind Extraction (Data Owner) line) is almost nine times that of normal extraction. The overhead at $\mathcal{U}$ side (Blind Extraction (User) line) doubles that at $\mathcal{DO}$ side.

To test Decrypt, we assume $\gamma' = \gamma$, i.e., all attributes should be involved in the decryption. Since all threshold gates in $\mathcal{T}_{\gamma'}$ should be conjunctive gates, we make them conjunctive in the random access tree $\mathcal{T}_\gamma$ as well. Fig. 3 (Decryption Speed line) shows the speed to recover Y^s. We find that decryption overhead increases linearly with $|\gamma|$ and it is even cheaper than extraction. The reason is because pairing operation and exponentiation in $\mathbb{G}_2$ is faster than exponentiation in $\mathbb{G}_1$ [1]. Fig. 5 shows the speed of computing f_x for all leaf node x, which is necessary for the optimization of decryption. Its speed is almost linear with the product of $|\gamma|$, tree height and tree degree. Note this part of operation can be conducted offline and only needs to be computed once for one type of access tree. The performance of $\text{Dec}_{\mathcal{H}(Y^s)}^{sym}(E)$ is same as $\text{Enc}_{\mathcal{H}(Y^s)}^{sym}(m)$ as shown in Fig. 4.

As to Test performance, it highly depends on the access tree. During the following test, the performance is recorded in the worst case, i.e. all possible subtrees $\mathcal{T}_{\gamma'}$ of $\mathcal{T}_\gamma$ are tried. Fig. 3 shows the conjunction-only Test and disjunction-only Test performance. As we can see, they all increases linearly with $|\gamma|$. The reason why they are almost the same is because conjunction-only Test has 1 test involving $|\gamma|$ pairing and $|\gamma|$ exponentiation in $\mathbb{G}_2$ while disjunction-only Test has $|\gamma|$ tests involving 1 pairing. To further test Test operation, we use random access tree. We restrict $|\gamma|$ to be 10, which is usually enough for normal query, and set each threshold gate in the tree randomly. Fig. 6 shows the results of 100 test cases. As we can see the maximum Test time is 170ms and the average Test time is 85ms. In cloud computing scenario, multiple Test operations can run simultaneously and therefore spending average 85ms on each record is acceptable.

---

[1] In our benchmark of Type A pairing family in [31], one exponentiation in $\mathbb{G}_1$ takes 1.9 ms, one exponentiation in $\mathbb{G}_2$ takes 0.18 ms while one group pairing takes 1.4 ms.

8 Limitation

The proposed scheme has some limitation and it should be considered in future work. First it only supports equality testing. Practical privacy-preserving comparison is not available yet. Second, it only hides concrete value in the conditional expression and the structure $\mathcal{T}_\gamma$ is revealed to the adversary. Third, join operations between two tables are not supported. Fourth, if the set of possible attribute values in γ is small, the adversary can always try to encrypt something under all possible values and run Test over the encryptions to see if there is a match. This would reveal v_γ within $tk_{(\mathcal{T}_\gamma, \mathbf{v}_\gamma)}$. However, the complexity of such brute force attacks against this intrinsic weakness of public key-based searchable encryption, grows exponentially with $|\gamma|$. Fifth, $\mathcal{DO}$ is required to be online to help $\mathcal{U}$ extract search tokens and decryption keys. However, we expect that this functionality can be finished by some secure hardware that can be safely installed at $\mathcal{U}$ side without compromising $msk_{\mathcal{DO}}$.

9 Conclusion

This paper provides an overview of privacy challenges facing cloud storage and develops a novel encryption scheme for coping with these challenges. The scheme hides the plaintext of database and user's query content from the cloud server. It allows data owner to do content-level fine-grained access control by issuing users appropriate search tokens and decryption keys. The scheme also supports blind retrieval of search tokens and decryption keys in the sense neither data owner nor cloud server learns the query content. Additional feature of user input authorization by CA can also be supported. Our evaluation shows that its performance falls within the acceptable range.

References

1. Goyal, V., Pandey, O., Sahai, A., Waters, B.: Attribute-based encryption for fine-grained access control of encrypted data. In: ACM CCS 2006 (2006)
2. Belenkiy, M., Camenisch, J., Chase, M., Kohlweiss, M., Lysyanskaya, A., Shacham, H.: Randomizable proofs and delegatable anonymous credentials. In: Halevi, S. (ed.) CRYPTO 2009. LNCS, vol. 5677, pp. 108–125. Springer, Heidelberg (2009)
3. Lu, Y., Tsudik, G.: Enhancing data privacy in the cloud, http://eprint.iacr.org/2011/158
4. Chor, B., Kushilevitz, E., Goldreich, O., Sudan, M.: Private information retrieval. Journal of the ACM (JACM) 45(6), 965–981 (1998)
5. Rabin, M.: How to exchange secrets by oblivious transfer. Harvard Aiken Computation Lab, Tech. Rep. TR-81 (1981)
6. Reardon, J., Pound, J., Goldberg, I.: Relational-complete private information retrieval. University of Waterloo, Tech. Rep. CACR 2007-34 (2007)
7. Olumofin, F., Goldberg, I.: Privacy-preserving queries over relational databases. In: Atallah, M.J., Hopper, N.J. (eds.) PETS 2010. LNCS, vol. 6205, pp. 75–92. Springer, Heidelberg (2010)
8. Song, D., Wagner, D., Perrig, A.: Practical techniques for searches on encrypted data. In: S&P 2000 (2000)
9. Chang, Y.C., Mitzenmacher, M.: Privacy preserving keyword searches on remote encrypted data. In: Ioannidis, J., Keromytis, A.D., Yung, M. (eds.) ACNS 2005. LNCS, vol. 3531, pp. 442–455. Springer, Heidelberg (2005)

10. Yang, Z., Zhong, S., Wright, R.N.: Privacy-preserving queries on encrypted data. In: Gollmann, D., Meier, J., Sabelfeld, A. (eds.) ESORICS 2006. LNCS, vol. 4189, pp. 479–495. Springer, Heidelberg (2006)
11. Golle, P., Staddon, J., Waters, B.: Secure Conjunctive Keyword Search over Encrypted Data. In: Jakobsson, M., Yung, M., Zhou, J. (eds.) ACNS 2004. LNCS, vol. 3089, pp. 31–45. Springer, Heidelberg (2004)
12. Boneh, D., Crescenzo, G.D., Ostrovsky, R., Persiano, G.: Public key encryption with keyword search. In: Cachin, C., Camenisch, J.L. (eds.) EUROCRYPT 2004. LNCS, vol. 3027, pp. 506–522. Springer, Heidelberg (2004)
13. Sahai, A., Waters, B.: Fuzzy identity-based encryption. In: Cramer, R. (ed.) EUROCRYPT 2005. LNCS, vol. 3494, pp. 457–473. Springer, Heidelberg (2005)
14. Bethencourt, J., Sahai, A., Waters, B.: Ciphertext-policy attribute-based encryption. In: S&P 2007 (2007)
15. Ostrovsky, R., Sahai, A., Waters, B.: Attribute-based encryption with non-monotonic access structures. In: CCS 2007 (2007)
16. Waters, B.R., Balfanz, D., Durfee, G., Smetters, D.K.: Building an encrypted and searchable audit log. In: NDSS 2004 (2004)
17. Shi, E., Waters, B.: Delegating capabilities in predicate encryption systems. In: Aceto, L., Damgård, I., Goldberg, L.A., Halldórsson, M.M., Ingólfsdóttir, A., Walukiewicz, I. (eds.) ICALP 2008, Part II. LNCS, vol. 5126, pp. 560–578. Springer, Heidelberg (2008)
18. Shi, E., Bethencourt, J., Chan, T.-H.H., Song, D., Perrig, A.: Multi-dimensional range query over encrypted data. In: S&P 2007 (2007)
19. Boneh, D., Waters, B.: Conjunctive, subset, and range queries on encrypted data. In: Vadhan, S.P. (ed.) TCC 2007. LNCS, vol. 4392, pp. 535–554. Springer, Heidelberg (2007)
20. Katz, J., Sahai, A., Waters, B.: Predicate encryption supporting disjunctions, polynomial equations, and inner products. In: Smart, N.P. (ed.) EUROCRYPT 2008. LNCS, vol. 4965, pp. 146–162. Springer, Heidelberg (2008)
21. Green, M., Hohenberger, S.: Blind identity-based encryption and simulatable oblivious transfer. In: Kurosawa, K. (ed.) ASIACRYPT 2007. LNCS, vol. 4833, pp. 265–282. Springer, Heidelberg (2007)
22. Camenisch, J., Neven, G., Shelat, A.: Simulatable adaptive oblivious transfer. In: Naor, M. (ed.) EUROCRYPT 2007. LNCS, vol. 4515, pp. 573–590. Springer, Heidelberg (2007)
23. Koblitz, N.: Elliptic curve cryptosystems. Mathematics of Computation (1987)
24. Paillier, P.: Public-key cryptosystems based on composite degree residuosity classes. In: Stern, J. (ed.) EUROCRYPT 1999. LNCS, vol. 1592, p. 223. Springer, Heidelberg (1999)
25. Camenisch, J., Stadler, M.: Efficient group signature schemes for large groups. In: Kaliski Jr., B.S. (ed.) CRYPTO 1997. LNCS, vol. 1294, pp. 410–424. Springer, Heidelberg (1997)
26. Chaum, D., Evertse, J.-H., van de Graaf, J.: An improved protocol for demonstrating possession of discrete logarithms and some generalizations. In: Price, W.L., Chaum, D. (eds.) EUROCRYPT 1987. LNCS, vol. 304, pp. 127–141. Springer, Heidelberg (1988)
27. Chaum, D.: Zero-knowledge undeniable signatures. In: Damgård, I.B. (ed.) EUROCRYPT 1990. LNCS, vol. 473, pp. 458–464. Springer, Heidelberg (1991)
28. Boudot, F.: Efficient proofs that a committed number lies in an interval. In: Preneel, B. (ed.) EUROCRYPT 2000. LNCS, vol. 1807, p. 431. Springer, Heidelberg (2000)
29. Boneh, D., Boyen, X.: Efficient selective-ID secure identity-based encryption without random oracles. In: Cachin, C., Camenisch, J.L. (eds.) EUROCRYPT 2004. LNCS, vol. 3027, pp. 223–238. Springer, Heidelberg (2004)
30. Boneh, D., Boyen, X.: Short signatures without random oracles. In: Cachin, C., Camenisch, J.L. (eds.) EUROCRYPT 2004. LNCS, vol. 3027, pp. 56–73. Springer, Heidelberg (2004)
31. Lynn, B.: PBC: The Pairing-Based Cryptography Library., http://crypto.stanford.edu/pbc/
32. OpenSSL, http://www.openssl.org/

Longitude: A Privacy-Preserving Location Sharing Protocol for Mobile Applications*

Changyu Dong and Naranker Dulay

Department of Computing
Imperial College London
{changyu.dong,n.dulay}@imperial.ac.uk

Abstract. Location sharing services are becoming increasingly popular. Although many location sharing services allow users to set up privacy policies to control who can access their location, the use made by service providers remains a source of concern. Ideally, location sharing providers and middleware should not be able to access users' location data without their consent. In this paper, we propose a new location sharing protocol called Longitude that eases privacy concerns by making it possible to share a user's location data blindly and allowing the user to control who can access her location, when and to what degree of precision. The underlying cryptographic algorithms are designed for GPS-enabled mobile phones. We describe and evaluate our implementation for the Nexus One Android mobile phone.

1 Introduction

Location sharing is an increasingly popular function of social-networking services, allowing users to share their location with family and friends. Examples include Google Latitude [1], Yahoo Fire Eagle [2], and Loopt [3]. Perhaps the biggest user concern about location sharing services is privacy. Many services allow the users to control who will have access to their location data, over what period of time, and to what degree of precision. However, for many users, the service providers are also a source of concern. Will not the location sharing service use location data to the detriment of the user?

Users' location data is normally saved by the service provider. Unfortunately, this allows providers to track, profile and target users [4,5] as well as aggregrate the data and sell it to others. The typical approach to informing users is to provide a lengthy webpage that states what the service provider may do with the data. The webpage is usually written in a sufficiently obfuscated way to ensure that few users will bother reading it, and often to hide the fact that providers want to give themselves a high degree of access to the data. A related, but important concern, is that the service provider may be the target of network intrusions and untrustworthy insiders, as well as requests from law-enforcement agencies [6].

---

* This work was supported by UK EPSRC research grant EP/F023294/1 - PRiMMA: Privacy Rights Management for Mobile Applications.

I. Wakeman et al. (Eds.): IFIPTM 2011, IFIP AICT 358, pp. 133–148, 2011.

This paper describes a protocol called Longitude for location sharing that uses cryptography to limit service provider access to location data. It is aimed at providers on the Internet or middleware to provide location sharing blindly without the hassle of compliance to data protection and location data requests. It ensures that users are able to share their location but are not tracked. Note that the protocol is not a replacement for traditional location-services like Google maps that translate locations into maps.

Naively, a user (Alice) could encrypt her location before sending it to the location sharing provider (Luke), effectively protecting it from Luke or other adversaries. Alice would have to securely disseminate the key to her friends (Bob and Carol) and revoke it if she wanted to prevent access to any friend or if the key was disclosed. Rather than a common shared key, Alice could establish pair-wise secret keys with each of her friends or use asymmetric keys, both requiring a great deal more additional storage, computation and communication overheads. A more flexible approach is needed, particularly for resource-constrained mobile devices.

Longitude has the following characteristics:

1. Privacy preserving. Longitude enables location-sharing providers or middleware to disseminate user location data blindly. The data is specially encrypted. Alice can control which of her friends can see her location, at what times and to what degree of precision.
2. Simple key management: Alice only needs to keep her own key on her mobile device. She can remove any of her friends at any time without affecting other friends. The revocation process can be done by Alice without requiring any interactions with her friends.
3. Lightweight cryptography. Most of the computationally intensive cryptographic operations in Longitude are done by the service provider, not on the mobile device. Computation and battery life for mobile devices can be optimised further by precomputing cryptographic material when the mobile device is connected to a power source.
4. Constant communication overhead. Longitude's communication costs do not increase with the number of friends (receivers). No matter how many friends a user has, each piece of location data is encrypted and sent only once. Therefore, the overhead of data communication is minimised.

The paper is organised as follows: in Section 2, we summarise the related work; in Section 3, we discuss the system and security model as well as the initial assumptions; in Section 4, we present Longitude, how to fine control user privacy and issues related to user revocation; in Section 5, we explain the underlying cryptographic techniques; in Section 6, we describe and evaluate a prototype implementation of Longitude for Android phones; in Section 7, we conclude the paper and discuss our future plans.

2   Related Work

Location sharing services have attracted a lot of attention from industry [1,2,3], and the development of GPS-enabled mobile phones makes it easy to sense and share user location. According to [7], these services can be categorised into two types: (1) purpose-driven, in which the requester has a specific need for the users location, e.g. coordinating meetings, arranging transportation, sending reminders, and (2) social, in which location information is shared simply because it is interesting or fun to do so. However, users are concerned about their privacy and according to [8], existing industry guidelines and implementations do not adequately address these concerns .

Previous research on location privacy has focused on anonymisation. For example, in [9], the authors describe a middleware system which delays and reorders messages from users within a mix zone to confuse an observer. In [10], a mechanism called cloaking is proposed that conceals a user within a group of k people. To achieve this, the accuracy of the disclosed location is reduced so that a user is indistinguishable from at least $k - 1$ other users. In [11], k-anonymity is achieved by an ad-hoc network formed by the user and surrounding neighbours, while [12] shows how to achieve k-anonymity in a distributed environment where there are multiple non-colluding servers. Anonymisation has a fundamental difference with location sharing. The goal of anonymisation is to prevent others from relating a location to a user; on the other hand, the goal of location sharing is to let authorised users know where a user is. Therefore, anonymisation is not directly applicable here.

Most existing location sharing services do offer the users some form of controls over their privacy. In [8], the authors examine 89 location sharing services and the most widely adopted privacy controls are white list, being invisible, blacklist, group-based permission and providing less detailed location. Several research projects in this area have tried to provide more expressive and effective policy-based privacy controls. For example, Locaccino [13] allows users to specify more fine grained policies based on temporal and spatial restrictions. The pawS system [14] allows a user to use P3P policies to define their location privacy settings and negotiate with the location service provider. The main drawback in all such approaches is that the users must trust the provider, its privileged employees and the security of the infrastructure. The user's privacy will also be compromised if the service provider is required to disclose the data to a law-enforcement agency.

In a location sharing services, the provider usually acts as a broker to disseminate the location information to the authorised receivers. In most of the cases the provider does not need to know the data content in order to provide this service. In [15] a system for sharing user location is described which provides protection from the provider. Users use pairwise symmetric key encryption or asymmetric key encryption to prevent the provider from learning their location. However, the user needs to store multiple keys. Moreover the user has to send multiple copies of the same data, each encrypted under a different key in order to let all her friends be able to get her location. The overheads of key management, computation and communication increase linearly with the number of friends.

Some work [16,17,18,19] has been done dealing with the problem of preserving privacy in proximity services. Proximity service is a sub-type of location sharing service which notifies and displays a friend's location if the friend is nearby. While in Longitude we consider the more general location sharing where a user can see a friend's location no matter the friend is near or far away from the user.

3   Models and Assumptions

3.1   Systems Model

The Longitude protocol has the following parties: the location-sharing service provider and the set of users registered with the provider. We assume that each user has a GPS-enabled mobile phone that can sense the user's current location and send it to the provider. The provider stores the location and along with some user configuration data. Users define which other users are authorised to receive their location. Authorised receivers can be removed at any time by the user. Users can also define the precision of the location that will be seen by a particular receiver, e.g. accurate to 1km, 5km, 10km, 100km.

3.2   Security Model

We consider the service-provider to be honest-but-curious. That is, the service provider will follow the protocol correctly, but will try to find out as much secret information as possible. To simplify the presentation in the paper we assume that there are mechanisms in place which ensure integrity and availability of the stored data. We also assume that there is a proper authentication mechanism which allows the user to identify the service provider and their friends and vice versa. In addition, we assume that each user securely protects their cryptographic key on their mobile device. Since location data will be transmitted through public networks and wireless networks, we assume that it is possible that an unauthorised user can intercept the data.

4   Longitude Protocol

4.1   Overview

We first describe how the protocol works in general. The protocol is depicted in Figure 1. In the figure we only show two users, Alice and Bob.

The design of Longitude is based on proxy re-encryption [20]. In a proxy re-encryption scheme, a ciphertext encrypted by one key can be transformed by a proxy function into the corresponding ciphertext for another key without revealing any information about the keys and the plaintext. Applications of proxy re-encryption include access control systems [21] and searchable data encryption [22]. The details of the proxy re-encryption scheme used in Longitude will be presented in Section 5.

To share her location with Bob, Alice and Bob must first register with the location service provider (Luke). During registration, Alice and Bob also obtain public cryptographic parameters and generate a public/private key pair locally on their mobile devices. After registration, Bob can send a request to Alice asking her to allow him to see her location. The request can be done out of band without involving Luke. In the request, Bob provides a copy of his public key. If Alice agrees, she computes a re-encryption key using Bob's public key and her own private key (explained in detail in section 5). She also decides how accurate the location should be for Bob and generates a corresponding precision mask (explained in section 4.2). The re-encryption key

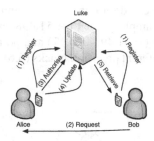

Fig. 1. Overview of Longitude Protocol

and the precision mask are sent to Luke, and act as an authorisation policy that allows Bob to retrieve Alice's location. Alice can now send encrypted location data to Luke. Bob's public key can also be discarded by Alice. Luke only stores a user's most recent location. The previous location is overwritten by a newly received location. When Bob wants to know where Alice is, he sends a request to Luke, who retrieves Alice's last encrypted location, applies the re-encryption key and policies defined by Alice then sends it to Bob. Bob can then decrypt the location received from Luke and process it as needed, e.g. to display Alice's location on a map.

4.2   Location Encryption and Location Granularity

Proxy re-encryption, though very efficient, is still too time-consuming to encrypt large volumes of data. To overcome this, in Longitude the actual data is encrypted by a more efficient hybrid encryption scheme, where a secure symmetric stream cipher is chosen to encrypt the location data under a random key and the random key is then encrypted using the proxy re-encryption scheme. The stream cipher also allows Luke to modify part of the ciphertext without rendering it undecryptable. In particular we can use this to allow Alice to define the granularity that her location is seen by different friends.

A location consists of a latitude and longitude. Both parts are represented in the format of decimal degrees. Obviously, a pair (51.49875, -0.17917) gives more accurate information about Alice's location than just (51.4, -0.1). In Longitude, we use this to allow Alice to define precision masks for each friend (see Figure 2). Before encryption, locations are encoded as a pair of fixed-length ASCII strings. Each String has 11 characters in the format of "siiifffff" where "s" is for the sign, "iii" is for the integral part and "ffffff" is for the fractional part. For example 51.49875 is encoded as "+0514987500". When using a stream cipher to encrypt, the stream cipher generates a stream of random bits. The location strings are also converted into bits and XORed with the random bit stream. Precision masks govern how many digits will be released to friends. Each precision mask is a pair of integers from 0 to 11. Luke simply truncates the encrypted location to the length specified by the precision mask before returning it to a friend. The truncated encrypted location information can still be decrypted after that because the decryption is another XOR. The benefits of using precision masks are two fold: (1) Alice does not have to encrypt the same location at different precision levels for different friends (2) applying the precision mask does not require Luke to first decrypt the data, so Luke can do it blindly. An example of using precision masks is shown in Figure 2. In the example, point 1 (+051.4987500, -000.1791700) is Alice's actual location , while point 2 (+051.49, -000.17) and point 3 (+051.4, -000.1) are the displayed locations for two different precision masks (6,6) and (5,5), i.e. what would be sent to two different friends.

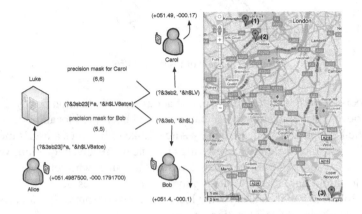

Fig. 2. Applying precision mask to encrypted location

Alice can also specify time-based policies to further control her privacy. An example of such a policy could be "My co-workers should not see my location during weekends". The policies are specified by Alice as constraints and uploaded to Luke. The policies do not need to be encrypted because they contain no location data (although they might contain other sensitive information). Luke is responsible for checking and enforcing these policies when Alice's location is requested by her co-workers.

4.3   Friend Revocation

If Alice wishes, she can revoke Bob from accessing her location. In Longitude, revocation can be accomplished in two different ways.

The first is called weak revocation. In this case, Alice simply sends a request to Luke asking that Bob should not receive her location any more. Luke then removes the corresponding re-encryption key. Since Alice's key pair and Bob's key pair are generated independently, it is easy to prove that after the re-encryption key has been removed by Luke, Bob will not be able to decrypt any of subsequent location updates from Alice.

Weak revocation has low overhead and is secure if Luke and Bob do not collude. However, if Luke colludes with Bob and does not remove the re-encryption key, Bob will still be able to track Alice. To prevent collusion, Alice can use strong revocation by updating her keys. Updating only changes two components in her keys and leaves the other parts unchanged. Alice also updates the re-encryption keys for all friends except Bob. After Alice has done this, Bob's re-encryption key will not be able to decrypt future locations encrypted using Alice's new public key. Note this process does not require Alice to interact with any of her friends. The update can be done by Alice herself using existing information. If Alice is authorised to receive location updates from her friends, those friends do not need to be involved either. The re-encryption keys they generated for Alice are still valid because these keys are generated using an unchanged component in Alice's public key. The details of the key update algorithm can be found in Section 5.

5   Proxy Re-encryption

The proxy re-encryption scheme used in Longitude is adapted from [21]. The scheme has many desirable features, for example, the proxy function is unidirectional and the user only needs to store her own key. We extended the scheme with a new key structure, support for user revocation and redesigned re-encryption and decryption functions. Our scheme is also provably secure under the conventional Decisional Bilinear Diffie-Hellman (DBDH) assumption [23], while the security of the original scheme is based on a special extension of the DBDH assumption. The proxy re-encryption scheme consists of 8 functions:

- The **Setup** function needs to be run once by the location service provider to initialise the service. It generates public parameters which will be used from then on. The provider does not need to keep any secret information after running this function.
- The **Keygen** function is run on the user's mobile device when the user registers. It also only needs to be run once.
- The **Encrypt** function is run on the user's device to encrypt the location data which is going to be sent to the provider.
- The **RekeyGen** function is run on the user's device to generate the re-encryption key for an authorised friend.

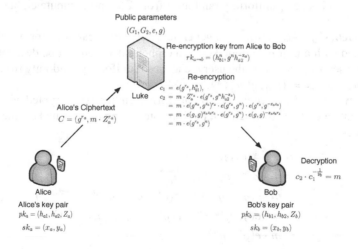

Fig. 3. The proxy re-encryption scheme

- The **ReEncrypt** function is run by the provider to transform location ciphertexts sent to friends.
- The **Decrypt** function is run on a friend's device to decrypt the locations received from the provider.
- The **KeyUpdate** function is run to update the user's key pair during strong revocation.
- The **ReKeyUpdate** function is run to update a re-encryption key during strong revocation.

5.1 Cryptographic Scheme

Our scheme is constructed on top of bilinear pairings. We briefly review bilinear pairings. We use the following notation:

- G_1 and G_2 are two cyclic groups of prime order q.
- g is a generator of G_1.
- e is a bilinear pairing $e : G_1 \times G_1 \to G_2$ which has the following properties:
  1. Bilinearity: for all $u, v \in G_1, a, b \in \mathbb{Z}_q$, we have $e(u^a, v^b) = e(u, v)^{ab}$.
  2. Non-degeneracy: $e(g, g) \neq 1$.
  3. Computable: There exists an efficient algorithm to compute $e(u, v)$ for all $u, v \in G_1$.

We now describe the proxy re-encryption algorithm in detail. The encryption/decryption scheme is shown in Figure 3.

- **Setup**(k): Given the security parameter k, choose two groups G_1, G_2 of prime order q and a bilinear pairing $e : G_1 \times G_1 \to G_2$. Then choose a random generator $g \in G_1$. Finally set the public parameter $param = (G_1, G_2, e, g)$ for the system.
- **Keygen**($param$): User i chooses x_i, y_i, z_i uniformly randomly from $\mathbb{Z}_q$ and computes $h_{i1} = g^{y_i}, h_{i2} = g^{z_i}, Z_i = e(g^{x_i}, g^{z_i})$. The user's public key is $pk_i = (h_{i1}, h_{i2}, Z_i)$, the user's private key is $sk_i = (x_i, y_i)$.
- **Encrypt**($m, pk_i, param$): To encrypt a message (e.g. location) with the user i's public key, choose r_i uniformly randomly from $\mathbb{Z}_q$, and compute ciphertext $C = (g^{r_i}, m \cdot Z_i^{r_i})$.
- **RekeyGen**($sk_a, pk_b, param$): To generate a key which can transform a ciphertext encrypted with a user a's public key to a ciphertext which can be decrypted using another user b's private key, the user a chooses n uniformly randomly from $\mathbb{Z}_q$, and computes $rk_{a\to b} = (h_{b1}^n, g^n h_{a2}^{-x_a})$.
- **ReEncrypt**($C_a, rk_{a\to b}, param$): To transform a ciphertext encrypted with a's public key into a ciphertext which can be decrypted using b's private key, the provider computes:

$$c_1 = e(g^{r_a}, h_{b1}^n),$$
$$c_2 = m \cdot Z_a^{r_a} \cdot e(g^{r_a}, g^n h_{a2}^{-x_a})$$
$$= m \cdot e(g^{x_a}, g^{z_a})^{r_a} \cdot e(g^{r_a}, g^n) \cdot e(g^{r_a}, g^{-x_a z_a})$$
$$= m \cdot e(g, g)^{x_a z_a r_a} \cdot e(g^{r_a}, g^n) \cdot e(g, g)^{-x_a z_a r_a}$$
$$= m \cdot e(g^{r_a}, g^n)$$

The new ciphertext $C_b = (c_1, c_2)$.

- **Decrypt**(sk_i, C_i): The re-encrypted ciphertext is decrypted as follows: $c_2 \cdot c_1^{-\frac{1}{y_i}} =$
  $m \cdot e(g^{r_i}, g^n) \cdot e(g^{r_i}, h_{i1}^n)^{-\frac{1}{y_i}} = m \cdot e(g, g)^{r_i n} \cdot e(g, g)^{-r_i y_i n \frac{1}{y_i}} = m$
- **KeyUpdate**($sk_i, pk_i, param$): The user only needs to change two components in
  the pair: the secret key will be changed from (x_a, y_a) to (x'_a, y_a) where x'_a is a
  random integer from Z_q and the public key will be changed from (h_{a1}, h_{a2}, Z_a) to
  $(h_{a1}, h_{a2}, Z_a^{\frac{x'_a}{x_a}})$.
- **ReKeyUpdate**($rk_{a \to b}, param$): For a re-encryption key $(h_{b1}^n, g^n h_{a2}^{-x_a})$, the user
  raises both of the values to the power of $\frac{x'_a}{x_a}$, where x'_a is the random integer generated in the KeyUpdate function. The new re-encryption key can be effectively
  written as $(h_{b1}^{n'}, g^{n'} h_{a2}^{-x'_a})$ where $n' = n \cdot \frac{x'_a}{x_a}$.

5.2   Security against an Unauthorised User

Our scheme is semantically secure against an unauthorised user. The notion of secure
against an unauthorised user is captured through the following game.

Game$_1$: The adversary $\mathcal{A}$ is an unauthorised user:

Game Setup: The challenger runs **Setup**(k) to generate the public parameter (G_1, G_2, e, g) given the security parameter k. It also uses **Keygen**($param$)
to generate an arbitrary number of public/private key pairs $pk_i/sk_i =$
$(h_{i1}, h_{i2}, Z_i)/(x_i, y_i)$. Then the challenger randomly choose a pair pk_a/sk_a.
   The public parameter and all the public keys are given to $\mathcal{A}$.

Phase 1: $\mathcal{A}$ is given oracle access to **Encrypt**($\cdot, pk_i, param$). The adversary outputs a pair of message m_0, m_1 of the same length.

Challenge: The challenger randomly chooses $b \leftarrow \{0, 1\}$ and then a ciphertext
$C =$**Encrypt**($m_b, pk_a, param$) is returned to $\mathcal{A}$.

Phase 2: $\mathcal{A}$ continues to have oracle access to **Encrypt**($\cdot, pk_i, param$).

Guess: $\mathcal{A}$ outputs a bit b' and wins the game if $b' = b$.

Theorem 1. *The proxy encryption scheme is semantically secure against an unauthorised user, i.e. for all PPT adversaries $\mathcal{A}$, there exists a negligible function negl such
that:*

$$Pr[Succ_{\mathcal{A}}^{game_1}(k)] \leq \frac{1}{2} + negl(k)$$

The proof of Theorem 1 relies on the Decisional Bilinear Diffie-Hellman (DBDH) assumption [23] which is stated as follows: given $g, g^\alpha, g^\beta, g^\gamma \in G_1$ and $r \in G_2$, every
probabilistic polynomial time adversary $\mathcal{A}$ has only a negligible probability in deciding
whether $r = e(g, g)^{\alpha\beta\gamma}$ or not, i.e.:

$$Pr[\mathcal{A}(g, g^\alpha, g^\beta, g^\gamma, e(g, g)^{\alpha\beta\gamma}) = 1] - Pr[\mathcal{A}(g, g^\alpha, g^\beta, g^\gamma, e(g, g)^\delta) = 1] \leq negl(k)$$

Proof. Let's consider the following PPT adversary $\mathcal{A}'$ who attempts to solve the DBDH
problem using $\mathcal{A}$ as a sub-routine. $\mathcal{A}'$ is given a tuple $(G_1, G_2, e, g, g^\alpha, g^\beta, g^\gamma, r)$ such
that $g, g^\alpha, g^\beta, g^\gamma \in G_1$ and $r \in G_2$. $\mathcal{A}'$ does the following:

Game Setup: $\mathcal{A}'$ sets $param = (G_1, G_2, e, g)$. $\mathcal{A}'$ also chooses $y_a \in Z_q$ randomly and sets $pk_a = (g^{y_a}, g^\gamma, e(g^\alpha, g^\gamma))$. $\mathcal{A}'$ then chooses an arbitrary number of random integers $(x_i, y_i, z_i) \in Z_q$ and computes $pk_i = (g^{y_i}, g^{z_i}, e(g^{x_i}, g^{z_i}))$. The public parameters and all the public keys are given to $\mathcal{A}$.

Phase 1: Whenever $\mathcal{A}$ requires oracle access to **Encrypt**$(\cdot, pk_a, param)$, $\mathcal{A}'$ chooses a random integer $r_a \in Z_q$ and encrypts the message using the corresponding public key as $(g^{r_a}, m \cdot e(g^\alpha, g^\gamma)^{r_a})$. At the end of phase 1, $\mathcal{A}$ outputs two messages m_0, m_1 of the same length.

Challenge: $\mathcal{A}'$ randomly chooses $b \leftarrow \{0, 1\}$ and sends $(g^\beta, m \cdot r)$.

Phase 2: Whenever $\mathcal{A}$ requires oracle access to **Encrypt**$(\cdot, pk_a, param)$, $\mathcal{A}'$ chooses a random integer $r_a \in Z_q$ and encrypts the message using the corresponding public key as $(g^{r_a}, m \cdot e(g^\alpha, g^\gamma)^{r_a})$.

Guess: $\mathcal{A}$ outputs a bit b'.

If $b' = b$, $\mathcal{A}'$ outputs 1, otherwise outputs 0. There are two cases:

Case 1: $r = e(g, g)^\delta$ for some random δ. In this case the probability of $b' = b$ is exactly $\frac{1}{2}$. So we have $Pr[\mathcal{A}'(g, g^\alpha, g^\beta, g^\gamma, e(g, g)^\delta) = 1] = \frac{1}{2}$.

Case 2: $r = e(g, g)^{\alpha\beta\gamma}$. In this case, $(g^\beta, m \cdot r)$ is a proper ciphertext for $\mathcal{A}$ and the probability of $b' = b$ is the same as $Succ_{\mathcal{A}}^{game_1}(k)$. So we have $Pr[\mathcal{A}'(g, g^\alpha, g^\beta, g^\gamma, e(g, g)^{\alpha\beta\gamma}) = 1] = Succ_{\mathcal{A}}^{game_1}(k)$.

Since the DBDH problem is hard, we have

$$Pr[\mathcal{A}'(g, g^\alpha, g^\beta, g^\gamma, e(g, g)^{\alpha\beta\gamma}) = 1] - Pr[\mathcal{A}'(g, g^\alpha, g^\beta, g^\gamma, e(g, g)^\delta) = 1] \leq negl(k)$$

After substitution, the above in-equation becomes $Succ_{\mathcal{A}}^{game_1}(k) - \frac{1}{2} \leq negl(k)$ and hence $Succ_{\mathcal{A}}^{game_1}(k) \leq \frac{1}{2} + negl(k)$.

5.3   Security against the Proxy

Our scheme is also semantically secure against the proxy (provider). This notion is captured by **Game$_2$** which differs from **Game$_1$** only in the game setup step. In **Game$_2$**, the challenger also gives a set of re-encryption keys to the adversary.

Theorem 2. *The proxy encryption scheme is semantically secure against the proxy i.e. for all PPT adversaries $\mathcal{A}$, there exists a negligible function negl such that:*

$$Pr[Succ_{\mathcal{A}}^{game_2}(k)] \leq \frac{1}{2} + negl(k)$$

Proof. The proof here is very similar to the proof of Theorem 1 except that in the **Game Setup** step, $\mathcal{A}'$ needs to generate a set of proxy keys and send them to $\mathcal{A}$. To generate a re-encrypt key $rk_{a \to b}$, $\mathcal{A}'$ chooses n, n' randomly from Z_q and set $rk_{a \to b} = (h_{b1}^n, g^{n'})$. Note that this re-encryption key is not correctly formed, but it has the same distribution as a correctly formed re-encryption key. Therefore $\mathcal{A}$ cannot distinguish this simulation from a real-world attack in which all values have the correct form. In other words, the view of $\mathcal{A}$ is indistinguishable from a real-world attack. The rest of the proof is the same as the previous proof.

6 Implementation and Evaluation

6.1 Implementation

We implemented Longitude in Java for testing and evaluation purposes. The architecture of a small application and location sharing service using Longitude is as shown in Figure 4.

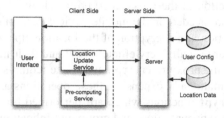

Fig. 4. The architecture of the Prototype Application

The client side has three components: (1) a user interface which provides the basic functionality for displaying user locations visually and performing management and configuration tasks; (2) a location update service which runs in the background to sense user location, encrypt it and send it to the server on schedule; (3) a pre-computing service which runs in the background only when external power has been connected to the device (see Section 6.2). The client side runs on the Android platform [24].

The server side has persistent data storage for location data and user configurations including re-encryption keys, precision masks and time-based policies. A daemon runs on the server and receives updates and request from clients. It can run on any system with Java 1.1 or above.

We did not find any cryptographic library in Java which supports bilinear pairing, so we implemented our own pairing library[1]. The algorithm implemented for pairing computation was the BKLS algorithm in Jabobian coordinates as described in [25]. We built all the underlying algebraic structures such as finite fields and elliptic curves using the BigInteger class in standard Java. We used the AES implementation provided by SunJCE.

The security parameters are taken from [26]. Namely, G_1 is an order-q subgroup of a non-supersingular elliptic curve over a finite field F_p, where q is a 160-bit prime and p is a 512-bit prime. G_2 is a subgroup of the finite field F_{p^2}. The overall security of this setting is roughly equivalent to 1024-bit RSA. We used AES-OFB [27,28] as the stream cipher. A key length of 128-bit was used.

6.2 Optimisation

Performance is an important issue for mobile applications. To enable location sharing service, users need to run a client-side application using the protocol on their mobile device. The application typically needs to be run in the background to collect and update

---

[1] Jpair: http://sourceforge.net/projects/jpair/

location data periodically. If the application consumes too much resource, it will slow down the foreground applications and will drain the battery.

Comparing to the location sharing services, the major performance overhead using Longitude comes from the cryptographic operations. To minimise the performance impact, Longitude is designed to distribute these operations between the mobile device and the server. To encrypt the location, 2 operations are needed on the mobile device: encryption of the location using the stream cipher and encryption of the random key using the **Encrypt** function of the proxy encryption scheme. To decrypt location ciphertext, 2 operations are needed on the mobile device: decryption of the random key using the **Decrypt** function and decryption of the location ciphertext using the stream cipher. Stream ciphers are usually very efficient [29] and their impact on performance is negligible. Although the proxy re-encryption scheme requires bilinear pairing operations which are computationally expensive, these operations are done on the server. The **Encrypt** and **Decrypt** functions which are performed on the user's mobile device require only group exponentiations and group multiplications. More precisely, the **Encrypt** function requires only 1 exponentiation in group G_1, 1 exponentiation and 1 multiplication in group G_2. The **Decrypt** function requires only 1 exponentiation and 1 multiplication in group G_2.

The **Encrypt** function is optimised further using the offline/online cryptography paradigm [30,31]. The ciphertext produced by the function is in the form of $(g^{r_a}, m \cdot Z_a^{r_a})$ where m is the location plaintext, g and Z_a are components in the public key and r_a is a random integer. The function can be naturally divided into two phases: a pre-computing (offline) phase and a final-encryption (online) phase. The pre-computing phase can be performed when the mobile device is being charged and no foreground application is running. In this phase multiple $(g^{r_a}, Z_a^{r_a})$ pairs are computed and stored. In the final-encryption phase when the application needs to send a location update to the server, a pair which is pre-computed in the pre-computing phase is retrieved from local data storage and a multiplication is performed to assemble the final ciphertext $(g^{r_a}, m \cdot Z_a^{r_a})$. The used pair is then erased from the device. In this way we can significantly improve the performance and reduce the energy consumption at the cost of some additional storage space, as we will see in Sections 6.3 and 6.4.

6.3 Performance Evaluation

The performance overhead of Longitude mainly comes from the cryptographic operations. Here we present our performance evaluation of these cryptographic operations in terms of execution time. All the numbers are the average time in milisecond for 10 executions.

The results of the client side tests are summarised in Table 1. The client runs on a Nexus One phone which has a 1GHZ Qualcomm QSD8250 CPU and 512 MB DRAM. From the table we see that the most time-consuming operation is the user key pair generation operation, which takes about 1.7 seconds. This should not be a problem because the user only runs it once when starting to use the service. Similarly, the other key generation and key update operations are slow but run only occasionally. The frequently used operations are encryption and decryption . The stream cipher encryption and decryption are very fast and can be done in 0.6 and 1 millisecond respectively. The public

Table 1. Speed & energy consumption of Cryptographic operations on Nexus One Phone

Operation	Time (ms)	Energy (mJ)
User Key Pair Generation	1693	945
Re-encryption Key Generation	1160	635
Public Key Encryption: Pre-computing Phase	427	245
Public Key Encryption: Final-encryption Phase	0.3	0.2
Stream Cipher Encryption	0.6	0.2
Public Key Decryption	32	10.5
Stream Cipher Decryption	1	0.7
Strong Revocation: User Key Update	94	14.6
Strong Revocation: Re-encryption Key Update	697	395

key decryption operation is much faster comparing to the public key encryption operation. As we can see, the optimisation we mentioned in section 6.2 can improve the performance significantly. The final-encryption phase is extremely fast, less than 1 ms.

The only cryptographic operation that runs at the service provider is the re-encryption operation. We measured this on a MacBook Pro laptop with an Intel Core2 Duo 2.5 GHZ CPU and 4 GB RAM. The operation takes 42 milliseconds.

6.4   Energy Consumption

We also measured the energy consumption of the client side cryptographic operations on the Nexus One. The measurement was done using PowerTutor [32]. The results are shown in Table 1 and given in Millijoules.

The capacity of the standard battery of Nexus One (1400mAh, 3.7V) is 18648 Joules. Therefore, 1000 full encryptions (including the pre-computing, the final-encryption and the stream encryption operations) will consume about 1.3% of the battery energy. If the pre-computing is done beforehand, then only the final-encryption and the stream encryption operations are needed for real-time encryption. In this case, 1000 encryptions will consume only 0.002% of the battery energy. The space overhead of storing 1000 precomputed values is about 200 KB. For decryption, 1000 decryptions (including the public key decryption and the the stream decryption operation) will consume 0.06% of the battery energy.

An interesting question is how long can 1000 pre-computed values last? Will they run out before the next recharge? In most cases, no. Apparently, the more frequently the phone updates its location, the faster the stored values will be exhausted. However, GPS and wireless radio are energy consuming. Therefore, the more frequently the phone updates its location, the shorter the battery life is. For a heavy user who updates his location every minute, the battery usually lasts less than a day. While 1000 precomputed values last 16.7 hours in this case. If the update frequency is 10 minutes, then the battery will last 2-3 days while 1000 pre-computed values will last about 7 days.

6.5   Communication Overhead

The location ciphertexts produced by the stream cipher have the same length as the location plaintexts. Therefore the communication overhead comes from the encrypted random stream cipher key. The ciphertext of a encrypted key consists of an elliptic curve point and an element in the field F_{p^2}. In our setting where p is 512-bits, the size of the ciphertext is about 1500 bits after point compression [33]. Further optimisation is possible by choosing elliptic curves with a larger embedding degree and by using compressed pairings [34].

6.6   Security Evaluation

In Section 5 we proved that Longitude's proxy re-encryption is semantically secure, which means that an adversary cannot get any information about the user's location by directly examining the ciphertext. However, there are three possible indirect attacks.

Since location data is sent through the Internet, an adversary may be able to infer the user's location given the user's IP address. Fortunately, this attack only allows the adversary to get an imprecise location, usually to the level of city or organisation. In addition, most mobile operators provide only a NATed Internet access, which means that an adversary will only see the gateway's IP address thus it is even harder for the adversary to infer the user's location. Therefore, in Longitude we did not implement any IP obfuscation mechanism. If needed, an external service such as Tor [35] could be used to provide anonymised communication.

If a query for a user's location is followed by a location-based query to another service provider, for example, a map-service, like Google Maps, then it's possible for the location sharing service to collude with the other service to correlate the two requests to discover a user's location. To counter this attack, the application would need to use offline data or perform requests to several *suitably* random locations.

Although precision masks allow users to be imprecise about their location, they do not prevent a recipient or intelligent software from inferring a more precise location, for example, by using background knowledge (user's home, workplace, favourite shops, previous locations). Depending on the circumstances and the intent of the user, Longitude mobile applications could generate precision masks more intelligently using viable but incorrect locations. However, even with cleverer concealment it's always possible that a recipient will learn the user's exact location and rightly or wrongly infer that the user is deliberately concealing their exact location from them, leading to a loss of trust and perhaps the recipient reciprocating or taking some other action.

7   Conclusion and Future Work

In this paper, we presented a new privacy preserving location sharing protocol called Longitude. The most significant features of Longitude are that the location sharing provider only processes encrypted locations that it unable to decrypt, supports different granularities of locations for different receivers, and low key management, computation and communication overheads. In addition, Longitude's proxy re-encryption scheme is provably secure and the cryptographic functions optimised for mobile platforms. A prototype was implemented in Java on the Nexus One Android mobile phone and the CPU-time and energy consumption were evaluated.

One type of privacy policy which has proven to be useful in location sharing services are selective location-based policies. For example, Alice may, when at home, only want her families to be able to track her but not her friends. This type of policy can be easily implemented if the location sharing service provider has access to the user's location. But how could we support this type of policy is the provider only holds encrypted data? We plan to investigate this problem further, looking at schemes such as searchable encrypted data [22] and attributed-based encryption [36]. We would also like to explore how to provide more services upon encrypted data, as suggested in [37].

References

1. Google Latitude, http://www.google.com/latitude
2. Yahoo fire eagle, http://fireeagle.yahoo.net/
3. Loopt, http://www.loopt.com/
4. Raphael, J.: Three Reasons Why I Won't Be Using Google Latitude (2009), http://www.pcworld.com/article/158953
5. Turoczy, R.: Google latitude: Ready to tell your friends (and google) where you are? (2009), http://www.readwriteweb.com/archives/google_latitude_location_aware.php
6. Gralla, P.: Privacy group asks ftc to investigate google (2009), http://www.pcworld.com/businesscenter/article/161497/privacy_group_asks_ftc_to_investigate_google.html
7. Tang, K.P., Lin, J., Hong, J.I., Siewiorek, D.P., Sadeh, N.: Rethinking location sharing: Exploring the implications of social-driven vs. purpose-driven location sharing. In: UbiComp (2010)
8. Tsai, J.Y., Kelley, P.G., Cranor, L.F., Sadeh, N.: Location-sharing technologies: Privacy risks and controls (2010), http://cups.cs.cmu.edu/LBSprivacy/files/TsaiKelleyCranorSadeh_2009.pdf
9. Beresford, A., Stajano, F.: Location privacy in pervasive computing. Pervasive Computing, IEEE 2(1), 46–55 (2003)
10. Gruteser, M., Grunwald, D.: Anonymous usage of location-based services through spatial and temporal cloaking. In: MobiSys (2003)
11. Hashem, T., Kulik, L.: Safeguarding location privacy in wireless ad-hoc networks. In: Krumm, J., Abowd, G.D., Seneviratne, A., Strang, T. (eds.) UbiComp 2007. LNCS, vol. 4717, pp. 372–390. Springer, Heidelberg (2007)
12. Zhong, G., Hengartner, U.: A distributed k-anonymity protocol for location privacy. In: IEEE International Conference on Pervasive Computing and Communications PerCom 2009, pp. 1–10 (9-13, 2009)
13. Locaccino, http://www.locaccino.org
14. Langheinrich, M.: A privacy awareness system for ubiquitous computing environments. In: Borriello, G., Holmquist, L.E. (eds.) UbiComp 2002. LNCS, vol. 2498, pp. 237–245. Springer, Heidelberg (2002)
15. Freudiger, J., Neu, R., Hubaux, J.P.: Private sharing of user location over online social networks. In: 3rd Hot Topics in Privacy Enhancing Technologies, HotPETs 2010 (2010)
16. Ruppel, P., Treu, G., Küpper, A., Linnhoff-Popien, C.: Anonymous user tracking for location-based community services. In: Hazas, M., Krumm, J., Strang, T. (eds.) LoCA 2006. LNCS, vol. 3987, pp. 116–133. Springer, Heidelberg (2006)
17. Zhong, G., Goldberg, I., Hengartner, U.: Louis, lester and pierre: Three protocols for location privacy. In: Borisov, N., Golle, P. (eds.) PET 2007. LNCS, vol. 4776, pp. 62–76. Springer, Heidelberg (2007)

18. Mascetti, S., Freni, D., Bettini, C., Wang, X.S., Jajodia, S.: Privacy in geo-social networks: proximity notification with untrusted service providers and curious buddies. CoRR abs/1007.0408 (2010)
19. Siksnys, L., Thomsen, J.R., Saltenis, S., Yiu, M.L.: Private and flexible proximity detection in mobile social networks. In: Mobile Data Management, pp. 75–84 (2010)
20. Blaze, M., Bleumer, G., Strauss, M.J.: Divertible protocols and atomic proxy cryptography. In: Nyberg, K. (ed.) EUROCRYPT 1998. LNCS, vol. 1403, pp. 127–144. Springer, Heidelberg (1998)
21. Ateniese, G., Fu, K., Green, M., Hohenberger, S.: Improved proxy re-encryption schemes with applications to secure distributed storage. ACM Trans. Inf. Syst. Secur. 9(1), 1–30 (2006)
22. Dong, C., Russello, G., Dulay, N.: Shared and searchable encrypted data for untrusted servers. In: DBSec., pp. 127–143 (2008)
23. Boneh, D., Franklin, M.K.: Identity-based encryption from the weil pairing. SIAM J. Comput. 32(3), 586–615 (2003)
24. Android platform, http://www.android.com/
25. Chatterjee, S., Sarkar, P., Barua, R.: Efficient computation of tate pairing in projective coordinate over general characteristic fields. In: Park, C.-s., Chee, S. (eds.) ICISC 2004. LNCS, vol. 3506, pp. 168–181. Springer, Heidelberg (2005)
26. Scott, M.: Computing the tate pairing. In: Menezes, A. (ed.) CT-RSA 2005. LNCS, vol. 3376, pp. 293–304. Springer, Heidelberg (2005)
27. NIST: NIST FIPS-197: Specification for the Advanced Encryption Standard
28. NIST: NIST SP 800-38A: Recommendation for Block Cipher Modes of Operation
29. Fournel, N., Minier, M., Ubéda, S.: Survey and benchmark of stream ciphers for wireless sensor networks. In: Sauveron, D., Markantonakis, K., Bilas, A., Quisquater, J.-J. (eds.) WISTP 2007. LNCS, vol. 4462, pp. 202–214. Springer, Heidelberg (2007)
30. Even, S., Goldreich, O., Micali, S.: On-line/Off-line digital signatures. In: Brassard, G. (ed.) CRYPTO 1989. LNCS, vol. 435, pp. 263–275. Springer, Heidelberg (1990)
31. Guo, F., Mu, Y., Chen, Z.: Identity-based online/Offline encryption. In: Tsudik, G. (ed.) FC 2008. LNCS, vol. 5143, pp. 247–261. Springer, Heidelberg (2008)
32. Zhang, L., Tiwana, B., Qian, Z., Wang, Z., Dick, R., Mao, Z.M., Yang, L.: Accurate online power estimation and automatic battery behavior based power model generation for smartphones. In: Proceedings of CODES+ISSS (2010)
33. IEEE: IEEE P1363: Standard specifications for public key cryptography
34. Scott, M., Barreto, P.S.L.M.: Compressed pairings. In: Franklin, M. (ed.) CRYPTO 2004. LNCS, vol. 3152, pp. 140–156. Springer, Heidelberg (2004)
35. Tor, http://www.torproject.org/
36. Lewko, A., Okamoto, T., Sahai, A., Takashima, K., Waters, B.: Fully secure functional encryption: Attribute-based encryption and (Hierarchical) inner product encryption. In: Gilbert, H. (ed.) EUROCRYPT 2010. LNCS, vol. 6110, pp. 62–91. Springer, Heidelberg (2010)
37. Popa, R.A., Zeldovich, N., Balakrishnan, H.: Cryptdb: A practical encrypted relational dbms. Technical Report MIT-CSAIL-TR-2011-005, MIT (2011)

An Empirical Evaluation of the Compliance of Game-Network Providers with Data-Protection Law

Thorben Burghardt[1], Klemens Böhm[1], Markus Korte[1], and Simon Bohnen[2]

[1] Karlsruhe Institute of Technology, 76131 Karlsruhe, Germany
firstname.lastname@kit.edu
[2] University of Regensburg, 93053 Regensburg, Germany
firstname.lastname@jura.uni-regensburg.de

Abstract. Game consoles have become ubiquitous, not only for gaming but also as media servers, internet gateways etc. In combination with online networks, consoles feature online gaming in an unprecedented fashion. To participate in the networks and to personalize the services offered, the providers collect, process and forward personal information. This puts user privacy at risk. In this work we analyze the privacy policies of the online networks Playstation-Network, Xbox-Live and Wii, the three major providers. More specifically, we test the compliance of the policies to the current legal situation. We also evaluate if the providers fulfill the fundamental right of a user to obtain information on him. Our results are that all providers commit several violations, and in many cases their practices are not transparent.

Keywords: privacy, study, game networks.

1 Introduction

Today, game consoles have become ubiquitous. They are highly versatile and not limited to high-performance game playing as such, but feature surfing the Internet, acting as Media Servers [1] etc. Online networks, for multiplayer games in particular, have become popular. Users playing against each other register at such game networks, normally with their names, email addresses, age information, a gamer tag etc. (*inventory data*). The network then manages user authentication, payment, matching similar users for online sessions etc. (*usage data*). The console vendors Sony Playstation, Microsoft Xbox or Nintendo Wii offer such networks. Network providers also exchange information with social network sites (SNS) [2]. Further, network providers run shops and can store interests in products, purchases, shipping address etc. Thus, network providers can create comprehensive user profiles. This puts user privacy at risk.

It is not only the acquisition of personal information that threatens user privacy. Game-network providers also forward this data to others, in the following ways: First, depending on the game, a network provider forwards the user requests to the provider hosting the game servers (game-server provider). Second,

I. Wakeman et al. (Eds.): IFIPTM 2011, IFIP AICT 358, pp. 149–164, 2011.
© IFIP International Federation for Information Processing 2011

several games embed in-game advertisement: Advertisers place real ads on the virtual advertising panels, e.g., for perimeter advertising in sports games. Advertisers then pay for their ads based on complex payout functions [3]. Third, individuals can exchange information between their social-network profiles and their game-network profiles. For instance, people can automatically upload their levels achieved in a game or their trophies won.

So far, while others have studied the privacy practices of SNS [4], this is not the case for game networks. Game networks are different from SN, in various ways: There are several parties responsible for the service provision, e.g., for authentication, playing, purchasing for a game, and these parties are tightly interwoven. Further, the parties responsible for the service provision vary for nearly every game available, and they differ in design, technology, utilization, and intent. Thus, results from SNS do not readily carry over to game networks.

In this work, we study privacy issues in game networks. In particular, we ask 'Is it feasible for a user to understand which party has which personal data?' (Q1). In other words, we analyze if privacy practices are transparent. With respect to the tight connection of game networks and SNS we ask 'Are there privacy threats arising from the connection of game-network providers and SNS?' (Q2). Finally, 'What might help to improve the privacy of the user?' (Q3). To answer the questions, we compare the privacy policies of game-network providers to the requirements stemming from data-protection law. The game networks we consider are the Playstation-Network (PSN), Xbox-Live (XBL) and Wii-Internet-Services (WIS), the three most popular networks by far. The legislative body relevant for our evaluation is the German data-protection law. As the EU is currently harmonizing data protection among its member states, our results are relevant beyond Germany. We evaluate which information the game-network providers acquire according to their privacy policies, whom they forward the information to, and if they inform the user about data usage according to data-protection law – the most powerful mechanism users have in the EU to control the flow of their personal information. In the name of real players we ask the providers which data they have stored and forwarded and evaluate their responses. The study has taken place between February and August 2010.

The impact of our work is high: The privacy practices of game-network providers have not yet been analyzed sufficiently. This is crucial as there are millions of gamers affected, and the information processed may be sensitive.

Paper structure: Section 2 contains some background information and explains the legal situation. We also report on related work. Section 3 describes our study setup, Section 4 gives our evaluation results. We propose measures to protect user privacy in Section 5. Section 6 concludes.

2   Background

In this section we give background information on game consoles and online networks. Then we describe in-game advertisement. Finally, we briefly discuss the statutory framework on data protection relevant for game consoles.

2.1 Parties Providing Online Gaming

While games with the first generations of consoles have been purely local, to-day's consoles all feature online gaming. This requires user management, payment mechanisms, hosting of the games, matching similar users for online sessions (matchmaking) etc. In this section we describe the parties involved in online games. These are the game-network provider, the game-server provider, ad servers and third-party providers.

Game-network provider. The game network is the gateway to any online access via a console. The network management handles the authentication and authorization of users and offers relevant services. For instance, it provides updates, manages groups of friends, sells updates, games, add-ons etc. Microsoft calls its network 'Xbox-Live' (XBL), Sony 'Playstation Network' (PSN) and Nintendo 'Wii Internet Services' (WIS). At all networks, users have to register before they can access it. PSN and XBL offer one network for all services. WIS distinguishes between Nintendo Club and the Nintendo Shop and states in the privacy policy that, without the user consent, information is not consolidated. It is important that not participating in the network as a player is unrealistic: The providers offer relevant patches, updates and extensions online, i.e., over their networks. Patches are available several times a month, some required for the games and some for the console itself. Downloading these patches, storing them on a disk and installing them manually, as is technically feasible, would not be practical.

Game-server provider. Game-server providers host the games. They mediate between players, i.e., create game sessions and assign users to them, etc. Games can be hosted by the game-network providers or by independent companies, e.g., the *game publisher.* For instance, Activision, the publisher of 'Call of Duty', also provides the servers hosting the game. In the case of independent companies, the game-network providers automatically forward (personal) information to the game publishers. The connection between the game server and the game network is often hidden from the user. In other words, a user does not need to know which company in which country operates the game server. This is good from a usability perspective, however, it is difficult with respect to data-protection law.

Ad-servers provider. Ad servers serve ads shown in games. We will describe in-game advertisement in Section 2.2. Both game-network providers and game-server providers can connect to ad servers and display ads.

Third-party provider. The console and game-network providers have recently started (November 2009) to integrate third-party services. These include Twitter, a music-recommendation service, and Facebook. This might raise new privacy threats: The data available to game-network providers and game-server providers (game publishers) allows them to build comprehensive user profiles. For SNS, this is well known [4]. The connection between both allows game-network providers and game publishers to learn details on their players from the SNS, e.g., habits, friends, interests. The SNS in turn can learn how often a user plays which game, at which time. The SNS can see this by trophies uploaded, game statistics etc. Thus, not only the trophies can threaten privacy, but also metadata like the upload timestamp. Further, companies providing ads for both game networks and SNS might learn from this as well, e.g., by linking IP information they obtain from the game-network provider for billing purposes.

XBL offers access to all these third-party services, e.g., users can upload images like game screenshot [5] and can browse Facebook photos. PSN users can send game statistics and information on items shopped to Facebook [2], upload videos to Youtube, and browse photos at Facebook and Picasa[1],[2]. WIS does not offer such a third-party integration.

2.2 In-Game Advertisement

Several games feature in-game advertisement (IGA). A unique selling point of IGA is that players accept it as making games more realistic [6]. We distinguish two variants of IGA: Static and dynamic in-game advertisement. The first variant is hard-coded, i.e., part of the game, and can be refreshed with software updates. With the dynamic variant in turn, ads are loaded from ad networks on-the-fly. Advertisers then pay based on complex payout functions. Both the Sony and Microsoft console feature dynamic advertisement. Sony has integrated the IGA Worldwide and Double Fusion in-game advertising networks. Microsoft uses the network of its subsidiary Massive Inc. and 18 further providers[3]. The effectiveness of IGA depends on how good the ad-placement algorithm predicts the interests of the users. This in turn brings ad-network providers to learn as much as possible about their customers, i.e., to collect sensitive personal information.

2.3 Legal Background

Since the EU Directive 95/46/EC has been issued, all EU member states have established data-protection regulations for services on the Internet. Many countries try to define regulations independent from the technology they apply to. Thus, first we have to find out which law is the relevant one for the parties involved in offering online services for consoles. This includes the relevant country and the law within the country.

With respect to [7], game networks are subject to the German Telemedia Act (Telemediengesetz, TMG). This law is relevant for services on the Internet if the service is a Telemedia service in terms of §1 p. 1 s. 1 TMG. It applies to all electronical services of information or communication except for telecommunication services (§3 No. 24, German Telecommunication Act, TKG), telecommunication supported services after §3 No. 25 TKG and broadcasting services (§2 German

---

[1] http://de.playstation.com/ps3/support/system-software/detail/
item289447/Update-Features-(Ver-3-40)/

[2] http://blog.us.playstation.com/2010/06/28/
playstation-3-system-software- update-v3-40-available-soon-2/

[3] http://privacy.microsoft.com/de-de/fullnotice.mspx

Broadcast Services State Treaty, RStV). The game-network providers and the game-server providers do not fall under these exceptions, so the TMG is relevant.

The scope of the TMG for international data processing depends on the home-state regulation in §3 p. 1 TMG. It says that (1) the German law is the relevant one if the provider is located in Germany. However, it further says that (2) if the provider is outside of Germany but within the EU, the law of the country from which the provider offers the service is the relevant one (§3 p. 3 TMG, §1 p. 5 Federal Data Protection Act, BDSG). For XBL and WIS (1) holds as they are located in Germany. For PSN however and according to (2), the British privacy law has to be applied because their domicile is not Germany but the UK.

With the TMG and the BDSG being the relevant legislative body and according to 95/46/EC, a provider has to fulfill several requirements. We will investigate to which extent providers act according to them. 95/46/EC harmonizes data protection within the EU, i.e., in this work we refer to German law (also in the PSN case) but this will hold for EU legislation as well.

2.4 Related Work

Game networks have not yet been studied sufficiently with respect to privacy. [7] describes the legal issues relevant for overlay networks, which, by subsumption, also hold for game networks. [4,8] describe large networks of interconnected users. However, they refer to social networks where users tend to establish the contacts explicitly. The assignment of users to game sessions in contrast takes place automatically, based on player characteristics. Others, e.g. [9], analyze in-game advertisement, but leave data protection aside. [10,11] investigate website advertisement and investigate privacy threats related. This as well cannot easily be mapped to game networks: Game networks use complex payout functions requiring a lot of personal information, much more than website advertisement.

3   Study Procedure

In this section we describe the two steps of our evaluation: first, the analysis of the privacy policies and, second, the request for information. Further, we describe differences between the game-network providers we have investigated.

Privacy-Policy Analysis. An important design decision of this study is to analyze the privacy policies of the providers (and nothing else) to learn about the privacy practices of providers. This is to avoid relying on insider knowledge regarding the data processing at the providers and to keep our study objective. Further, law requires providers to inform users of data collection and processing in advance. Thus, users assess providers by characteristics accessible from an external perspective, i.e., the privacy policy, and we do so as well. In more concrete terms, we analyze the privacy policies and the general terms of usage. Some providers have more than one privacy policy, e.g., a general and a specific one, as they call them. We consider all of these policies. We evaluate the providers according to the following criteria: the availability of a privacy policy, the law they deem relevant, information on data collection and forwarding, information on automated data processing like cookies, the way they integrate in-game advertisement, information on the right to opt-out, giving and revoking consent, and the availability of a contact address.

Non-Transparency vs. Violation. With any assessment of the provider we will state whether the practice of the provider fits our interpretation of the law. In several cases the practice might be, but is not necessarily a violation of the law. We would need further details, or it would require a court (of ultimate resort) decision to decide if this was a violation. In any case, it is not transparent for the user what the provider does with the data. In the assessment we will use the words 'non-transparency' and 'violation', denoting them with ▲ and ⚡ respectively.

Request for Information. An individual has the right to request from a provider which personal information it has stored about him. The provider has to reply immediately, i.e., within two weeks realistically [12]. This arguably is one of the most important mechanisms to track one's personal information. To test its effectiveness, we ask PSN, XBL and WIS for personal information on behalf of real players. We also do this with several game publishers. We have sent our requests via postal letters, and we have identified ourselves (the requester) with our MAC and IP address, the serial number of the device and the user-account name. We have requested any information that the provider stores *about* the requester, the *attribute names* and *attribute values*, and the *purpose of the acquisition* of the data. Further, we have requested *which data* has been forwarded, to *whom* and for which *purpose*. We have considered any response received until now.

A common approach to substantiate results would be to repeat the experiment, i.e., send several requests. In our case however, the providers might see what our intention is and behave differently, compared to 'normal' requests. To observe realistic behavior, we have contacted a provider at most two times.

Game-Network Providers. We analyze the three game-network providers PSN, XBL and WIS. The WIS privacy policy has a distinctive characteristic: It claims that no information WIS acquires can be linked to an individual, as long as the Wii-shopping-channel account is not connected to the Club-Nintendo account. A user can connect both in his personal settings. So WIS acquires data but states to be unable to identify individuals by it. To better compare the three game-network providers, we will investigate the case of connected WIS accounts if not stated differently.

4   Evaluation

We now evaluate the privacy practices of the game-network providers. We then focus on privacy threats that might result from connecting SNS and game networks (Section 4.2). Last, we investigate how PSN, XBL and WIS deal with the right of individuals to access their personal data (Section 4.3).

4.1 Privacy Policy

We now report on our evaluation of the privacy policies of game-network providers according to the criteria from Section 3. For citations we use another font.

Table 1. Overview privacy-policy analysis

Assessment criteria	PSN	XBL	Wii
Relevant law			
Privacy policy available	▲		▲
Data acqu. (kind of data)	▲	▲	
Data acqu. (scope of data)	↯	↯	
Data acqu. (purpose)		▲	
Data acqu. (usage data)	↯		
Data forwarding		▲	
Automated processing	↯	▲	↯
In-game advertisement		▲	
Giving & revoking consent	↯	▲	↯
Contact address		▲	

Table 2. Usage-data attributes

Attribute	PSN	XBL	Wii
IP address	✓	✓	✓
MAC address	✓		
console id	✓	✓	
user id	✓	✓	✓
settings	✓		✓
time/date of usage	✓	✓	✓
games played	✓	✓	✓
chat usage	✓		
content accessed	✓		✓
game statistics	✓	✓	
friend list	✓		
products purchased	✓		✓
credit card inform.	✓		

Relevant Law. The relevant law is the TMG. *XBL* does not state anything about the relevant law, *WIS* says that the contract the user agrees to when registering is subject to German law. Both is acceptable, as no information on the relevant law is required, but if it exists, it has to be correct. *PSN* in contrast says in their general terms that, to the extent permitted by law, they will handle all claims by the law of England. According to Section 2.3, this is valid.

Availability of privacy policy. §13 p.1 s.3 TMG: *Each customer must be able to obtain the privacy policy easily and at any time.*

Though all network providers do have privacy policies, users already encounter several difficulties when they simply want to see them. The *PSN* privacy policy can be found easily. In the policy itself PSN refers to a page where the most current version is available. However, it points to a dead URL[4]. For *XBL*, users can find a link to the privacy policy. It consists of a general policy, valid for all Microsoft services, a compressed version and a special one for individual services, e.g., for XBL. For *WIS*, due to the separation of the game network and the shop, finding the privacy policy is difficult. It exists stand alone for the Wii-Shop-Channel and as a part of the general terms for the game network. However, the section in the general terms is marked with the wrong caption. Further, when selecting the German language and then opening the policy, it is different from the one shown when Nintendo picks a language automatically.

We classify the PSN practice and the WIS practice as non-transparent.

[4] http://network.eu.playstation.com/legal

Information on data acquisition. §13 p.1 s.1 TMG: *A provider has to inform on (i) the kind of data, (ii) the scope and (iii) the purpose of data acquisition and usage. The purpose specification can be omitted when obvious.*

Kind of data. The legislator requires the providers to state attribute names or meaningful categories, e.g., shipping address, of data which they collect for the registration. *PSN* names attributes, e.g., name and e-mail address, and meaningful categories, e.g., postal address. However, they also refer to attributes *like* .... Thus, it is not clear if the list is complete, i.e., we see an non-transparency. *XBL* states attribute names and meaningful categories as well. However, they list the attributes acquired in the general privacy policy, which covers access to websites as well as Microsoft services for mobile phones etc. Thus, since it is not clear which attributes XBL collects, this is an non-transparency as well. The *WIS* policy names the attributes necessary for a registration.

Scope of data (storage time). In the *PSN* privacy policy we do not find a hint on how long data is stored or on how to delete it. This is a violation. *XBL* gives no information on how long the data is stored either, i.e., this is a violation as well. *WIS* provides an email address which a user can contact to delete the data.

Purpose. *PSN* states explicitly which purpose they acquire personal data for, e.g., for network gaming, community functions etc. *XBL* states several purposes, ranging from providing the requested service to advertisement. Again, as Microsoft states the purpose in the general policy, it is unclear if this holds for the XBL game network as well. We classify this as non-transparent. *WIS* clearly states the purposes access to websites, registration for a newsletter and email subscription.

Information on the acquisition of usage data. Besides the data providers acquire when registering at the service (inventory data), providers also acquire data when individuals use the service (usage data). All providers list the attributes of the usage data collected. This includes the IP address, the usage behavior etc. (see Table 2). *PSN* states that, to enforce the general terms of use, they may store any information on chat and speech data, without informing the user beforehand. This is a violation. They do so without any well-founded suspicion and, as this clause is 'surprising', it also violates the German Civil Code.

Forwarding of data. §13 p. 1 s. 1 TMG: *Each provider has to state which personal data is forwarded to others.*

PSN states three kinds of receivers of personal information. The first ones are companies providing the PSN service. PSN states that the receivers have to act according to the PSN privacy policy, and that PSN regards herself responsible for the data. Second, other subsidiaries of Sony Computer Entertainment have access to the data. In this case, PSN does not state the purpose of data forwarding. As PSN is a worldwide service, data is forwarded to countries outside the European Economic Area, i.e., countries with different data-protection laws. PSN informs on this. Third, PSN also forwards personal data to game communities, third-party publishers and social network sites at the time when a user accesses it. Here, it is important that the PSN states that the receiver of the data is responsible for the personal data, i.e., another policy takes effect. *XBL* states to forward data to other countries as well. According to their privacy policy, personal data can be stored and processed in any country where Microsoft has a related company or a branch, or where their service providers have offices. Microsoft states to act according to the Safe-Harbor Agreement. It establishes that the data transfer to the US complies with the EU directive 95/46/EC. Normally, this agreement is relevant for EU subsidiaries of Microsoft only. But from the Microsoft privacy policy, a user gains the impression that this holds for companies outside of the EU and the US as well. We deem this non-transparent. *WIS* states that they do not sell personal information and use it only for its own purposes and the ones of their subsidiaries.

Summary. All providers are international and have subsidiaries they forward personal data to. A user is not able to find out which companies belong to a provider. Thus, the data flow is non-transparent. However, since relationships of companies are likely to change over time, it is adequate to name the receivers of the data in forms of categories. It then depends on how the providers handle requests for information (Section 4.3) whether this is a violation.

Information on automated data processing. §13 p.1 s.1, s.2 TMG: *Each provider has to inform about the automated processing of personal data if the processes give way to the identification of an individual. In particular, the obligation to inform includes (i) the kind of data, (ii) the storage period (scope) and (iii) the purpose of processing.*

PSN uses cookies to acquire specific information about the users, to track the access and usage of PSN, to deliver the service and to store the relevant language. The formulation specific is vague. Further, there is no information on the storage time, i.e., if session or persistent cookies are used, for how long, or on how to remove them. This is a violation. *XBL* uses cookies for the login to specific services, for the personalization of the service and to place adequate advertisement. XBL states to use session cookies, which will be removed when logging out or closing the browser, and persistent cookies. XBL explains how to remove cookies. We deem this sufficient to meet the storage-time requirement. Further, Microsoft states which information is stored in the cookies. Thus, Microsoft informs on the kind, purpose and scope of cookie usage. Microsoft uses also Webbeacons, i.e., content like transparent one-pixel images users download (unknowingly) and providers then track. Microsoft uses this for statistical purposes, for cobranding services and advertisement. Further, under certain circumstances, Microsoft uses Webbeacons of third parties that build statistics. XBL says that no such Webbeacons are allowed on Microsoft websites that give way to the collection of personal data. On the other hand, XBL states that they build aggregated statistics. This is comparable to web-statistics tools which violate data-protection law in Germany [13]. Here, further details are required to decide if this is a violation. However, formulations like specific services or under certain circumstances are non-transparent. *Wii* states to use cookies to collect information on the websites a user visits and the products he is interested in. Further, Wii states to use cookies to check if a user is already registered, and permanent cookies to store the preferred language of the user. Webbeacons are also used, e.g., to track users. Wii does not say how long cookies are stored, i.e., violates the law. The purpose Wii states is to provide content interesting for the user and for marketing purposes.

In-Game Advertisement. *PSN* states to create personalized profiles to predict the user intent and interests. To do so, PSN states to store the IP address, the MAC address, the position in the game where the ad is placed, how long the ad has been visible, its size and the perspective the user has seen it from. This information is not only stored by PSN, but PSN also forwards it to companies that place the ads. However, it becomes clear to the user what kind of information PSN processes and forwards. *XBL* does not explicitly use the term in-game advertisement. They state that many services offered by Microsoft partners are supported by advertisement. Due to the very general overall privacy policy it is difficult to understand if Microsoft as the game-server provider uses in-game advertisement. We classify this as non-transparent. The *WIS* privacy policy does not mention in-game advertisement or personalized ads.

Opt-Out. §15 p.3 TMG: *If the provider informs the user on his right to opt-out, the provider is allowed to build usage profiles for the purpose of advertisement, market research, and to adjust the service to market needs.*

Regarding this point, all providers behave in line with law. *PSN* creates pseudonymous profiles. However, they inform the user on his right to opt-out from receiving marketing information. They refer to the account-setting page, where the user can disable this. *XBL* creates pseudonymous and personalized profiles. They also refer to a page where the user can deactivate personalized advertisement. Users can do so for the device they currently use or for their entire account, i.e., their Live-ID. This allows to deactivate personal and pseudonymous profiles. *WIS* creates pseudonymous profiles as well and explains how to opt-out.

Giving and revoking consent §12 p.1, §13 p.2 TMG: *Acquisition and usage of personal data are allowed only if permitted by law, or if the user consents. It must become clear which purpose the user consents to, and which practice is already legitimated by (any) law. Further, the user has to be aware of the fact that he is consenting. The user must be informed that he can revoke his consent at any time.*

In particular, requesting the consent of the user is required when building personalized profiles, acquiring more data than necessary to provide the service and when forwarding personal information to non EU countries. All providers request user consent to their privacy practices.

   PSN creates personalized profiles, acquires more data than necessary to provide a service, e.g., the postal address, and forwards data. Thus, giving consent is required. PSN also requests the consent for using cookies. It does not become clear which purpose that requires a consent they use cookies for. The PSN privacy policy states that using their service after a modification of the privacy policy is equivalent to giving consent consciously. The same holds for the forwarding of personal information. This is a violation of the law. Further, PSN does not inform the user that he can revoke his consent. This is another violation. According to its privacy policy, *XBL* creates personalized profiles, forwards data to companies not necessary to offer the service, and collects data not necessary to this end. Thus, user consent is required. However, a user cannot see in detail from their privacy policy which practices actually do require consent. We classify this as non-transparent. As mentioned before, XBL offers an interface to revoke the consent for advertisement. Further, they inform the users that they can revoke the consent. This is in line with the law. *WIS* explicitly states in a paragraph purposes which they request consent for. This is transparent. However, a closer look shows that this paragraph also includes practices that do not require user consent. For instance, this is the case when the provider uses personal information to improve a website. Again, a user cannot see what exactly the consent is required for, and what is legitimated by law anyhow. As we have explained, Wii distinguishes between two kinds of accounts, one for playing and one for the shop. They state that by connecting both accounts a user automatically consents to building a personalized profile. However, this implicit kind of giving consent is a violation. In line with law, Wii points out that the user may revoke his consent.

Summary. All providers request user consent, as required by law, considering their purposes. However, they do not make clear what is already legitimated by law, and which practices require consent. Further, giving consent must be consciously, but this is not always the case.

Contact Address §15 p.1 no. 1, no. 2 TMG: *Providers have to provide a contact information.*

The *PSN* and *WIS* privacy policies contain concrete contact addresses. *XBL* states how to contact a person responsible for data protection, a phone number, a web form and a postal address. When using the web form however, one has to consent to the privacy policy before being able to ask questions regarding the policy itself. Further, the privacy policy referenced in the form cannot be correctly displayed with Firefox. Last, the contact form the policy displayed refers to is different from the one we came from. Overall, we deem this non-transparent.

4.2   Interconnection of Console Networks and Social Network Sites

The connection of game networks and SNS since 2009 are likely to raise new privacy threats. We analyze how the game-network providers address this issue in their privacy policy. *PSN* states that data can be forwarded to, say, SNS if one accesses such a service via one's PSN account. The purpose of the data forwarding, according to PSN, is to provide the services and related research and analysis. We do not know what research and analysis include and classify this as non-transparent. PSN states that, when forwarding data to a SNS (here Facebook), the privacy policy of the receiver is the relevant one. *XBL* does not explicitly use the terms 'social network site' or 'Facebook', but states to use cobranding and to offer some services referred to as alliance with other companies. We assume that, here as well, the privacy policy of the receiver is the relevant one. This conforms to law if XBL informs the user when data is transferred.

4.3   Request for Information

§13 p.7 TMG, §34 BDSG: *Each customer can ask a provider to inform her on her personal data. The provider has to list all data stored and forwarded.*

Table 3. Responses to the request for information

	PSN	Activision	Electronic Arts	Epic Games	Ubisoft	Rockstar Games	XBL	Activision	Electronic Arts	Ubisoft	WIS	Hudson Entert.
Response time	1m, 14d	↯	↯	↯	✓	14d	↯	↯	↯	20d	20d, 1m, 1m	↯
Data acquisition	−, ✓	↯	↯	↯	✓	↯	↯	↯	↯	✓	−, −,	↯
Data forwarding	−, ↯	↯	↯	↯	✓	↯	↯	↯	↯	✓	−, −,	↯
No Complaints	−, ▲	↯	↯	↯	✓	✓	↯	↯	↯	✓	−, −,	↯

Our evaluation covers all assessment criteria relevant according to law, as well as general information on the interaction with the provider. It states whom we obtained a response from, within which time window, if the provider has replied with the data acquired and stored, the data forwarded, the purpose of any data forwarding, the receiver, and if the request has been answered without complaints. Table 3 gives an overview. Multiple entries for the same provider means that we have had repeated interactions. For each player we will first describe our experiences with the game-network providers, the ones with the game publishers follow. Complementary information can be found on our web site[5].

We have approached the game-network providers and game-server providers in the name of three real players. In the name of a PS3 user we have asked PSN, Acitivision, Electronic Arts, Epic Games, Rockstargames and Ubisoft. For the Xbox user we have requested information from XBL, Activision, Electronic Arts, and Ubisoft, for the Wii users WIS and Hudson Entertainment.

PSN. We have sent 6 requests for information in the name of the PSN user.

---

[5] http://privacy.ipd.kit.edu

Game-Network Provider. *PSN* has answered our request after one month by requesting a copy of the passport and asking if they could limit the information sent to one year; we did agree. 14 days later we have received a detailed list of data acquired, stored and processed, together with a description on how to read the table, explanations of the database schema etc. This includes 15 inventory attributes (see Table 4).

Table 4. Inventory-data PSN   **Table 5.** Events PSN

Attributes 1	Attributes 2
Identifier	Last Deposit Amount
PSN Account ID	Last Deposit Date
Login Name	Account Update
Pseudonym	Reg. Console ID
Account Status	Gender
Address 1 – 3	Day Of Birth
City	Language
Zip Code	Account Creation
Province Code	Opt-In Direct
Country	Opt In-3rd-Party
Country Currency	EULA-Version
Wallet Balance	

Events 1	Events 2
Authentication	Verify (Payment)
Authorization	Activate Console
Authorize DRM	View Product
Create Account	Add to Cart
Change Payment Infor	View Category
Change Opt-In	Purchase Product
Credit Card Auth.	Download Content
Credit Card Charge	Redownload Store
Purchase	Purchase Info
Deposit - Charge	Create Session
Lookup Voucher	Delete Session

Besides the inventory data, PSN acquires two kinds of usage data: They call the first one transactions, the second one includes connection information to the network etc. Transactions refer to any action related to the Playstation store. For each transaction they store 57 attributes, including the name of the buyer, his day of birth, the product etc. Further, PSN has sent us an overview of the transactions, which we refer to in the following. Transactions, as far as we can see from the answer, refers to downloads, product sale, voucher redemption, and revenue realization. Product sale also includes access to demos of games etc. For any transaction, they store the transaction type, a time stamp, the identifier and pseudonym, the quantity, price, currency, the medium used to buy the product (e.g., PS3, PSP), the product name and a product category.

The second kind of usage data comprises 22 event types (see Table 5). The events have between 4 and 10 attributes, e.g., specifying the account ID, IP address, console ID, name of the credit-card owner etc. As one can see, the data PSN stores is not free of overlap. However, we present it here as given by the PSN response. For our PS3 user, PSN has reported 1760 events stored. This allows to build a comprehensive user profile.

Next, we look at the forwarding practices. PSN has stated in their response that, for purposes given in the privacy policy, data is forwarded to Sony-Computer-Entertainment companies and to external service providers. This is a violation, as this category is too unspecific.

Further, PSN states we cannot guarantee that the data provided is correct and complete. This is insufficient from a legal perspective.

Summing up, PSN has answered our request at the level of detail required by law, in a human readable way. Further, the attributes fit the ones in their privacy policy (cf. Table 2). However, they have not correctly informed us whom they have forwarded our data to, and state that the response might be incomplete.

Game Publisher. From the game publishers, only Ubisoft has answered, stating that they do not store any personal information and referring us to PSN. From all others we did not get any response. This violates the law.

XBL. We have sent 4 requests for information in the name of the Xbox user to XBL, to two different addresses, one in Germany, one in the USA. XBL has answered neither one. From the game publishers, again, Ubisoft has answered our request. They claim to not store any personal data. Activision did not respond. EA games gives a dead contact address in their privacy policy. We have sent a second request to another address but have not obtained any response. Summing up, except for Ubisoft, the providers violate the law.

WIS. We have sent 2 requests for information in the name of the Wii user.

Game-Network Provider. WIS has replied to our request after 20 days, requesting the serial number of our Wii and a copy of the sales slip. One month later, we have received a response that, to answer our request, the MAC address and IP address have to be correlated with our name. They have asked if we agree to this procedure. In their final response, WIS states that they deem the data-protection law not relevant for them, as they perceive the data they store as anonymous. They further say that, in fact, the personalization of the data stored had become possible with the name from our request. However, as they have stored credit card and purchasing information, they obviously have the possibility to correlate the usage data with individuals. Thus, the information stored is at least pseudonymous, i.e., one has the right to request that information. We do not classify this as a violation as WIS has answered our request.

WIS stores three kinds of information: basic information, shop-channel data, and two network-communication logs. See Table 6. Further, they explicitly state which data is stored and processed in which country by which company. Countries they name are Japan and the US.

Table 6. WIS data

basic data	shop data	network communic.
Wii number	purchasing points	game title
serial no	purchasing game	user nickname
device region	balance	login time
country	time / data	current IP
register date	name of game	time of msg.
Wifi MAC	current IP	
Bluetooth MAC		

The WIS response fulfills the requirements from law. However, in their second response WIS states that they will provide only such information where doing so is reasonable at a technical level. This is a violation.

Game-Publisher. We have sent a request for information to Hudson Entertainment. However, we got back the letter with the information that the forward time expired for the address used – the address we took from the privacy policy. We have sent another request to a different address, but did not receive any response. This is a violation.

Summing up, the request for information fails in practice. From 12 requests we have sent, providers have answered only 4, and some replies are incomplete. Further, with up to three months to come to results, users cannot effectively track their personal data.

4.4   Summary

Our evaluation shows that the means to track the flow of one's personal information are insufficient (Q1, Q2). This is due to often vague statements on which information is acquired, stored or processed, and to unspecific formulations regarding the potential receivers in case of data forwarding. The request for information, the most powerful means of a user to track her personal information, yields results that are particularly unsatisfactory.

5   Proposals

In this section we will answer Q3 (What might help to improve the privacy of the user?). We only focus on what we have not already deemed non-transparent or a violation. We derive our proposals from the evaluation just presented.

P1. The forwarding of personal information from the game-network provider or the game publisher to ad servers puts user privacy at risk. Actually, such information is transferred to prove when, where and for how long the ad impressions have been shown. Put differently, millions of users have to trust the game-network providers, game publishers and advertisers. A potential solution might be billing models where personal information is not transferred, or only in case of a breach of the agreement.

P2. Serving a privacy policy common for all services and specific ones for the individual services sounds wise, at least at first sight. However, we have observed that providers overload the common policy, like collecting any practice conceivable, so that the real practices become non-transparent. We propose that there should be individual policies for any service, or the common policy should only cover the practices common to all services addressed.

P3. Today's highly complex consoles require maintenance, i.e., software updates. We do not see any reason why a user has to be registered at the game network to download updates and fixes. We propose, in the style of the WIS distinction between shop and gaming data, a separation of entertainment, shop and maintenance services provided.

6   Conclusions

Game consoles and the corresponding online networks currently offer a variety
of different services. To provide these services, game-network providers collect
and process personal information. For advertisement, they also forward the information to third parties. This puts user privacy at risk.

In this paper we have analyzed the privacy policies of Sony Playstation, Microsoft Xbox-Live and Nintendo Wii, and have compared them to their actual
data-processing practices, as far as they are observable from an outside perspective. Our results are that in many cases the provider practices are non-
transparent or even violate law. In particular, most providers which we have
sent a request for information to did not send any or only an incomplete answer.
Given these insights, we have compiled a list of proposals that might help to
make the practices more transparent and to protect user privacy.

References

1. Spiegel. Playstation 3 im Test – Das sexy Paradox (March 2007),
   http://www.spiegel.de/netzwelt/spielzeug/0,1518,473311,00.html
2. Sony Computer Entertainment America Inc. (SCEA). To offer richer online social
   experience to playstation®3 computer entertainment system owners with facebook
   integration (2009), http://www.scei.co.jp/corporate/release/091118_e.html
3. Interactive Advertising Bureau. In-Game Advertising Measurement Guidelines
   (2009),   http://www.iab.net/iab_products_and_industry_services/508676/
   guidelines/in-game
4. Gross, R., Acquisti, A.: Information Revelation and Privacy in Online Social Networks. In: WPES (2005)
5. Microsoft Press Pass. Xbox unveils entertainment experiences that put everyone
   center stage (2009), http://www.microsoft.com/Presspass/press/2009/jun09/
   06-01E3PR.mspx
6. IGA Worldwide: Landmark IGA-Nielsen Study: 82% of Consumers React Positively to Receiving Contextual In-Game Ads During Game Play
   (June   2008),   http://www.igaworldwide.com/aboutus/pr/pressreleases/
   landmark-iga-nielsen-study.cfm
7. Raabe, O., Dinger, J.: Telemedienrechtliche informationspflichten in p2p-overlay-
   netzen und bei web-services. Computer und Recht (2007)
8. Zhou, B., Pei, J.: Preserving privacy in social networks against neighborhood attacks. In: ICDE (2008)
9. Yang, M., et al.: The effectiveness of 'in-game' advertising: Comparing college students? explicit and implicit memory for brand names. Journal of Advertising (2006)
10. Yan, J., et al.: How much can behavioral targeting help online advertising? In:
    WWW. ACM, New York (2009)
11. Haddadi, H., Guha, S., Francis, P.: Not all adware is badware: Towards privacy-
    aware advertising. In: Godart, C., Gronau, N., Sharma, S., Canals, G. (eds.) I3E
    2009. IFIP Advances in Information and Communication Technology, vol. 305,
    pp. 161–172. Springer, Heidelberg (2009)
12. Bundesdatenschutzgesetz: Bdsg; kommentar (2010)
13. Unabhängiges Landeszentrum für Datenschutz Schleswig-Holstein. Daten-
    schutzrechtliche Bewertung des Einsatzes von Google Analytics. ULD (2009)

Physiological Measurement of Trust-Related Behavior in Trust-Neutral and Trust-Critical Situations

Karin Leichtenstern, Nikolaus Bee, Elisabeth André, Ulrich Berkmüller, and Johannes Wagner

Human Centered Multimedia, Universitätsstr. 6a, D-86159 Augsburg
{Leichtenstern,Bee,Andre,Wagner}@hcm-lab.de

Abstract. In this paper we present results of a user study that we conducted with 21 subjects to investigate whether initial user trust is accompanied by unconscious bodily responses which enable more objective measurements than user reports. In particular, we recorded the user's eye gaze and heart rate to evaluate whether users respond differently when interacting with a web page that is supposed to build initial trust as opposed to a web page that lacks this capability. Our results indicate that there are significantly different response patterns to trust-critical and trust-neutral situations during the interaction with a web page depending on whether the web page has helped users form initial trust or not. Knowledge of trust-related behavior can help to manage user trust at the runtime of the system since different usage phases can continuously be interpreted in order to detect situations which need to be considered to re-cover user trust.

Keywords: Subjective and Objective Measurement, Physiological Data, Trust-related Behavior Measurement, Eye Gaze and Heart Rate.

1 Introduction and Related Work

Trust is a major factor to ensure that a computing system will find acceptance among users. For human to human and similarly for human to computer relationships, we learn to appreciate other people or computing systems and thus, in process of time, we acquire knowledge about their actions and behavior. This is a basis for trust and a mechanism to reduce social complexity [4]. If a human does not have previous knowledge and experience in another human or computing system, a social dilemma emerges since humans are often forced to interact with other unknown humans or things. In this context, we talk about *initial trust* [7] if a user is able to form trust based on her first impression towards an unknown interaction partner. For instance, when interacting with web pages in the Internet, users often do not have previous knowledge about the web pages and their vendors. If the web page does not succeed in building up initial user trust, the user will probably avoid using it and its services. Research has focused on these issues and other problems related to trust in several disciplines, such as

I. Wakeman et al. (Eds.): IFIPTM 2011, IFIP AICT 358, pp. 165–172, 2011.

sociology, psychology, economy and computer science (e.g. [8]). Typically, these different disciplines have several perspectives on trust and consequently definitions. One common agreement is that trust is multi-dimensional consisting of subjective trust triggers, such as the user's willingness of vulnerability, benevolence, reliability, competence, honesty, and openness. These subjective triggers can lead to different levels of attention and engagement as perceived states of user trust in a computing system [3]. There is evidence that trust increases the users willingness to acquire new knowledge (e.g. [6]) since they overcome the feelings of insecurity and risk [8]. We therefore hypothesize that a web page which succeeds in establishing initial user trust is also more likely to motivate users to study its content which potentially can be measured by increased levels of attention and engagement. Various studies indicate that attention and user engagement can be measured using physiological data (e.g. [10]).

In this paper we investigate whether the perceived user behavior of initial trust can be measured by making use of objective measuring methods. Applying observation methods instead of inquiry methods can solve two major issues: (1) Not the user's subjective trust opinion is measured by inquiry methods but instead their actual trust-related behavior by observation methods which potentially provide more realistic and genuine user data. (2) Also, the user's trust behavior is not assessed after the usage but continuously while interacting with the system. By having access to body sensors (e.g. wearable sensors, such as as a pulse meter embedded in clothes) and external sensors (e.g. an eye tracker), the user's attention and engagement might be assessed and thereby indirectly the level of trust. Then, if necessary, the level of user trust can be re-covered by self-adaptively optimizing the system, such as by providing more system transparency or user control. In the following we present a first step towards investigating these trust-related behaviour. We present a user experiment where 21 users were interacting with two web pages in a trust-neutral and a trust-critical phase. One of these web pages was expected to support the formation of initial trust while the other was not. While interacting with the two web pages, physiological data of the user's heart rate (HR) were captured as well as their eye gaze behavior. Later on, the data was analyzed by means of SPSS and discussed how trust-related behavior by means of attention and engagement can be measured objectively.

2   Implementing Initial Trust

In order to objectively investigate initial trust in web pages, we decided to implement two versions of a web page which pretended to provide free software downloads, such as games or office tools. One web page called *WorldofApps* was expected to support initial trust since it followed approved trust guidelines whereas the other web page called *LoadIt* did not support these trust guidelines and thus potentially lacked initial trust. The applied trust guidelines are mainly based on recommendations of Nielsen et al. [9] and Fogg et al. [2]. Among other guidelines, we addressed guidelines in terms of the web page's credibility

Fig. 1. WorldofApps that potentially forms initial user trust (left) and LoadIt that potentially lacks initial trust (right)

by providing contact information and an imprint. Additionally, we considered guidelines with respect to usability, such as an intuitive and easy to use navigation. Since initial or immediate trust is strongly linked to an appropriate and professional appearance [5], we also took into account a calm and serious layout and design for the web page *WorldofApps* (see Figure 1 left) whereas the web page *LoadIt* provided several blinking images and texts (see Figure 1 right). The reliability of the user interface was also covered by dead links for *LoadIt*.

3 The Experiment

The main objective of the experiment was to investigate whether trust is accompanied by typical heart rate and eye gaze patterns. Therefore, we used our two introduced web pages which potentially form initial trust (*WorldofApps*) or not (*LoadIt*) and conducted an experiment.

As independent variable we defined *the applied user interface* with two levels: user interface with initial trust and user interface with a lack of initial trust. The dependent variable was *the initial user trust* in the user interface which was investigated subjectively and objectively. We decided to also subjectively measure trust by a questionnaire in order to validate whether *WorldofApps* was more likely perceived as trustworthy than *LoadIt* and thus whether the two web pages could form initial user trust or not. Our questionnaire based on common trust dimensions which are considered as factors of trust (e.g. [1]). The subjects had to rate their perceived level of the trust dimensions (correctness, security, reliability, credibility, basic usability and appearance) for the corresponding web page on a five point scale from strongly disagree to strongly agree. Additionally, we also asked for a rating of the web page's overall trust level. Thus, we also added a statement in terms of the overall user trust. For objectively measuring the users' behavior we applied sensors for measuring heart rate and an eye tracker to record the users' eye gaze behavior. As group design, we applied the within subjects design and thus each user had to participate in both levels of the independent variable. To prevent positioning effects we counterbalanced the order of the levels.

In the experiment we asked 21 participants (two female and 19 male) with a strong professional background in computer science to complete different tasks with our two web pages and *Amazon*. They were aged between 21 and 27 ($M = 24.8$, $SD = 1.97$). Before we started the experiment, we asked the subjects for a permission to capture physiological and audio-visual data while they were completing their tasks. Then we equipped them with our sensors, re-calibrated the eye tracker and started the capturing. The experiment always started by first filling-in a questionnaire with questions addressing demographics and then by browsing *Amazon* as a period of familiarization. We also used *Amazon* for the users to relax and get used to browsing the Internet for our setting. The participants had to browse *Amazon* for new products for approximately two minutes. Afterwards, the subjects had to fill-in our second questionnaire regarding statements in terms of the subject's perceived trust dimensions and overall user trust for *Amazon*. We also asked for trust ratings of *Amazon* since we expected these ratings as a typical baseline for a trustworthy web page. Followed by the period of familiarization, eleven subjects started by using *WorldofApps* and later on used *LoadIt* while the other ten subjects used *LoadIt* first. For both web pages, the subjects first were asked to freely browse on the web page for about two minutes. We consider this browsing phase as a trust-neutral phase since it did not contain serious trust-critical situations. After the browsing phase, the subjects had to download two predefined software products from the respective web page which took on average 55.4 seconds for *WorldofApps* and 75.4 seconds for *LoadIt*. In contrast to the browsing phase, the download phase contained serious trust-critical situations since the computer might be harmed by the download of a corrupted software product. That is the reason why we call the download phase a trust-critical phase. After the browsing and download phase the participants had to fill-in our questionnaire for the corresponding web page.

4   Subjective Validation of Initial Trust

The results of the questionnaire validate that our participants perceived *WorldofApps* as trustworthier than *LoadIt* (see Fig. 2). A one-way repeated measured ANOVA test showed significant results in all categories: correctness ($F(2, 40) = 73.56$, $p < 0.001$), security ($F(1.4, 27.5) = 94.14$, $p < 0.001$ with sphericity corrections by Greenhouse-Geisser), reliability ($F(2, 40) = 92.5$, $p < 0.001$), credibility ($F(2, 40) = 125.59$, $p < 0.001$), basic usability ($F(2, 40) = 55.13$, $p < 0.001$) and appearance ($F(2, 40) = 75.80$, $p < 0.001$). For each trust dimension the Bonferroni post-hoc tests revealed significant differences between the web pages of *Amazon* and *LoadIt* as well as between the web pages *WorldofApps* and *LoadIt* with $p < 0.001$. For the trust dimensions about security ($p < 0.001$) and credibility ($p < 0.05$) we also had significant differences between *Amazon* and the web page *WorldofApps*.

In terms of overall user trust, we also found highly significant differences between the three web pages ($F(2, 40) = 144.30$, $p < 0.001$). The Bonferroni post-hoc test revealed significant differences between *Amazon* and *WorldofApps* ($p = 0.001$) and between these two web pages and *LoadIt* (each with $p < 0.001$).

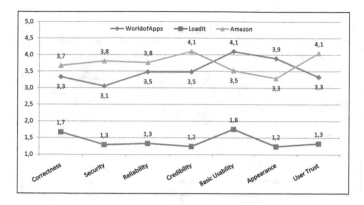

Fig. 2. Results of the Questionnaire (Trust Dimensions and User Trust)

As expected we observed that *WorldofApps* and *Amazon* achieved similar high values of the trust dimensions and the overall user trust which confirms our assumption that the web page *WorldofApps* helps forming initial user trust. In contrast to these two web pages, *LoadIt* failed in all categories which seems to indicate a low level of initial user trust. The bad results of *LoadIt* also appeared when analyzing the feedback of the subjects. Several subjects mentioned that they were reluctant to download software from the bad web page since they were afraid about also downloading a virus or a trojan. One subject even refused to download software from *LoadIt*.

5   Results of the Objective Data

The captured physiological data was split into three sections each with a duration of 30 seconds. The first section (*Browse Begin*) began 15 seconds after the browsing task started and the second section (*Browse End*) ended 15 seconds before this task was finished. The third section (*Download*) began 15 seconds after the download task started which was directly following the browsing task. We decided to use the offset of 15 seconds for each section to reduce interfering factors which are caused by the transition from one phase to another. The trust-neutral phase (browsing task) is covered by the first and second section and the trust-critical phase (download task) is covered by the third section. For the analysis of the objective data we applied two-sided pairwise *t*-tests. One of our 21 subjects was excluded for the analysis of the objective data since some problems occurred with the sensors during the capturing.

The eye tracker (SMI iView X RED) recorded the users' eye gaze with 50 Hz. We computed the average fixation times from the raw gaze data within the single sections (see Fig. 3). We could not find significant differences between the fixation time of the trustworthy web page in comparison to the web page with little initial trust. However, the fixation time computed in milliseconds during the section *Browse Begin* of the trustworthier web page ($M = 353, SD = 118$) was higher (1) compared to the web page with little initial trust ($M = 294,$

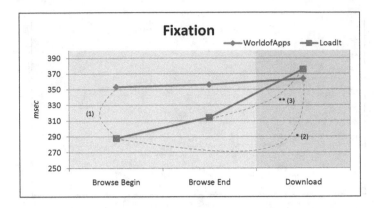

Fig. 3. Fixation time in milliseconds during the three sections. *Green* area indicates the trust-neutral phase and the *red* area the trust-critical phase. ($^{*}p < 0.05$, $^{**}p < 0.01$).

$SD = 96$), $t(18) = 1.8, p = 0.085, r = 0.40$ with a medium effect size. Within the three sections of *LoadIt*, we found a significant increase (2) between *Browse Begin* ($M = 287, SD = 100$) and *Download* ($M = 376, SD = 110$), $t(18) = -2.6, p < 0.05, r = 0.53$ with a large effect. And further we also found a significant increase (3) between *Browse End* ($M = 310, SD = 77$) and *Download* ($M = 376, SD = 110$), $t(18) = -3.3, p < 0.01, r = 0.61$ also with a large effect size. Overall, the users devoted more continuous attention to the web page that succeeded in building initial user trust than to the web page that failed to do so. Only in trust-critical moments, namely when users had to download software the level of attention increased for the little trustworthy web page and achieved the level of attention of the trustworthy page.

The heart rate was computed by measuring the length between the interbeat intervals and averaged within the three sections (see Fig. 4). Comparing the

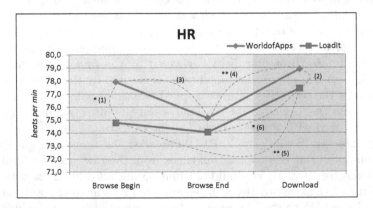

Fig. 4. Heart rate in beats per minute during the three sections. *Green* area indicates the trust-neutral phase and the *red* area the trust-critical phase. ($^{*}p < 0.05$, $^{**}p < 0.01$).

heart beats per minutes of *WorldofApps* ($M = 77.9, SD = 10.8$) with *LoadIt* ($M = 74.8, SD = 10.6$) during *Browse Begin* reveals a significant decrease (1) with a large effect size ($t(19) = 2.5, p < 0.05, r = 0.50$). A decrease (2) between *WorlofApps* ($M = 78.9, SD = 9.7$) and *LoadIt* ($M = 77.4, SD = 9.4$) also appeared during *Download* with a medium effect size ($t(19) = 2.0, p = 0.060, r = 0.42$). Within the three sections of the trustworthy web page, the heart rate was higher (3) at *Browse Begin* ($M = 77.9, SD = 10.8$) compared to *Browse End* ($M = 75.1, SD = 9.0$) with a medium effect size ($t(19) = 1.9, p = 0.077, r = 0.39$). After *Browse End* there was a significant increase (4) towards *Download* ($M = 78.9, SD = 9.7$) with a large effect size ($t(19) = -3.5, p < 0.01, r = 0.63$). Within the three sections of the web page without initial trust, the heart rate was significantly lower (5) at *Browse Begin* ($M = 74.8, SD = 10.6$) compared to *Download* ($M = 77.4, SD = 9.4$) with a large effect size ($t(19) = -3.5, p < 0.01, r = 0.63$). And there is also a significant increase (6) between *Browse End* ($M = 74.1, SD = 9.1$) and *Download* ($M = 77.4, SD = 9.4$) with a medium effect size ($t(19) = -2.4, p < 0.05, r = 0.48$). Based on the results it seems that higher values of the heart rate go along with higher engagement with a task completion. This higher engagement, in turn, seems to be an indicator of a user interface's success to build initial user trust, particularly, since the pattern of higher heart rates appeared independent on whether the users were interacting in a trust-neutral (browsing) or trust-critical (downloading) phase. Furthermore, we found a significant pattern if users changed from a trust-neutral to a trust-critical phase which appeared similarly for a web page that succeed in building initial user trust and also for the web page that failed to do so. Consequently, the heart rate seems to be also an indicator if users change in situations that require more user trust. A further insight is that a trustworthy web page seems to have a relax phase when browsing (trust-neutral phase) since the heart rate decreased until the end of the browsing phase. In contrast to that, the phenomena of a relax phase was not observed for the web page with a lack of initial trust.

6   Conclusion

Based on the results of our experiment we found significantly measured patterns of the user's eye gaze fixation time and heart rate when interacting with a user interface that was subjectively rated as trustworthy or untrustworthy. Additionally, we found significant patterns if users complete trust-neutral tasks (browsing) or trust-critical tasks (downloading) for the trustworthy and untrustworthy rated systems. The results of our user study indicate that users do not take user interfaces with a lack of initial trust seriously which turned out to be reflected by reduced attention and engagement to complete a task. Once the user has changed from a trust-neutral (browsing) to a trust-critical phase (downloading), the user's attention and engagement was significantly increased when using a systems that lacks of initial trust. In this situations the users seem to be forced to change their behavior towards an increased level of engagement and attention for not being harmed by the system. As far as we know we are the first who did investigations of the user's actual trust-related behavior by means of physiological data. Our work provides a first step towards the development of methods that continuously measure user trust based on behavioral data. Such methods bear the advantage over traditional trust measurements that they enable a more objective assessment of user trust. They are not based on subjective self reports which have to be provided by users either after the interaction or cause an interruption of the experience. During the usage time, our methods provide important knowledge about the users and their behavior in order to automatically manage user trust by means of self-adaptations, such as by presenting more system transparency and user control. In future work we would like to validate our results by means of a setting that has several changes between trust-critical and trust-neutral situations.

Acknowledgement

This research is sponsored by *OC-Trust* (FOR 1085) of the German research foundation (DFG).

References

1. Chen, S., Li, J.: An empirical research on consumer trust in e-commerce. In: IEEC 2009: Proceedings of the 2009 International Symposium on Information Engineering and Electronic Commerce, pp. 56–61. IEEE Computer Society, Los Alamitos (2009)
2. Fogg, B.J., Marshall, J., Laraki, O., et al.: What makes web sites credible?: a report on a large quantitative study. In: CHI 2001: Proceedings of the SIGCHI conference on Human factors in computing systems, pp. 61–68. ACM, New York (2001)
3. Hughes, L.W., Avey, J.B., Norman, S.M.: A study of supportive climate, trust, engagement and organizational commitment. Journal of Business & Leadership: Research, Practice and Teaching 4(2), 51–59 (2008)
4. Luhmann, N.: Vertrauen; ein Mechanismus der Reduktion sozialer Komplexitat. F. Enke, Stuttgart (1968)
5. Lumsden, J.: Triggering trust: to what extent does the question influence the answer when evaluating the perceived importance of trust triggers? In: BCS HCI 2009: Proceedings of the 2009 British Computer Society Conference on Human-Computer Interaction, pp. 214–223. British Computer Society (2009)
6. Mayer, R.C., Davis, J.H., Schoorman, F.D.: An integrative model of organizational trust. The Academy of Management Review 20(3), 709–734 (1995)
7. McKnight, D., Cummings, L., Chervany, N.: Initial trust formation in new organizational relationships. The Academy of Management Review 23(3), 473–490 (1998)
8. McKnight, D.H., Choudhury, V., Kacmar, C.: Developing and validating trust measures for e-commerce: An integrative typology. Info. Sys. Research 13(3), 334–359 (2002)
9. Nielsen, J., Snyder, C., Molich, R., Farrell, S.: E-Commerce User Experience. Nielsen Norman Gr. (2001)
10. Pecchinenda, A., Smith, C.A.: The affective significance of skin conductance activity during a difficult problem-solving task. Cognition & Emotion 10(5), 481–504 (1996)

Trusted Principal-Hosted Certificate Revocation

Sufatrio[1] and Roland H.C. Yap[2]

[1] Temasek Laboratories, National University of Singapore, Singapore
tslsufa@nus.edu.sg
[2] School of Computing, National University of Singapore, Singapore
ryap@comp.nus.edu.sg

Abstract. Public Key Infrastructure is a key infrastructure for secure and trusted communication on the Internet. This paper revisits the problem of providing timely certificate revocation focusing on the needs of mobile devices. We survey existing schemes then present a new approach where the principal's server functions as the directory for *its own* revocation information. We evaluate the properties and trust requirements in this approach, and propose two new schemes, CREV-I and CREV-II, which meet the security requirements and performance goals. Evaluation of CREV shows it is more lightweight on the verifier and more scalable at the CA and the principals while providing near real-time revocation.

1 Introduction

Public Key Infrastructure (PKI) is a primary infrastructure relied on for disseminating trust as well as ensuring secure communications and transactions over the Internet. Certificate revocation, namely giving notice that a public and private key pair is no longer valid despite still being within its validity period, is a major challenge in PKI [1,2]. In X.509 based PKI [3,4], certificate revocation is conducted mainly by two standardized mechanisms, namely Certificate Revocation List (CRL) [4] and Online Certificate Status Protocol (OCSP) [5]. These two mechanisms, however, have their own shortcomings. CRL imposes a high bandwidth requirement on the verifier, and (generally) provides a low timeliness guarantee. It is common for a Certification Authority (CA) to update its CRL only *daily* (as suggested in [6]). OCSP offers a potentially real-time recency assurance, but puts a high online computational requirement on the CA.

This paper revisits the problem of providing timely and lightweight certificate revocation taking into account two important *emerging trends*. Firstly, the growth of Internet-connected mobile devices requires a revocation mechanism to be *lightweight on the verifier* due to the limited resources on the device. Secondly, the growth in volume and value of Internet transactions increases the need for revocation services with *higher* timeliness guarantees (i.e. much less than a day).

In this paper, we first survey various existing certificate revocation schemes and characterize them using our framework for classifying revocation schemes. We identify a new design choice which is not well-investigated to date, and then propose revocation schemes based on placing trust on a *principal* as a scalable distribution point for more timely revocation information. The rationale is that a

I. Wakeman et al. (Eds.): IFIPTM 2011, IFIP AICT 358, pp. 173–189, 2011.

verifier needs to place trust on the principal with respect to the ensuing communication/transactions anyway. Unlike existing schemes employing repository(ies) as revocation distribution points, having principal as a personal repository brings the following unique advantages to the parties involved:

- For each validity time interval, the CA needs to produce revocation information for a principal only *once*, and then sends/pushes the information to the principal. This significantly reduces the CA's workload as there are usually far fewer principals than verifiers. The CA's overhead thus becomes independent from the number of queries from verifiers.
- A principal stores its latest revocation information for its own verifiers to access and verify. Compared to a centralized repository approach, this offers more locality of processing, decentralization, and more balanced overheads, allowing more scalable revocation while meeting the security requirements.
- Verifiers do not need to contact the CA (or repository) to validate a certificate. Rather, they deal directly with the relevant principal. This will give more privacy protection than OCSP. Yet, the CA can still revoke a principal's certificate since all revocation information originates from the CA. When a principal cannot be contacted, other existing revocation mechanisms can still alternatively be used.

In addition, the setting also addresses the incentive problem on certificate revocation information management and dissemination [2].

We analyze our proposed schemes, CREV-I and CREV-II, to show that they meet the security and trust requirements as well as the performance goals. We then evaluate our schemes together with several well known existing schemes to show that our CREV schemes can provide near real-time timeliness (e.g. 10 minutes) while being lightweight on the verifier and more scalable than OCSP.

The rest of this paper is organized as follows. Section 2 presents a framework for analyzing revocation schemes. Section 3 describes our two CREV schemes, and analyzes their trust and security requirements. Section 4 compares the performance of CREV with several existing ones. Section 5 finally concludes.

2   A Framework for Classifying Revocation Schemes

Throughout this paper, we refer to the subject of a certificate as *principal*, the principal of an Extended Validation Certificate (EVC) as *EVCP*, and the party verifying certificates as *verifier*. *Certificate Status Information (CSI)* [7] denotes the CA's released information pertinent to the validity of a certificate. CSI thus encompasses CRL data, OCSP messages, and hash tokens in CRS/NOVOMODO [8,9]. *Certificate Management Ancillary Entity (CMAE)* denotes the designated repository from which a verifier may obtain the CSI. The *revocation latency* is the bound on the time between a CA making a revocation record and when that information becomes available to the verifiers. A low revocation latency means a high *revocation timeliness guarantee*. In a per-certificate revocation scheme, such as CRS/NOVOMODO, OCSP and ours, we assume that the CA will not unnecessarily delay publishing the CSI for a revocation event.

We now specify the *security* and *performance* requirements of a revocation scheme. In this paper, we consider a certification system based on X.509 PKI model [3,4] where an issued certificate is valid *throughout* its issued lifetime unless otherwise revoked by means of the revocation mechanism in place. We simply refer to the CA as the issuer of a CSI. A certificate revocation scheme should provide the following security guarantees:

(Sec_1) **CSI availability:** makes a pertinent CSI available to each verifier that wishes to validate a not-yet-expired certificate issued by the CA.

(Sec_2) **Authenticity of CSI:** allows the verifier obtaining a CSI related to a certificate to verify (using strong cryptographic techniques) that the CSI originates from the CA and its integrity is preserved. The verifier must also be able to unambiguously determine the revocation status of the certificate.

(Sec_3) **Revocation timeliness:** specifies the validity period of the CSI, which must be less than a pre-determined maximum time bound.

(Sec_4) **Definition of revocation mechanism and CSI access point:** ensures that the certificate revocation mechanism(s) operated by the CA, together with the identity (including its accessible address on the network) of the access point where the CSI can be obtained, is clearly defined in the signed message portion of the certificate.

(Sec_5) **Assurance on certificate principal identity:** provides trustworthiness on the identity of the principal of a certificate (i.e. name, domain name). This is intended to protect against impersonation (e.g. phishing) attacks.

(Sec_6) **Privacy of verifiers:** ensures the privacy of verifiers validating a principal. Although the CA is trusted for managing certificates, the CA's knowledge on transactions involving a certificate can constitute a privacy leak.

In addition, the performance of the revocation scheme is critical in practice, especially on mobile devices. Thus we have the following performance goals:

($Perf_1$) **Scalability of the CA and CSI-Repository:** The bandwidth, storage and computational costs incurred on the CA and the CSI repository(ies) should scale well with the number of verifiers served.

($Perf_2$) **Performance constraints of the verifier:** Verifiers such as mobile devices impose special constraints in that they require revocation to be lightweight, i.e. low in computational, storage and bandwidth costs.

($Perf_3$) **Incentives for CSI dissemination:** There should be strong and clear economic incentives for the entities involved in the dissemination of CSI.

2.1 A Framework for Certificate Revocation Schemes

We characterize certificate revocation schemes based on the following four important design options:

(P_1) **Placement of directory:** The *directory* holding a copy of CSI issued by the CA, can be placed in either: the *CMAE* as a designated repository, the *verifier*, or the *principal*. Some schemes do not employ a directory, e.g. NOVOMODO [9] and OCSP where the CA is the Responder.

Table 1. Design choices in revocation schemes – options P_1 and P_2

Directory Placement	CSI Coverage Scope		
	All CA's Certs	**Subset of Certs**	**Individual Cert**
No directory (handled by CA)			NOVOMODO [9], OCSP [5], H-OCSP [10], MBS-OCSP [11]
CMAE	CRL [4], HS [12], CRT [13], 2-3 tree CRT [14]	Partitioned CRL, CSPR [15]	CRS [8]
Verifier	CPR [16], BCPR[17]		
Principal			***CREV-I, CREV-II***

(P_2) **Scope of released CSI:** A released CSI is verifiable to determine the revocation status(es) for either: *all* certificates, *a subset of* certificates, or *a single* certificate issued by the CA. CRL data gives the status of either all (as in standard CRL) or a subset of (as in Partitioned CRL or also known as CRL Distribution Points [4]) certificates. In contrast, the CSI in CRS, NOVOMODO or OCSP accounts for an individual certificate.

(P_3) **Positive or negative status representation:** The CA can state the status of certificates using either a *negative* (black-listing) approach, or *positive* approach where the status of each certificate is explicitly stated. Note the negative approach can only work when the scope of CSI is for all CA's certificates or a well-defined subset of CA's certificates.

(P_4) **Use of linked CSIs for subsequent status updates:** A CSI usually comes signed by the CA. The signed CSI may contain additional information aimed at allowing subsequent (periodic) release of more compact and unsigned CSI to update the status of certificate(s), e.g. the tip of a hash chain in CRS or the root and several interior node values of a Merkle Hash Tree in [10,11]. We characterize a revocation scheme based on *whether or not* it employs linked additional information for subsequent status updates.

We have purposely omitted several possible design options, such as periodic versus non-periodic CSI issuance, and pull versus push CSI access between the CA/CMAE and verifiers. This is because we assume standard X.509-based PKI practices as well as typical PKI-based applications. Thus, we focus on the information flow and representation of the CSI, which we believe are the main factors that characterize a revocation scheme.

Table 1 characterizes numerous existing revocation schemes based on properties P_1 and P_2. We also make the following observations. For revocation schemes with the principal as the directory, a per-certificate CSI is generally preferred as a principal is usually concerned with its own verifiers. Per-certificate CSI is also usually better for performance. Revocation schemes with CSI for all certificates can be transformed into subset-based schemes as long as the certificate space can be partitioned clearly. Transformation into per-certificate (individual) CSI is possible only if a positive CSI representation is employed. Having either the

CA or CMAE(s) as the directory is simply a matter of repository delegation. However, for high timeliness or online revocation schemes (e.g. OCSP), a CMAE must have access to the revocation statuses hosted by the CA, and must be as trusted as the CA with respect to informing the certificate status.

2.2 Survey of Existing Certificate Revocation Schemes

CRL [4] is presently the most widely supported revocation scheme. However, it is also widely known to have serious shortcomings. Firstly, the CRL may eventually grow to a cumbersome size in very large PKIs [18]. Secondly, the downloaded CRLs may be mostly useless since more than 90% of the information can be irrelevant to the verifiers [18]. Lastly, CRL (generally) does not offer adequate timely revocation guarantees. There are several improvements on the basic CRL mechanism, such as CRL Distribution Points, Delta CRLs, and Indirect CRLs [4]. However, all these schemes still put the same requirement on the verifier to obtain a complete or subset of revocation list, including the unrelated entries.

OCSP [5] was proposed to provide more timely certificate status checking. It returns the status of an inquired certificate in an online fashion. However, it imposes high computational and network requirements on OCSP Responder [19]. Furthermore, there is a privacy problem since the Responder knows all verifiers dealing with a principal. Several modifications have been proposed on OCSP. Like our scheme (CREV-I), H-OCSP [10] and MBS-OCSP [11] employ a hash-chaining technique. However, they require the CA to cater for a *potentially large number of verifiers* while CREV-I reduces it to just the EVC principals. Thus, the CA's bandwidth and storage requirements in [10,11] remain high.

Certificate Revocation Status (CRS) [8] makes revocation more efficient by periodic release of compact hash-chain information. It assumes the use of a CMAE. The CA chooses a one-way hash function $H()$, a time interval period d, and the length of a hash chain ℓ. The lifetime of the certificate is: $d(\ell+1)$. The CA then includes the following into a certificate: $HashAlgID$ (defining $H()$), d, ℓ, issue and expiration times, and two numbers Y and N for "valid" and "revoked" status respectively. The CA generates two secret random numbers Y_0 and N_0, with $Y = H^\ell(Y_0)$ and $N = H(N_0)$. On the i-th time interval after the certificate's issuance, the CA sends to the CMAE(s): a signed timestamped string containing all serial numbers of issued and not-yet-expired certificates; and V_i for each certificate, where: $V_i = H^{\ell-i}(Y_0)$ if a certificate is valid, or $V_i = N_0$ if it is revoked. The CMAE sends V_i in reply to a query from a verifier. The verifier checks the certificate status by comparing $H(V_i)$ with N, or $H^i(V_i)$ with Y. NOVOMODO [9] extended CRS using SHA-1 and avoids centralized CMAE(s).

Aiello et al. [12] proposed an improvement to CRS called "Hierarchical Scheme" (HS) to reduce the CA-to-CMAE communication. Yet, it can significantly increase the certificate size. Kocher [13] proposed Certificate Revocation Tree (CRT) employing Merkle Hash Tree (MHT). It however has a high computational cost to update the CRT. Naor and Nissim [14] extended the CRT by using a more suitable data structure, a 2-3 tree. In these three schemes, the data structures maintain the statuses of *all* certificates.

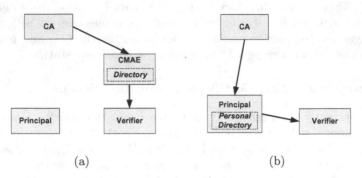

(a)   (b)

Fig. 1. Comparison of CSI communication flow: (a) typical revocation schemes (with CMAE); (b) Revocation setting with principal as the directory as in CREV schemes

Certificate Push Revocation (CPR) [16] and Beacon CPR (BCPR) [17] suggest placing the directory at the verifiers. Although the schemes may work for highly connected and high-bandwidth verifiers, it seems impractical otherwise and even less so for mobile verifiers. They also suggest placing the cache on the ISPs, but that begs a question of economic incentive for the ISPs to do so.

Certificate Space Partitioning with Renewals (CSPR) [15] was proposed to reduce the high CA-to-CMAE communication cost such as in CRS. The CA divides its certificates into partitions, and signs the CSI for each partition which contains the *status bits* of all certificates in the partition. If there is no status change for the certificates in a partition, the CA renews the partition by releasing hash-chain information whose tip is embedded in the partition's CSI. CSPR employs *CMAEs* as directories, whereas CREV uses *principals* as directories.

3   CREV: Principal-Hosted Revocation

Using our framework, we have identified a new design option where the directory for *an individual* certificate is placed at the respective *principal's server*. The principal's server thus acts as a distribution point for its own CSI. This is advantageous as it allows for the co-location of web/transaction server with the corresponding CSI distribution point. Note that CREV schemes can co-exist with other schemes such as timely CRL. Hence, if an EVCP's server happens to be temporarily unavailable, the verifier can resort to other revocation mechanisms, such as downloading the CRL.

Figure 1 depicts the CSI communication flow between the parties involved. In this setting, we propose additional requirements for security and efficiency:

(Req_1) **Principal's domain and server:** A principal must have an exclusively controlled domain name and the associated publicly-accessible server.

(Req_2) **Per-certificate CSI with positive representation:** Since a principal provides a CSI access service only to its own verifiers, it requires a positive status representation to confirm the goodness (*"liveness"*) of a certificate.

3.1   CREV Revocation Schemes

We propose two revocation schemes, called CREV-I and CREV-II, which make use of the principal-hosted revocation setting. CREV schemes leverage on the availability of the *Extended-Validation Certificates (EVCs)* from the CA/Browser Forum so as to ensure a verified domain name and the associated server (Req_1).

Two existing revocation schemes, CRS/NOVOMODO and OCSP, meet the Requirement Req_2. We enhance these two schemes, resulting in the two CREV schemes, to also achieve the previously stated Requirements Sec_1–Sec_6 and $Perf_1$–$Perf_3$. CREV-I takes advantage of available online schemes like OCSP. For each EVC, the CA produces *only one* OCSP Response per time interval, which is sent and subsequently hosted by the EVC principal's server. CREV-II improves CREV-I by making use of hash-chaining technique for lightweight subsequent updates. Unlike in CRS/NOVOMODO, CREV-II sets up a *session-based* hash-chaining service between the CA and an EVCP. Hence, it shortens the length of the hash chain for a faster verifier's operation and a significantly reduced CA's storage requirement.

To identify the availability of a CREV revocation scheme, we define the following extension to an EV Certificate:

$$CREV\ Extension ::= CREV\ Scheme, Transfer\ Mechanism \qquad (1)$$

CREV Scheme identifies the used CREV scheme, and *Transfer Mechanism* defines the CSI transfer mechanism, e.g. HTTP. The CSI for the EVC is accessible on the EVCP's server on the pre-determined URI (explained later).

With respect to Properties P_1–P_4, CREV realizes the following options:

- (P_1:) The directory is placed in the (server belonging to the) *principal*.
- (P_2:) The released CSI provides assurance for *a single certificate*.
- (P_3:) The status of a certificate is stated using a *positive* representation.
- (P_4:) CREV-I does not employ any linked CSI technique, whereas CREV-II makes use of a hash chain technique. We do not consider a scheme using MHT since it can potentially increase the size of the certificate.

3.2   CREV-I: Session-Based Online Status Scheme

CREV-I takes advantage of a CA's ability to support an online status notification service such as OCSP. Unlike OCSP, the CA in CREV-I produces *only one* OCSP Response for an EVCP per time interval (regardless of the number of verifiers). To support CREV-I, the CA includes the following in a certificate: (i) *CREV Extension* (Eq. 1); and (ii) *CREV-I Extension*, which contains: URI for CA's nonce (URI_{CA_nonce}) and URI for the latest OCSP Response (URI_{latest_OCSP}).

Similar to OCSP, the CA's availability for a request message might be attacked with denial of service by a flood of requests to the CA, including replaying previously valid request messages. To deal with this, we require every incoming *SubscriptionRequest* message (see CREV-I Step 1 below) to be signed by the EVCP. We also require the message to carry T, which is either: a timestamp of the current time, or a CA's nonce accessible from URI_{CA_nonce}. This nonce is regularly updated by the CA at a pre-determinedly short time interval.

The following protocol establishes a CSI subscription session between CA and EVCP. We assume that serial number (S_No) and CA's name (CA_ID) are sufficient to identify a unique certificate. The notation $\langle M \rangle_{K_A^{-1}}$ denotes a message M which is signed using the private key of principal A (i.e. K_A^{-1}); whereas $nonce_X$ denotes a nonce from X.

1. $EVCP \rightarrow CA$: "Subscription Request"= $\langle$ SubsReq, EVCP_ID, CA_ID, $\quad\quad\quad\quad\quad\quad$ S_No, T, $nonce_{EVCP}$, t_{EVCP}, d_{EVCP}, SigAlgID $\rangle_{K_{EVCP}^{-1}}$.

   where: $SubsReq$ = header indicating a Subscription Request message;
   $EVCP\_ID$ = identity (i.e. domain name) of the EVCP;
   T = either a timestamp, or CA's nonce accessible on URI_{CA_nonce};
   t_{EVCP} = EVCP's proposed lifetime of the established session;
   d_{EVCP} = EVCP's proposed time interval between two OCSP Responses;
   $SigAlgID$ = identification for the signing algorithm.

2. CA $\quad\quad\quad\quad$: If T or K_{EVCP}^{-1} is incorrect, then abort.

3. $CA \rightarrow EVCP$: "Subscription Reply"= $\langle$ SubsReply, EstStatus, CA_ID, $\quad\quad\quad\quad\quad\quad$ EVCP_ID, S_No, $nonce_{EVCP}$, CertStatus, d_{CA}, $\quad\quad\quad\quad\quad\quad$ SessStart, SessExpiry, $nonce_{CA}$, SigAlgID $\rangle_{K_{CA}^{-1}}$.

   where: $SubsReply$ = header indicating a Subscription Reply message;
   $EstStatus$ = status indicator for a successful subscription establishment;
   $CertStatus$ = status of the EVC;
   d_{CA} = selected time interval between two consecutive OCSP Responses.
   The session's lifetime $(t_{CREV\_I}) = SessExpiry - SessStart$.

4. $EVCP$ $\quad\quad\quad$: if $nonce_{EVCP}$ or K_{CA}^{-1} incorrect,
   $\quad\quad\quad\quad\quad\quad$ or $EstStatus$ is unsuccesful, then abort.

5. $EVCP \rightarrow CA$: "Subscription ACK"= $\langle$ SubsACK, EVCP_ID, CA_ID, $\quad\quad\quad\quad\quad\quad$ S_No, $nonce_{CA}$, SigAlgID $\rangle_{K_{EVCP}^{-1}}$.

   where: $SubsACK$ = header indicating a Subscription ACK message.

6. $EVCP$ $\quad\quad\quad$: Establish an update association with CA.

7. CA $\quad\quad\quad\quad$: If $nonce_{CA}$ and K_{EVCP}^{-1} is incorrect, then abort.

After Step 7, the CA starts delivering (pushing) OCSP Response messages to the EVCP every d_{CA} time interval for ℓ_{CA} times, or until the certificate is revoked. Upon receipt of every OCSP Response from the CA, the EVCP puts it at URI_{latest_OCSP}. Note that the periodically released OCSP Responses contain no requester's nonce. As such, the EVCP and the verifier must verify the freshness of an OCSP Response by checking the included values of `thisUpdate` and `nextUpdate` to be current. The CA must properly set a Response's validity period (i.e. `nextUpdate - thisUpdate`) to d_{CA}.

3.3   CREV-II: Session-Based Hash-Chaining Scheme

Despite their benefits, CRS and NOVOMODO can incur significant overheads when the hash chains employed are rather long since the length of the hash chain increases with timeliness. The verifiers need to perform more repeated hash computations, and the CA must allocate more storage for the hash chains. CREV-II improves CRS/NOVOMODO by setting up a *session-based* hash-chaining service between the CA and an EVCP. The idea is that each EVCP and the CA establish a secure session using the "*Session Establishment*" protocol given below. Thus, CREV-II employs a hash chain, but the length of the hash chain is much shorter. CREV-II also represents an improvement over CREV-I by allowing lightweight subsequent status updates using a (one-way) hash chain.

In a published certificate, the CA includes: (i) *CREV Extension* (Eq. 1); and (ii) *CREV-II Extension*, which contains: URI for the CA's nonce (URI_{CA_nonce}), URI for the *Session Reply* message ($URI_{hashchain\_session}$), and URI for the hash-chain token (URI_{hash_token}). The following protocol is executed by the CA and EVCP to establish a hash chain session on a valid EVC.

1. $EVCP \rightarrow CA$: "*Session Request*" = $\langle SessReq, EVCP\_ID, CA\_ID, S\_No,$
   $T, nonce_{EVCP}, SigAlgID \rangle_{K_{EVCP}^{-1}}$.
   where: $SessReq$ = header indicating a Session Request message;
   T = timestamp or a CA's nonce accessible at URI_{CA_nonce}.
2. CA : If T or K_{EVCP}^{-1} is incorrect, then abort.
3. $CA \rightarrow EVCP$: "*Session Reply*" = $\langle SessReply, ReplyStatus, CA\_ID,$
   $EVCP\_ID, nonce_{EVCP}, S\_No, CertStatus, HashAlgID,$
   $d, Y, N, SessStart, SessExpiry, nonce_{CA}, SigAlgID \rangle_{K_{CA}^{-1}}$.
   where: $SessReply$ = header indicating a Session Reply message;
   $ReplyStatus$ = status indicator for a successful session establishment;
   $HashAlgID, d, Y, N$ = hash chain parameters in CRS (see Section 2.2);
   $SessStart$ and $SessExpiry$ = the start and end times of the session.
4. $EVCP$: If $nonce_{EVCP}$ or K_{CA}^{-1} incorrect, or $ReplyStatus$ is unsuccesful, then abort.
5. $EVCP \rightarrow CA$: "*Session ACK*" = $\langle SessACK, EVCP\_ID, CA\_ID, nonce_{CA},$
   $S\_No, SigAlgID \rangle_{K_{EVCP}^{-1}}$.
   where: $SessACK$ = header indicating a Session ACK message.
6. $EVCP$: Put *Session Reply* from Step 3 at $URI_{hashchain\_session}$;
   Establish an association for hash chain updates with CA.
7. CA : If $nonce_{CA}$ and K_{EVCP}^{-1} is incorrect, then abort.
   Start providing timely hash-chain token updates until the session expires, or the EV certificate is revoked.

The established session is good for time interval $t_{CREV\_II} = SessExpiry - SessStart$. For a valid certificate, on the i-th time interval (for $1 \leq i \leq \ell_{CREV\_II}$) after $SessStart$, the CA releases the latest hash chain token (V_i) to the EVCP as in CRS/NOVOMODO. The EVCP always puts the most recent V_i that it receives from the CA at URI_{hash_token}.

The verifier obtains the *Session Reply* from the specified $URI_{hashchain\_session}$, and V_i from URI_{hash_token}. It validates K_{CA}^{-1} in the *Session Reply*, and determines that the EVC is still valid if $H^i(V_i) = Y$, or that the EVC is revoked if $H(V_i) = N$. Note that the length of the hash chain in a CREV-II session is $\ell_{CREV\_II} = \frac{t_{CREV\_II}}{d} - 1$, which is much smaller than CRS/NOVOMODO. Thus, the workload for the verifier's repeated hash operations is much reduced. The CA also stores and keep tracks of a much shorter (session-wide) hash chain.

3.4   Evaluating CREV on the Requirements

We now evaluate how the CREV schemes satisfy the trust and security requirements Sec_1–Sec_6:

- (Sec_1:) By definition, each EVC is required to have the associated publicly-available server. This server is expected to be continuously up and running in order to provide related online service(s). Given a reliable communication channel between the CA and this server, the CSI is thus available for access.
- (Sec_2:) The OCSP Response in CREV-I is always signed by the CA. In CREV-II, the periodically released hash tokens are unsigned. However, due to the signed hash chain tip and the use of one-way hash chain, a verifier can easily verify as to whether a hash token originates from the CA.
- (Sec_3:) The validity of an OCSP Response in CREV-I can be determined by checking the values of thisUpdate and nextUpdate (as two fields in the standard OCSP Response). The timeliness guarantee of hash token updates in CREV-II can be seen from the *Session Reply* message signed by the CA.
- (Sec_4:) The employed revocation scheme can be identified from the *CREV Extension*, in which the EVC principal serves as the CSI access point.
- (Sec_5:) Our use of EV certificates provides a strong protection on both the principal's name and server against impersonation attacks.
- (Sec_6:) Since a verifier obtain the CSI of an EVCP directly from its server, with whom the verifier will potentially conduct online transactions afterwards, CREV schemes do not reveal the status queries to any other third party including the CA. The EVCP may find out the (addresses of) verifiers who obtains its CSI but do not proceed with any online transactions afterwards. However, the information obtained by the EVCP in this case is negative in nature, e.g. who did not (proceed to) use the provided service. There is still less information about the verifiers than the CA (which is an external party with respect to the transactions) can obtain in OCSP.

Now we analyze how CREV addresses the performance requirements:

- ($Perf_1$:) In CREV, the EVCP servers are self-managed (i.e. independent from the CA), and deal only with *their own* respective verifiers. Thus, the workload of CSI access is now distributed to the EVCP's servers, which are expected to have sufficient capacity to meet the respective transaction volumes. As such, potential bottlenecks (such as the CA in OCSP) is avoided.
- ($Perf_2$:) Due to our use of per-certificate CSI, the verifier's bandwidth requirement is low. Only one signature verification operation by the verifier is needed in CREV-I. CREV-II makes use of a session-based hash chaining in order to reduce the verifier's required repeated hash operations.
- ($Perf_3$:) An EVCP's server has a strong incentive to provide reliable and timely CSI access service for its *own* transactions. Also notice that the CA

provides the service to EVCPs. Hence, CREV also allows for a workable economic model in which the CA charges EVCPs, rather than the verifiers, for the rendered CSI services. It also has economic advantages to schemes employing the verifier's ISP as directory [16,17]. CREV thus addresses the incentive problem on CSI management and dissemination [2].

We remark that the overhead of session management is incurred only between the CA and EVCPs. Nevertheless, there are far fewer EVCPS than verifiers. Thus, we expect the overhead to be manageable. Later, we show that the CA's cryptographic overheads of CREV schemes are much lower than OCSP.

We project that the CREV schemes are practical even with near a real-time timeliness guarantee from 10 to 1 minute. A 10-minute guarantee may already be considered short-lived in many environments. A 1-minute guarantee could be even considered as being "indistinguishable" from a real-time service due to potential clock time differences among the entities [9]. The recency requirements in CREV are set by the CA and EVCP, and not the verifier. But, with a high timeliness guarantee, a verifier receives greater assurance.

4   A Performance Evaluation of CREV

We evaluate CREV schemes with others using a simple analytical model to measure the costs with a single-CA system during the *steady-state condition*, i.e. when certificate expiration is balanced by the new certificates added. This approach is commonly adopted by many papers [20,21]. It allows us to focus on the stable behavior of the revocation schemes and omit external variable factors. Since we consider a certification system with a uniform certificate lifetime β, the steady-state condition thus takes place after β days from the *first* certificate generation in the system, i.e. the time interval $(\beta, +\infty)$.

The commonly made assumptions when analyzing revocation schemes under the steady state, which we also make, are below. The total number of principals and the corresponding valid certificates (N) is constant. Certificates have the same lifetime (of β days), where b percent of N certificates are revoked within β days. The revocation of a certificate occurs at the half of its lifetime. The time interval between two successive CRL releases (Δt) is constant, which is the same as the time interval between two successive certificate generations (ΔX). Certificate issuance takes place at a constant rate (of $\frac{N \cdot \Delta t}{\beta \cdot 1,440}$ per issuance). (We use time units in minutes, and $1,440 =$ the number of minutes in a day). When a certificate is revoked, a new certificate is issued immediately to replace it.

Using a model where $\Delta X = \Delta t$, we thus consider the situation where the certificate issuance and the CRL release take place continuously. Table 2 summarizes the notation and parameter values used in our analytical evaluation.

Performance Comparison Metrics. We use the following notation to denote various costs incurred in a particular revocation scheme: $Ovh_A =$ computation time needed by entity A (in seconds), $Bw_{A-B} =$ network bandwidth needed from entity A to B (in MB), and $Stor_A =$ storage needed on A (in MB). The entities involved are: CA, Ver (indicating a verifier), $CMAE$, and $EVCP$.

Table 2. Notation and parameter values used in the performance model

Symbol	Description	Unit	Value(s)	
N	Number of valid (non-revoked) and not-yet-expired certificates	-	100,000	
β	Issued lifetime of a certificate	days	365	
b	Percentage of certificates revoked	-	$0.1 = 10\%$	
δ	Revocation latency	mins	60	10
$\Delta X = \delta$	Time interval between two successive certificate generations	mins	60	10
$\Delta t = \delta$	Time interval between two successive CRL releases	mins	60	10
$d = \delta$	Time interval for periodic hash-token release	mins	60	10
t_{CREV_I}, t_{CREV_II}	Session lifetime in CREV-I and CREV-II	mins	720	180
U	Total number of CRL and hash-token releases per day	-	$1,440/\delta$	
V	Number of verifiers	-	30,000,000	
Q_{V_daily}	Average daily queries needed by a verifier	-	30	
$Q_{V\_issued\_daily}$	Average daily queries *issued* by a verifier	-	$min(U, Q_{V\_daily})$	
Q_{daily}	Total average daily queries received by CA/CMAE	-	$V \cdot Q_{V\_issued\_daily}$	
$Q_{per\_cert\_daily}$	Average daily queries on a certificate	-	Q_{daily}/N	

To compare different schemes, we use the following cost metrics:

1. Certificate creation cost: Ovh_{CA}.
2. Update costs: Ovh_{CA}, Ovh_{CMAE} (Ovh_{EVCP}) and $Bw_{CA-CMAE}$ ($Bw_{CA-EVCP}$).
3. Query costs: Ovh_{CA}, Ovh_{CMAE} (Ovh_{EVCP}), $Bw_{CMAE-Ver}$ ($Bw_{EVCP-Ver}$) and Ovh_{Ver}.
4. Storage requirement at one point in time: $Stor_{CA}$ and $Stor_{CMAE}$ ($Stor_{EVCP}$).
5. Timeliness: the revocation latency (δ), which also represents the *window of vulnerability* of the revocation scheme.

For metrics (1) to (3), we measure the total *cost per day*. We use $D\_\langle Cost \rangle$ to denote *the daily cost* of a cost metric. In order to have a more compact notation, we abuse the notation slightly and write $\forall A$ for all instances of entity A, and $\exists A$ for a single instance of A. Thus, for example, $D\_Bw_{CMAE-\exists Ver}$ denotes the daily bandwidth cost between a CMAE and a single verifier, whereas $D\_Bw_{CMAE-\forall Ver}$ is the daily bandwidth needed by a CMAE to all the verifiers.

4.1 A Simple Performance Model for Revocation Schemes

We derive the costs for the following schemes using a simple analysis model: CRL (with one CMAE employed), OCSP (with the CA as the Responder), CRS (with one CMAE employed), and our two CREV schemes. For bandwidth calculation, we do not consider the cost due to the underlying network transfer mechanism(s). We use L_{Msg} to denote the length of message portion Msg. Due to space reasons, we describe the costs compactly as the derivations are straightforward.

In our evaluation, we use revocation latency (δ) of 1 hour and also 10 minutes. The number of average daily queries *needed* by a verifier (Q_{V_daily}) is 30 (see Table 2). We assume that the queries from a verifier are issued throughout the day with uniformly distributed time intervals. Since a verifier can cache the revocation information as long as it is still valid, the number of daily queries *actually issued* by a verifier is: $Q_{V\_issued\_daily} = min(\frac{M}{\delta}, Q_{V\_daily})$, where $M = 1,440$ is the number of minutes in a day. The total number of daily queries issued by *all* verifiers is therefore: $Q_{daily} = V \cdot Q_{V\_issued\_daily}$. In all the schemes below, the *daily* cost of certificate creation is: $D\_Ovh_{CA} = (\frac{N}{\beta} + \frac{N \cdot b}{\beta}) \cdot C_{sign}$.

CRL (with a CMAE). The size of CRL is: $L_{CRL} = L_{CRL\_fields} + \lfloor Nb/2 \rfloor \cdot L_{CRL\_entry}$, where $L_{CRL\_fields} = 400$ bytes is the length of the CRL header and signature, and $L_{CRL\_entry} = 39$ bytes is the length of each entry in CRL [22]. With $U = \frac{M}{\delta}$ as the total number of CRL updates in a day, the daily update costs are: $D\_Bw_{CA-CMAE} = U \cdot L_{CRL}$, $D\_Ovh_{CA} = U \cdot C_{sign}$, and $D\_Ovh_{CMAE} = U \cdot C_{verify}$.

The daily query costs of CRL are: $D\_Bw_{CMAE-\exists Ver} = Q_{V\_issued\_daily} \cdot L_{CRL}$, $D\_Bw_{CMAE-\forall Ver} = Q_{daily} \cdot L_{CRL}$, $D\_Ovh_{CA} = 0$, $D\_Ovh_{CMAE} = 0$, and $D\_Ovh_{Ver} = Q_{V\_issued\_daily} \cdot C_{verify}$.

The storage requirements are: $Stor_{CA} = Stor_{CMAE} = L_{CRL}$. Finally, the revocation latency is δ minutes.

OCSP (with the CA as OCSP Responder). There is no update cost between the CA and CMAE, since no CMAE is involved. With $L_{OCSP\_Resp} = 459$ bytes as the length of OCSP Response [22], the daily query costs (due to status reply) are: $D\_Bw_{CA-\forall Ver} = Q_{daily} \cdot L_{OCSP\_Resp}$, $D\_Bw_{CA-\exists Ver} = Q_{V\_issued\_daily} \cdot L_{OCSP\_Resp}$, $D\_Ovh_{CA} = Q_{daily} \cdot C_{sign}$, and $D\_Ovh_{Ver} = Q_{V\_issued\_daily} \cdot C_{verify}$. The storage requirement is: $Stor_{CA} = 0$. The revocation latency of OCSP can be close to zero when desired.

CRS (with a CMAE). We set the time interval for periodic hash-token release $d = \delta$ minute(s). The length of the hash chain is thus: $\ell = \frac{\beta M}{\delta} - 1$. Here, we assume that the CA stores the whole hash chain for all the valid certificates in its storage. An amortization technique such as [23] can be used to reduce its storage requirements, but at the cost of additional online processing for the CA.

We use $L_{CRS\_fields} = 161$ bytes to denote the length of the CA's timestamp and signature, and $L_{S\_No} = 7$ bytes to denote the length of a certificate's serial number [22]. The bandwidth cost for a *single* CRS update between CA and CMAE is: $Bw_{CA-CMAE} = L_{CRS\_fields} + ((N + \lfloor Nb/2 \rfloor) \cdot (L_{S\_No} + L_{hash}))$. With $U = \frac{M}{\delta}$, the total daily update costs become: $D\_Bw_{CA-CMAE} = U \cdot Bw_{CA-CMAE}$, $D\_Ovh_{CA} = U \cdot C_{sign}$, and $D\_Ovh_{CMAE} = U \cdot C_{verify}$.

Under the steady-state condition, there are N valid certificates and $Nb/2$ (or $0.05N$ when $b=0.1$) revoked certificates in the system. The majority of the certificates are thus valid.[1] The expected average overhead of a verifier in validating *one* hash token is: $Ovh_{Ver} = \frac{\ell+1}{2} \cdot C_{hash}$. The corresponding daily query costs are: $D\_Bw_{CMAE-\forall Ver} = Q_{daily} \cdot L_{hash}$, $D\_Bw_{CMAE-\exists Ver} = Q_{V\_issued\_daily} \cdot L_{hash}$, $D\_Ovh_{CA} = 0$, $D\_Ovh_{CMAE} = 0$, and $D\_Ovh_{Ver} = Q_{V\_issued\_daily} \cdot Ovh_{Ver}$.

For the storage costs, note that the CA can remove the subchains it has released. Thus, the storage requirements in CRS are: $Stor_{CA} = \frac{N\delta}{\beta M} \cdot \frac{\ell^2+3\ell}{2} \cdot L_{hash} + \lfloor Nb/2 \rfloor \cdot L_{hash}$, and $Stor_{CMAE} = Bw_{CA-CMAE}$.

CREV-I. The CA sends an OCSP Response message every $d_{CA} = \delta$ minutes. In a day, each EVCP thus performs $S = \frac{M}{t_{CREV\_I}}$ session establishments, and receives $U = \frac{M}{\delta}$ OCSP Response messages. We use $L_{CREV\_I\_Msgs} = 1{,}577$ bytes to denote the length of all messages in a session establishment, L_{OCSP_Resp} to denote the length of an OCSP Response message, and L_T to denote the length of the timestamp or a CA's nonce.

The total daily update costs are: $D\_Bw_{CA-\forall EVCP} = N \cdot (S \cdot L_{CREV\_I\_Msgs} + U \cdot L_{OCSP\_Resp})$, $D\_Bw_{CA-\exists EVCP} = S \cdot L_{CREV\_I\_Msgs} + U \cdot L_{OCSP\_Resp}$, $D\_Ovh_{CA} = N \cdot S \cdot (2 \cdot C_{verify} + C_{sign}) + N \cdot U \cdot C_{sign}$, and $D\_Ovh_{EVCP} = S \cdot (2 \cdot C_{sign} + C_{verify}) + U \cdot C_{verify}$.

The total daily query costs are as follows: $D\_Bw_{EVCP-\forall Ver} = Q_{per\_cert\_daily} \cdot L_{OCSP\_Resp}$, $D\_Bw_{EVCP-\exists Ver} = Q_{V\_issued\_daily} \cdot L_{OCSP\_Resp}$, with $D\_Ovh_{CA} = 0$, $D\_Ovh_{EVCP} = 0$, and $D\_Ovh_{Ver} = Q_{V\_issued\_daily} \cdot C_{verify}$.

The storage requirements are: $Stor_{CA} = 0$ and $Stor_{EVCP} = L_T + L_{OCSP\_Resp}$.

CREV-II. We set the hash-chain update interval in CREV-II (d) to δ minutes. Each EVCP thus performs $S = \frac{M}{t_{CREV\_II}}$ session establishments daily, and receives $U = S \cdot \ell_{CREV\_II} = \frac{M}{\delta} - S$ hash-token updates daily. We use $L_{CREV\_II\_Reply} = 605$ bytes to denote the length of *Session Reply* message, and $L_{CREV\_II\_Msgs} = 1{,}615$ bytes to denote the length of all messages in a session establishment of CREV-II.

The total daily update costs are: $D\_Bw_{CA-\forall EVCP} = N \cdot (S \cdot L_{CREV\_II\_Msgs} + U \cdot L_{hash})$, $D\_Bw_{CA-\exists EVCP} = S \cdot L_{CREV\_II\_Msgs} + U \cdot L_{hash}$, $D\_Ovh_{CA} = N \cdot S \cdot (2 \cdot C_{verify} + C_{sign})$, and $D\_Ovh_{EVCP} = S \cdot (2 \cdot C_{sign} + C_{verify}) + U \cdot C_{hash}$.

The expected verifier's average query cost is: $Ovh_{Ver} = \frac{\ell_{CREV\_II}+1}{2} \cdot C_{hash} + C_{verify}$. The total daily costs are: $D\_Bw_{EVCP-\forall Ver} = Q_{per\_cert\_daily} \cdot (L_{hash} + L_{CREV\_II\_Reply})$, $D\_Bw_{EVCP-\exists Ver} = Q_{V\_issued\_daily} \cdot (L_{hash} + L_{CREV\_II\_Reply})$, $D\_Ovh_{CA} = 0$, $D\_Ovh_{EVCP} = 0$, and $D\_Ovh_{Ver} = Q_{V\_issued\_daily} \cdot Ovh_{Ver}$.

The storage requirements are: $Stor_{CA} = \frac{N}{\ell_{CREV\_II}} \cdot \frac{\ell_{CREV\_II}^2 + 3\ell_{CREV\_II}}{2} \cdot L_{hash}$, and $Stor_{EVCP} = L_T + L_{CREV\_II\_Reply} + L_{hash}$.

---

[1] Furthermore, in practice, queries on revoked certificates are expected to decrease over time due to the increasing usages of the valid replacement certificates.

Table 3. Cost comparison of various schemes with $\delta = 1$ hour. U and Q denote the costs due to update and query respectively.

Entity	Daily Costs	Unit	CRL	OCSP	CRS	CREV-I	CREV-II
CA	D_Ovh_{CA} (U+Q)	sec	0.036	1.07×10^6	3.39×10^{-5}	3876	324
	$Stor_{CA}$	MB	0.19	0	8355.24	0	13.35
	$D\_Bw_{CA-CMAE}$ (U)	MB	4.47	-	64.89	-	-
	$D\_Bw_{CA-\forall EVCP}$ (U)	MB	-	-	-	1351.36	350.00
	$D\_Bw_{CA-\forall Ver}$ (Q)	MB	-	3.15×10^5	-	-	-
CMAE	D_Ovh_{CMAE} (U+Q)	sec	0.0017	-	0.0017	-	-
	$Stor_{CMAE}$	MB	0.19	-	2.70	-	-
	$D\_Bw_{CA-CMAE}$ (U)	MB	4.47	-	64.89	-	-
	$D\_Bw_{CMAE-\forall Ver}$ (Q)	MB	1.34×10^8	-	1.37×10^4	-	-
EVCP	D_Ovh_{EVCP} (U+Q)	sec	-	-	-	0.0078	0.0061
	$Stor_{EVCP}$	MB	-	-	-	4.53×10^{-4}	6.11×10^{-4}
	$D\_Bw_{CA-\exists EVCP}$ (U)	MB	-	-	-	0.014	0.0035
	$D\_Bw_{EVCP-\forall Ver}$ (Q)	MB	-	-	-	3.15	4.29
Verifier	D_Ovh_{Ver} (Q)	sec	0.0017	0.0017	0.042	0.0017	0.0017
	$D\_Bw_{CA-\exists Ver}$ (Q)	MB	-	0.011	-	-	-
	$D\_Bw_{CMAE-\exists Ver}$ (Q)	MB	4.47	-	4.58×10^{-4}	-	-
	$D\_Bw_{EVCP-\exists Ver}$ (Q)	MB	-	-	-	0.011	0.014
Revocation Latency		mins	60	≈ 0	60	60	60

4.2 Performance Evaluation of CREV and Other Schemes

We evaluated the models in Sect. 4.1 with parameter values for the two scenarios given in Table 2. The objective here is to have a quantitative comparison of the costs incurred by the various schemes under common conditions and basic costs.

All hash values are generated using SHA-1, and signatures are created using RSA with a 1024-bit modulus. The overheads of the basic cryptographic operations, based on the Crypto++ 5.6.0 Benchmarks (http://www.cryptopp.com/benchmarks.html) on Intel Core-2 PC with 1.83 GHz CPU, are as follows: C_{sign} − 1.48 ms as the cost of a digital signature (RSA-1024) generation;

Table 4. Cost comparison of various schemes with $\delta = 10$ minutes

Entity	Daily Costs	Unit	CRL	OCSP	CRS	CREV-I	CREV-II
CA	D_Ovh_{CA} (U+Q)	sec	0.21	1.33×10^6	2.03×10^{-4}	2.26×10^4	1296
	$Stor_{CA}$	MB	0.19	0	5.01×10^4	0	19.07
	$D\_Bw_{CA-CMAE}$ (U)	MB	26.83	-	389.35	-	-
	$D\_Bw_{CA-\forall EVCP}$ (U)	MB	-	-	-	7506.56	1491.55
	$D\_Bw_{CA-\forall Ver}$ (Q)	MB	-	3.94×10^5	-	-	-
CMAE	D_Ovh_{CMAE} (U+Q)	sec	0.01	-	0.01	-	-
	$Stor_{CMAE}$	MB	0.19	-	2.70	-	-
	$D\_Bw_{CA-CMAE}$ (U)	MB	26.83	-	389.35	-	-
	$D\_Bw_{CMAE-\forall Ver}$ (Q)	MB	1.68×10^8	-	1.72×10^4	-	-
EVCP	D_Ovh_{EVCP} (U+Q)	sec	-	-	-	0.034	0.024
	$Stor_{EVCP}$	MB	-	-	-	4.53×10^{-4}	6.11×10^{-4}
	$D\_Bw_{CA-\exists EVCP}$ (U)	MB	-	-	-	0.075	0.015
	$D\_Bw_{EVCP-\forall Ver}$ (Q)	MB	-	-	-	3.94	5.36
Verifier	D_Ovh_{Ver} (Q)	sec	0.0021	0.0021	0.32	0.0021	0.0022
	$D\_Bw_{CA-\exists Ver}$ (Q)	MB	-	0.013	-	-	-
	$D\_Bw_{CMAE-\exists Ver}$ (Q)	MB	5.59	-	5.72×10^{-4}	-	-
	$D\_Bw_{EVCP-\exists Ver}$ (Q)	MB	-	-	-	0.013	0.018
Revocation Latency		mins	10	≈ 0	10	10	10

$C_{verify} = 0.07$ ms as the cost of a digital signature (RSA-1024) verification; and $C_{hash} = 0.40\,\mu s$ as the cost of computing a hash (SHA-1).

Table 3 and Table 4 show the overheads of the all revocation schemes under the evaluation scenarios. The daily computational overhead for certificate creation (of $\frac{N(1+b)}{\beta}$ certificates), D_Ovh_{CA}, is 0.45 second in all the schemes.

We can see that CREV schemes offer a good trade-off between the costs incurred on the CA, CMAE and EVCP, while incurring low costs on the verifier. Even for δ=10 minutes, the CA's daily computational cost (D_Ovh_{CA}) in CREV-I is 2.26×10^4 seconds ($\sim$6 hrs), much lower than 1.33×10^6 seconds ($\sim$370 hrs) in OCSP. Due to the use of hash chaining, CREV-II incurs an even much lower D_Ovh_{CA}. Compared with other schemes, CREV schemes are thus more viable for deployment when a near real-time timeliness guarantee is needed.

5   Conclusion

We have presented two lightweight and practical certificate revocation schemes, called CREV, based on a principal-hosted CSI revocation setting. We have also analyzed the trust and security requirements of the new setting, and how CREV can address them. Our cost analysis has shown the practicality of CREV when compared to several existing schemes even under the near real-time timeliness guarantee of 10 minutes. CREV offers a good balance of costs incurred on all the entities, while being very lightweight on the verifier. Furthermore, it provides good incentives for the involved entities to provide a secure and trusted revocation service. Thus, CREV gives a more scalable revocation service for real-time needs, and also addresses the constraints of mobile devices.

References

1. Lopez, J., Oppliger, R., Pernul, G.: Why Have Public Key Infrastructures Failed so Far? Internet Research 15(5), 544–556 (2005)
2. Gutmann, P.: PKI: It's Not Dead, Just Resting. Computer 35(8), 41–49 (2002)
3. ITU-T Recommendation X.509: Information Technology - Open Systems Interconnection - The Directory: Public-key and Attribute Certificate Frameworks (2000)
4. Cooper, D., Santesson, S., Farrell, S., Boeyen, S., Housley, R., Polk, W.: Internet X.509 Public Key Infrastructure Certificate and Certificate Revocation List (CRL) Profile. RFC 5280 (2008)
5. Myers, M., Ankney, R., Malpani, A., Galperin, S., Adams, C.: X.509 Internet Public Key Infrastructure Online Certificate Status Protocol - OCSP. RFC 2560 (1999)
6. VeriSign, Inc., VeriSign Certification Practice Statement Version 3.8.1 (2009)
7. Iliadis, J., Gritzalis, S., Spinellis, D., de Cock, D., Preneel, B., Gritzalis, D.: Towards a Framework for Evaluating Certificate Status Information Mechanisms. Computer Communications 26(16), 1839–1850 (2003)
8. Micali, S.: Efficient Certificate Revocation. Technical report, MIT-LCS-TM-542b, Massachusetts Institute of Technology (1996)
9. Micali, S.: NOVOMODO: Scalable Certificate Validation and Simplified PKI Management. In: PKI Research Workshop (2002)

10. Muñoz, J.L., Forné, J., Esparza, O., Soriano, B.M.: Using OCSP to secure certificate-using transactions in M-commerce. In: Zhou, J., Yung, M., Han, Y. (eds.) ACNS 2003. LNCS, vol. 2846, pp. 280–292. Springer, Heidelberg (2003)
11. Berbecaru, D.: MBS-OCSP: An OCSP based Certificate Revocation System for Wireless Environments. In: Signal Processing and Information Technology (2004)
12. Aiello, W., Lodha, S., Ostrovsky, R.: Fast digital identity revocation. In: Krawczyk, H. (ed.) CRYPTO 1998. LNCS, vol. 1462, p. 137. Springer, Heidelberg (1998)
13. Kocher, P. C.: On Certificate Revocation and Validation. In: Financial Cryptography (1998)
14. Naor, M., Nissim, K.: Certificate Revocation and Certificate Update. In: USENIX Security (1998)
15. Goyal, V.: Certificate Revocation Using Fine Grained Certificate Space Partitioning. In: Financial Cryptography and Data Security (2007)
16. Solworth, J. A.: Instant Revocation. In: European PKI workshop on Public Key Infrastructure: Theory and Practice (2008)
17. Solworth, J. A.: Beacon Certificate Push Revocation. In: Computer Security Architecture Workshop (2008)
18. Scheibelhofer, K.: PKI without Revocation Checking. In: PKI R&D Workshop (2005)
19. Lioy, A., Marian, M., Moltchanova, N., Pala, M.: PKI Past, Present and Future. International Journal of Information Security 5, 18–29 (2006)
20. Lim, T.-L., Lakshminarayanan, A.: On the Performance of Certificate Validation Schemes Based on Pre-Computed Responses. In: GLOBECOM (2007)
21. Zheng, P.: Tradeoffs in Certificate Revocation Schemes. ACM Computer Communication Review 33(2), 103–112 (2003)
22. Perlines Hormann, T., Wrona, K., Holtmanns, S.: Evaluation of Certificate Validation Mechanisms. Computer Communications 29(3), 291–305 (2006)
23. Jakobsson, M.: Fractal Hash Sequence Representation and Traversal. IEEE International Symposium on Information Theory, 437–444 (2002)

On Tradeoffs between Trust and Survivability Using a Game Theoretic Approach

Jin-Hee Cho and Ananthram Swami

U.S. Army Research Laboratory, Communication and Information Sciences Directorate,
2800 Powder Mill Rd., Adelphi, MD 20783
{jinhee.cho,ananthram.swami}@us.army.mil

Abstract. Military communities in tactical networks must often maintain high group solidarity based on the trustworthiness of participating individual entities where collaboration is critical to performing team-oriented missions. Group trust is regarded as more important than trust of an individual entity since consensus among or compliance of participating entities with given protocols may significantly affect successful mission completion. This work introduces a game theoretic approach, namely Aoyagi's game theory based on positive collusion of players. This approach improves group trust by encouraging nodes to meet unanimous compliance with a given group protocol. However, when any group member does not follow the given group protocol, they are penalized by being evicted from the system, resulting in a shorter system lifetime due to lack of available members for mission execution. Further, inspired by aspiration theory in social sciences, we adjust an expected system trust threshold level that should be maintained by all participating entities to effectively encourage benign behaviors. The results show that there exists the optimal trust threshold that can maximize group trust level while meeting required system lifetime (survivability).

Keywords: economic modeling, trust network, positive collusion, aspiration, rationality, wireless mobile networks.

1 Introduction

Collaboration is critical in team-oriented missions. This is particularly important in military communities engaged in tactical operations where it is important to maintaining group solidarity based on the trustworthiness of the individual entities. Communal compliance to a common protocol can significantly affect successful mission completion. In the military, group trust is often considered to be more important than the trust of any single entity. Rewards and penalties are natural ways of enforcing or encouraging expected behaviors.

Economic models have been used to support decision making problems such as efficient resource allocations or encouraging cooperative behaviors in the communication and networking field [17]. We employ a game theoretic approach, namely *Aoyagi*'s game theory [2], to introduce the concept of positive collusion that has been used in economics. This approach improves group trust by using positive

I. Wakeman et al. (Eds.): IFIPTM 2011, IFIP AICT 358, pp. 190–205, 2011.

collusion to encourage unanimous compliance with a given group protocol. That is, the entire system is penalized or rewarded regardless of which individual entity misbehaved or behaved, so that group members are stimulated to pressure each other to reach their common goal [16]. As motivation, consider the scenario in which a commander expects all participating members in a mission team to maintain an expected trust threshold. The overall trust metric is based on trust components derived from the characteristics of the composite network. The trust components include processing delay per packet, cooperativeness (i.e., packet dropping or forwarding), data integrity (i.e., message forgery or modification or lying), and inherent rationality referring to the degree of willingness to follow a given protocol in order to maximize an entity's utility. Further, we assume that an entity is cognitive in that it will make a decision to improve its behavior only when the changed behavior will immediately or ultimately increase its own trust or group trust as well as help the system avoid penalties.

This work is also inspired by aspiration theory in social sciences in that an appropriate aspiration (or goal) level given to a group will effectively increase the group's performance without letting group members feel frustrated or failed. Hoppe [10] defined *aspiration* as "a person's expectations, goals, or claims on his own future achievement." He emphasized that determining "success" or "failure" does not depend only on its objective goodness, but also on whether the level of aspiration may be reached or not. The underlying idea is that entities work hard to avoid failure where failure is defined as being below the aspiration level, a standard set implicitly or explicitly by peers or the community at large. Aspiration theory has been used in fields such as psychology [8], sociology [3], education [16], economics [7], and computer science (artificial intelligence) [9].

Economic theories are popularly applied where resources are restricted such as in wireless networks (e.g., mobile ad hoc networks, sensor networks, wireless tactical networks) [11], [12]. Very recently, Ng and Seah [14] used *Aoyagi*'s game theory to improve cooperation of nodes in resource-restricted wireless networks where nodes are more likely to be selfish. In [14], a node's selfishness is assessed by examining its packet forwarding or dropping behaviors. Our work differs from [11], [12], [14] in that we consider multi-layer composite trust as behaviors to improve and investigate the tradeoff between trust and system survivability.

Aspiration level has been used as an attribute that an agent considers to express its preference [4], [9]. However, our work applies a group aspiration level based on the idea that individuals tend to follow the collective norm of the group to which they belong. Our work models a wireless tactical network where an entity is a mobile device carried by a human being (e.g., soldier) and identifies optimal trust threshold (as the goal level for members to achieve) to maximize group trust while meeting system survivability.

The main contributions of this paper are as follow. First, we employ a unique game theoretic approach, called *Aoyagi*'s game theory, to model a tactical network where a trusted commander desires participating entities to follow a given protocol with the goal of reaching an acceptable system trust level. Second, we propose a composite trust metric that captures various aspects of an entity in a composite network comprising communication, information, social, and cognitive networks. Third, inspired by aspiration theory from social sciences, we adopt aspiration level (i.e., trust threshold in this study) to effectively stimulate an entity towards desired behaviors. Fourth, we develop a mathematical model using Stochastic Petri Nets (SPN) [5] to study the tradeoff between group trust and system survivability in the presence of misbehaving nodes and under resource constraints. Lastly, we identify the optimal trust threshold that maximizes group trust level while meeting system survivability.

The rest of this paper is organized as follows. Section 2 describes the system designs, assumptions, proposed composite trust metric, system failure conditions, and computations of performance metrics. Section 3 shows our performance model developed using SPN techniques and how to compute the metrics in our SPN model. Section 4 discusses numerical results obtained from our SPN model, and provides physical interpretations. Section 5 concludes this paper and suggests future research directions.

2   System Model

We consider a wireless tactical network where a trusted third party, called a commander node (CN), coordinates or gives orders to member nodes in the network, the so called "mission group." Communications in the network may require multiple hops. A group maintains a symmetric key, called a group key, in order to maintain secrecy (forward and backward secrecy) among legal members [15]. We assume that when nodes are evicted from the mission group, a new key is distributed to the remaining members by the CN based on a centralized key management protocol [15] Each node disseminates its beacon message (e.g., "I am alive") to stay connected to the group. Each node is also assumed to periodically disseminate packets related to group activities in terms of group communication, trust update, and neighbors' monitoring.

The network is heterogeneous where each node can have different characteristics such as different degree of cooperativeness (propensity to forward packets), integrity (message forgery or modification, or lying), processing delay per packet, and rationality (willingness to follow a given protocol). Except for the processing delay, the three characteristics are assumed to be drawn from a uniform distribution with a prescribed range, and are assumed known in advance to the CN. These four characteristics are reflected as components of our proposed composite trust metric, discussed in Section 2.1. Note that an entity is assumed to be a mobile device carried by a human (e.g., soldier). We model dynamically changing behaviors related to cooperativeness, data integrity, and capability in processing delay. However, we model a node's rationality as a static trust value that affects the attitude to improve its behavior. This is because we assume that an entity's rationality or disposition does not change over the short period of mission duration. Further, we assume that an entity's willingness to comply with a common protocol is related to its rationality, seeking to increase its utility by avoiding penalty. If the entity is an attacker and has a different goal such as disrupting the entire system, it may not improve its behaviors to attain the given trust threshold. However, in this case, the system penalizes the misbehaving node by evicting it, ultimately eliminating any chance of participation in any group activities as a legal member. Thus, a smart attacker may not easily manifest misbehaviors that can be promptly penalized by the system.

In our proposed protocol, we follow a rule similar to that described in *Aoyagi*'s game theory with some modifications. All nodes are expected to maintain the trust threshold given by the CN. The trust threshold is an expected goal that each node needs to achieve in order to avoid penalty. Each node periodically reports its self-computed trust value to the CN, the so called "public signal." The CN collects trust values of all participating nodes based on each node's self-reported *public* signals and computes the group trust, an average trust level of all group members. Only when *all* nodes say they are observing the target trust level, do they not receive any penalty. We call this the "collusion phase." We use "collusion" as a positive term different from "collusion" among compromised nodes. Otherwise, a certain number of the nodes that are not maintaining the given trust threshold will be evicted from the mission group. We call this "feedback phase," meaning that some nodes are penalized by being evicted and the existing members need to improve their behaviors so as not to be penalized again. The CN checks the degree of rationality of the nodes and evicts a certain portion of them.

On the other hand, a rational node also may lie to avoid the penalty even if it is not maintaining the given trust threshold. Further, a node may not follow the rule in order to achieve its attack goals if it is an attacker. To alleviate this effect, we assume that each node is capable of monitoring its neighboring nodes (e.g., via Pathrater [13]) based on direct observations and can detect whether public signals of its neighbors are true; nodes report lying behaviors to the CN. If a lying node is reported, even if all nodes claim compliance to the given trust threshold, the CN will proceed with "feedback phase" so that the lying nodes are all evicted from the system and the remaining member nodes may need to improve their behaviors. Since each node's direct monitoring capability is not perfect, we also consider false positive and false negative probabilities of the monitoring mechanism of each node.

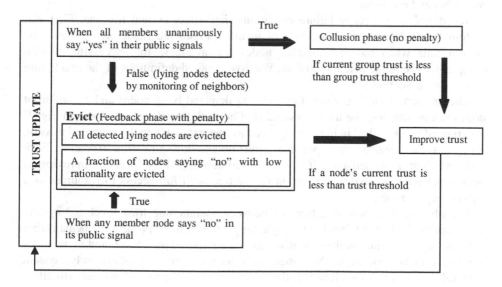

Fig. 1. The proposed protocol

In our model, each node is required to keep its trust level above the threshold as noted earlier; in addition, the average trust level of the group must exceed a desired value which we call the group trust threshold. Thus even if an individual node's trust value exceeds the individual trust threshold, it could make an extra effort to improve the average group trust level. Upon the end of each trust update, the CN will inform the current group trust level to group members. Thus, each node can make use of the informed current group trust value to decide whether it will improve its behaviors, as explained in Fig. 1. There is no penalty if the group threshold is not met, so far as all nodes are maintaining the given trust threshold individually. Fig.1 describes the proposed protocol. Notice that all detected lying nodes are evicted without forgiveness. However, if a node is not maintaining the prescribed trust threshold, but honestly says so, then it is only penalized if its rationality is low. We model a node's ability to change its behaviors is directly proportional to its degree of rationality since nodes with low rationality are assumed to be not capable of changing their behaviors sufficiently. Hence, a fraction of the honest but underperforming nodes with lowest rationality values are evicted from the mission group. This discourages a node's lying behavior by giving higher penalty than not lying. We assume that a node does not lie about its trust status when it is above the trust threshold. That is, we do not consider the case when a node with the trust value above the trust threshold says "no" in its public signal to trigger the feedback phase.

We assume that a node's misbehaviors including dropping packets or modifying messages are only observed in packets related to group communications for mission execution, and not other activities such as disseminating packets related to trust update or neighbor monitoring. The trust update related packets (i.e., public signals by group members, group trust values by the CN) are assumed to be acknowledged by recipients and error-free.

We define two security failure conditions that affect system lifetime. First, the system fails when a certain fraction of member nodes are malicious. Second, the system fails when too few member nodes are available for successful mission completion due to the eviction process. We give detailed definitions of the two failure conditions in Section 2.2.

The mission group is penalized by evicting detected lying nodes and a fraction of nodes not maintaining the trust threshold (but honestly saying so) as shown in Fig. 1. The procedure described in Fig.1 is regarded as one game where the proposed mission group plays a repeated game upon every trust update during mission execution. Each node, as a *self-interested agent* [6], seeks to maintain high trust level by improving its benign behaviors so that it can stay in the system with full access to resources as a legal group member.

We observe that there is a tradeoff between maintaining trust level and system survivability. If the trust threshold is high, the system is more prone to be penalized; it will take a longer time for the system to reach the required trust level, and more nodes are likely to be evicted in this longer convergence period. Consequently, system survivability will be low. However, the efforts to reach the trust threshold will allow surviving entities to increase their trust level ultimately.

2.1   Composite Trust Metric

We consider four components of trust derived from four different network layers: communication, information, social, and cognitive networks in order to assess the trustworthiness of a node. The four trust components are:

- **Communication trust** is based on a node's capability to process data measured by the *delay* incurred in forwarding or processing a packet. It could be affected by queue length, congestion at downstream nodes, and quality of outgoing links. This trust component can be computed from the number of packets received by the node.
- **Information trust** is based on *data integrity*, whether or not a node modifies or forges received messages or lies (e.g., lying about its trust status). This property can be computed by examining the integrity of the packets sent by the node.
- **Social trust** is assessed from the degree of *cooperativeness* of a node, and can be estimated from the frequency of packet forwarding or dropping by the node.
- **Cognitive trust** is a measure of *rationality* which is defined as the degree of willingness to follow a given protocol. This information is assumed to be known to the CN based on prior knowledge about the node population.

Recall that this work defines rationality as the willingness to comply with a common protocol. Note that rationality is represented as a static value that stays constant for the entire mission execution, based on the conjecture that disposition of human beings will only change very gradually, assuming that the mission duration is relatively short, less than a day. We relate a node's rationality with the willingness to improve the other three trust components. That is, a node with high rationality will change its behavior more aggressively to improve cooperativeness or data integrity. This relationship (rationality versus cooperativeness or data integrity) is justified in that each entity desires to reduce the possibility of failure by improving its behaviors with the goal of reaching the given trust threshold. Thus, the "rationality" component will indirectly affect the overall trust by influencing the attitude to improve cooperativeness and data integrity behaviors, as shown in Equation 2.

A node's self-reported trust value to the CN is based on three trust components, cooperativeness, data integrity, and processing delay where cooperativeness and data integrity are updated based on its rationality. The self-reported trust value of node i at time t is given as:

$$T_i(t) = w_1 P_i^{cooperativeness}(t) + w_2 P_i^{data-integrity}(t) + w_3 P_i^{delay}(t). \qquad (1)$$

Each of the above three trust components is a real number in the range of $[0, 1]$ and the weights sum to unity: $w_1 + w_2 + w_3 = 1$. A node will change its behaviors in terms of the cooperativeness and data integrity trust components, if and only if its projected trust value ($PT_i^X(t)$) is larger than its current trust value ($T_i(t - \Delta t)$) and either its current trust value is less than the trust threshold (T_{th}) or the current group trust (average trust of all member nodes) is less than the group trust threshold (T_{th}^{group}), as shown in Equation 2 below. Trust component X value of node i at time t is obtained by:

$$PT_i^X(t) = T_i^X(t - \Delta t) + f_{feedback}(t)P_{i,change}^X(t)$$

$$P_{i,change}^X(t) = c[P_i^{rationality}(1 - P_i^X)]$$

$$f_{feedback}(t) = \begin{cases} 1 \text{ if } (T_i(t - \Delta t) < T_{th} \text{ || } GT(t - \Delta t) < T_{th}^{group}) \\ 0 \text{ otherwise} \end{cases}$$

$$PT_i(t) = w_1 PT_i^{cooperativeness}(t) + w_2 PT_i^{data-integrity}(t) + w_3 PT_i^{delay}(t) \qquad (2)$$

$$if((PT_i(t) - T_i(t - \Delta t)) > 0 \&\& (T_i(t - \Delta t) < T_{th} \text{ || } GT(t - \Delta t) < T_{th}^{group}))$$

$$T_i(t) = PT_i(t);$$

$$else \ T_i(t) = T_i(t - \Delta t);$$

$$1 \geq T_{th}^{group} > T_{th} > 0, \qquad \Delta t = T_{update}$$

Here P_i^X is the original value of trust component X (cooperativeness or data integrity). $P_i^{rationality}$ represents node i's rationality initially given; $P_{i,change}^X(t)$ estimates how much node i can improve its behavior X upon each feedback and c is a constant. If the node's current trust level is below the trust threshold (T_{th}) or the current group trust level is below the group trust threshold (T_{th}^{group}), then the node accepts the feedback ($f_{feedback}(t) = 1$). Otherwise, the node stays in the previous trust at time $t-\Delta t$. As noted in Equation 2, we assume that the group trust threshold T_{th}^{group} is larger than the individual threshold T_{th}.

The processing delay trust component is based on the number of packets received by a node which is affected by the number of group members and their cooperative behaviors. This trust component value is estimated as:

$$P_i^{delay}(t) = \min [D/N_i^{packet}(t), 1] \qquad (3)$$

where D is an allowed constant time delay. $N_i^{packet}(t)$ is computed based on the number of packets node i received for forwarding to other nodes or as a destination node related to all system activities (i.e., monitoring, beacon, public signal, group communication, and trust update). The expected number of packets received or forwarded by a node can be estimated via its path centrality. Note that $PT_i^{delay}(t)$ in Equation 2 is also computed based on Equation 3.

2.2 Failure Conditions

We define "system survivability" or "lifetime" as the time to first system or security failure: loss of system integrity or loss of service availability. Therefore, the system fails when either of the two conditions below is true.

- **Failure Condition 1 (FC1):** The system fails when the fraction of member nodes that are malicious (i.e., modify or forge message, or lie) exceeds the system tolerance level ($TH_{malicious}$), leading to a security failure, *loss of system integrity*. FC1 is computed by:

$$M_{system}(t) = \sum_{i \in G(t)}^{all} (1 - P_i^{data-integrity}(t))$$

(4)

$$FC1 = \begin{cases} 1 \text{ if } M_{system}(t) > TH_{malicious} \\ \quad\quad 0 \text{ otherwise} \end{cases}$$

Here $G(t)$ is the set of member nodes at time t and $TH_{malicious}$ is the maximum number of malicious nodes that can be tolerated; and $M_{system}(t)$ is the average number of malicious nodes in the system.

- **Failure Condition 2 (FC2):** The system fails if the total number of evicted nodes exceeds a threshold ($TH_{mission}$). Equivalently, failure occurs when too few member nodes are available for successful mission completion. This leads to system performance failure, called *loss of service availability*. FC2 is computed by:

$$FC2 = \begin{cases} 1 \text{ if } N_{evicted}(t) > TH_{mission} \\ \quad\quad 0 \text{ otherwise} \end{cases}$$

(5)

$N_{evicted}(t)$ is the number of nodes evicted by time t and $TH_{mission}$ is the minimum number of nodes required for successful mission completion.

2.3 Metrics

We use two metrics to measure performance: system survivability and overall group trust.

System Survivability Probability ($P_{survivability}(t)$): This metric indicates the probability that the system is alive at time t. This is defined by:

$$P_{survivability}(t) = \begin{cases} 0 \text{ if FC1 or FC2 is true;} \\ \quad 1 \text{ otherwise;} \end{cases}$$

(6)

Overall Group Trust ($T_{group}(t)$): This metric refers to the average group trust. Trust value of each node, $T_i(t)$, is computed via Equation 1 and $T_{group}(t)$ is calculated as:

$$T_{group}(t) = \frac{\sum_{i \in G(t)}^{all} T_i(t)}{|G(t)|}$$

(7)

$G(t)$ is the set of current members at time t.

3 Performance Model

We have developed a mathematical model using Stochastic Petri Nets (SPN) [5]. This section describes our SPN model of the proposed system and its lifecycle. Further, this section addresses how the metrics (system survivability and overall group trust) are computed in our SPN. c

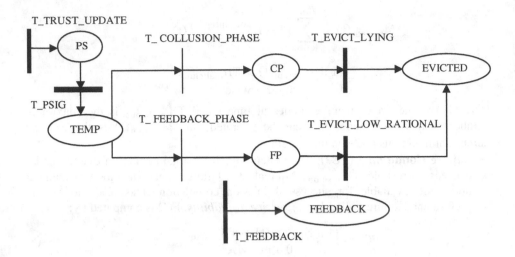

Fig. 2. SPN Model

Fig. 1 describes our SPN model; Places (i.e., PS, TEMP, CP, FP, EVICTED, FEEDBACK in ovals) indicate token holders to indicate the status of the system. Transitions (e.g., T_TRUST_UPDATE, T_PSIG, etc.) refer to events that occur at a certain rate. A token in Place PS indicates that a new session for trust update is initiated. The public signals from the nodes are periodically disseminated to the CN with the transition rate T_PSIG, $1/T_{ps}$ where T_{ps} is the public signal interval. When the transition T_PSIG is triggered, a temporary place holder TEMP will obtain a token. When all nodes say "yes" indicating they observe the given trust threshold in their public signals, the immediate transition T_COLLUSION_PHASE is triggered and Place CP obtains a token. The immediate transition is triggered with only a probability without time given and indicated with a thin line distinguished from other transition rates in Fig. 1. The probability given in the immediate transition T_COLLUSION_PHASE is computed by:

$$\text{probv(T\_COLLUSION\_PHASE)} = P_{collusion}(t)$$

$$P_{collusion}(t) = \prod_{i \in G(t)} P_i^{collusion}(t) \tag{8}$$

$$\text{where } P_i^{collusion}(t) = \begin{cases} (1 - P_i^{data-integrity}(t)) \text{ if } T_i(t) < T_{th} \\ 1 \text{ otherwise} \end{cases}$$

The probability in the immediate transition T_COLLUSION_PHASE is computed based on each node's lying probability based on the data integrity trust component. $G(t)$ represents the set of member nodes in the system at time t.

When Place CP has a token meaning all nodes say "yes," the CN also screens the public signals based on the information reported by neighboring nodes of each target node. When any lying nodes are detected by their neighboring nodes (either true negatives or false positives), they all will be evicted from the system with the rate

$1/T_{\text{monitor}}$ in the transition T_EVICT_LYING. The number of nodes to be evicted ($N_{\text{evicted}}^{\text{lying}}$) by triggering the transition T_EVICT_LYING is computed by:

$$N_{\text{evicted}}^{\text{lying}} = N_{\text{lie}}(t)(1 - P_{\text{fn}}) + N_{\text{good}}(t)P_{\text{fp}}$$

$$N_{\text{lie}}(t) = \sum_{i \in S(t)}^{\text{all}} 1, \quad N_{\text{good}}(t) = G(t) - N_{\text{lie}}(t) \tag{9}$$

$S(t)$ is the set of member nodes whose trust value is below the trust threshold at time t. $N_{\text{lie}}(t)$ is the number of lying nodes having trust values below the trust threshold and $N_{\text{good}}(t)$ is the number of member nodes with trust values above the trust threshold at time t. $G(t)$ represents the set of member nodes in the system at time t. P_{fn} and P_{fp} are the false negative and false positive probabilities of a monitoring mechanism preinstalled on each node.

If any node honestly says "no" meaning it is not maintaining the given trust threshold, the immediate transition T_FEEDBACK_PHASE fires and accordingly Place FP has a token. The probability of the immediate transition T_FEEDBACK_PHASE is computed by:

$$\text{probv}(T\_FEEDBACK\_PHASE) = 1 - P_{\text{collusion}}(t) \tag{10}$$

$P_{\text{collusion}}(t)$ and T_{ps} are explained as shown in Equation 8.

When Place FP has a token, the CN only identifies nodes that have trust values below the trust threshold and low rationality. Further, depending on the number of group members in the system, a certain fraction of nodes that are below the trust threshold with the lowest rationality will be evicted from the system with the rate $1/T_{\text{monitor}}$ in the transition T_EVICT_LOW_RATIONAL where T_{monitor} is the monitoring interval. The nodes to be evicted here are computed as:

$$N_{\text{evicted}}^{\text{low-rational}} = \min\left[\sum_{i \in IR(t)}^{\text{all}} 1, \ G(t)P_{\text{th}}^{\text{rationality}}\right] \tag{11}$$

$IR(t)$ is the set of member nodes with trust values below the trust threshold at time t and returns the lowest rational node first. $G(t)P_{\text{th}}^{\text{rationality}}$ is an upper bound to limit the number of nodes to be evicted and $P_{\text{th}}^{\text{rationality}}$ is a constant in the range of (0, 1).

When the transition T_FEEDBACK is triggered with the rate $1/T_{\text{update}}$ where T_{update} is the trust update interval, a token is taken to Place FEEDBACK which accumulates tokens over time. mark(FEEDBACK), meaning the number of tokens in Place FEEDBACK, represents the maximum feedback each node can accept for improving its trust value from its initially given trust value. Since each node's trust value is different, only some of member nodes will accept the feedback with the maximum of mark(FEEDBACK) depending on their trust status (discussed in Equation 2). The transition T_FEEDBACK only fires (returns 1) when the following conditions are met:

$$\text{If (mark(FEEDBACK)} < \text{MAX\_FEEDBACK}$$

$$\&\& \left(T_i(t - \Delta t) < T_{th} \,||\, GT(t - \Delta t) < T_{th}^{group} \right) \text{ return 1;} \qquad (12)$$

$$\text{return 0 otherwise;}$$

MAX_FEEDBACK is a constant to limit the amount of feedback for the entire mission duration. Equation 12 explains that a feedback is issued when any member node does not reach the trust threshold or the current group trust does not reach the group trust threshold.

We made the states reaching FC1 or FC2 absorbing states such that all transitions are halted when either failure condition is met. Two metrics in Section 2.3 are computed using built-in functions of SPN Package version 6 [5] as follows.

System survivability probability is computed as:

$$P_{survivability}(t) = \sum_{i \in S}^{all} P_i(t) S_{alive}(t) \text{ where } S_{alive}(t) = \begin{cases} 0 \text{ if FC1 or FC2 is true;} \\ 1 \text{ otherwise;} \end{cases} \qquad (13)$$

S is the set of allowable states of the system (e.g., possible states that are generated by SPN to represent the status of the system such as collusion phase or feedback phase at time t) and $P_i(t)$ is the probability of the system being in state i. $S_{alive}(t)$ returns a binary value where 0 represents system failure and 1 otherwise, representing a reward assignment to each state i defined in the system.

Overall group trust is calculated as:

$$T_{group}(t) = \Sigma_{i \in S}^{all} P_i(t) P_{group}(t) \text{ where } P_{group}(t) = \frac{\Sigma_{j \in G(t)}^{all} T_j(t)}{|G(t)|} \qquad (14)$$

S and $P_i(t)$ are similarly defined as in Equation 13. G (t) is the set of current members at time t. $P_{group}(t)$ is used as a reward assignment to each state i.

In addition to the two metrics above, we also show the results using a combined metric, the so called "trust-survivability" metric. This metric indicates the overall group trust only when the system is alive. This metric is computed by:

$$T_{survivability}(t) = \sum_{i \in S}^{all} P_i(t) \, P_{trust-survivability}(t) \qquad (15)$$

$$P_{trust-survivability}(t) = \begin{cases} 0 \text{ if FC1 or FC2 is true;} \\ P_{group}(t) \text{ otherwise;} \end{cases}$$

S and $P_i(t)$ are defined as in Equation 13. $P_{trust-survivability}(t)$ is used as a reward assignment to each state i. As we shall see in Section 4, this metric enables us to identify the optimal threshold based on the tradeoff between system survivability and group trust.

4   Numerical Results and Analysis

This section shows the results obtained from our analytical model and explains the physical meanings of the observed results. In particular, we identify the optimal trust threshold that maximizes overall group trust while meeting required system survivability. Table 1 summarizes the key default design parameter values used.

Table 1. Default design parameter values used

Parameter	Meaning	Value
$T_{monitor} = T_{ps} = T_{update}$	Time interval used for disseminating message related to monitoring, public signal, or trust update	300 sec.
$P_{fp} = P_{fn}$	False positive or negative probability	0.05
T_{th}	Trust threshold	0.7
T_{th}^{group}	Group trust threshold	$T_{th} + 0.1$
Initial Trust Distribution	Initial trust values given to the node population in terms of cooperativeness, data integrity, and rationality based on uniform distribution	[0.6, 1]
N_{init}	Initial number of nodes	100 nodes
MAX_FEEDBACK	Maximum value of feedback	20
$TH_{mission}$	Minimum number of member nodes for mission execution; used in FC1	60
$TH_{malicious}$	Maximum number of malicious nodes out of the total member nodes; used in FC2	$N_{init}/3$
d	Allowed constant time delay in computing processing delay in Equation 3	600 sec.
c	A constant used in $P_{i,change}^{X}(t)$	1/20

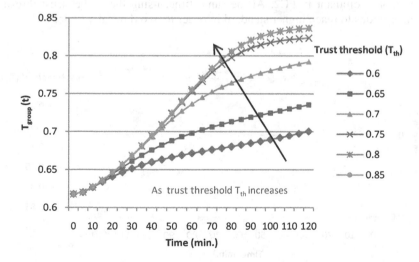

Fig. 2. Group trust metric over time for various trust thresholds (T_{th})

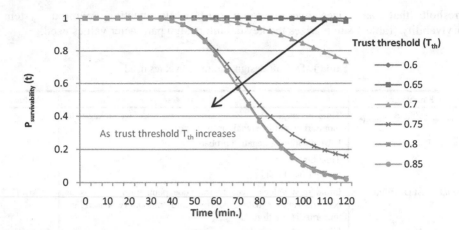

Fig. 3. System survivability metric over time for various trust thresholds (T_{th})

Figs. 2 and 3 show the evolution of the two metrics over time as the trust threshold varies. Fig. 2 demonstrates that when higher trust threshold is used, higher overall group trust is observed. On the other hand, Fig. 3 shows that as higher trust threshold is used, system survivability is lowered. As previously pointed out, the tradeoff between trust and survivability can be clearly observed in Figs. 2 and 3. When higher trust threshold is used, a node fails more frequently to reach the trust threshold. This leads to more nodes being evicted and consequently lowers the system lifetime. This effect is more dominant in FC2. At the same time, using the higher trust threshold encourages nodes to reach higher standard in order to avoid penalty (eviction).

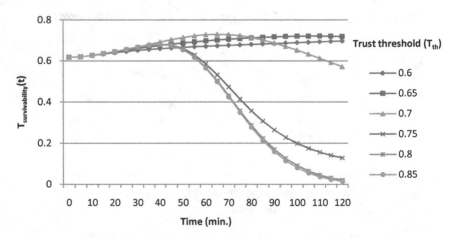

Fig. 4. Trust-survivability metric over time for various trust thresholds (T_{th})

Fig. 4 shows the trust-survivability metric that identifies the optimal trust threshold (T_{th}) as the trust threshold varies. Notice that the optimal trust-survivability is observed at $T_{th} = 0.7$ when time < 80 min. Further, when $T_{th} = 0.6$ or 0.65, the metric increases monotonically within the 2 hour mission duration.

Next we study how sensitive the optimal trust threshold (T_{th}) is to different initial trust values (ITD: initial trust distribution) in the node population. Recall that the trust components for cooperativeness, data integrity and rationality are drawn from a uniform distribution over [LB, 1]. In this example, we study the impact of varying LB. Fig. 5 shows the time-averaged group trust value for the 2 hour mission duration as LB varies. Each curve shows that higher group trust is observed at higher T_{th}. One noticeable observation is that even if LB is low, the node population with lower minimum trust (e.g., ITD = [0.5, 1]) performs better than the one with higher minimum trust (e.g., ITD = [0.55, 1] or [0.6, 1]) in some cases. For example, with T_{th} < 0.8, the node population with ITD = [0.5, 1] performs better than the one with ITD = [0.55, 1]. Further, with T_{th} < 0.7, the node population with ITD = [0.5, 1] even performs better than the one with ITD = [0.6, 1].

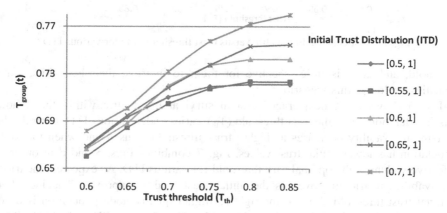

Fig. 5. Group trust metric versus trust threshold (T_{th}) for various ITD

The mission group is penalized when any member node is below the trust threshold but the group trust may be above the group trust threshold. This encourages nodes to improve their behavior further. But if the trust threshold is low, nodes easily reach the

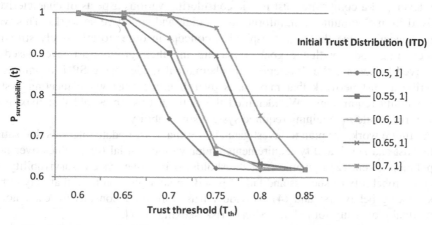

Fig. 6. System survivability metric versus trust threshold (T_{th}) for various ITD

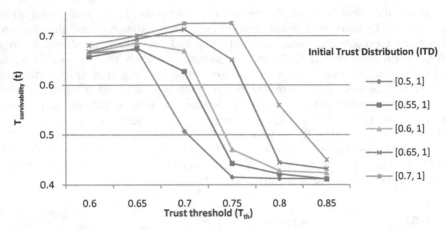

Fig. 7. Trust-survivability metric versus trust threshold (T_{th}) for various ITD

threshold, and there is little incentive for them to improve their behaviors, since penalties are low in this scenario.

Fig. 6 shows the time-averaged system survivability metric within the 2 hour mission duration when the trust threshold (T_{th}) varies under various ITD. Overall, the system survivability decreases as higher trust threshold is used and when the node population has lower initial trust values. Fig. 7 combines Figs. 5 and 6 in order to effectively identify the optimal trust threshold for various ITD. As expected, the trust-survivability metric improves as the initial trust quality improves. The identified optimal trust threshold shifts to the right as higher quality node population is used. For example, the optimal threshold is observed at $T_{th} = 0.65$ for ITD = [0.5, 1], [0.55, 1], and [0.6, 1], at $T_{th} = 0.7$ for ITD = [0.65, 1], and at $T_{th} = 0.75$ for ITD = [0.7, 1].

6   Conclusions and Future Work

We developed a composite trust metric considering various aspects of characteristics derived from communication, information, social, and cognitive networks. This work used *Aoyagi*'s game theory and aspiration concept in order to effectively stimulate participating nodes with the goal of maximizing their group trust level based on improved behaviors. We developed a mathematical model using SPN techniques to describe a trust network that maximizes overall group trust while meeting system survivability requirement. We identified the optimal trust threshold that maximizes group trust while maintaining required system survivability.

As future work, we plan to investigate (1) optimal trust update intervals that satisfy both trust and survivability requirements under various initial trust values over node population given; (2) dynamic trust thresholds to improve system survivability; (3) overall probability of success and failure based on an aspiration level that may induce risk-seeking behaviors; and (4) individual trust threshold considering each node's individual propensity for risk-aversion or risk-seeking [1, 7].

References

1. Atkinson, J.W.: Motivational determinants of risk-taking behavior. Psychological Review 64(6) part I, 359–372 (1957), available online (May 29, 2007)
2. Aoyagi, M.: Collusion in dynamic Bertrand oligopoly with correlated private signals and communication. Journal of Economic Theory 102(1), 229–248 (2002)
3. Berman, Y.: Occupational aspirations of 545 female high school seniors. Journal of Vocational Behavior 2(2), 173–177 (1972), available online (July 27, 2004)
4. Bellosta, M., Brigui, I., Kornman, S., Vanderpooten, D.: A multi-criteria model for electronic auctions. In: Proc. 2004 ACM Symposium on Applied Computing, Nicosia, Cyprus, pp. 14–17 (March 2004)
5. Ciardo, G., Fricks, R.M., Muppala, J.K., Trivedi, K.S.: SPNP Users Manual Version 6. Department Electrical Engineering. Duke University, Durham (1999)
6. Dash, R.K., Jennings, N.R., Parkes, D.C.: Computational-mechanism design: a call to arms. IEEE Intelligent Systems 18(6), 40–47 (2003)
7. Diecidue, E., Ven, J.: Aspiration level, probability of success and failure, and expected utility. Int'l Economic Review 49(2), 683–700 (2008)
8. Festinger, L.: Wish, expectation, and group standards as factors in influencing level of aspiration. Journal of Abnormal and Social Psychology 37(2), 184–200 (1942), available online (May 15, 2007)
9. Han, Q., Arentze, T., Timmermans, H., Janssens, D., Wets, G.: An agent-based system for simulating dynamic choice-sets. In: Proc. 2008 Spring Simulation Multiconference, Ottawa, ON, Canada, pp. 26–33 (April 13-16, 2008)
10. Hoppe, F.: Success and failure. In: Rivera, D. (ed.) Field Theory as Human Science, pp. 324–422. Gardner Press, New York (1976), originally work published in 1931
11. Klein, M., Moreno, G.A., Parkes, D.C., Plakosh, D., Seuken, S., Wallnau, K.C.: Handling interdependent values in an auction mechanism for bandwidth allocation in tactical data networks. In: Proc. 3rd Int'l Workshop on Economics of Networked Systems, Seattle, WA, pp. 73–78 (August 2008)
12. Mainland, G., Parkes, D., Welsh, M.: Decentralized, adaptive resource allocation for sensor networks. In: Proc. 2nd Symposium on Networked Systems Design and Implementation, Boston, MA, vol. 2, pp. 315–328 (May 2005)
13. Marti, S., Giuli, T., Lai, K., Baker, M.: Mitigating routing misbehavior in mobile ad hoc networks. In: Pro. 6th Annual ACM/IEEE Mobile Computing and Networking, Boston, MA, pp. 255–265 (August 2000)
14. Ng, S.K., Seah, W.K.G.: Game-theoretic approach for improving cooperation in wireless multihop networks. IEEE Transactions on Systems, Man, and Cybernetics-Part B: Cybernetics (2010)
15. Perrig, A., Tygar, J.D.: Secure Broadcast Communication in Wired and Wireless Networks. Kluwer Academic Publishers, Boston (2002)
16. Quaglia, R.J., Cobb, C.D.: Toward a theory of student aspirations. Journal of Research in Rural Education 12(3), 127–132 (1996)
17. Rue, R., Pfleeger, S.L.: Making the best use of cyber-security economic models. IEEE Security and Privacy 7(4), 52–60 (2009)
18. Sahner, R.A., Trivedi, K.S., Puliafito, A.: Performance and Reliability Analysis of Computer Systems. Kluwer Academic Publishers, Boston (1996)

Prob-Cog: An Adaptive Filtering Model for Trust Evaluation

Zeinab Noorian[1], Stephen Marsh[2], and Michael Fleming[1]

[1] University of New Brunswick, Canada
[2] Communications Research Centre, Canada
{z.noorian,mwf}@unb.ca, stephen.marsh@crc.gc.ca

Abstract. Trust and reputation systems are central for resisting against threats from malicious agents in decentralized systems. In previous work we have introduced the Prob-Cog model of multi-layer filtering for consumer agents in e-marketplaces which provide mechanisms for identifying participants who disseminate unfair ratings by cognitively eliciting the behavioural characteristics of e-marketplace agents. We have argued that the notion of *unfairness* does not exclusively refer to deception but can also imply differences in dispositions. The proposed filtering approach goes beyond the inflexible judgements on the quality of participants and instead allows environmental circumstances and the human dispositions that we call optimism, pessimism and realism to be incorporated into our trustworthiness evaluation procedures. In this paper we briefly outline the two layers before providing a detailed exposition of our experimental results, comparing Prob-Cog to FIRE and the personalized approach under various attacks and normal situations.

1 Introduction

Open e-marketplaces are uncertain places. These uncertainties contribute to misunderstandings amongst the agents that inhabit them [4]. While malicious agents exist, the recommendations of even honest agents who are unknown must be considered to be unreliable. Strategies for managing the uncertainties exist. In particular, in order to diminish the risk of being misled by unfair advisers, a consumer agent seeks advice from participants with the most similar ratings [3],[13].

In previous work [7] we amended this common view of trustworthiness [10],[15] by introducing a new definition for *unfairness*. Unfairness can be examined across two categories: 1) *intentional*, a) participants consistently act malevolently and b) participants occasionally engage in deceitful activities. And 2) *unintentional*, as a result of a) lack of personal experiences and b) various behavioural characteristics resulting in different rating attitudes.

Our algorithm uses a two-layered filtering approach combining cognitive and probabilistic views of trust [4] to mainly target the intentional group of unfair advisers. We showed that modeling the trustworthiness of advisers based on a strict judgement of the quality of their recommendations is not complete unless

I. Wakeman et al. (Eds.): IFIPTM 2011, IFIP AICT 358, pp. 206–222, 2011.

it is accompanied by the analysis of their dispositions. Thus, through the comprehension of their rating attitudes, a consumer agent could take appropriate steps to evaluate them.

In this paper, we provide an overview of the algorithm before presenting new experimental results to show its efficacy in filtering unfair advisers whilst still managing the problem of unfairness to new or unknown others. We then describe the adaptive approach of the Prob-Cog model in determination of the employed threshold parameters in different environmental circumstances. Our experimental results show the utility of our approach in classification of various participants and, specifically, how consumers could detect more honest advisers in a community where the majority of participants are unfair. Our Prob-Cog filtering model can therefore be seen as an effective approach in modeling the reputation of advisers in a dynamic agent-oriented e-commerce application.

2 Related Works

Several reputation systems and mechanisms have been proposed for modeling the trustworthiness of advisers and coping with the problem of unfair ratings in multi-agent online environments. Below we provide a description on two representative approaches: FIRE and the personalized model. More detailed overviews of other existing trust and reputation systems can be found in [7],[8].

The FIRE Model [3] is a decentralized trust and reputation system designed for open multi-agent systems such as e-commerce applications. In FIRE, trust is evaluated within the context of a number of different information components:1) *Interaction Trust* (IT) that is built from the direct experience of buying agents ; 2) *Witness Reputation* (WR) that is based on the direct observation of selling agents' performance by third-party agents; 3)*Certified Reputation* (CR) which consists of certified references disclosed by selling agents; and 4) *Role-based Trust* (RT), which models the trust across predefined role-based relationships between two participants. In this trust model, each component has a deterministic trust formula with a relevant rating weight function [8]. These weight functions are designed such that they reflect intrinsic characteristics of their components. For example, in the IT component, the weight function is merely based on the recency of the reputation information, whereas in WR the weight is calculated based on the credibility of its reputation providers. To evaluate the credibility of reputation providers, FIRE has developed an adaptive mechanism to detect and filter out inaccurate reports. It defines an adaptive inaccuracy tolerance threshold based on the selling agents' performance variation to specify the maximal permitted differences between the actual performance and the provided ratings. Credibility ratings of the reputation providers are tuned to be inversely proportional to the differences, i.e., the higher the differences are, the lower their credibility.

Zhang [15] proposed a personalized approach for handling unfair ratings in centralized reputation systems. It provides public and private reputation components to evaluate the trustworthiness of advisers. Depending on the availability of reputation information, consumer agents would determine the weight of private and public reputation components differently. In the personalized approach, advisers share their subjective opinions over a common set of providers. To estimate the credibility of advisers, consumers estimate the recency of their ratings using the concept of a time window [15] and exploit a probabilistic approach to calculate the expected value of advisers' trustworthiness based on their provided ratings.

Our work differs from them in a number of ways. Unlike other models[3],[9],[10], [15] which mainly evaluate the credibility of advisers based on the percentage of unfair ratings they provided, the Prob-Cog model takes initiative steps to aggregate several parameters in deriving the trustworthiness of advisers. That is, in addition to the similarity degree of advisers' opinions, it further aggregates their behavioural characteristics and evaluates the adequacy of their reputation information in its credibility measure. In this model, every consumer with different behavioural characteristics is able to objectively evaluate the similarity degree of advisers through a multi-criterion rating approach. Consumer agents could adaptively predict the trustworthiness of advisers using different credibility measures well-suited for various kinds of advisers. Prob-Cog provides a consumer with the ability to simply adjust the influence of each view of trust based on its own preferences and determines the influence of each layer in its decision making. Besides, while in most existing models [9],[11],[13],[15] the evaluation of the adopted thresholds are not addressed explicitly, in this model we explore some determinant factors which are important in evaluating the adopted thresholds effectively.

3   The Prob-Cog Filtering Algorithm

In the Prob-Cog model, consumers analyze the neighbours' trustworthiness based on two types of information. The first, which helps build the first layer of our filtering algorithm, is used to identify malicious participants with a complementary model of deception[14] who lie significantly in their ratings. It also detects newly-joined agents with insufficient personal experiences. The second helps consumers to recognize the behavioural characteristics of their neighbours. As such, it will be able to subjectively evaluate their degree of trustworthiness. Note that, in the second layer of the model, consumers take an analytical approach in order to detect deceitful participants with volatile dispositions who cheat opportunistically. By hiding their true intentions, this group of deceitful participants impose greater risk and insecurity to the system compared with those with a frequently deceptive attitude[1],[6],[8].

Below we provide an overview of the formal model. A more detailed exposition can be found in [7].

3.1   First Layer: Evaluating the Competency of Neighbours

A consumer agent C sends a query to its neighbours $N = \{N_1, N_2, ..., N_i\}$ requesting information about providers $P = \{P_1, P_2, ..., P_q\} \subseteq \{P_1, P_2, ..., P_m\}, q \leq m$ on interactions occurring before a time threshold T (which diminishes the risk of changeability in a provider's behaviour), and with a Quality of Service (QoS) threshold Ω to imply C's belief about an acceptable minimum level of trust.

Neighbour N_k responds by providing a rating vector $R_{(N_k,P_j)}$ for each provider. It contains a tuple $\langle r, s \rangle$ which indicates the number of successful (r) and unsuccessful (s) interaction results with provider P_j respectively. In the first layer of Prob-Cog, neighbours are asked to provide merely a *binary rating*: "1" means that P_j is reputable and "0" means not reputable. Thus, considering the consumer's QoS threshold, they will send reputation reports as a collection of positive and negative interaction outcomes. Once the evidence is received, for each $R_{(N_k,P_j)}$, C calculates the expected value of the probability of a positive outcome for a provider P_j [9] as:

$$E(pr_r, P_j) = \frac{r+1}{r+s+2} \tag{1}$$

For an e-marketplace we use $E(pr_r, P_j)_{Par}$ where $Par \in \{C\} \cup N$ implies participants of the community.

Clearly, $0 < E(pr_r, P_j)_{Par} \leq 1$ and as it approaches 0 or 1, it indicates *unanimity* in the body of evidence[5]. That is, particularly large values of s or r provide better intuition about an overall tendency and service quality of providers. In contrast, $E(pr_r, P_j)_{Par} - 0.5$, (i.e, $r = s$) signifies the maximal conflict in gathered evidence resulting in increasing the uncertainty in determining the service quality of providers. Based on these intuitions, we are able to calculate the degree of reliability and certainty of ratings provided by neighbours.

Let x represent the probability of a successful outcome for a certain provider. Based on the Definitions(2) and (3) in [12], the *Reliability degree* of each $R_{(N_k,P_j)}$ is defined as:

$$c(r, s) = \frac{1}{2} \int_0^1 \left| \frac{x^r(1-x)^s}{\int_0^1 x^r(1-x)^s \, dx} - 1 \right| \, dx \tag{2}$$

Similar to $E(pr_r, P_j)_{Par}$, we can use $c(r, s)_{Par}$.

Following [12], reliability is a minimum when $E(pr_r, P_j)_{Par} = 0.5$. As such, the less conflict in their ratings, the more reliable the neighbours would be. However, in Prob-Cog, C would not strictly judge the neighbours with rather low reliability in their $R_{(N_k,P_j)}$ as deceptive participants since this factor could signify both dishonesty of neighbours and the dynamicity and fraudulent behaviour of providers. That is, some malicious providers may provide satisfactory quality of service in some situations when there is not much at stake and act conversely in occasions associated with a large gain. As such, even though they retain a certain level of trustworthiness, their associated reliability degree is low.

To address this ambiguity, C computes the $E(pr_r, P_j)_C$ and $c(r, s)_C$ of its personal experiences, $R_{(C,P_j)}$, for a common set of providers. Through the comparison of neighbours' metrics with its own, it would select those with a similar rating pattern and satisfactory level of honesty as its *advisers*. More formally, it measures an average level of dishonesty of N_k by:

$$\overline{d}_{(N_k)} = \frac{\sum_{j=1}^{|P|} | E(pr_r, P_j)_C - E(pr_r, P_j)_{N_k} |}{|P|} \tag{3}$$

It may also happen that a truthful neighbour lacks in experience. Thus, despite its inherent honesty, its reliability degree is low and it is not qualified to play the role of adviser. To address this, we introduce an uncertainty function $\overline{U}_{(N_k)}$ to capture the intuition of information imbalance between C and N_k as follows:

$$\overline{U}_{(N_k)} = \frac{\sum_{j=1}^{|P|} \mid (c(r,s)_C - c(r,s)_{N_k})_{P_j} \mid}{|P|} \tag{4}$$

In light of the uncertainty function, the opinions of deceptive neighbours who attempt to mislead consumer agents by supplying a large number of ratings are discounted. Similarly, this model hinders short-term observations of newly-joined agents from having influence on a consumer agent's decision making process. Given the formulae 3 and 4, the *competency degree* of N_k is calculated by reducing its honesty based on its certainty degree:

$$Comp_{(N_k)} = (1 - \overline{d}_{(N_k)}) * (1 - \overline{U}_{(N_k)}) \tag{5}$$

Consumer C determines an incompetency tolerance threshold μ which indicates an acceptable level of a neighbour's incompetency. It further chooses the neighbours with $(1 - Comp_{(N_k)}) \leq \mu$ as its potential advisers and filters out the rest.

To attain partial perception on overall quality of the environment, a consumer C evaluates an approximate dishonesty of participants based on its observation of the quality of its neighbours in this layer. It calculates an Approximate Dishonesty Coefficient $ADC_{(C)}$ as the ratio of detected incompetent neighbours to all of its neighbours as follows:

$$ADC_{(C)} = \frac{|\{N_k|(1 - Comp_{(N_k)}) > \mu , k \leq i\}|}{|N|} \tag{6}$$

It is worthwhile to note that, since in this layer we target the participants with a significant lying pattern, detecting fraudulent agents with oscillating rating attitudes is left for the next layer.

3.2   Second Layer: Calculating a Credibility Degree of Advisers

In the first phase of the Prob-Cog model a consumer agent has obtained a rough estimate of the honesty level of neighbours and selects a subset of them as its advisers. However, the open e-marketplace allows various kinds of participants with distinctive behavioural characteristics [2] to engage in the system. Besides, the multi-dimensional rating system provides tools for a consumer agent to objectively evaluate the performance of service providers across several criteria with different degrees of preference. Evidently, the measured QoS is mainly dependent on how much the criteria with a high preference degree are fulfilled[8]. Owing to the different purchasing behaviour of the agents, it is expected that preference degrees vary from one participant to another, resulting in dissimilar assessment of the quality of the *same* service. As such, computing the credibility of advisers regardless of their behavioural characteristics and rating attitudes, and merely based on their subjective opinions would not sufficiently ensure high quality judgements of their trustworthiness.

In the second layer of Prob-Cog, C gives credits to advisers to the extent that their evaluation of each criterion of a negotiated context is similar to its own experiences. For this purpose, it asks advisers about mutually agreed criteria over which they have bargained with *highly-reliable* providers whose reputation value has been recently released in the form of binary ratings. They also are requested to include the time of the latest interaction with such information so as to give a higher weight to more recent feedback. For this we adopt the concept of forgetting factor presented in [9],[15] and define the recency factor as:

$$T_{(C,A_k)P_j} = \frac{1}{\lambda^{T_{A_k}-T_C}} \tag{7}$$

Here, T_{A_k} and T_C indicate the adviser's and consumer's time windows when they had an experience with the same provider. Also, the λ represents the forgetting parameter and $0 < \lambda \leq 1$. When $\lambda = 1$, there is no forgetting and all the ratings are treated as though they happened in the same time period. In contrast, $\lambda \approx 0$ specifies that ratings from different time windows will not be significantly taken into account. Similarly to [15], in this filtering algorithm, the recency factor is characterized with a discrete integer value where 1 is the most recent time period and 2 is the time period just prior. Also, it is presumed that the adviser's ratings are prior to those a consumer agent supplies so that $T_{A_k} \geq T_C$.

Adviser A_k responds with an interaction context $IC_{(A_k,P_j,T_A)}$ that contains a tuple of *weight* and *value*: $\{W_i.V_i | i = 1..n\}$ and the latest interaction time T_A for each provider. Given A_k's interaction context, a consumer agent would estimate the possible interaction outcomes of an adviser based on its own perspective. That is, C will examine its $IC_{(C,P_j,T_C)}$ -which contains pairs of weight and value: $\{Y_i.R_i | i = 1..n\}$- and replace A_k's preferences W_i with its personal preference degrees Y_i. Based on this, the interaction context of A_k is updated to: $IC'_{(A_k,P_j,T_A)} = \{Y_i.V_i | i = 1..n\}$. We formalize the difference of C and A_k in assessing a provider P_j as follows:

$$Diff_{(C,A_k)P_j} = 1 - \frac{\sum_{i=1}^{n} Y_i \times R_i}{\sum_{i=1}^{n} Y_i \times V_i} \tag{8}$$

Based on Equations 7 and 8, C would calculate the *average* differences between the transaction result of A_k and its own experiences with a same set of providers as:

$$\overline{Diff}_{(C,A_k)} = \frac{\sum_{j=1}^{|P|} | Diff_{(C,A_k)P_j} | * T_{(C,A_k)P_j}}{|P|} \tag{9}$$

In the Prob-Cog model of filtering, we take a further step and embrace the diversity in participants as an influential factor in our credibility measures. For this purpose, C captures the overall tendency of A_k in evaluating the providers'

QoS as:

$$Tendency_{(C,A_k)} = \frac{\sum_{j=1}^{|P|} Diff_{(C,A_k)P_j}}{|P|} \tag{10}$$

A positive value of $Tendency_{(C,A_k)}$ indicates that an adviser has the attitude of overrating providers while a negative value declares that an adviser has a tendency to underrate providers.

Further, an adaptive threshold β is used to determine behavioural patterns of advisers such that if A_k's $IC'_{(A_k,P_j,T_A)}$ is compatible with those experienced by C ($\overline{Diff}_{(C,A_k)} \leqslant \beta$), they will be counted as *credible* advisers. In Prob-Cog, C determines the outlook of the advisers by analyzing $\overline{Diff}_{(C,A_k)}$. If it is marginally greater than β with a negative $Tendency_{(C,A_k)}$, the corresponding adviser's attitude is identified as *pessimistic*. Similarly, in case their differences marginally exceed β with a positive $Tendency_{(C,A_k)}$, the respective adviser's attitude is recognized as *optimistic*. We define a marginal error ϵ as a ratio of β and it is subjectively determined by a consumer agent. If A_k's $IC'_{(A_k,P_j,T_A)}$ significantly deviates from the consumer agent's direct experiences, they will be detected as *malicious* advisers with *deceitful* behavioural models.

The classification mechanism of the behavioural pattern of A_k based on C's interaction context is formally presented as follows:

$$BP_{(C,A_k)} = \begin{cases} Credible: & \overline{Diff}_{(C,A_k)} \leqslant \beta \\ Optimistic: & \beta < \overline{Diff}_{(C,A_k)} \leqslant \beta + \epsilon \ \& \ Tendency_{(C,A_k)} > 0 \\ Pessimistic: & \beta < \overline{Diff}_{(C,A_k)} \leqslant \beta + \epsilon \ \& \ Tendency_{(C,A_k)} < 0 \\ Deceitful: & \overline{Diff}_{(C,A_k)} > \beta + \epsilon \end{cases} \tag{11}$$

Given the $BP_{(C,A_k)}$, the credibility measure $CR_{(C,A_k)}$ is formulated as:

$$CR_{(C,A_k)} = \begin{cases} 1 - \overline{Diff}_{(C,A_k)}: & BP_{(A_k)} = Credible \\ (1 - \overline{Diff}_{(C,A_k)}) \times e^{-\theta * \overline{Diff}_{(C,A_k)}}: & BP_{(A_k)} = Optimistic \\ (1 - \overline{Diff}_{(C,A_k)}) \times e^{-\sigma * \overline{Diff}_{(C,A_k)}}: & BP_{(A_k)} = Pessimistic \\ 0: & BP_{(A_k)} = Deceitful \end{cases} \tag{12}$$

Here, θ and σ represent the optimistic and pessimistic coefficients respectively. Coefficients θ and σ are formalized with reference to the consumer's disposition as:

$$\theta = \begin{cases} max\{|\ Diff_{(C,A_k)P_i}\ |\ |i = 1...m\} & Risk\text{-}Averse\ consumer \\ min\{|\ Diff_{(C,A_k)P_i}\ |\ |i = 1...m\} & Risk\text{-}Taking\ consumer \end{cases} \tag{13}$$

$$\sigma = \begin{cases} min\{|\ Diff_{(C,A_k)P_i}\ |\ |i = 1...m\} & Risk\text{-}Averse\ consumer \\ max\{|\ Diff_{(C,A_k)P_i}\ |\ |i = 1...m\} & Risk\text{-}Taking\ consumer \end{cases} \tag{14}$$

The coefficient parameters ensure that the recommendation of advisers with volatile behaviour who have a high variability in their opinions is heavily discounted.

4   Evaluating Threshold Parameters

In the Prob-Cog, we combine cognitive and probabilistic views of trust such that each might have different weights depending on the consumer's endogenous factors, such as willingness and preferences. That is, some consumers might assign a great deal of influence on the probabilistic evaluation results while having less interest in the inclusion of the factor of behaviour in their evaluation. The priority of either view is projected into different thresholds dedicated to each layer. In this model, the values of the adopted thresholds are attributed to many factors such as: 1) the variation of the providers' performance, 2) percentage of neighbours with dishonest attitude and 3) the influence of the cognitive approach on the consumer's perspective ($Inf_{view:cog}$).

To optimally estimate β in the second layer, C needs to acquire enough information about the potential reasons for a reporter's inaccuracy. For example, variation in providers' performance can be served as a measure of reporters' inaccuracy[3]. Thus, the inaccuracy tolerance threshold β is evaluated by capturing the mean variation in providers' quality of products. However, for the precise calculation of the provider's performance variation, in this model C only selects highly-reliable providers whose $c(r, s) > 0.50$. Based on this principle, the variation of a provider P_j can be calculated as follows:

$$dev(C, P_j) = \sqrt{\frac{\sum_{r_i \in \Re(C,P_j)}(v_i - \bar{v})^2}{|\Re(C, P_j)|}} \qquad (15)$$

And β is estimated as:

$$\beta = \frac{\sum_{j=1}^{|P|} dev(C, P_j)}{|P|}$$

where $dev(C, P_j)$ is the standard deviation of provider P_j's performance in the last interactions experienced by C. v_i is the value of the rating r_i which is the rating of C provided for P_j and $0 \le v_i \le 1$. And $\bar{v}$ is a mean value of all the rating values in the set of ratings $\Re(C, P_j)$ which is a collection of r_i.

Depending on the value of $Inf_{view:cog}$, consumers show different levels of interest in modeling the behavioural patterns of advisers. To satisfy their interests, ϵ is designed to give consumers an opportunity to detect different dispositions of advisers. However, initializing ϵ not only depends on $Inf_{view:cog}$ but also relies on β and the approximate dishonesty coefficient of participants ($ADC_{(C)}$) that is estimated in the first layer. More explicitly, in a dynamic environment where providers indicate highly-variant behaviour, a high value of β increases the risk that deceptive reporters remain undetected. In such conditions, ϵ should be automatically adjusted to a low value in order to protect consumers against spurious participants. As such, consumer C would compute ϵ as:

$$\epsilon = (1 - ADC_{(C)})e^{-\beta} Inf_{view:cog} \qquad (16)$$

As aforementioned, the incompetency tolerance threshold μ should be evaluated in such a way to be able to expel neighbours with significant dishonesty or unreliability. Hence, we get the intuition that μ should be assigned a higher value than the second layer thresholds $(\beta + \epsilon)$ so as to be able to target only major dishonest participants. It also should be aligned with the cognitive preferences of consumers. That is, since a high value of $Inf_{view:cog}$ signifies the importance of the second layer's evaluation mechanism and behavioural modeling, a higher value of μ is desirable so as to reduce the number of filtered participants in the first layer and gives opportunity to consumers to cognitively evaluate the trustworthiness of advisers based on their behavioural characteristics in the second layer. Based on these principles, μ is calculated as follows:

$$\mu = n * (\beta + e^{-\beta} Inf_{view:cog}) \tag{17}$$

where $n > 1$.

5   Experimental and Comparison Results

In this section we explore the performance of our Prob-Cog model confronting different scenarios and attacks in comparison with two representative approaches: the FIRE model[3] and the personalized approach[15]. We picked out the important features of each model and conducted experiments to analyze how our model compares in similar conditions. For example, some experiments are dedicated to studying the effectiveness of different approaches dealing with dynamicity in an environment like the situation when providers change their behaviours. We also evaluate the accuracy of different models coping with a majority of unfair participants and indicate how exploitation of the cognitive view of trust could improve the performance in such situations. We further compare various approaches in addressing the bootstrapping problem of newcomers having limited experiences.

5.1   Performance Measurement

To measure the performance of different approaches, we have used the Matthews Correlation Coefficient (MCC)[16] to evaluate the quality of various approaches in differentiation between honest and dishonest participants. MCC is a precise metric and it gives a single value for the quality of binary classification and is calculated as follows:

$$MCC = \frac{(t_p.t_n) - (f_p.f_n)}{\sqrt{(t_p + f_p)(t_p + f_n)(t_n + f_p)(t_n + f_n)}} \tag{18}$$

where in this paper t_p represents the number of advisers correctly detected as dishonest, t_n signifies advisers correctly detected as honest. Also, f_p represents honest advisers misclassified as dishonest and f_n signifies dishonest advisers that are incorrectly classified as honest advisers. The MCC value is between $[-1, +1]$. A coefficient of +1 indicates accurate detection, a coefficient of 0 indicates an average detection quality and -1 indicates the worst possible detection.

5.2 Cold Start

Consider the scenario when consumer agent C has recently joined the system and intends to bootstrap its relationship with its neighbours. In the Prob-Cog model, C relies only on its few personal experiences. On the other side, in the personalized approach[15], C relies heavily on the public knowledge component when its personal knowledge is scarce. Exploiting public knowledge sounds promising when the majority of participants are honest. However, when an environment is controlled by a majority of deceptive participants, using public knowledge would be misleading.

The first experiment demonstrates C's performance in classification of participants when it has a limited number of personal experiences using Prob-Cog model and the personalized approach. It involves 100 advisers and 3 providers. We vary the percentage of dishonest advisers from 0% to 95% in an e-marketplace. We then measure an average MCC value for the Prob-Cog model and the personalized approach with 10 and 40 experiences commonly rated by both consumer C and advisers for the same set of providers. Results are presented in Figure 1. It indicates that the personalized approach produces high MCC when the majority of participants are honest while its performance degrades as the percentage of dishonest participants increases in an e-marketplace. It also implies that as the amount of personal knowledge increases, the resistance of C against misleading opinions of the majority of participants increases considerably. Figure 1 also shows that the Prob-Cog model consistently yields high performance in every condition since public knowledge does not have any influence on its evaluation mechanism.

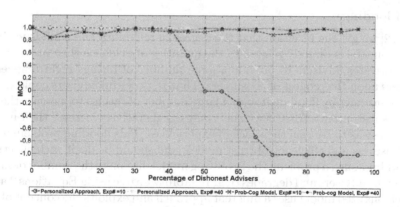

Fig. 1. Performance comparison of personalized & Prob-Cog approaches in classification of advisers

Dealing with insufficiency of personal experiences should not be restricted to consumer agents. Rather, it may happen that advisers with inadequate experiences unintentionally disseminate inaccurate information throughout an e-marketplace. Trust models must provide consumers with a mechanism to detect advisers with few experiences and reduce their influence in a consumer's decision making process.

The next experiment demonstrates how the Prob-Cog model evaluates the competency level of an intrinsically *honest* but inexperienced adviser with various amounts of experience. It involves one consumer C asking adviser N about its common experiences with 2 and 50 providers. N provides various percentages (0% to 100%) of differences in number of common experiences, presented by a normal distribution. The results indicate that the competency of even an honest adviser degrades as its number of experiences decreases (Figure 2). We also observe that C can effectively evaluate the competency level of N even with a limited set of providers.

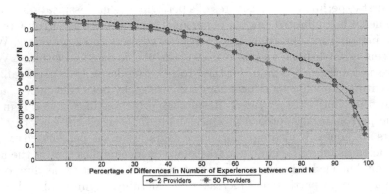

Fig. 2. Competency degradation of adviser N having different percentages of common experiences

5.3   Flooding

From [12] we get the intuition that the degree of reliability and confidence in advisers' opinions is directly related to the quantity of evidence they provide. This issue motivates advisers to provide a large number of ratings regarding certain providers upon the request of consumers. That is, deceitful advisers could manipulate a consumer by flooding it with a large number of ratings to increase their reliability substantially. Also, newcomers may exaggeratively increase their number of ratings so as to conceal their lack of experiences. This flooding problem affects the robustness and efficiency of trust models and should be dealt with effectively.

To address such a problem, the Prob-Cog model discounts the number of ratings provided by advisers and degrades their reliability degree using Equations 2 and 4. The personalized model uses a different approach and exploits the concept of time window. It considers those ratings of advisers that are provided in a same period of time as the ratings of the consumer more valuable and underestimates others.

The next class of experiment involves two consumers: 1) consumer C_1 with few experiences and 2) consumer C_2 with sufficient experiences. We examine the accuracy of the Prob-Cog model in classifying the advisers in a situation where different percentages of advisers from 0% to 100% flood consumers by providing 100-150 more ratings than C_1 and C_2. From the results in Figure 3 we can see that C_2 with sufficient experiences is more robust than C_1 with few experiences

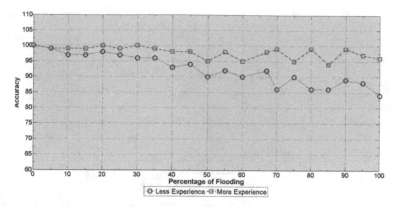

Fig. 3. The accuracy degree of Prob-Cog model dealing with different percentages of flooding

against the flooding attack of advisers. However, this attack does not have any significant negative impact on the overall performance of the Prob-Cog model.

5.4 Providers with Varying Behaviors

Our Prob-Cog model adopts a promising mechanism for capturing the variation in providers' performances. We have conducted specific experiments to demonstrate how our approach can accurately classify advisers in such an environment where providers continuously change their behaviour. This set of experiments involves 100 advisers which are divided in three groups: 1) 50% honest, 2) 25% deceitful who lie a small percentage of the time, and 3) 25% malicious with significant dishonesty. In this environment, providers have different levels of variation in their performance ranging from 5% to 100%.

To examine the effectiveness of our approach compared with other models, we consider four different threshold evaluation mechanisms: 1) fixed low threshold $\beta = 0.5$ as is used in the personalized approach [15], 2) fixed high threshold $\beta = 1.0$, 3) auto β which is exploited in the FIRE model [3] and 4) adaptive $\beta + \epsilon$ which is used by the Prob-Cog model in the second layer[1].

The results of this experiment are plotted in Figure 4, indicating the consumer's accuracy in classifying different groups of advisers. Specifically, the second approach with fixed $\beta = 1.0$ performs worst when the mean variation of the providers' performance is low. In contrast, the performance of the first approach with fixed $\beta = 0.5$ degrades as providers change their performance significantly. By having the ability to monitor the actual variations of the providers' performances, only the third and the last approach can maintain a high level of classification accuracy. However, the Prob-Cog model outperforms other approaches as it fairly achieves maximum classification accuracy by integrating the factor of behaviour in its evaluation.

---

[1] In this experiment, we assume that none of the advisers are filtered in the first layer so that $ADC_{(C)} = 0$

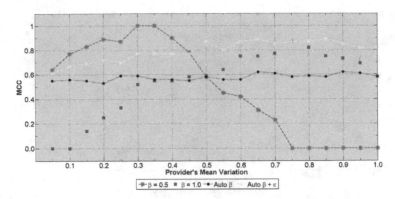

Fig. 4. Classification of advisers across different variations in providers' behaviours

The next experiment aims to highlight the influences of the cognitive view of trust in advisers' classifications. We learn that different $Inf_{view:cog}$ values yield different performances in various conditions. More explicitly, in case consumers deal with low-variance providers, a high value of $Inf_{view:cog}$ degrades the classification accuracy significantly. However, it shows better results as the providers' performance variation rose from 50% to 100%. As it is implied in Figure 5, assigning an average influence $Inf_{view:cog} = 0.5$ to the cognitive approach ensures consistent high performance throughout the experiment.

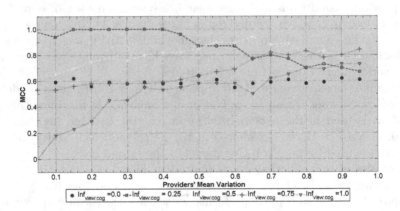

Fig. 5. Accuracy of advisers' classification having different cognitive preferences

5.5   Unbalanced Environment with Dishonest Majority

Trust models should be able to effectively cope with the problem of unfair ratings. They specifically should perform ideally in a situation where a majority of participants act dishonestly in an environment. In the following series of experiments we examine the performance of the personalized approach and the Prob-Cog model in classifying participants when 5% to 90% of them are dishonest.

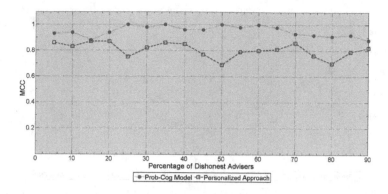

Fig. 6. The Prob-Cog model vs Personalized approach Performance

In this environment providers change their performance from 35% to 45%. We consider two patterns for dishonesty: 1) a deceitful pattern which includes 50% dishonest participants and 2) a complementary pattern which covers the remaining percentage of dishonest participants. We also assume that in both models consumer C has an adequate number of experiences[2] and advisers' ratings are provided in the same time window as consumer C. We adjust the $Inf_{view:cog}$ of the Prob-Cog model and the trustworthiness threshold of the personalized approaches to 0.5.

Results are shown in Figure 6. We can see that the classification performance of the Prob-Cog model is higher than the personalized approach across different percentages of dishonest participants. This is mainly due to the static approach of the personalized approach in determination of the trustworthiness threshold. That is, it might happen that in the environment where providers vary their QoS, this model labels honest participants as dishonest. This issue shows its significant deficiency when the majority of dishonest participants prevail in the environment, resulting in the detection of fewer honest advisers.

To better perceive the reasons behind the performance leaks, we compute the error rates (FPR and FNR) of these two models in detecting honest and dishonest participants dealing with different population tendency. Based on Figure 7, we observe that in the Prob-Cog model, when the majority of advisers are honest, the low value of $ADC_{(C)}$ in the first layer increases the effect of the cognitive dimension. As such, the high value of ϵ relatively amplifies the probability of misclassification of dishonest advisers as honest so that $FNR \geq 0$.

On the other hand, in this model when a majority of advisers turn out to be dishonest, it adaptively reduces ϵ so as to degrade the influence of the cognitive dimension and behavioural modeling in trustworthiness evaluation. Even though this strategy helps consumer C to detect a high percentage of deceitful participants, there is a chance that honest advisers with low credibility will be

---

[2] Based on this assumption, the weight of the public knowledge component in the personalized approach is negligible.

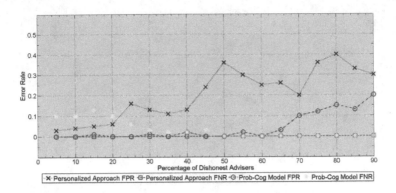

Fig. 7. The Error Rate of Prob-Cog model vs Personalized approach

misclassified as dishonest, resulting in a reduction of the classification perfor-mance ($FPR \geq 0$).

In the personalized approach when C has sufficient personal experiences and the threshold is assigned to a low value, it can perfectly detect dishonest par-ticipants so that ($FNR = 0$). However, since this model does not capture the providers' variations, C would highly misclassify honest advisers as malevolent ($FPR > 0$). In these series of experiments we observed that with the employment of the Prob-Cog approach we are able to detect *more* honest advisers compared with other approaches.

6   Summary of the Results

We have carried out a set of experiments to compare overall performance of three representative approaches: FIRE, the personalized approach and the Prob-Cog model in different scenarios. We measure their accuracy in detecting honest advisers when a majority of advisers are unfair, providers vary their behaviours in different degrees and consumers lack in personal experiences. We notice that the Prob-Cog model performs the best as it is able to better classify advisers in the aforementioned situations in comparison with other approaches. We have shown that, owing to the limited observation of the environment, it is not a sensible idea to exploit public knowledge as the environment might be controlled by a majority of dishonest participants. We noticed that the Prob-Cog model could successfully differentiate honest participants from dishonest ones in the cold start problem. We also verified how our approach effectively detects advisers with insufficient experiences and reduces their competency degree proportionately.

7   Conclusion and Future Work

In this paper, we present an adaptive multi-layered filtering algorithm that en-ables consumers with different behavioural attitudes to subjectively evaluate the trustworthiness of a variety of advisers in an e-marketplace. In the Prob-Cog model, the genuine beliefs and behavioural characteristics of participants are cognitively modeled and integrated in their trustworthiness evaluation metrics.

The principles of the two-layer filtering algorithm detect and disqualify various types of participants such as: malicious agents with a complementary rating pattern, newcomers with insufficient experiences, and fraudulent participants who retain a minimum level of trust to cheat opportunistically. In the Prob-Cog model, consumers can dynamically adjust the influence of the cognitive view of trust pertaining to their behavioural patterns to amplify or reduce the effect of different dimensions on credibility measures. This model also provides consumers with a mechanism to adaptively determine the value of the thresholds' parameters based on the observations of the quality of providers and environmental conditions. To demonstrate the effectiveness and capabilities of our approach, we focused on the experimental comparison with two representative approaches: the personalized approach and FIRE. We specifically examined some prominent scenarios, including ones dealing with participants' lack of experience, advisers flooding consumers with lots of ratings, providers' dynamicity and an environment with a majority of dishonest participants. Such empirical studies are useful for highlighting the importance of the capabilities of our Prob-Cog model.

Notably, results indicate that through the proper adaptation of the employed thresholds, consumers are able to identify more honest advisers compared with other approaches in different environmental circumstances, specifically when a majority of participants are unfair and when reliable advisers are scarce. One possible avenue for future work is to develop a provider classification mechanism which exploits the Prob-Cog model to evaluate the qualification of the participating providers in an e-marketplace.

References

1. Barber, K., Fullam, K., Kim, J.: Challenges for trust, fraud and deception research in multi-agent systems. In: Falcone, R., Barber, S.K., Korba, L., Singh, M.P. (eds.) AAMAS 2002. LNCS (LNAI), vol. 2631, pp. 8–14. Springer, Heidelberg (2003)
2. Castelfranchi, C., Falcone, R., Piunti, M.: Agents with anticipatory behaviors: To be cautious in a risky environment. In: ECAI (2006)
3. Huynh, T.D., Jennings, N.R., Shadbolt, N.R.: An integrated trust and reputation model for open multi-agent systems. In: AAMAS, pp. 119–154 (2006)
4. Falcone, R., Castelfranchi, C.: Generalizing trust: Inferencing trustworthiness from categories. In: AAMAS-TRUST, pp. 65–80 (2008)
5. Hang, C.-W., Wang, Y., Singh, M.P.: An adaptive probabilistic trust model and its evaluation. In: AAMAS, vol. 3, pp. 1485–1488 (2008)
6. Kerr, R., Cohen, R.: Smart cheaters do prosper: defeating trust and reputation systems. In: AAMAS, vol. 2, pp. 993–1000 (2009)
7. Noorian, Z., Marsh, S., Fleming, M.: Multi-layer cognitive filtering by behavioral modeling. In: Proceedings of the 10th International Conference on Autonomous Agents and Multiagent Systems (AAMAS 2011), Taipei, Taiwan, May 2-6, pp. 871–878. ACM, New York (2011)

8. Noorian, Z., Ulieru, M.: The state of the art in trust and reputation systems: A framework for comparison. J. Theor. Appl. Electron. Commer. JTAER 5(2), 97–117 (2010)
9. Jøsang, A., Ismail, R.: The Beta reputation system. In: Proceedings of the 15th Bled Electronic Commerce Conference (2002)
10. Teacy, W.T.L., Patel, J., Jennings, N.R., Luck, M.: TRAVOS: Trust and reputation in the context of inaccurate information sources. Journal of Autonomous Agents and Multi-Agent Systems (2006)
11. Wang, Y., Vassileva, J.: Bayesian network-based trust model. Web Intelligence, 372–378 (2003)
12. Wang, Y., Singh, M.P.: Formal trust model for multiagent systems. In: IJCAI (2007)
13. Xiong, L., Liu, L.: PeerTrust: Supporting reputation-based trust for peer-to-peer electronic communities. IEEE Transactions on Knowledge and Data Engineering 16, 843–857 (2004)
14. Yu, B., Singh, M.P.: Detecting deception in reputation management. In: AAMAS 2003: Proceedings of the second international joint conference on Autonomous agents and multiagent systems, pp. 73–80 (2003)
15. Zhang, J., Cohen, R.: Evaluating the trustworthiness of advice about seller agents in e-marketplaces: A personalized approach. Journal of Electronic Commerce Research and Applications (2008)
16. Zviling, M., Leonov, H., Arkin, I.T.: Genetic algorithm-based optimization of hydrophobicity tables. Bioinformatics 21(11), 2651–2656 (2005)

Privacy-Respecting Reputation for Wiki Users

Benjamin Kellermann[1], Stefanie Pötzsch[1], and Sandra Steinbrecher[1,2]

[1] Technische Universität Dresden, Faculty of Computer Science,
D-01062 Dresden, Germany
{Benjamin.Kellermann,Stefanie.Poetzsch}@tu-dresden.de
[2] SAP Research Dresden,
Chemnitzer Strasse 48, D-01187 Dresden, Germany
steinbrecher@acm.org

Abstract. Wikis are popular tools for creation and sharing of content. Integrated reputation systems allow to assess expertise and reliability of authors and thus to support trust in the wiki content. Yet, results from our empirical study indicate that the disclosure of user reputation evokes privacy issues. As a solution for this conflict between the need to evaluate trustworthiness of users and protecting their privacy, we present a privacy-respecting reputation system for wikis that we realized as OpenSource-Extension for the wiki software MediaWiki.

Keywords: Empirical Study, Privacy, Reputation System, Wiki.

1 Introduction

A wiki gives users the possibility to create a common information basis. Technically it is implemented as a collection of HTML pages, usually called *wiki articles*, that are generated, modified, and reviewed by wiki users. A very popular example is the online encyclopaedia Wikipedia. In January 2011, Wikipedia was available in 276 languages or dialects, among which English (more than 3.5 million articles and more than 13 million registered users) was the largest one.[1] This means, Wikipedia covers more articles than the famous and still in print available Encyclopaedia Britannica (about 65 thousand articles).

Wikis enable every user to contribute to the content with only her web browser. This leads to the drawback that it becomes difficult for readers to assess quality of content, and/or expertise of authors respectively. Wikis are aware of this problem and give users the possibility not only to change others' articles but to tag an article, e.g., with a number of stars and/or adding a written comment. Examples for MediaWiki – the software used to implement Wikipedia – are the extensions ReaderFeedback, Rating or Discussion.[2] This helps other readers to decide on how much they trust in the article.

Furthermore, the background of the users who create and also of those who rate an article are important. Here reputation systems common for other Internet

---

[1] http://en.wikipedia.org/wiki/Wikipedia:About
[2] These extensions are available from http://www.mediawiki.org/wiki/Extension.

I. Wakeman et al. (Eds.): IFIPTM 2011, IFIP AICT 358, pp. 223–239, 2011.

applications, e.g., electronic marketplaces like eBay[3] can be used to help wiki users to build up a reputation about their expertise, that they can use as authors and raters of articles. Having a user's reputation publicly available helps others to assess the trustworthiness of this user. However, this reputation is an aggregate of the user's personal properties/expertise/knowledge and conveys personal data, which means that privacy concerns may evoke and should be addressed. In this paper - after discussing background and related work on privacy-respecting reputation systems in Section 2 - we present an empirical study on users' privacy awareness with respect to their reputation in a wiki (Section 3). From the results of the study and existing work we deduce requirements focused on user reputation systems for wikis in Section 4. Based on the study and the derived requirements we propose a reputation system for wikis that allows users to find a balance between their need for privacy and other users' need to assess trustworthiness. In Section 5 we outline the design and implementation of our user reputation system for the wiki system MediaWiki and evaluate how it can fulfill the previously explained requirements in Section 6. The main focus of our work in contrast to previous work is giving the user the choice to balance his wish for privacy with the trustworthiness the content he creates has for others.

2   Background and Related Work

In the scenario of a wiki users may take the following roles:

- *readers* read articles others wrote (possibly with evaluating ratings others gave to the article),
- *authors* write articles or contribute to existing ones, and
- *raters* rate others' articles (usually after reading them).

In this scenario we want to integrate a user reputation system. Reputation systems for an interaction system need to provide the following protocols [1]:

1. Centralized communication protocols that allow users to:
   - provide ratings about other users,
   - obtain reputation of other users from the reputation server.
2. A reputation computation algorithm to derive users' reputation based on received ratings, and possibly other information.

Earlier work about reputation systems focuses on the e-commerce scenario that reflects such an interaction system with buying and selling products, e.g., [2,3,4]. In our scenario where the interactions between users are only implicitly given by reading/writing content an interesting question is whether

1. users get ratings explicitly from other users or
2. users get ratings implicitly from ratings given to the content they wrote.

---

[3] http://www.ebay.com

User reputation and trustworthiness of content alternatively can also be created from system-based observations about the users' behavior. This approach was the one followed for calculating the reputation of content and users in wikis recently: Dondio et al. suggested an algorithm to automatically calculate the overall trustworthiness of a wiki article based on statistical data [5]. Adler and Alfaro [6] present a system for Wikipedia that computes an editor's reputation by observing whether subsequent users preserve the changes that were made. Recommer Systems are slightly different from Reputation Systems by especially recommending content to users. A popular technique used to do so is collaborative filtering, this means using the input from other users in determining what is useful information for a user. The WRS (Wikipedia Recommender System) [7] is a rating-based personalized recommender system that uses trust metrics to give not only general information but personalised recommendations by comparing a user with other users and then calculating a trust profile of their expertise.

It has been studied from the legal perspective that user reputation can be seen as personal data [8] and should be protected by technical means [9]. This is contradicting to personalising reputation/recommendation data for users by a system. In [10] a small survey among 13 persons indicated that these participants do not feel comfortable to publish their real names within online communities and that half of them regard their reputation as privacy-sensitive data. Besides, there exists no empirical study on how privacy aware users are about their reputation in the context of a wiki. The other direction on how much content- and author-related information actually influences users' perceived trustworthiness of a Wikipedia article is already studied by [11]. Privacy usually covers three aspects: *anonymity of providing ratings, anonymity of obtaining other users' reputation*, and *anonymity of users who are rated and whose reputation is obtained*.

Anonymity services - as suggested in [12] - can only protect the users obtaining reputation. In order to obtain anonymity of users rating and being rated, it needs to be ensured that many users are indistinguishable by an attacker, so that they are in large anonymity sets. For anonymity of users who are rated and whose reputation is obtained, others should not be able to link interactions with the same user. The possibility of recognizing users by reputation is limited if the set of possible reputations is limited [13] or if the reputation is only published as an estimated reputation [14]. Transaction pseudonyms can be used to avoid linkability between transactions [15, 13]. In order to obtain anonymity of raters, interactions and ratings related to these interactions need to be unlinkable. This can be reached by a reputation provider who only calculates a new user reputation after it collected not only one but several ratings [16], or who only publishes an estimation of the actual reputation [14]. Further, a rater can be anonymous against the reputation provider by using convertible credentials [10] or electronic cash [15,17] or involve Trusted Third Parties similarly for separating interactions and ratings while preventing attacks [18,19].

But to the best of our knowledge there exists no design and implementation of a user reputation system that shows the trade-off between trust and privacy requirements in wikis and allows users to make a decision on which to favor.

3   User Reputation and the Need for Privacy

In the previous section we pointed out that a user's reputation is an aggregate of her personal expertise, skills and reliability based on previous behavior and thus may be classified as personal data. According to [20], it is important what is deemed sensitive or personal data in the perception of the individual rather than if it can be evaluated by third parties (e.g., lawyers, computer specialists). Considering that individuals often claim to have a huge need for privacy but behave differently (see also the *privacy paradox* [21]), we decided to conduct a larger study with experimental part to learn how users actually treat their own reputation value compared to other personal data items. In the following we briefly sketch the design of the study and report key results.

3.1   Study Design

The web-based study consisted of an experiment and a standardized questionnaire. Invitations to participate in the study were posted in forums and blogs on the Internet and we also distributed flyers in a university library. All participants who completed the study were offered the chance to win vouchers for an online shop. For the experiment, all participants were asked to rate the same articles from a wiki about books and literature according to three given categories. Before participants actually accessed the wiki articles, they did a short literature quiz. By answering four multiple choice questions about famous writers and books, they received between zero and four points. These points are considered as a participant's *reputation*. Participants further were asked to indicate name, age and place of residence. When rating the wiki articles subsequently, each participant decides whether her name, age, place of residence, and/or reputation should be published together with her rating of the wiki article.

Half of the participants were randomly assigned to the experimental group. Together with each wiki article, privacy-awareness information were displayed to the experimental group (i.e., information about who can see which data). The other half of the participants belonged to the control group and did not receive privacy-awareness information. After finishing this first part of the study, all participants filled' in the questionnaire. In this questionnaire we asked about perceived privacy in the wiki, experience with wikis, ratings systems and the Internet in general. We used questions from the applied privacy concerns and protection scale [22] to investigate general caution, privacy concerns and applied protection measures. Finally, we asked about demographic data and whether subjects had given their real name, place of residence and age at the beginning.

We calculated the *Perceived Privacy Index* (PPX)[4] from participants' answers to the questions how public, how private, how anonymous and how identifiable

---

[4] The questionnaire contained the questions: "Please indicate to which extent the following adjectives describe your feelings while using the wiki: 0 % (not at all) — 100 % (very much)?" (originally asked in German). The PPX is composed of the adjectives "public" (scale inverted), "private", "anonymous", "identifiable" (scale inverted).

they have felt in the wiki. Each item was measured on a 0 to 100 % slider scale. The higher the PPX value, the more private a participant has felt.

3.2 Results

After excluding data sets from few participants who admitted not to have seriously participated in the study, 186 valid responses were further analyzed.

30 % of the participants agreed to publish their real name together with their rating of a wiki article. The disclosure of their real age was okay for 57 %, real place of residence for 55 % and 63 % agreed to have their reputation value published. This means, for each data item there was a considerable share of participants who wished to keep this information private. If participants indicated later in the standardized questionnaire that they did not provide true information in one of the first three categories, we treated this data item as not disclosed. Since the reputation value was calculated from answers in the literature quiz, lying was impossible here.

Further, we used a linear regression model [23] to calculate how the disclosure of these four data items and a few other factors influence user's perceived privacy in the wiki. Results are listed in Table 1 and reveal that availability of privacy-awareness information and application-independent measures, like privacy concerns, general caution and protection measures, did not play a significant role for perceived privacy in the wiki. Yet, there are two factors that significantly decrease perceived privacy: the fact that a user has published her name and the fact that a user has published her reputation value. While it is not surprising that a user feels less private after disclosing her real name, we found that also disclosing the own reputation value has a similar effect on perceived privacy. According to the results it is to say that the reputation value is deemed an even more sensitive data than age or place of residence. Further unreported models show that also including combinations of data items, e.g., age published + reputation value published, have no additional effect.

In line with findings from the small survey in [10], the results of our empirical study underline that a user's reputation (even if only a numerical value) needs to be treated as personal data item, i.e., the user should have control over the disclosure of this information. Therefore we will present a privacy-respecting reputation system based on the ideas proposed in [10] but addressing and showing specifically the trade-off between privacy and trust requirements.

4   Requirements

4.1   Functional Requirements

The goal of a wiki is collecting valid and trustworthy information. The first means to reach this is editing/changing articles by other (possibly more knowledgeable) authors. Therefore many articles in Wikipedia have a long changing history.

---

[5] Intercept indicates the basic value of PPX when all predictors are equal to zero.

Table 1. Regression models for perceived privacy index (n=186)

PPX (dependent var.)	estimate	std. error	p-value
Application-specific predictors			
Privacy-awareness inform. available	4.57	12.01	0.704
Name published	−46.66	14.49	0.002 **
Age published	−13.54	16.77	0.420
Place of residence published	−21.65	16.06	0.179
Reputation value published	−39.99	14.04	0.005 **
Application-independent predictors			
General caution	0.22	1.79	0.902
Technical protection	−0.47	1.47	0.750
Privacy concerns	−1.35	1.10	0.223
Intercept[5]	288.93	33.47	

sign. levels: $*** p < 0,001$; $** p < 0,01$; $* p < 0,05$

Even information valid at some point in time might change and then the wiki article needs to be changed. But usually many articles will converge to a version containing mostly valid information. Using a content rating system with positive ratings, such acrticles can be marked as such. If the article contains unvalid information the person detecting this can improve or even remove content.

Incentives to improve content can be given by an additional user reputation system. The reputation computation algorithm from the user reputation system uses the content ratings from the content rating system as input to calculate the reputation of users who wrote this article. Users might even receive a monetary compensation for a good reputation. As for many other examples in our society where choices are made certificate-based we assume the following requirement to hold:

Positive integers as ratings and reputation: The rating protocol of the content rating system gets only positive integers as inputs and transfers it to positive reputation of content. The reputation computation algorithm of the user reputation system uses the ratings from the articles a user wrote to calculate her reputation.

Advantages and disadvantages of positive reputation systems depending on the user population are discussed in [24]. The main impact is that it encourages a user population of the wiki that creates valid content of high quality. In the long run all active wiki users would have a maximum reputation value. Low reputation corresponds to not contributing (in a positive way) to the quality of the wiki. To help newcomers [25] to start they can bring in certificates from outside the wiki that are transferred to reputation, e.g., a master in medicine might result in some initial reputation for a medical wiki.

Possibility of non-zero initial reputation: The reputation computation algorithm should be able to transfer a certificate a user got outside the wiki to an initial reputation inside the reputation system

As users have different areas of expertise we assume that wiki, user reputation system and content rating system agree on areas of expertise all articles, ratings, and reputations are linked with:

Area-specific reputation: The reputation system allows to set up different areas of expertise and users can have different reputations in these areas.

We abstract from a concrete classification of areas but refer to [26] for a comparison of several approaches. We only assume an agreement on metadata (tags) for areas of expertise defined for all system components. These areas of expertise should have a tree structure with 'general' as root and certain specific expertise as children. E.g. 'medicine' inherits from 'general' and might have 'gynecology' and 'surgery' as children, which again may have specialized children. All articles in the wiki are tagged with these areas (resp. paths in the tree of areas) as well as user reputation always will be linked to such an area. E.g. an article about breast cancer will be tagged with the expertise path 'general → medicine → gynecology'. Wikipedia already realises this with its Categorys[6], but they are organised as general graph. For reasons of simplicity we assume a tree, but it can easily be extended to a general graph.

The reputation computation algorithm of a user reputation system needs to be accurate and self-correcting. This means that it should consider all ratings given in an appropriate way by considering at the same time various attacks [27]. There exist numerous proposals for such algorithms [1] with respective advantages and disadvantages. For our scenario we assume a rating algorithm of the content rating system and a reputation computation algorithm of the user reputation system with the following features:

Influence of rater on user reputation: The higher the reputation of a rater is the more influence it will usually have on the perceived trustworthiness of the rating for others. For this reason the respecting rater's reputation should be used when calculating a user's reputation.

Influence of time on user reputation: To encourage users to contribute to the wiki continuously their reputation should be aged.

Availability of user reputation with content: As users want to estimate directly the quality of content the reputation of users who edited or rated this article should be stored with the content.

Beneath the functional requirements the scenario has privacy and security requirements that are partly contradicting and need to be balanced according to the principles of multilateral security [28]. We list the most important ones in the following. But due to the contradiction our system can only fulfill them partly.

4.2   Security Requirements

The following security requirements most important for our scenario of a user reputation system in a wiki are derived from [27, 17]. They need to be met by

---

[6] http://en.wikipedia.org/wiki/Special:Categories

the protocols for providing ratings to the content rating system and obtaining user reputation from the user reputation system:

Integrity of content and ratings: Users want content and ratings given to it to be preserved from manipulations.
Accountability of raters: Raters should be accountable for their ratings.
No self-rating: It should be impossible that users rate themselves [25].

4.3   Privacy Requirements

As we could see from the study in Section 3 both users' real names and reputation should be protected by technical means. For the real name the corresponding requirements are similar to [27, 17]:

Anonymity/pseudonymity of raters and authors: Users want to rate and provide content anonymously or under a pseudonym to not necessarily allow others to link this rating to their real name.
Anonymity of readers: Users want to read content and evaluate corresponding user reputation anonymously.

Privacy of reputation can mean keeping the reputation confidential what would contradict the availability of reputation and therefore is no option. The better alternative is to relax the sensitivity of reputation as identifying or linkable attribute of users. This can be described by the following requirements:

Anonymity/pseudonymity of users for showing reputation: Users want to show reputation only pseudonymously or even anonymously.
Unlinkability of users for rating and writing content: Users want to be unlinkable when rating and writing content, also for showing reputation.

It needs to be communicated to users whether a user reputation system has these privacy options to relax their privacy awareness about reputation (cp. Section 3).

5   Infrastructure and Design

Our scenario needs three major system components to be in place: The first component is the wiki itself where we decided to use MediaWiki. Second, for the content rating system, there are already some extensions to MediaWiki available where we chose the ReaderFeedback[7] extension.

As third component for the privacy and security requirements we use the privacy-enhancing identity management system PRIME [29] as it was used in [10] to assist users in controlling their personal data. This data can be certified by third parties in the form of credentials. Credentials can be convertible [30] and might be used with various unlinkable pseudonyms. The implementation used by

---

[7] http://www.mediawiki.org/wiki/Extension:ReaderFeedback

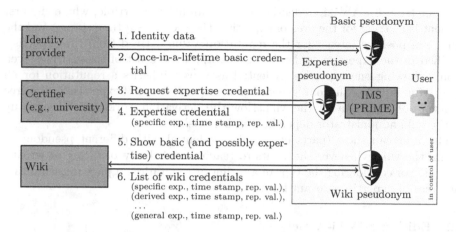

Fig. 1. Registration process enabling unlinkability of a user and her pseudonyms

PRIME for the credential realization is IdentityMixer[8]. This allows for balancing privacy requirements with accountability of users as discussed in [10].

To reach (pseudonymous) accountability of all data and credentials a public-key-infrastructure is needed. For our scenario we assume all actions and ratings to be secured by (pseudonymous) digital signatures. Additionally we assume all communication to be secured by encryption and anonymised by using an anonymity service to reach confidentiality and anonymity of all ratings and actions performed against outsiders.

The user reputation system needs to be integrated in all three system components as we will describe in the following for all actions users can perform. An illustration, how the communication flow of the components is done is shown for the example of editing a wiki article in Fig. 3.

5.1 Registration

A user registers a basic pseudonym with an identity provider by declaration of some identity data (step 1 in Fig. 1). After verifying the data the identity provider issues a basic credential to her (step 2 in Fig. 1). This credential has the meaning, that the identity provider checked the identity data, is willing to disclose it in the case of the user's misbehavior, and that the credential is issued per user only once in her life.

When the user gains some expertise in an area that can be certified by an independent certifier (e.g., a university) she may ask the certifier (step 3 in Fig. 1) under her expertise pseudonym for a respective expertise credential (step 4).

When the user wants to register in a wiki under a wiki pseudonym she sends the wiki her basic credential (and possibly her expertise credential(s) (step 5 in Fig. 1). The wiki provider creates a list of wiki credentials and sends it back to

---

[8] http://prime.inf.tu-dresden.de/idemix/

the user (step 6). A wiki credential contains an attribute-triple, where the first element is a string for the area of expertise, the second is a time stamp, and the third is a positive integer for the reputation value derived from the expertise, certified in the expertise credential. There might be a list of these triples even if only showing one expertise credential as a user inherits a reputation for all areas lying in the path from 'general' to her specific area of expertise in the tree structure of metadata for the wiki. How the derivation works can be setup up by the wiki administrator depending on her wishes.

The user can show (parts of) a wiki credential with different pseudonyms within the wiki whenever she wants to reach unlinkability of rating or writing content. For considering the type of a rating or reputation, a page must indicate the areas of expertise relevant for it.

5.2   Editing a Wiki-Article

After editing a page (step 1 in Fig. 3), a user is asked which reputation will be shown to others reading the content (step 3). Here it comes clear why we only allow positive ratings because the user would suppress negative one here. There are actually two choices she can make:

First she decides which areas of expertise to choose the reputation from. As the area of the content is fixed, a user may choose the credential, which is specific to the content or an inherited one. A more specific credential will have more impact on the content, a more general one has the benefit of higher anonymity. E.g., if the content is about gynecology, a surgeon might use her credential about medicine or a general knowledge credential.

Second as the reputation is a positive value she can decide on which value smaller or equal to her reputation value in the area she wants to show. For this reason we make use of credentials that allow greater-than-proofs [31]. E.g., when having a reputation value of 63, an author may prove that she has a value greater than 20 or greater than 50 or that she actually has 63. The higher a reputation value is, the more impact it will have on the reputation value of the content but as the number of authors having at least this reputation decreases with increasing reputation value, the anonymity of the author decreases as well.

As every user has to decide on this trade-off on her own, a so called "Send Personal Data Dialog" asks the user for her reputation value and tries to display the trade-off in a graphical way. This dialog is shown in Fig. 2(a). The calculation logics used to show the degree of anonymity is based on the number of credentials with a similar reputation value the wiki server saw recently to calculate the user's anonymity. This is the user's current anonymity set for showing this reputation value. Note that the server does not get the actual reputation value from the user in this dialogue, but only provides the user with the data she got from other users when showing reputation to calculate the user's anonymity. Based on this data the user can calculate her possible anonymity as an estimation and displays it to the user. This problem of only estimating anonymity is inherent existent in privacy-enhanced identity management [32] as there exists no global authority that has all user data and can calculate a user's anonymity exactly.

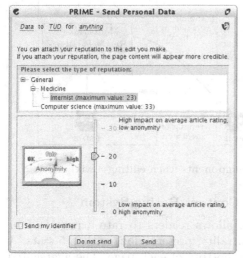

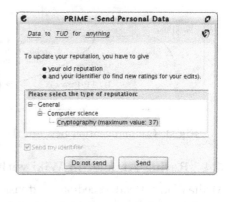

(a) Attaching reputation to the content.   (b) Collecting new ratings

Fig. 2. Two dialogs which show, how personal data is sent

After the user made her choice which reputation to show the wiki server receives the reputation value and can offer it to other users for calculation of anonymity.

In addition to the choices which areas of expertise and which ratings to show, the user can decide on whether she wants to indicate the wiki pseudonym she registered with the wiki to collect reputation. This gives her the possibility to benefit w.r.t. the increase of her reputation value, whenever other raters give a high rating to the page. However, giving the wiki pseudonym makes her linkable. The decision about sending the wiki pseudonym is done with a checkbox shown in Fig. 2(a) ('Send my identifier') on the bottom. This process is driven by the user's own decision whether she wants to collect these ratings or not, both at the time of editing an article by giving a linkable pseudonym and after the article is rated if she includes this rating in her wiki credential.

5.3 Collecting Reputation

If an author provided her identifier, she may collect reputation, given to articles she wrote. She therefore has to show the wiki pseudonym again. The dialog asking for this pseudonym is shown in Fig. 2(b). After showing the old wiki credential, the server issues a new reputation triple. There are a number of possibilities for calculation of reputation [1]. Our reputation system is able to handle ones based on positive ratings with the possibility to weight ratings depending on the rater('s) reputation and to decrease reputation depending on its age indicated in the time stamp of a wiki credential. Both aspects can be configured within our implementation by the wiki administrator.

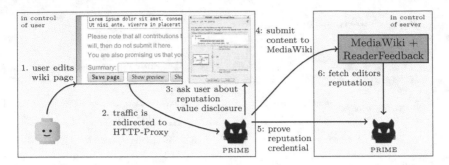

Fig. 3. Communication between the components when editing a wiki article

5.4   Rating Articles in Wiki with Content Rating System

MediaWiki's ReaderFeedback extension allows readers to rate a page in four categories (reliability, completeness, neutrality, presentation) with 1–5 stars. A rating form is shown to the user on the bottom of each page. The aggregated reputation displayed is a daily and selected interval average rating. We modified this extension to collect the user's reputation together with the ratings of a page.

A dialog similar to the one shown in Fig. 2(a) asking for the reputation to show is displayed when a user wants to submit her rating. As for writing content the user has to make a trade-off between showing expertise or remaining anonymous.

5.5   Reading Content in Wiki with User and Content Rating System

Readers have the possibility to view the average rating in the four categories the articles was rated on as in the ReaderFeedback extension. Additionally the detailed list of authors the content had (with their revealed user reputation at this point) and the ratings (with their raters and reputation) can be shown (Fig. 4). The raters' reputation is shown on top of the table below the name or pseudonym of the rater. The different icons represent the reputation type shown (e.g., the syringes represent a certain reputation in medical area). The stars below the raters are the ratings, which were given to a single revision of the page. If an author indicated some reputation together with a page edit, this reputation is shown beneath the authors name or pseudonym.

6   Evaluation

In the following we analyse to which extent the requirements from Section 4 could be met with the prototype.

6.1   Functional Requirements

Positive integers as ratings and reputation: This is given by design of the ReaderFeedback-Extension and our user reputation system based on this.
Possibility of non-zero initial reputation: The expertise credentials allow for indicating prior certified knowledge.

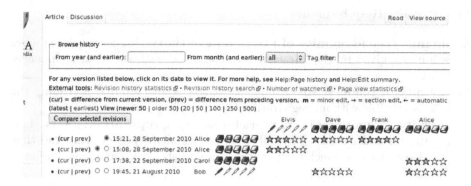

Fig. 4. Example of ratings given to a specific article

Area-specific reputation: The construction of the reputation credential in the form of (area of expertise, time stamp, rating)-triples allows for separating different areas of expertise.

Influence of rater on user reputation: This can be considered by the reputation computation algorithm if the rater agrees to reveal his reputation.

Influence of time on user reputation: This can be considered by the reputation computation algorithm as the wiki credentials contain a timestamp.

Availability of user reputation with content: The users' reputation at the time of editing or rating a wiki article is shown with it. Further updates are not considered.

6.2 Security Requirements

Integrity of content and ratings: As all ratings and content are signed integrity is given.

Accountability of raters: Accountability with the help of the identity provider is given as well as she can reveal the user's identity in the case of misuse. Within the registration process, the user shows her basic credential. Based on this credential, she gets only one wiki credential, which can be converted once by the user to avoid linkability to this registration. This has the advantage that the wiki server can verify if a revision is already rated by an author and update old ratings if necessary. Also self-ratings are prevented and users can collect their ratings to be included in their reputation.

No self-rating: Self-rating is contradicting to the privacy requirements. It therefore is prevented only partially. If users cannot be linked between their areas of expertise, a user can rate her specialized expertise credential with a more general one. However, as the granularity of the ontology has not necessarily to be too fine-grained, a user may not get many ratings (e.g., if the tree from general to specialized is surgery – medicine – general, a user may rate the surgery credential twice) As every user gets only one non-convertible credential from the identity provider, acting with two different wiki credentials which rate one user is prevented.

6.3   Privacy Requirements

Anonymity/pseudonymity of raters and authors: Pseudonymity of users is initially given by the infrastructure combined with the identity management.

Anonymity of readers: Anonymity of readers is also assured if reading the wiki is possible without registration.

Anonymity/Pseudonymity of users for showing reputation: Users show reputation under a pseudonym if they write under a pseudonym. And they can determine how much of their reputation to show to remain anonymous.

Unlinkability of users for rating and writing content. For rating and writing content the users resp. the wiki provider can determine the unlinkability of users depending on the credentials used and on the reputation shown as we will outline in the following.

- **Unlinkability for different articles:** The wiki provider issues one credential per user and article. The user can convert the credentials once to assure unlinkability. The wiki provider learns from issuing the credentials the pages a user is interested in (except a user fetches credentials for all pages by default or some dummy-credentials in addition to the real ones). Still this has the advantage that the wiki server can verify, if a revision is already rated by an author and update old ratings if necessary. Also self-ratings are prevented and users can collect their ratings to be included in their reputation. Ratings received under different pseudonyms can be aggregated.
- **Unlinkability for versions of an article:** As wiki articles change frequently users might also want to be unlinkable for different versions. To achieve this the wiki provider issues additionally a number of one-show credentials (containing the user's reputation) in a specific time period. With these credentials the user may rate a number revisions of an article in the specific period, proving her reputation anonymously. This makes the user unlinkable but she is not able to collect her ratings afterwards and whatever she does under these one-time pseudonyms does not influence her reputation.
- **Unlinkability with respect to reputation:** Even if users are unlinkable for different (versions of) articles or ratings with respect to showing credentials they still might be linkable by their reputation if always showing the same one or one following deterministic rules. According to [13] the set of pseudonyms $\mathcal{P}$ at time t in a system is split into several subsets regarding the relation "has the same reputation". The set $\mathcal{P}_{t,r} = \{p_{t,i}|rep(t,p_{t,i}) = r.\}$ with the pseudonyms having the reputation $r \in R$ is the anonymity set a user has for re-using a pseudonym if we assume an attacker who knows the reputation of all users at a time (like the wiki provider does). This anonymity set can be increased in our system if a user shows a smaller than her actual reputation value. Then her anonymity set will be $\mathcal{P}_{t,\geq r} = \{p_{t,i}|rep(t,p_{t,i}) \geq r.\}$ with $|\mathcal{P}_{t,\geq r}| \geq |\mathcal{P}_{t,r}|$ as all reputations only increase.

7 Conclusion and Future Work

In this paper we have investigated the privacy needs of users with respect to their reputation in a wiki in comparison to other personal data. As results of our empirical study shew that users' reputation value should be treated as personal data item we built a framework that allows users to balance their need for privacy and others' wish for trustworthiness of content by the usage of metadata to indicate users' areas of expertise. Still the design of the framework uses the assumption the platform MediaWiki makes for the reputation computation of content. Future studies need to show which set of possible reputation values users like most and how areas of expertise can be related.

References

1. Jøsang, A., Ismail, R., Boyd, C.: A survey of trust and reputation systems for online service provision. Decision Support Systems 43(2), 618–644 (2007)
2. Schafer, J.B., Konstan, J.A., Riedl, J.: E-commerce recommendation applications. Data Min. Knowl. Discov. 5(1-2), 115–153 (2001)
3. Resnick, P., Zeckhauser, R.: Trust among strangers in internet transactions: Empirical analysis of ebay's reputation system. The economics of the internet and e-commerce. Advances in Applied Microeconomics 11, 127–157 (2002)
4. Livingston, J.A.: How valuable is a good reputation? A sample selection model of internet auctions. The Review of Economics and Statistics 87(3), 453–465 (2005)
5. Dondio, P., Barrett, S., Weber, S., Seigneur, J.-M.: Extracting trust from domain analysis: A case study on the wikipedia project. In: Yang, L.T., Jin, H., Ma, J., Ungerer, T. (eds.) ATC 2006. LNCS, vol. 4158, pp. 362–373. Springer, Heidelberg (2006)
6. Adler, B.T., de Alfaro, L.: A content-driven reputation system for the wikipedia. In: WWW 2007: Proceedings of the 16th international conference on World Wide Web, pp. 261–270. ACM, New York (2007)
7. Lefévre, T., Jensen, C.D., Korsgaard, T.R.: Wrs: The wikipedia recommender system. In: Ferrari, E., Li, N., Bertino, E., Karabulut, Y. (eds.) IFIPTM 2009. IFIP Advances in Information and Communication Technology, vol. 300, pp. 298–301. Springer, Heidelberg (2009)
8. Bygrave, L.: Data Protection Law, Approaching Its Rationale, Logic and Limits. Kluwer Law International, The Hague (2002)
9. Mahler, T., Olsen, T.: Reputation systems and data protection law. In: eAdoption and the Knowledge Economy: Issues, Applications, Case Studies, pp. 180–187. IOS Press, Amsterdam (2004)
10. Pingel, F., Steinbrecher, S.: Multilateral secure cross-community reputation systems. In: Furnell, S.M., Katsikas, S.K., Lioy, A. (eds.) TrustBus 2008. LNCS, vol. 5185, pp. 69–78. Springer, Heidelberg (2008)
11. Kittur, A., Suh, B., Chi, E.H.: Can you ever trust a wiki?: impacting perceived trustworthiness in wikipedia. In: CSCW, pp. 477–480. ACM, New York (2008)

12. Pavlov, E., Rosenschein, J.S., Topol, Z.: Supporting privacy in decentralized additive reputation systems. In: The Second International Conference on Trust Management, Oxford, United Kingdom, pp. 108–119 (March 2004)
13. Steinbrecher, S.: Design options for privacy-respecting reputation systems within centralised internet communities. In: 21st IFIP International Information Security Conference. IFIP, vol. 201, pp. 123–134. Springer, Heidelberg (2006)
14. Dellarocas, C.: Immunizing online reputation reporting systems against unfair ratings and discriminatory behavior. In: Proceedings of the 2nd ACM conference on Electronic commerce, pp. 150–157. ACM Press, New York (2000)
15. Androulaki, E., Choi, S.G., Bellovin, S.M., Malkin, T.: Reputation systems for anonymous networks. In: Borisov, N., Goldberg, I. (eds.) PETS 2008. LNCS, vol. 5134, pp. 202–218. Springer, Heidelberg (2008)
16. Dellarocas, C.N., Dini, F., Spagnolo, G.: Designing reputation (feedback) mechanisms. In: Dimitri, N., Piga, G., Spagnolo, G. (eds.) Handbook of Procurement, Cambridge University Press, Cambridge (2006)
17. Schiffner, S., Clauß, S., Steinbrecher, S.: Privacy and liveliness for reputation systems. In: Martinelli, F., Preneel, B. (eds.) EuroPKI 2009. LNCS, vol. 6391, pp. 209–224. Springer, Heidelberg (2010)
18. Kerschbaum, F.: A verifiable, centralized, coercion-free reputation system. In: WPES, pp. 61–70. ACM, New York (2009)
19. Schiffner, S., Clauß, S., Steinbrecher, S.: Privacy, liveliness and fairness for reputation. In: Černá, I., Gyimóthy, T., Hromkovič, J., Jefferey, K., Králović, R., Vukolić, M., Wolf, S. (eds.) SOFSEM 2011. LNCS, vol. 6543, pp. 506–519. Springer, Heidelberg (2011)
20. Adams, A.: The implications of users' privacy perception on communication and information privacy policies. In: Proceedings of Telecommunications Policy Research Conference, Washington, DC (1999)
21. Pötzsch, S.: Privacy Awareness: A Means to Solve the Privacy Paradox? In: Matyáš, V., Fischer-Hübner, S., Cvrček, D., Švenda, P. (eds.) IFIP WG 9.2, 9.6/11.6, 11.7/FIDIS. IFIP Advances in Information and Communication Technology, vol. 298, pp. 226–236. Springer, Heidelberg (2009)
22. Taddicken, M.: Measuring Online Privacy Concern and Protection in the (Social) Web: Development of the APCP and APCP-18 Scale. In: 60th Annual ICA Conference (International Communication Association), Singapur (June 2010)
23. Wirtz, M., Nachtigall, C.: Deskriptive Statistik. Statistische Methoden für Psychologen, vol. 1. Juventa-Verlag (2008)
24. Whitmeyer, J.M.: Effects of positive reputation systems. Social Science Research 29(2), 188–207 (2000)
25. Friedman, E., Resnick, P.: The social cost of cheap pseudonyms. Journal of Economics and Management Strategy 10, 173–199 (1999)
26. Jensen, C.D., Lefévre, T.: Classifying areas of expertise in the wikipedia recommender system. Online Paper at IFIPTM (2010), http://www.ifip-tm2010.org/lib/exe/fetch.php?media=shortpaper08.pdf
27. ENISA: Position Paper. Reputation-based Systems: a security analysis (2007), http://www.enisa.europa.eu/act/it/oar/reputation-systems/ reputation-based-systems-a-security-analysis/at_download/fullReport
28. Rannenberg, K., Pfitzmann, A., Müller, G.: IT security and multilateral security. In: Müller, G., Rannenberg, K. (eds.) Multilateral Security in Communications (Technology, Infrastructure, Economy), vol. 3, pp. 21–29. Addison-Wesley, München (1999)

29. Casassa-Mont, M., Crosta, S., Kriegelstein, T., Sommer, D.: Architecture v2. Deliverable D14.2.c, PRIME (March 2007),
https://www.prime-project.eu/prime_products/reports/arch/
pub_del_D14.2.c_ec_WP14.2_v1_Final.pdf
30. Chaum, D.: Showing credentials without identification. In: Pichler, F. (ed.) EUROCRYPT 1985. LNCS, vol. 219, pp. 241–244. Springer, Heidelberg (1986)
31. Camenisch, J., Van Herreweghen, E.: Design and implementation of the idemix anonymous credential system. In: CCS, pp. 21–30. ACM, New York (2002)
32. Clauß, S.: A framework for quantification of linkability within a privacy-enhancing identity management system. In: Müller, G. (ed.) ETRICS 2006. LNCS, vol. 3995, pp. 191–205. Springer, Heidelberg (2006)

Security and Privacy in E-consumer Protection in Victoria, Australia

Huong Ha

University of Newcastle, Singapore
artp6075singapore@yahoo.com

Abstract. Governments in many countries have actively promoted both regulatory and self-regulatory approaches to govern e-commerce and to protect e-consumers. Nevertheless, the desired outcomes of e-consumer protection have not fully materialised. Although there are many research projects about e-commerce, security, privacy, trust, etc., few relate to e-consumer protection. In addition, most projects on e-consumer protection only focus on individual issues, rather than examining the entire coverage of the protection of e-consumers. This paper, a theoretical one, aims to fill these gaps by (i) identifying five issues in e-consumer protection, (ii) discussing the current regulatory and non-regulatory framework of e-consumer protection, (iii) examining the effectiveness of this current framework, and (iv) proposing how this framework can be improved to address current and future problems. This paper will use Victoria, Australia as a case study and takes into account the view of all stakeholders.

Keywords: E-consumer, e-consumer protection, e-retailing, jurisdiction, privacy, security, redress, regulation, self-regulation.

1 Introduction

It is no doubt that e-commerce has generated several benefits to e-users, and it is still a popular platform for commercial transactions in the next few years. The volume of e-transactions is expected to reach over US$71 billion by 2012 [1]. However, e-commerce also raises many problems for e-users and the operations of the e-market, especially consumer protection [2]. This paper has identified five issues relating to the protection of consumers in the online market (or e-consumer protection), which are the barriers for the development of e-commerce. They are (i) information disclosure and verification, (ii) security, (iii) jurisdiction, (iv) redress, and (v) privacy.

To address these issues, the Australian government has implemented a mixture of approaches, including government regulation and guidelines, self-regulation by industry, professional associations and businesses. However, the effectiveness of the current regulatory framework of e-consumer protection has not been adequately assessed. In addition, the self-regulatory approach has not worked for e-consumers. The number of consumer complaints about online purchases and payment has steadily increased [3]. Although many works and research have attempted to address issues in e-consumer protection, most of them only focus on individual issues. Also, there is

I. Wakeman et al. (Eds.): IFIPTM 2011, IFIP AICT 358, pp. 240–252, 2011.

insufficient academic work analysing the current state of e-consumer protection and assessing the effectiveness of the current e-consumer protection in Australia. Thus, this paper aims to (i) identify five issues in e-consumer protection, (ii) examine the current regulatory and non-regulatory framework of e-consumer protection, (iii) evaluate this current framework, using Victoria (Australia) as a case study, and (iv) recommend how e-consumer protection can be enhanced.

Overall, although this is a theoretical paper, it will contribute to identify positive and negative impacts of the current regulatory framework on e-consumer protection. This paper is important as protecting e-consumers means protecting e-businesses which, in turn, can improve the online global market. It will also trigger further research on how to protect global e-consumers more effectively.

2 Five Issues in E-consumer Protection

Due to the differences between the offline and online market places, consumers have to face more risks when shopping online. Apart from the common issues faced in traditional forms of commerce, e-consumers have to deal with the five issues relating to e-transactions, namely (i) information disclosure, (ii) security, (iii) jurisdiction, (iv) redress, and (v) privacy. These issues are important and interdependent. Although no issue is more critical than others, this paper focuses on two main issues, security and privacy, given the nature of the online market and e-consumer protection.

Information Disclosure and Verification
In the online market place, e-consumers are disadvantageous as they have to provide all information required via the Internet, while they do not know about e-retailers. E-consumers have to make decision with limited or asymmetric information. Thus, information about the registration status and the location where e-retailers register their business must be displayed on their website [4]. E-consumers must also know the description about goods/services as they will purchase based on the description of goods/services provided on websites. Without sufficient and precise information, e-consumers are unable to make informed decisions [5]. In addition, information about transaction processes, refund, exchange, delivery, etc. must also be available to e-consumers as they have to pay in advance and have to make decision without having a chance to negotiate with e-retailers. All terms and conditions must be presented precisely and simply to help e-consumers to make their best choices [6].

Security
Security embraces two issues: data and payment security. Data security refers to the protection of personal identity and information (contact number, income, etc.). Personal information and identity may be collected for many purposes or even for committing crimes [7] [8]. Online payment is a special feature of e-retailing. To enjoy the convenience of shopping online, buyers have to pay mainly by credit cards. Global e-consumers have been increasingly concerned about the misuse of credit card information and the theft of credit card details. In Australia, the security of online payment is one of the main reasons discouraging consumers to shop online [9]. Charge back is another sub-issue. Many e-customers do not know how to collect the

refund or the amount of money wrongly charged by e-retailers if e-retailers ignore their requests [10].

Jurisdiction
Consumers encounter higher level of risks relating to security, privacy, fraudulence, and scam when they are online. It is more difficult to address these cyber misdeeds due to different legal frameworks from different countries. Consumers face two key issues when they buy from sellers locating in different jurisdictions: (i) which regulation they should follow, and (ii) which government bodies will resolve any subsequent dispute [11]. Since cross-border trade involves in many countries, jurisdiction concern needs to be addressed at multilateral levels of government.

Redress
E-consumers will not shop online if there is no redress mechanism available [12]. This kind of fear grows bigger in the online market when the transactions are done across nations. Ironically, many customers may find it too troublesome to ask for a refund or an exchange when the quality of goods/services is not acceptable or products purchased are not delivered. Customers are often afraid that costs spent for redress may be higher than the amount of compensation [13]. In the offline market, many options are available to consumers when they need to seek compensation for defective goods purchased [14]. Nevertheless, traditional ways of resolving disputes may not be applicable in the global e-market. For example, consumers may not be able to return products purchased to e-retailers due to the distance and cost involved. Therefore, addressing redress concern may contribute to facilitate online transactions.

Privacy
E-consumers are very concerned about the misuse of personal details via illegal collection and dissemination of such information [15] [16]. To make this situation worse, many e-traders in Australia do not publish privacy policies on their websites [17]. There are two main privacy concerns: (i) e-consumers' personal particulars and their credit card details will be used by unauthorised persons or by authorised persons without their consent or knowledge; and (ii) their e-mail address and correspondence will be unlawfully accessed and used for unknown purposes [18]. Paradoxically, some customers do not hesitate giving their particulars to e-retailers or promoters in exchange for some economic gain such as discount or cheaper purchases.

3   The Current Regulatory and Non-regulatory Framework of E-consumer Protection

Consumer protection aims to protect the benefits of consumers in commercial transactions [19]. Since online transactions are cross-border, the protection of consumer must be exercised at three levels: international, national and state levels.

International and National Initiatives to Protect e-Consumers
Electronic transactions have obtained the same status as other forms of transactions as they have been legally recognized by the *Model Law on Electronic Commerce*

enacted by the United Nations Commission on International Trade Law, the *Commonwealth Electronic Transactions Act 1999* and the *Victorian Electronic Transactions Act 2000* [20]. Hence, e-consumers must receive equal protection as consumers in traditional markets [21].

The United Nations General Assembly adopted the principles of consumer protection in 1985 [22]. These guidelines provide the direction for member countries to develop, strengthen and modify the legal framework and policies related to e-consumer protection in their countries. The UN guidelines also seek strong cooperation among all stakeholders to develop a healthy global online market. This resolution consists of six general principles and seven guidelines aiming to achieve the above objectives. Nonetheless, this set of guidelines is applicable to consumer protection in general, not particular to e-consumers.

The 1999 *OECD Guidelines for Consumer Protection in the Context of Electronic Commerce* aim to (i) promote a conducive online environment for all players to increase cross-border trade; (ii) provide direction for countries to align their e-consumer protection policies with international laws and practices; (iii) call for self-regulation by and active participation from all stakeholders; and (iv) call for equal protection of consumers in both the online and offline markets [23] [24]. The OECD *guidelines* suggest eight principles of consumer protection in B2C e-commerce.

The Australian government has addressed the issues arisen in e-commerce by introducing the national guidelines, *"Building Consumer Sovereignty in Electronic Commerce: a Best Practice Model for Business"* (the BPM) [25] which complements the five principles of consumer protection discussed in *Policy Framework for Consumer Protection in Electronic Commerce (1999)*. This BPM aims to enhance consumer sovereignty by encouraging stakeholders to adopt a self-regulatory approach and to exercise their social responsibility to protect consumers. The BPM does not apply to overseas traders and neither does it include e-auction [26].

These three sets of guidelines share a common element of calling for voluntary compliance and self-reviewing of national consumer protection policies [27].

Current Measures to Protect E-consumers in Victoria, Australia

This section examines the current regulatory and non-regulatory framework to address fives issues in consumer protection in e-retailing in Victoria, Australia.

Information Disclosure and Verification

In Australia, information disclosure and fair trading in both offline and online markets are regulated by the *Trade Practices Act 1974* (TPA 1974) which aims to protect the welfare of all stakeholders nationally [28]. Under the TPA 1974, businesses must avoid misleading advertising, fraudulence and other unfair and dishonest practices such as unauthorized billing or selling faulty products [29] [30].

Consumer protection is highlighted in Part V of the TPA 1974. Although the TPA 1974 originally aims to protect consumers and promote fair trade practices in traditional commerce, many of its provisions in Part V can be applied in e-commerce [31]. The TPA 1974 can only partially address the issues relating to information disclosure. Besides, the TPA 1974 does not cover all types of companies and all businesses in Australia [32]. Another source of legislation is acts enacted by states and territories, such as the *Victorian Fair Trading Act 1999, South Australian Fair Trading Act 1987, New South Wale Fair Trading Act 1987,* and others.

Security

Addressing security concern to counteract cyber threats and vulnerabilities can positively affect the global economic growth [33]. This task requires strong cooperation and collaboration among all sectors and among nations. At national level, security concern is addressed by both the public and the private sectors.

The Commonwealth government introduces several measures to ensure confidentiality, integrity and availability in the online environment [34]. The first measure is the enactment of legislations relating to security. These legislations include the *Commonwealth Cybercrime Act 2001* (amended in 2004), the *Australian Security Intelligence Organisation Act 1979*, the *Crimes Act 1914*, the *Criminal Code Act 1995* and the *Telecommunications (Interception) Act 1979.* These Acts aim to prevent potential cyber attacks of security systems of businesses and government agencies. According to the *Cyber Crime Act 2001*, some individuals and agents may by exempted from this Act [35]. The *Security Legislation Amendment (Terrorism) Act 2002* deals with potential attacks by terrorists via the cyberspace [36]. Nevertheless, there is an absence of initiatives of states in the combat against cyber-crimes. For example, Victoria does not pass any legislation relating to security or identity theft.

The Australian government also works closely with industry to set up "a Business-Government Task Force on Critical Infrastructure" which oversees problems associated with cyber-security [37]. The National Information Infrastructure (2000) was introduced to promote the cooperation of all stakeholders and create a reliable online environment [38]. Launched in April 2003, the Trusted Information Sharing Network for Critical Infrastructure Protection engages an "all-hazards" approach to tackle current and potential vulnerabilities [39]. *OnSecure* website (2003) by the government offers a convenient and secure platform for inter-departmental use. The public can also access its public site at www.onsecure.gov.au to obtain information about e-security threats [40]. The private sector exercises social responsibility by introducing more inclusive hi-tech solutions. These solutions range from e-cash, e-certificates, to e-signatures which enable customers to protect their details in e-purchases. Bio-technology is also explored to enhance data and payment security [41]. Surprisingly, Victoria does not enact specific legislation relating to security. There is no record of the participation of consumer associations in e-security projects.

Jurisdiction

So far, jurisdiction concern has not been received sufficient attention at the international and national levels. The *TPA 1974* and the *Victoria Fair Trading (Amendment) Act 2003* mainly apply to businesses registered in Australia. Even the *OECD Guidelines* and the Australia BPM only emphasize self-regulation by businesses and industry. Only the Free Trade Agreements (FTAs) between Australia and Singapore, Australia and Thailand as well as Australia and USA state clearly the responsibility of each party in the protection of e-consumers [42]. Most FTAs do not specify any mechanisms or collaboration to address problems relating to e-transactions. Although these FTAs acknowledge the importance of consumer laws and policies of counterpart countries in the facilitation of international trade, they do not really demonstrate how jurisdiction concern can be tackled.

Redress

The dispute resolution framework in Australia includes three stages: (i) settlement between e-customers and e-retailers, (ii) settlement via a third party, and (iii) settlement via an independent Ombudsman or going to court.

If customers are not happy with the online purchase, they can directly complain to e-retailers who will address problems via their internal dispute resolution processes. However, many customers find it difficult to settle the matter with e-retailers from different jurisdictions [43]. They may not pursue the case if it is too time consuming.

If the problems are not solved at the first stage, e-consumers can employ Alternative Dispute Resolution schemes (ADRs) or Online Dispute Resolutions (ODRs) by external parties [44]. ADRs/ODRs can provide users with cheap, expedient and effective solutions and help to avoid jurisdiction problems [45]. The Australian Competition and Consumer Commission (ACCC) [46] provides e-consumers and e-retailers with dispute resolutions before these parties have to involve in litigation. The Australian National Alternative Dispute Resolution Advisory Council [47], a government-linked agency, also helps users to manage commercial disputes. At state level, Consumer Affairs Victoria [48] also provides ADR schemes. In some instance, these government agencies will refer unresolved cases to the ACCC or the Australian Securities and Investments Commission for investigation and settlement [49]. Some popular organisations offer industry-based dispute resolution schemes are the Telecommunications Industry Ombudsman, the Australian Direct Marketing Association (ADMA) and the Internet Industry Association (IIA). Schemes offered by international consumer associations are mainly online. Consumer International, an international consumer association, helps consumers to "exercise their rights and responsibilities" in dispute resolution [50]. Other international online ODR services are *Sentinel*, the American Better Business Bureau, CyberSettle, SquareTrade, etc. [51].

Finally, if consumers do not satisfy with the outcome of an ADR procedure, they can approach an independent Ombudsman to help their cases resolved or they can seek legal action through the Small Claim courts or other courts [52].

Privacy

In Australia, personal privacy is protected based on two main mechanisms, namely (i) common laws, and (ii) self-regulatory approach by firms and industries [53].

Common Laws. The *Commonwealth Privacy Act 1988* applies to the public sector, and the *Privacy Amendment (Private Sector) Act 2000* covers the rest in the handle of personal information [54] [55]. These acts require that personal data must be collected, used and stored confidentially. Recipients must be informed about the purposes of the collection of their personal data. The *Spam Act 2003* states that sending of "unsolicited commercial electronic messages" [56] with an Australian link and using "address-harvesting software" (spyware) is prohibited [57]. However, many government agencies, registered political parties, religious organisations, small businesses (revenue of less than $3 million), the media, etc. are excluded from its coverage [58]. Finally, only Australian citizens and permanent residents are protected under these Acts [59]. Another privacy act is the Commonwealth *Telecommunications Act* which specifies the responsibilities of service providers in terms of the usage and the disclosure of customers' personal information [60]. Victoria only passed the *Information Privacy Act* in 2000 which regulates the handling of personal information, but excluding "personal health information", in the public sector [61].

Self-regulation. Currently, there are two industry associations that introduce voluntary codes of practice dealing with spam. They are the ADMA and the IIA. The ADMA also appoints an independent Code Authority to monitor the compliance of its members with the code of practice [62]. Both sets of code of practice mainly apply to their members and code subscribers (if any), though non-members can adopt these codes. Other initiatives from the private sector include services relating to audits of privacy policies and privacy seals [63]. The audits ensure that private enterprises adhere to their own privacy policies.

4 The Effectiveness of the Current Regulatory and Non-regulatory Framework in E-consumer Protection

Facts and Figures

Internationally, 64% of the respondents will not shop online [64]. In another global survey, 42% of the respondents received spam e-mails which accounted for more than 50% of their e-mails [65]. In Australia, 3,317 complaints relating to e-transactions were lodged with the ACCC in 2001 and 2002. 19.17% of these were complaints about online issues such as deceptive advertising, guarantee and refund [66] [67]. Until June 2003, 2,899 similar complaints, accounted for 5.4% of total complaints, were recorded [68]. The amount of money lost due to online fraud was AU$980 million with 806,000 victims in 2007 in Australia [69]. The loss due to online scams was A$839,365 in 2008, and A$544,694 in 2009 [70]. Also, "Internet shopping trustmarks in 2005" was assessed as "little effectiveness" by Australia [71].

In Victoria, 183 e-commerce complaints were handled by Consumer Affairs Victoria in 2002. This figure indicated an increase of 45.24% of complaints compared to year 2001. 41% of these complaints were related to e-sales; 35% were related to "domain name services", and 24% of the complaints were about "Internet Service Providers" [72]. In the survey in May 2003 by Consumer Affairs Victoria, only 4% of 380 Australian trader websites posted information about procedures to handle complaints [73]. It should be noted that the statistics are not updated as only 25% of fraud cases was reported to policy or the respecitve authorities or agencies [74].

What Works and What Does Not Work?

The findings indicate that government acts and regulations do not cover all aspects of e-consumer protection. For example, many individuals and organisations are excluded from the *Cyber Crime Act 2001* and others. Such individuals and organisations may take advantage of the legal loophole for their personal gain. In addition, guidelines and code of practice are not mandatory and must be backed up by government regulation. However, states heavily rely on national legislation and guidelines for e-consumer protection as there is inadequate government regulation at the state level. Besides, there is insufficient involvement and coordination among stakeholders. For instance, in Victoria, few activities relating to e-consumer protection by civil society have been recorded. The private sector also provides limited contribution to address issues concerning security and privacy.

E-consumers would purchase online if they trust e-retailers. Trust is one of the business strategies of reputable e-retailers to retain existing customers and to attract new customers. Thus, self-regulation by e-retailers would strengthen the trade relationship between e-consumers and e-retailers. Nevertheless, the degree of employing self-regulatory approaches varies from one e-retailer to another, either in the same industry or in different industry. This causes confusion to e-consumers, and makes it difficult for the respective government agencies to monitor.

Generally, limited effectiveness has been achieved in e-consumer protection. Consumers can obtain fair treatment in business transactions when they can get sufficient and precise information about products and services, about e-retailers and about all terms and conditions. In the offline market, customers can get such information by various channels. However, the overloaded or underloaded information on the Internet make it difficult for customers to make good decisions [75]. Trans-national online incidents diminish consumer confidence in the e-market, directing consumers to decide that they must only have business relationships with well-known, local vendors [76]. Therefore, consumers will engage in online shopping only when they are ensured that they will be well protected and when the potential gain from online shopping will exceed the level of risks they have to face.

5 Recommendations to Improve E-consumer Protection

The above discussion suggests that special conditions are required to ensure the level of consumer protection in the online environment the same as in the offline market. While many legislative provisions and regulatory frameworks have been implemented to address consumer protection in traditional commerce, very few have demonstrated their effectiveness and efficiency in the protection of e-consumers. Besides, the current policy framework does not really adhere to the *OECD Guidelines* and the five Australian principles of consumer protection in e-commerce. Thus, recommendations to improve e-consumer protection are discussed as follows.

Firstly, government regulations and acts should cover as much as possible all aspects of e-consumer protection. The online marketplace evolves rapidly, and thus enforcement of regulations must be frequently monitored, and regulations must be revised to respond to changes and meet the needs of e-consumers in the online environment. Also, projects aiming to enhance e-consumer protection should focus on both macro and micro levels as online incidents will affect both e-consumers and e-retailers, and the whole industry. Importantly, governments must ensure that consumers in both traditional and online marketplaces receive equal protection [77].

Secondly, the online marketplace is cross-border and cross-jurisdiction. It is impossible for any single individual or agency, either in the public or private sector, to provide e-consumer protection without cross-support and external assistance.

Hence, international and national collaboration is required to enable all stakeholders to share information about online incidents and how to deal with such incidents.

Finally, it is not feasible for governments to police the website of each and every e-retailer to ensure that regulations and policies are complied with. In addition, e-consumers would carry out transactions with e-retailers who can provide good quality of products and services, with reasonable price and flexible terms and conditions. In other words, e-consumers will deal with only trustworthy e-retailers. Therefore, adoption of both regulatory and self-regulatory measures may help e-retailers to retain existing e-customers and to attract new e-customers.

6   Conclusion

In brief, due to the cross-border nature and the speed of e-transactions, e-consumers have to face five additional issues when shopping online, namely (i) information disclosure and verification, (ii) security, (iii) jurisdiction, (iv) redress, and (v) privacy. These issues are interdependent and important to the development of the online market. However, security and privacy are more pertinent to e-consumer protection.

This paper has discussed the current regulatory and non-regulatory framework to protect e-consumers in Victoria, Australia. There are strengths and weaknesses in this framework and its implementation. There is also no empirical evidence whether this current framework is still valid, given the rapid development of the e-market and whether e-consumers are aware of what kind of protection which national and local governments can provide them and whether they are confidence in such protection. Thus, there is a need for further research on e-consumer protection. Further and systematic researches on consumer protection in e-retailing from the standpoint of e-consumers will certainly facilitate the advance of a theoretical framework and practical approaches to solve stagnant problems in e-consumer protection.

Acknowledgment. The author would like to thank Associate Professor Ken Coghill (Department of Management, Monash University) and Dr. Ann Maharaj (Department of Econometrics and Business Statistics, Monash University) for their academic guidance and great support in many aspects to complete her PhD thesis successfully.

References

1. eCommerce Report (2011), http://www.ecommercereport.com.au/?p=183
2. Fairfax Media (2011), http://www.bordermail.com.au/_blogs/national-comment/online-shopping-vs-bricks-and-mortar/2012288. aspx?storypage=2
3. Ha, H.: E-security and the Roles of the Police in E-consumer Protection - Australia Case. In: The 2nd Istanbul Conference on Democracy and Global Security, Turkey (June 14-16, 2007)
4. The Expert Group on Electronic Commerce (2003), http://www.ecommerce.treasury.gov.au/bpmreview/content/DiscussionPaper/01_Summary.asp

5. Quo, S.: Spam: Private and Legislative Responses to Unsolicited Electronic Mail in Australia and the United States. ELaw - Murchdoch University 11(1), 45 (2004)
6. Ha, H.: Three-Sector Governance System Model to Address Fives Issues of Consumer Protection in B2C E-commerce in Victoria, Australia. In: 19th ANZAM Conference, Canberra (December 7-10, 2005)
7. Grabosky, P., Smith, R.G., Dempsey, G.: Electronic Theft: Unlawful Acquisition in Cyberspace. Cambridge University Press, Cambridge (2001)
8. Identity Theft Resource Center News (2009),
   `http://www.idtheftcenter.org/artman2/uploads/1/`
   `ITRaC_NEWS_Q4_2009.pdf`
9. Ha, H., Coghill, K., Maharaj, E.A.: Policy Framework for Protection of E-consumers' Privacy in Australia. In: Chen, K.C., Fadlalla, A. (eds.) Online Consumer Protection: Theories of Human Relativism, pp. 123–150. Idea Group, Inc., USA (2008)
10. Ha, H.: Three-Sector Governance System Model to Address Fives Issues of Consumer Protection in B2C E-commerce in Victoria, Australia. In: 19th ANZAM Conference, Canberra (December 7-10, 2005)
11. Burns, E. (2005),
    `http://www.clickz.com/stats/sectors/email/article.php/3571381`
12. Endeshaw, A.: The Law Vis-A-Vis Electronic Commerce. In: Rahman, S.M., Rasinghani, M.S. (eds.) Electronic Commerce: Opportunity and Challenges. Idea Group Publishing, Hershey (2000)
13. Consumer Affairs Division: Dispute Resolution in Electronic Commerce. Commonwealth of Australia. The Department of Treasury, Canberra (2001)
14. Ha, H.: Three-Sector Governance System Model to Address Fives Issues of Consumer Protection in B2C E-commerce in Victoria, Australia. In: 19th ANZAM Conference, Canberra (December 7-10, 2005)
15. Moghe, V.: Privacy Management - a New Era in the Australian Business Environment. Information Management & Computer Security 11(2), 60–66 (2003)
16. Internet Society (2010), http://www.isoc.org/internet/issues/docs/privacy-survey_2010.pdf
17. Consumer Affairs Victoria: Online Shopping and Consumer Protection. Standing Committee of Officials of Consumer Affairs - E-commerce Working Party, Victoria (2004)
18. Jackson, M.: Internet Privacy. Telecommunications Journal of Australia 53(2), 21–31 (2003)
19. Quirk, P., Forder, J.: Electronic Commerce and The Law, 2nd edn. John Wiley & Sons Australia, Ltd., Queensland (2003)
20. Ha, H.: Three-Sector Governance System Model to Address Fives Issues of Consumer Protection in B2C E-commerce in Victoria, Australia. In: 19th ANZAM Conference, Canberra (December 7-10, 2005)
21. The Expert Group on Electronic Commerce (2003),
    `http://www.ecommerce.treasury.gov.au/bpmreview/content/Discu`
    `ssionPaper/01_Summary.asp`
22. The United Nations Department of Economic and Social Affairs (DESA): Guidelines for Consumer Protection. In: Resolution 39/248: The United Nations (1985)
23. OECD: Policy Brief: Electronic Commerce. OECD, Paris (2001)
24. Smith, R., Budd, C.: Consumer fraud in Australia: costs, rates and awareness of the risks in 2008. Australian Institute of Criminology, Australia (2009)
25. Hockey, J.: Building Consumer Sovereignty in Electronic Commerce: A best practice model for business. Commonwealth of Australia, Canberra (2000)

26. Hockey, J.: A Policy Framework for Consumer Protection in Electronic Commerce. Commonwealth of Australia, Canberra (1999)
27. Harland, D.: The Consumer in the Globalised Information Society. The Impact of the International Organisations. Australian Competition and Consumer Law Journal 7, 23 (1999)
28. Martin, J.: The Roles of the ACCC in Protecting Competition and Fair Dealing. In: Murray Hume Business Enterprise Centre, Albury-Wodonga (September 2, 2004)
29. Graeme, S.: 30 Years of Protecting Consumers and Promoting Competition. Keeping Good Companies 57(1), 38041 (2005)
30. Horvitz, R. (2002), http://www.slideshare.net/tomwinfrey/ecommerce-framework
31. Attorney-General's Department (Australia): Trade Practices Act 1974, vol. 1 (2005)
32. Productivity Commission: Australian and New Zealand Competition and Consumer Protection Regimes. Australian Government, Productivity Commission, Canberra (2004)
33. Ford, P.: Implementing a Culture of Security in Australia. Attorney-General's Department, Deputy Secretary Criminal Justice and Security, Canberra (2003)
34. Department of Communications, Information Technology and the Arts (2005a), http://www.dcita.gov.au/ie/e-security
35. Ha, H.: Three-Sector Governance System Model to Address Fives Issues of Consumer Protection in B2C E-commerce in Victoria, Australia. In: 19th ANZAM Conference, Canberra (December 7-10, 2005)
36. Ford, P.: Implementing a 'Culture of Security' in Australia. Attorney-General's Department, Deputy Secretary Criminal Justice and Security, Canberra (2003)
37. Directorate for Science Technology and Industry, and Committee for Information Computer and Communications Policy (2004), http://www.oecd.org/dataoecd/16/27/35884541.pdf
38. Department of Communications, Information Technology and the Arts (2005b), http://www.dcita.gov.au/ie/e-security?SQ_DESIGN_NAME= printer_friendly
39. Ford, P.: Implementing a 'Culture of Security' in Australia, p. 2. Attorney-General's Department, Deputy Secretary Criminal Justice and Security, Canberra (2003)
40. Hill, R., Ruddock, P. (2005), http://www.agimo.gov.au/media/2003/12/2936.html
41. Directorate for Science, Technology and Industry Committee on Consumer Policy: Report on Consumer Protections for Payment Cardholders. OECD, Paris (2002)
42. Australian Competition and Consumer Commission, http://www.accc.gov.au/content/index.phtml/itemId/563794 (undated)
43. Ha, H.: Three-Sector Governance System Model to Address Fives Issues of Consumer Protection in B2C E-commerce in Victoria, Australia. In: 19th ANZAM Conference, Canberra (December 7-10, 2005)
44. Schellekens, M., Van Der Wees, L.: ADR and ODR in Electronic Commerce. In: Prins, J.E.J., Ribbers, P.M.A., Van Tilborg, H.C.A., Veth, A.F.L., Van Der Wees, J.G.L. (eds.) Trust in Electronic Commerce. The Role of Trust Form a Legal, an Organizational and a Technical Point of View, Kluwer Law International, The Hagues (2002)
45. Tyler, M.C., Bretherton, D.: Country Experiences of ODR: Australia - A Report of Research Conducted for the Department of Justice, Victoria, Australia. In: The UNECE Forum on ODR (2003)

46. Australian Competition and Consumer Commission: Role and Activities (2005), http://www.accc.gov.au/content/index.phtml/itemId/54137/ fromItemId/3744
47. National Alternative Dispute Resolution Advisory Council (2007), http://www.nadrac.gov.au/www/nadrac/nadrac.nsf/Page/ About_NADRAC
48. Consumer Affairs Victoria: Victoria Leads the Way in Consumer Protection. Consumer Affairs Victoria, Melbourne (2005)
49. Neave, C.N., Pinnock, J.: Setting the Scene Industry-based Customer Dispute Resolution Schemes. In: ADR - A better way to do business conference, Sydney (September 4-5, 2003)
50. Consumers International: Annual Report 2004, p. 1. Consumer International, London (2004)
51. Consumer Affairs Division: Dispute Resolution in Electronic Commerce. Commonwealth of Australia, The Department of Treasury, Canberra (2001)
52. Neave, C.N., Pinnock, J.: Setting the Scene Industry-based Customer Dispute Resolution Schemes. In: ADR - A better way to do business conference, Sydney (September 4-5, 2003)
53. Moulinos, K., Iliadis, J., Tsoumas, V.: Towards Secure Sealing of Privacy Policies. Information Management & Computer Security 12(4), 350–361 (2004)
54. Jackson, M.: Internet Privacy. Telecommunications Journal of Australia 53(2), 21–31 (2003)
55. Curtis, K.: Privacy in Practice. In: The workshop at Centre for Continuing Legal Education. University of NSW, Sydney (March 9, 2005)
56. Quo, S.: Spam: Private and Legislative Responses to Unsolicited Electronic Mail in Australia and the United States. ELaw - Murchdoch University 11(1), 4 (2004)
57. Spam Act 2003. Act No. 129 of 2003 as amended, December 12, 2003-10 April 2004, p. 35 (2004)
58. Jackson, M.: Internet Privacy. Telecommunications Journal of Australia 53(2), 21–31 (2003)
59. Vasiu, L., Warren, M., Mackay, D.: Personal Information Privacy Issues in B2C E-Commerce: a Theoretical Framework. CollECTeR (2002)
60. Ha, H.: Three-Sector Governance System Model to Address Fives Issues of Consumer Protection in B2C E-commerce in Victoria, Australia. In: 19th ANZAM Conference, Canberra (December 7-10, 2005)
61. Moghe, V.: Privacy Management - a New Era in the Australian Business Environment. Information Management & Computer Security 11(2), 61 (2003)
62. Quo, S.: Spam: Private and Legislative Responses to Unsolicited Electronic Mail in Australia and the United States. ELaw - Murchdoch University 11(1), 45 (2004)
63. Egger, F.N.: Consumer Trust in E-Commerce: From Psychology to Interaction Design. In: Prins, J.E.J., Ribbers, P.M.A., van Tilborg, H.C.A., Veth, A.F.L., van der Wees, J.G.L. (eds.) Trust in Electronic Commerce. The Role of Trust form a Legal, an Organizational and a Technical Point of View, pp. 11–43. Kluwer Law International, The Hagues (2002)
64. PC Magazine: The Perils of Online Shopping. PC Magazine, p. 23 (August 23, 2005)
65. Consumers International: Annual Report 2004. Consumer International, London (2004)
66. Lundy, K. (2005), http://www.katelundy.com.au/October2002.htm#23October2002

67. Consumer Affairs Victoria: Online Shopping and Consumer Protection, p. 4. Standing Committee of Officials of Consumer Affairs - E-commerce Working Party, Victoria (2004)
68. Consumer Affairs Victoria: Online Shopping and Consumer Protection. Standing Committee of Officials of Consumer Affairs - E-commerce Working Party, Victoria (2004)
69. Australian Bureau of Statistics: Nearly $1 billion dollars lost by Australians to personal fraud. Australian Bureau of Statistics, Canberra (2008)
70. Dearden, J. (2009),
    http://www.aic.gov.au/events/aic%20upcoming%20events/2009/acft.aspx
71. Office of Fair Trading (UK) (2007),
    http://www.oft.gov.uk/shared_oft/reports/consumer_protection/oft921.pdf
72. Consumer Affairs Victoria: Online Shopping and Consumer Protection, p. 14. Standing Committee of Officials of Consumer Affairs - E-commerce Working Party, Victoria (2004)
73. Wentworth, E.
    http://www.nadrac.gov.au/www/nadrac/rwpattach.nsf/VAP/(3A6790B96C 927794AF1031D9395C5C20)~ADR+-+A+Better+Way+to+do+ Business+-+September+2003(2).PDF/$file/ADR+-+A+Better+Way+to+do+Business+-+September+2003(2).PDF
74. Smith, R., Budd, C.: Consumer fraud in Australia: costs, rates and awareness of the risks in 2008. Australian Institute of Criminology, Australia (2009)
75. Glenn, J.C., Gordon, T.J.: State of the Future, p. 2. American Council for the United Nations University, Washington, D. C (2005)
76. Majoras, D.P., Swindle, O., Leary, T.B., Harbour, P.J., Leibowitz, J.: The US SAFE WEB Act: Protecting Consumers from Spam, Spyware, and Fraud. A Legislative Recommendation to Congress, Federal Trade Commission, USA (2005)
77. Ruddock, P. (2006),
    http://www.ag.gov.au/agd/WWW/MinisterRuddockHome.nsf/Page/Media_Releases_2006_First_Quarter_31_January_2006_-_Australian _Law_Reform_Commission_to_review_Privacy_Act_-_0062006#

Proximity-Based Trust Inference for Mobile Social Networking*

Amir Seyedi, Rachid Saadi, and Valérie Issarny

ARLES Project-Team
INRIA CRI Paris-Rocquencourt, France
{name.surname}@inria.fr

Abstract. The growing trend to social networking and increased prevalence of new mobile devices lead to the emergence of mobile social networking applications where users are able to share experience in an impromptu way as they move. However, this is at risk for mobile users since they may not have any knowledge about the users they socially connect with. Trust management then appears as a promising decision support for mobile users in establishing social links. However, while the literature is rich of trust models, most approaches lack appropriate trust bootstrapping, i.e., the initialization of trust values. This paper addresses this challenge by introducing proximity-based trust initialization based on the users' behavioral data available from their mobile devices or other types of social interactions. The proposed approach is further assessed in the context of mobile social networking using users behavioral data collected by the MIT reality mining project. Results show that the inferred trust values correlate with the self-report survey of users relationships.

Keywords: Trust bootstrapping, mobile social network, small worlds.

1 Introduction

Portable devices have gained wide popularity and people are spending a considerable portion of their daily life using their mobile devices. This situation together with the success of social networking lead to the emergence of mobile social networking. However, anytime and anywhere interactions have a built-in risk factor. Development of trust-based collaborations is then the solution to reduce the vulnerability to risk and to fully exploit the potential of spontaneous social networking [5]. In our work, we aim at developing a trust management method for mobile social networking. Then, the challenge we are addressing here is how to initiate trust values and how to evaluate unknown mobile users using initiated trust values, to enable impromptu social networking.

Computational trust brings the human concept of trust into the digital world, which leads to a new kind of open social ecosystem [12]. In general, the notion of trust can be represented by a relation that links trustors to trustees. The

---

* Work supported by EU-funded project FP7-231167 CONNECT and by EU-funded project FP7-256980 NESSOS.

I. Wakeman et al. (Eds.): IFIPTM 2011, IFIP AICT 358, pp. 253–264, 2011.

literature [17] includes two main categories of relations to set trust values for trustees, namely: (i) direct-based and (ii) recommendation-based relation.

Most existing trust models focus on assessing recommendation-based relationships [18] and lack the bootstrapping stage, which is how to initialize direct trust in order to efficiently start the trust model operation. This is very problematic and challenging, since recommendation-based relationships are built upon bootstrapped direct-based relationships. Indeed, most solutions that address trust assessment make one of the following assumptions:

- Trust initialization is not a problem of the model; it is the responsibility of the actors of the system [8]. However, this task remains challenging, especially when it comes to evaluating trustees numerically (e.g., 0.1, 0.2, 0.15, etc.).
- The trust model initially evaluates trust relationships with a fixed value (e.g., 0.5 [9], a uniform Beta probabilistic distribution [10], etc.) or according to the trust disposition of the trustor [14] (i.e., pessimistic, optimistic, or undecided). In [16], trust is initialized by asking trustors to sort their trustees rather than assigning fixed trust values. There are other bootstrapping solutions [15, 2, 1] that assess trustees into different contexts (e.g., fixing a car, babysitting, etc.) and then automatically infer unknown trust values from known ones of similar or correlative contexts. However, if no prior related context exists, these solutions lack initialization of trust.

We have developed our trust model based on the hypothesis that it is possible to measure and bootstrap trust from human social behavior. Therefore, in this paper, we investigate a formal approach that quantifies human proximity from which possible trust relationships are transparently and automatically inferred and assessed on behalf of the trustor. We choose proximity between people as an effective measure for trust. Because, proximity between people is not only a matter of trust, but it increases trust affinity as well [4]. In other words, people spend more time with those whom they trust and, at the same time, if they start spending time with new people, it is likely that trust relationships will arise and evolve.

In order to better understand the contribution and evolution of proximity in the human society, consider the fact that a society is initiated by people who live in the same territory. Fukuyama [7], describing the role of trust in a society, mentions that people can build efficient economy and social organization, if they have wide and efficient trust networks. It shows clearly how trust and proximity of people are tied together to initiate a successful society. As a result, today we have different cultures and societies in the world simply because of their founders being at different location and proximity. Building on this social knowledge, this paper introduces a method for bootstrapping trust values in mobile environments, based on the *proximity* of people. However, in today's virtual world expanding the physical one, proximity is not just about the physical distance between people. Practically, while people who are physically close maybe detected using technologies such as Bluetooth [6], other types of proximity like phone calls, emails, social network interactions, etc. can be detected by the implementation of virtual sensors. We classify the range of proximity-based trust values semantically for further judgments based on these values. Then, the initiated trust values can be used to calculate similarity between people from the standpoint of trust. Similar people can make good recommendations to each other. Hence, they can evaluate not-directly-known users on each others behalf. So, when mobile users are about to interact with unknown users, they may acquire the trust knowledge through known similar users. The process should be feasible in a limited number of hops because of the small world phenomenon [13].

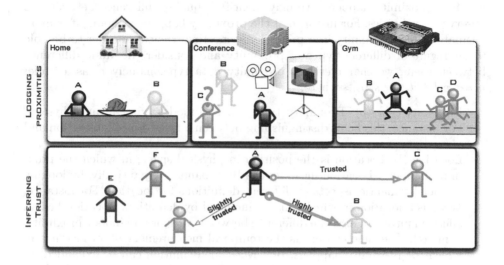

Fig. 1. User A evaluates others based on the observed proximity with others

The next section characterizes proximity towards trust assessment and is then followed by proposed proximity-based trust initialization in Section 3. Then, we evaluate the effectiveness of the proposed approach using the MIT reality mining dataset. Finally, we conclude in Section 5, summarizing our contribution and sketching our future work.

2   Trust and Proximity

We make the assumption that there is a strong correlation between proximity observations and real social relationship [6]. Proximity itself can be considered as a consequence of trust relationship, while at the same time the longer users are in proximity, the higher the probability of their friendship increases. Moreover, as noted by [4], proximity is a measure of trust as well as a cause to trust between users.

Thus, we argue that *proximity* is the *nearness* of any two persons in space or time. Let P be the proximity between two persons. Two persons are in *physical proximity* if the nearness happens in the same space and time. Two persons are in *virtual proximity* if the nearness happens only in the time dimension. Physical proximity can be detected by various technologies (e.g., blue-tooth, Wi-Fi, etc.) and likewise virtual proximity through monitoring of social activities (e.g., chat, SMS, voice call, liking a content on facebook etc.). The collected proximity-related data provides information such as when, where, how frequently, and for how long people were in the proximity of each other.

In general, the definition of proximity takes several forms (from physical to virtual) and differs according to context (work, home, etc.) as well as it can be quantified by duration or frequency. From a social point of view, from the context in which proximity happens, we may identify a quality difference between the observed proximities. For instance, if the proximity happens at home, it is more intimate than a proximity in a professional meeting. Hence, in order to be able to aggregate of different types of proximity and consider the value difference between them, we characterize a proximity data type, namely η, as a tuple: $\eta = < p, l, t, d_s, d_d, s, m >$ where,

- Proximity type (p): Proximity type has two modes, virtual and physical. For instance, this helps distinguishing between a face-to-face interaction and virtual proximity.
- Location (l): Location is the position in physical space, in which the proximity happens. Location meaning can be expanded semantically, by looking to social semantic aspects of different definitions for location. For instance, *home* is a location in which trust is included by definition. Location has an effect on intimacy, e.g., the difference between outdoor and indoor proximity.
- Time (t): The time context is the temporal measurement of an instance in which the proximity happens. However time definition can be expanded semantically. For instance, weekend or working time has different social values. We take into account the quality difference of proximity as time changes, e.g., during weekend, being in the proximity of friends is more likely and therefore is a more valuable proximity.
- Source device type (d_s): Device type helps to includes the nature of device in terms of mobility etc. e.g., mobile device like smart-phone versus laptop). The observed proximity from a mobile device is more reliable as people are more likely to have their mobile device always with them. Then, d_s is the source device that belongs to the observer user.
- Destination device type (d_d): d_d is the destination device of a user who has been observed.
- Sensing method (s) (e.g., physical sensors, virtual sensors): Sensing methods take into account the technology effect on measurement method. or example bluetooth detects people in a shorter range than wifi does. So the detected proximity by bluetooth is more reliable as it catches the closer users.
- Measurement type (m): Measurement type indicates the difference between duration and frequency of a proximity. Hence, we introduce a proximity coefficient, which is necessary for combining different types of proximity.

Proximity data types enable us to consider value difference between proximities. We in particular assign a coefficient for each proximity data. This can be done using techniques such as fuzzy logic; logic can decide the weight of specific proximity data types in terms of trust. Thus, several sources of proximity can be combined by a weighted average using their coefficients. Let k_{η_i} be the coefficient for an observed proximity of type η_i. k_{η_i} is calculated for any given η_i by logical aggregation of proximity data type parameters. $K = \{k_{\eta_1}, k_{\eta_2}, k_{\eta_3}, ...\}$ is the set of coefficients for different types of proximity, coefficients are bounded to the range of $[0, 1]$. Accordingly, K_B^A is the set of all proximity coefficients between users A and B. An example of three different proximity data types is shown in Table 1.

Table 1. Proximity Data Types

η	p	l	t	d_s	d_d	s	m
η_1	physical	anywhere	anytime	mobile	mobile	bluetooth	duration
η_2	physical	office	working time	mobile	laptop	WiFi	duration
η_3	virtual	anywhere	night	mobile	mobile	SMS	frequency

Given the above types of proximity we define proximity records as:

`ProximityRecord=<UserID,`η`, Value>`

where the `Proximity` tuple is composed by the `UserID`, which is the unique identifier of the observed user, η is the data type of the observed proximity; and `value` is the observed proximity, which is duration or frequency based on the data type. Hence, each user's device is assigned with a set of `Proximity` tuples called *observed set*, as exemplified in Table 2.

Table 2. An example of proximity duration data provided by user A device

UserID	η	Value
B	η_1	200h
C	η_1	20h
D	η_1	80h
E	η_1	30h
F	η_1	0,5h

3   Proximity-Based Trust Initialization

Proximity-based trust initiates trust values between nodes with a one-to-one trust relationship. Using an appropriate conversion method for various proximity data is the most challenging part of trust calculation. As a matter of fact, it is a difficult task to make a conversion from varied types of observed proximity to a range of trust values that are meaningful. For the conversion of proximity records to *Proximity-based trust* values, we use *standard score* formula. Standard score has a normalization effect on the amount of observed proximities according to the observer(user's) average activity.

3.1 Definitions

Normalization has several positive outcomes. First, social interaction quantity varies a lot according to user personality in a social network [11]; as a result the amount of proximity varies substantially for different nodes [6]. Second, there are multiple types of proximity; normalized scoring eases the process of combining trust values according to different proximity data types.

Definition 1 (Standard Score). *A* standard score *[3] indicates how many standard deviations* (σ)*, an observation or datum(x) is above or below the mean(μ):*

$$Z = \frac{datum - mean}{standard\ deviation} = \frac{x - \mu}{\sigma} \qquad (1)$$

As a result of using standard score, each peer normalizes trust values based on their average proximity duration with anyone. Therefore, each trust value is unbiased and bounded into a determined range, which hides the effect of variation of proximity duration due to peers having various behavior. Hence, by using standard score formula, we process the observed proximity as follows.

Definition 2 (Observed Set). *The Observed Set (OS) of a user includes all the users that have been detected in proximity of a given user.*

We use a time finite subset of observed proximities for trust evaluation. Therefore, we define the proximity window function as:

Definition 3 (Proximity Window Function). *The proximity window function $P_{\eta_i}^{w}(A, B)$ accumulates the proximity of user B monitored by user A during the time window $\underline{w}$ and with proximity type η_i.*

Definition 4 (Proximity-based Trust Function). *Proximity-based trust is basically calculated using* standard score *formula. The proximity-based trust function is denoted by $T_{\eta_i}^{t}$ and is formally defined as:*

$$T_{\eta_i}^{t} : \mathbb{U} \times \mathbb{U} \to \mathbb{R} \qquad \mathbb{U} : set\ of\ Users$$
$$(A, B) \to T_{\eta_i}^{t}(A, B)\ \mathbb{R} : set\ of\ real\ numbers$$

$$T_{\eta_i}^{t}(A, B) = \begin{cases} -\infty & if (B \notin OS_A) \\ \frac{P_{\eta_i}^{w}(A,B) - \mu_{\eta_i}^{w}}{\sigma_{\eta_i}^{w}} & if (B \in OS_A \wedge t \leq w) \\ (1 - \alpha) * T_{\eta_i}^{p}(A, B) + \alpha * \frac{P_{\eta_i}^{w}(A,B) - \mu_{\eta_i}^{w}}{\sigma_{\eta_i}^{w}} & if (B \in OS_A \wedge t > w) \end{cases}$$

$$(2)$$

where:

- $T_{\eta_i}^{t}(A, B)$ *is the proximity-based trust value given by user A for user B at the instant t with proximity data type of η_i.*
- $T_{\eta_i}^{p}(A, B)$ *is the past acquired proximity-based trust value by user A for user B at the instant $p = t - t\%w$ with proximity data type η_i.*
- $P_{\eta_i}^{w}(A, B)$ *is the cumulative proximity of B in the given period of time w with proximity data type η_i.*

- α is a coefficient which is in range of $]0,1[$ and defines how significant is the impact of new observed proximities on the last calculation of proximity based trust value.
- $\mu_{\eta_i}^w$ and $\sigma_{\eta_i}^w$ are, respectively, the observed period average and the standard deviation during the time window w with proximity data type η_i.

Definition 5 (Proximity-based Trust Aggregation Function). *The proximity-based trust aggregation function is for combining trust values, which is inferred from different proximity data types. It is formally defined as:*

$$T^t : U \times U \to \mathbb{R} \qquad U : set\ of\ Users$$
$$(A,B) \to T^t(A,B)\ \mathbb{R} : set\ of\ real\ numbers$$

$$T^t(A,B) = \begin{cases} -\infty & if(B \notin OS_A) \\[2em] \dfrac{\sum\limits_{i=1}^{|K_B^A|} k_{\eta_i} * T_{\eta_i}^t(A,B)}{\sum\limits_{i=1}^{|K_B^A|} k_{\eta_i}} & if(B \in OS_A) \end{cases} \qquad (3)$$

where $T_{\eta_i}^t$ and k_{η_i} are the trust value and the coefficient for proximity type η_i, respectively K_B^A is the set of coefficients for all the observed proximity types between users A and B. Thus, by using the equation 2, we consider only the proximity that occurs during time window w. Then, for a new time window, the latest assessed trust value $(T_{\eta_i}^p)$ is used to serve as an input for new trust assessment.

3.2 Semantical Trust Inference

Given T^t, we are able to infer trust relationships between users. For the moment we do so by splitting the trust scale equally into four sections with respect to the normal distribution probability density in each **area** and according to the experiments of trust calculation we did using real proximity data from [6] (Illustrated in Figure 2), we define four trust levels and each level includes 25 percent of the observed peers, namely: *Unknown Trust, Slightly trusted, Moderately trusted* and *Highly trusted.* Unknown Trust represents all the persons whose trust (T^t) is assessed into interval $] - \infty, -0.67[$. For this category, we consider that the system has insufficient information to infer trust. All the other that are assessed over -0.67 are considered as trusted entities and they are classified into three other categories: (i) people who may be slightly trusted (i.e., people assessed in range of $[-0.67, 0[$), (ii) people who may be moderately trusted (i.e., ones assessed into the range $[0, 0.67[$) and (iii) people who may be highly trusted (i.e., ones assessed into the range $[0.67, +\infty[$).

Then, according to our classification, which is based on density of peers in each score interval and exprimental results, we consider that a proximity-based trust

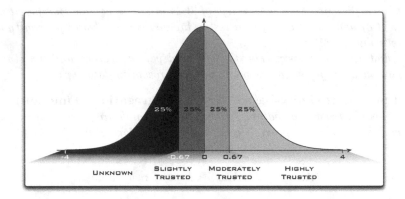

Fig. 2. Trust Scale for normalized Trust values

relationship is established if an inferred proximity-based trust value is higher than -0.67. We define this relation as follows:

Definition 6 (Proximity-based Trust relationship)
Let A and B be two users. If $T(A, B) \geq 0.67$, we say that the Trust relation is verified between A and B. Formally:

$$if \ T(A, B) \geq -0.67 \ then \ A \xrightarrow{T} B$$

Example: To explain our approach, we use the following example. User A has a mobile device with a proximity logging application. The observed set of user A is composed by: $OS_A = \{B, C, D, E, F\}$. Table 2 introduced in Section 2 shows an example of cumulative proximity duration that can be provided by user A device with η_1 proximity data type. For instance: $P_{\eta_1}^w(A, B) = 200h$. Considering an unbounded time window (i.e., $w = +\infty$), the proximity duration average is: $\mu_{\eta_1}^w = 66.1$. For calculating the standard deviation, we first compute the difference of each data point from the mean, and then square the result: $(200 - 66.1)^2 = 17929.21$, $(80 - 66.1)^2 = 193.21$. We repeat the same process for the other values. Then, we calculate the standard deviation by dividing the sum of these values by the number of values and take the square root:

$$\sigma_{\eta_1}^w = \sqrt{\tfrac{17929.21 + 2125.21 + 193.21 + 1303.21 + 4303.36}{5}} = 71.90$$

The proximity-based trust value for the user B with 200 hours of proximity is then calculated using Formula: 3, $T_{\eta_i}^t(A, B) = \frac{200 - 66.1}{71.90} = 1.86$

Therefore, a one-to-one trust relation is established between users A and B (i.e., $A \xrightarrow{T} B$), which means that $B \in Tee(A)$ and $A \in Tor(B)$. Moreover, A may highly trust B because $T^t(A, B) \geq 0.67$.

In next section we evaluate our approach experimentally using the MIT real mobility data.

4   Experimental Evaluation

A full-fledged evaluation of our approach needs a large-scale proximity dataset with different data types, in order to have possibilities for combining trust values from different types of observed proximity. Also, for a multi-hop trust estimation, large number of users is needed. That aside, a survey of trust and/or other social facts such as friendship between the observed users is needed to make a comparison between inferred trust values and real social facts. While to the best of our knowledge there is no such kind of vast proximity dataset publicly available, we have used the reality mining dataset[1] [6] as the only existing public dataset of mobile phone proximity records with self-report survey data. The reality mining project was developed by the MIT Media Lab during years 2004-2005 by using 100 Nokia 6600s with Context logging software. They have gathered 330,000 hours of continuous behavioral data logged by the mobile phones of the subjects. They also did a survey in which they asked users about friendship and whom are they going to meet.

To illustrate the capability of our approach, we answer the following question: To what extent the bootstrapped trust values are in correlation with real social facts(e.g. friendship)?

We run the evaluation with the following steps. First, we calculate the proximity-based trust values between users. Then, by comparing the calculated proximity-based trust values of each user to the answers he provided in the survey, we verify if the inferred trust values are coherent with friendship.

Table 3. Average $T^t(A, B)$ value for reported people in survey

Group	Average of minimum trust	Average of trust values
Friends	1.4070	2.0209
inLab	-0.3079	0.7696
outLab	0.0068	1.0460

From the reality mining dataset, we can calculate the proximity duration between two persons which has been detected by bluetooth. We apply the proximity-based trust function (Equation 2) to the proximity durations in order to obtain proximity-based trust values, $T^t(A, B)$, of each user. From the survey, each person predicts his possible future proximity with a friend, or if they are going to meet any other person inside or outside the lab. From this survey, we may tell that mentioned persons are either friends or they are important from the user point of view. We can make the judgment that it is probable that trust relationships exist between the reported users. For these groups (Friends, inLab, outLab), average trust value is shown in Table 3. To find out the relevance of the proximity-based trust values, as we can perceive, highest average of trust values are assigned to friends. Based on the given definitions (Figure 2), friends are

---

[1] http://reality.media.mit.edu/

Table 4. Average of similarity for reported people in survey

Group	Average of minimum similarities	Average of similarities
Friends	0.2913	0.4828
inLab	-0.0858	0.2520
outLab	0.0089	0.3372

assigned with highly trusted notion. For inLab group, which is the people that users meet inside the MIT Lab, the values are overall located in slightly trusted and moderately trusted classification. For outLab group, which usually consist of friends, family and friends of friends, that a person meets outside of working area, the values are around the barriers of highly trusted group. This experiment shows that trust values are related to the social strength of a relationship. For instance, highest values belong to friends. Additionally, we calculated similarity between users, which is used for the trust transitivity calculation. Table 4 shows that similarity values are behaving very similar to the proximity-based trust values, and they change with the characteristics of relationship. Knowing that similarity is a measure of trust, this arrangement evidences the social fact that friends are similar in their relationships and they are favorite recommender to each other.

The average of minimums is for showing the minimum value that is inferred by a user for each group.

Figure 3 shows the percentage of trust values in each semantical classification of trust, for the trust that is inferred for users in different groups of friends and known people inside and outside MIT Lab. Friends are removed from both

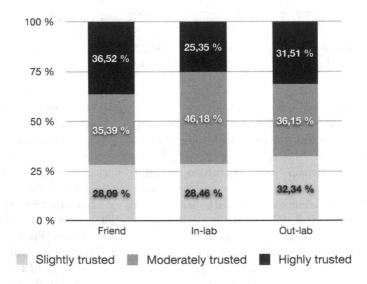

Fig. 3. Trust value distribution in different context of proximity

inLab and outLab groups. As we see, friends have the highest percentage of nodes assessed as highly trusted peers(36%), while inLab peers (e.g. colleagues) are often moderately trusted(46%). For the outLab group, the highly trusted nodes are more than inLab group, but the slightly trusted nodes are increasing. This can be commented by the fact that users meet more random people out of their working place and at the same time more intimate persons are around them than work.

5 Conclusion and Future Work

In this paper, we proposed a novel method to bootstrap trust values from proximity between the people which can also be used for trust inference for unknown users. This approach is suitable for mobile social networking applications. We formalized different types of proximity and introduced proximity data types. The evaluation using real proximity data shows that inferred values are correlated with real social facts. For future work, we aim at creation and evaluation of large dataset of different types of proximity. At the same time, user opinions of trust should be surveyed and included in such kind of dataset. We aim at using fuzzy logic for aggregation of different proximity, according to the level of contribution they can provide to trust value. Also, a large body of work exists in the domain of estimation and recommendation, they may be adapted and evaluated for trust recommendation and transitivity within this approach. Hence, for further evaluation of our approach, and in order to better investigate other available possibilities in trust assessment, we are looking into the deployment of this approach as part of the yarta middle ware framework[2]. Yarta middle ware support the development of mobile social applications.

References

1. Ahamed, S., Hoque, E., Rahman, F., Zulkernine, M.: Towards Secure Trust Bootstrapping in Pervasive Computing Environment. In: 11th IEEE High Assurance Systems Engineering Symposium HASE 2008, pp. 89–96 (2008)
2. Ahamed, S., Monjur, M., Islam, M.: CCTB: Context correlation for trust bootstrapping in pervasive environment. In: IET 4th International Conference on Intelligent Environments, pp. 1–8 (2008)
3. Aron, A.: Statistics for the behavioral and social sciences. Prentice Hall, Englewood Cliffs (1997)
4. Bruneel, J., Spithoven, A., Maesen, A.: Building Trust: A Matter of Proximity? Babson College Entrepreneurship Research Conference, BCERC (2007)
5. Capra, L.: Engineering human trust in mobile system collaborations. SIGSOFT Softw. Eng. Notes 29(6), 107–116 (2004)
6. Eagle, N., Pentland, A.S., Lazer, D.: Inferring friendship network structure by using mobile phone data. Proceedings of the National Academy of Sciences 106(36), 15274–15278 (2009)

---

[2] https://gforge.inria.fr/projects/yarta/

7. Fukuyama, F.: Trust: the social virtues and the creation of prosperity. Free Press, New York (1995)
8. Golbeck, J., Hendler, J.: Filmtrust: movie recommendations using trust in web-based social networks. In: 3rd IEEE Consumer Communications and Networking Conference, CCNC 2006, vol. 1, pp. 282–286 (2006)
9. Haque, M., Ahamed, S.: An Omnipresent Formal Trust Model (FTM) for Pervasive Computing Environment. In: Proceedings of the 31st Annual International Computer Software and Applications Conference, vol. 01, pp. 49–56. IEEE Computer Society, Los Alamitos (2007)
10. Jøsang, A., Pope, S.: Semantic constraints for trust transitivity. In: APCCM 2005: Proceedings of the 2nd Asia-Pacific conference on Conceptual modelling, pp. 59–68. Australian Computer Society, Inc., Australia (2005)
11. Kumar, R., Novak, J., Tomkins, A.: Structure and evolution of online social networks. In: Proceedings of the 12th ACM SIGKDD international conference on Knowledge discovery and data mining, KDD 2006, pp. 611–617. ACM, New York (2006)
12. Marsh, S.P.: Formalising trust as a computational concept (1994)
13. Newman, M.E.J., Watts, D.J., Strogatz, S.H.: Random graph models of social networks. Proceedings of the National Academy of Science 99, 2566–2572 (2002)
14. Perich, F., Undercoffer, J., Kagal, L., Joshi, A., Finin, T., Yesha, Y.: In reputation we believe: Query processing in mobile ad-hoc networks. In: Annual International Conference on Mobile and Ubiquitous Systems, pp. 326–334 (2004)
15. Quercia, D., Hailes, S., Capra, L.: TRULLO-local trust bootstrapping for ubiquitous devices. Proc. of IEEE Mobiquitous (2007)
16. Saadi, R., Pierson, J., Brunie, L.: T2D: A Peer to Peer trust management system based on Disposition to Trust. In: Proceedings of the 2010 ACM Symposium on Applied Computing, pp. 1472–1478. ACM, New York (2010)
17. Sabater, J., Sierra, C.: Review on Computational Trust and Reputation Models. Artificial Intelligence Review 24(1), 33–60 (2005)
18. Walter, F.E., Battiston, S., Schweitzer, F.: A model of a trust-based recommendation system on a social network. Autonomous Agents and Multi-Agent Systems 16, 57–74 (2008)

Trust-Threshold Based Routing in Delay Tolerant Networks

MoonJeong Chang[1], Ing-Ray Chen[1], Fenye Bao[1], and Jin-Hee Cho[2]

[1] Department of Computer Science,
Virginia Tech, 7054 Haycock Road, Falls Church, VA 22043, USA
{mjchang,irchen,baofenye}@vt.edu
[2] Computational and Information Sciences Directorate,
U.S. Army Research Laboratory, 2800 Powder Mill Road, Adelphi, MD 20783, USA
jinhee.cho@us.army.mil

Abstract. We propose a trust-threshold based routing protocol for delay tolerant networks, leveraging two trust thresholds for accepting recommendations and for selecting the next message carrier for message forwarding. We show that there exist optimal trust threshold values under which trust-threshold based routing performs the best in terms of message delivery ratio, message delay and message overhead. By means of a probability model, we perform a comparative analysis of trust-threshold based routing against epidemic, social-trust-based and QoS-trust-based routing. Our results demonstrate that trust-threshold based routing operating under proper trust thresholds can effectively trade off message delay and message overhead for a significant gain in message delivery ratio. Moreover, our analysis helps identify the optimal weight setting to best balance the effect of social vs. QoS trust metrics to maximize the message delivery ratio without compromising message delay and/or message overhead requirements.

Keywords: Delay tolerant networks, encounter-based routing, trust management, threshold-based routing, performance analysis.

1   Introduction

Delay Tolerant Networks (DTNs) are self-organizing wireless networks with the characteristics of large latency, intermittent connectivity, and limited resources (e.g., battery, computational power, bandwidth) [1]. Different from traditional networks such as mobile ad hoc networks, nodes in DTNs forward messages to a destination node in a *store-and-forward* manner [1] in order to cope with the absence of guaranteed end-to-end connectivity. In such environments, the key challenge is to select an appropriate "next message carrier" among all encountered nodes to maximize message delivery ratio while minimizing message overhead and delay. Further, we face additional challenges due to the lack of a centralized trust entity. The open, distributed, and dynamic inherent nature of DTNs also induces security vulnerability [2, 3]. In this paper, we consider a DTN in the presence of malicious and uncooperative nodes and propose a method for the selection of trustworthy message carriers with the goal of maximizing message delivery ratio without compromising message delay or message overhead in the context of DTN routing.

I. Wakeman et al. (Eds.): IFIPTM 2011, IFIP AICT 358, pp. 265–276, 2011.
© Springer-Verlag Berlin Heidelberg 2011

Most current DTN routing protocols are based on encounter patterns [4, 5]. The problem is that if the predicted encounter does not happen, then messages would be lost for single-copy routing, or flooded for multi-copy routing. Moreover, in the presence of selfish or malicious nodes, these approaches still could not guarantee reliable message delivery. Several recent studies [6-9] used reputation to select message carriers among encountered nodes and encouraged cooperative behaviors using credit incentives. However, a centralized credit management system which can be a single point of failure is typically required, as it is challenging to perform distributed credit management in a DTN in the presence of selfish or malicious nodes. On the other hand, there have been several social network based approaches [10-14] to select the best message carrier in DTNs. They considered social relationship and social networking as criteria to select message carriers in DTNs. However, no consideration was given to the presence of malicious or selfish nodes.

This work extends from our earlier work [15] on trust-based routing in DTNs. Unlike prior work cited above [4-14], we integrate *social trust* and *Quality of Service (QoS) trust* into a composite trust metric for determining the best message carrier among new encounters for message forwarding. In this work, we propose the design notion of trust thresholds for determining the trustworthiness of a node acting as a recommender or as the next message carrier, and analyze the best thresholds under which trust-threshold based routing (TTBR) in DTNs would perform the best. Our approach is distributed in nature and does not require a complicated credit management system. Each node will run TTBR autonomously to assess trust of its peers using the same trust threshold setting depending on application characteristics, and consequently select trustworthy nodes as carriers for message routing. Without loss of generality, we consider *healthiness* and *cooperativeness* for social trust to account for a node's trustworthiness for message delivery, and *connectivity* and *energy* for QoS trust to account for a node's QoS capability to quickly deliver the message to the destination node. We perform a comparative analysis of TTBR with epidemic routing [16], social-trust-based routing (for which only social trust metrics are considered) and QoS-trust-based routing (for which only QoS trust metrics are considered) and identify conditions including the best trust thresholds to be used under which trust-threshold based routing outperforms these baseline routing algorithms for a DTN consisting of heterogeneous mobile nodes.

2   System Model

We consider a DTN environment without a centralized trust authority. Every node may have a different level of energy and speed reflecting node heterogeneity. We differentiate uncooperative nodes from malicious nodes. An uncooperative node acts to maximize its own benefit regardless of the global benefit of the DTN. So it may drop packets arbitrarily just to save energy. Once a node becomes uncooperative, it stays as uncooperative. A malicious node acts maliciously with the intent to disrupt the main functionality of the DTN, so it can drop packets, jam wireless channel, and even forge packets. As soon as a malicious node is detected, the trust value of the malicious node will be set to zero, and thus excluding it as a message carrier for message forwarding. A node initially may be healthy but become compromised because of being captured, for example. Once a node is compromised, it stays as a malicious node.

We consider the following energy model. The energy level of a node is related to its social encountering activities. If a node becomes uncooperative, the speed of energy consumption by the node is slowed down. If a node becomes compromised, the speed of energy consumption by the node will increase since the node may perform attacks which may consume more energy.

A node's trust value is assessed based on direct observations through monitoring, snooping, or overhearing, and indirect information. To counter whitewashing or false information attacks, a node does not use status exchange information including encounter history information because a malicious node can provide fake encounter history information to other nodes [17]. For indirect information, a node uses recommendations obtained only from 1-hop neighbors to cope with fragile connectivity and sparse node density in DTNs. The trust of one node toward another node is updated upon an encounter event. Our trust metric consists of two aspects of trust relationship: *social trust* and *QoS trust*. *Social trust* is based on social relationships. We consider **healthiness** and **cooperativeness** to measure the social trust level of a node. Social network structure-based properties such as similarity, centrality, and betweenness are not considered because we do not use trust encounter histories exchanged to avoid self-promoting or false information attacks by malicious nodes. *QoS trust* is evaluated through the communication networks by the capability of a node to deliver messages to the destination node. We consider **connectivity** and **energy** to measure the QoS trust level of a node. We define a node's trust level as a real number in the range of [0, 1], with 1 indicating complete trust, 0.5 ignorance, and 0 complete distrust.

3   Trust-Threshold Based Routing

Our trust-threshold based routing algorithm builds upon the notion of peer-to-peer trust evaluation at runtime. A node will evaluate its peers dynamically and will use trust thresholds as criteria to determine if it can trust a node as a recommender or as a message carrier. Two trust thresholds are used: recommender threshold denoted by T_{rec} and message forwarding threshold denoted by T_f. In this paper, the trust value of node j evaluated by node i at time t, denoted as $T_{i,j}(t)$, is computed by a weighted average of healthiness, cooperativeness, connectivity, and energy as follows:

$$T_{i,j}(t) = w_1 T_{i,j}^{healthiness}(t) + w_2 T_{i,j}^{cooperativeness}(t) + w_3 T_{i,j}^{connectivity}(t)$$
$$+ w_4 T_{i,j}^{energy}(t) \tag{1}$$

Here $w_1, w_2, w_3,$ and w_4 are weights associated with healthiness, cooperativeness, connectivity and energy, respectively with $w_1 + w_2 + w_3 + w_4 = 1$. Specifically, node i will update its trust toward node j upon encountering node m at time t for the duration $[t, t + \Delta t]$ as follows:

$$T_{i,j}^X(t + \Delta t) = \beta_1 T_{i,j}^{direct,X}(t + \Delta t) + \beta_2 T_{i,j}^{indirect,X}(t + \Delta t) \tag{2}$$

Here X refers to a trust property. In Eq. 2, β_1 is a parameter to weigh node i's own trust assessment toward node j at time $t + \Delta t$, and β_2 is another parameter to weigh indirect information from the recommender. Note that $\beta_1 + \beta_2 = 1$.

$$T_{i,j}^{direct,X}(t + \Delta t) = \begin{cases} T_{i,m}^{encounter,X}(t + \Delta t), & if\ m = j \\ e^{-\lambda_d \Delta t} \times T_{i,j}^{X}(t), & if\ m \neq j \end{cases} \tag{3}$$

The direct trust evaluation of node j is given in Eq. 3 above by which if the new encounter (node m) is node j itself, then node i can directly evaluate node j because node i and node j are 1-hop neighbors. We use $T_{i,m}^{encounter,X}(t + \Delta t)$ to denote the assessment result of node i toward node m in trust property X based on node i's direct observations toward node m over the encounter interval $[t, t + \Delta t]$. Node i may also leverage its past experiences with node m over $[0, t]$ to help assess $T_{i,m}^{encounter,X}(t + \Delta t)$, especially if the current encountering interval is short. If node j is not the new encounter, then no new direct information can be gained about node j. So, node i will use its past trust toward node j obtained at time t decayed over the time interval Δt to model trust decay over time. We adopt an exponential time decay factor, $e^{-\lambda_d \Delta t}$ (with $0 < \lambda_d \leq 0.1$ to limit the decay to at most 50%). Below we describe how node i can assess $T_{i,m}^{encounter,X}(t + \Delta t)$ based on direct observations during its encounter with node m over the interval $[t, t + \Delta t]$:

- $T_{i,m}^{encounter,healthiness}(t + \Delta t)$: This provides the belief of node i that node m is not compromised based on node i's direct observations toward node m over the encounter interval $[t, t + \Delta t]$. Node i can monitor node m's unhealthiness evidences including dishonest trust recommendation, irregular packet patterns, and abnormal traffic over the new encounter period $[t, t + \Delta t]$ or even extend the time period to $[0, t + \Delta t]$ to help assess $T_{i,m}^{encounter,healthiness}(t + \Delta t)$. It can be computed by the number of bad experiences in healthiness over the total healthiness experiences.

- $T_{i,m}^{encounter,cooperativeness}(t + \Delta t)$: This provides the degree of node m's cooperativeness evaluated by node i based on direct observations over the encounter interval $[t, t + \Delta t]$. Node i can apply overhearing and snooping techniques to detect cooperativeness behavior, e.g., whether or not node m follows the prescribed hello or routing protocol, over the time period $[t, t + \Delta t]$ or even extend the time period to $[0, t + \Delta t]$. It can be computed by the number of bad experiences in cooperativeness over the total cooperativeness experiences.

- $T_{i,m}^{encounter,connectivity}(t + \Delta t)$: This provides the connectivity belief that node m will encounter node d (a node which may become a destination node in packet forwarding in the future). It can be computed by the number of encounters between node m and node d over the maximum number of encounters between node d and any other node over the time period $[0, t + \Delta t]$ all based on node i's observations. Note that node i can observe node m encountering node d only if both node m and node d are within 1-hop range of node i. Thus, by consulting its encounter history with all nodes, node i will be able to calculate $T_{i,m}^{encounter,connectivity}(t + \Delta t)$ for the connectivity of node m to node d. In particular, if node i observes that node d encounters node m most frequently among all nodes over the time period $[0, t + \Delta t]$, then $T_{i,m}^{encounter,connectivity}(t + \Delta t) = 1$. This means that node i highly trusts that node m will encounter node d often and is a good candidate for packet forwarding.

- $T_{i,m}^{encounter,energy}(t + \Delta t)$: This provides the belief of node i toward node m's energy status based on direct observations toward node m. Here energy represents competence. Node i can monitor node m's transmission signal strength over $[t, t + \Delta t]$ to estimate energy status of node m.

On the other hand, for indirect trust evaluation, only 1-hop neighbors of node i will be used as recommenders for scalability. We define the recommender trust threshold T_{rec} such that if $T_{i,j}(t) > T_{rec}$, node i will consider node j as a "trustworthy" recommender at time t.

The indirect trust evaluation toward node j is given in Eq. 4 below. R_i is the set containing node i's 1-hop neighbors with $T_{i,c}(t + \Delta t) > T_{rec}$ and $|R_i|$ indicates the cardinality of R_i. If the new encounter is node j, then there is no indirect recommendation available for node j, so node i will use its past trust toward node j obtained at time t with trust decay over Δt. If the new encounter is not node j and node i considers node c as a trustworthy recommender, i.e., $T_{i,c}(t + \Delta t) > T_{rec}$, then node c can provide its recommendation to node i for evaluating node j. In this case, node i weighs node c's recommendation with node i's trust toward node c. Moreover, the more recommendations from trustworthy nodes node i receives, the more accurate the trust value of node j can be. Using T_{rec} provides robustness against bad-mouthing or good-mouthing attacks since only recommendations from trustworthy nodes are considered.

$$
T_{i,j}^{indirect,\ X}(t + \Delta t)
= \begin{cases}
e^{-\lambda_d \Delta t} \times T_{i,m}^X(t), & if\ m = j \\
e^{-\lambda_d \Delta t} \times T_{i,j}^X(t), & if\ m \neq j\ and\ |R_i| = 0 \\
\dfrac{\sum_{c \in R_i}\{T_{i,c}^X(t + \Delta t) \times T_{c,j}^X(t + \Delta t)\}}{\sum_{c \in R_i} T_{i,c}^X(t + \Delta t)}, & if\ m \neq j\ and\ |R_i| > 0
\end{cases}
\tag{4}
$$

When node i encounters node m, it can use $T_{i,m}(t)$ to decide whether or not node m can be the next message carrier to shorten message delay or improve message delivery ratio. We consider a Ω–permissible policy with T_f as the minimum trust threshold for the selection of the next message carrier. That is, node i will forward the message to node m if $T_{i,m}(t + \Delta t) \geq T_f$ as well as $T_{i,m}(t)$ is in the top Ω percentile among all $T_{i,j}(t)$'s. This guarantees to select a trustworthy next message carrier. We consider only single-copy message routing, and buffer management is not considered in this paper.

4   Performance Model

We develop a probability model to analyze the performance of the proposed trust-threshold based routing protocol for DTN message forwarding. The probability model

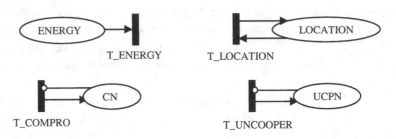

Fig. 1. SPN Model

is based on stochastic Petri net (SPN) techniques [18] due to its ability to handle a large number of states. The SPN model is shown in Fig. 1 consisting of 4 event subnets, namely, in clockwise order, energy, location, cooperativeness, and compromise. The purpose of the SPN model is to yield the ground truth status of a node (i.e., healthiness, cooperativeness, connectivity, and energy) in the presence of uncooperative and malicious nodes and to derive its trust relationships with other nodes in the system. Without loss of generality, we consider a square-shaped operational area consisting of $m \times m$ sub-grid areas with the width and height equal to radio range R. Initially nodes are randomly distributed over the operational area based on uniform distribution. Below we explain how we construct the SPN model for describing a node's ground truth status.

Location (Connectivity): We use the *location subnet* to describe the location status of a node. Transition T_LOCATION is triggered when the node moves to a randomly selected area out of four different directions (i.e., north, west, south, and east) from its current location with the rate σ_0/R based on the node's speed σ_0 and radio range R. To avoid end-effects, movement is bounced back. This information along with the location information of other nodes at time t provides us the probability of two nodes encountering with each other at any time t.

Energy: We use the *energy subnet* to describe the energy status of a node. Place *ENERGY* represents the current energy level of a node. An initial energy level of each node is assigned according to node heterogeneity information. A token is taken out when transition T_ENERGY fires. The rate of transition T_ENERGY indicates the energy consumption rate which depends on the ground truth status of the node (i.e., uncooperativeness and healthiness).

Healthiness: We use the *compromise subnet* to describe the healthiness status of a node. A node becomes compromised when transition T_COMPRO fires and then a token is put in place *CN* to represent the node has been captured and compromised. The rate to T_COMPRO is λ_{com}, the per-node compromising rate given as input to the SPN model.

Cooperativeness: We use the *cooperative subnet* to describe the cooperative status of a node. Place *UCPN* indicates whether a node is uncooperative or not. If a node becomes uncooperative, a token goes to *UCPN* by triggering T_UNCOOPER. The transition rate to T_UNCOOPER is $\lambda_{uncooper}$, the per-node uncooperative rate given as input to the SPN model.

The SPN model described above yields the "ground truth" status of each node, which facilitates the calculation of $T_{i,j}^X(t + \Delta t)$ in theoretical analysis as follows. When node i encounters node j, node i will assess node j in trust property X to yield $T_{i,j}^{encounter,X}(t + \Delta t)$. Node i can directly observe node j during the current encounter interval $[t, t + \Delta t]$ plus it may have accumulated past direct observations toward node j over $[0, t]$ prior to the current encounter. Thus, assuming that the "cooperativeness detection mechanism" described earlier in the protocol design is effective, node i's direct assessment on node j's cooperativeness will be close to the ground truth cooperativeness status of node j at time $t + \Delta t$. Consequently, $T_{i,j}^{encounter,cooperativeness}(t + \Delta t)$ in Eq. 3 can be estimated by the probability that place $UCPN$ in node j does not contain a token at time $t + \Delta t$. Similarly, node i can fairly accurately assess $T_{i,j}^{encounter,connectivity}(t)$ by consulting its encounter history with all nodes over the interval $[0, t + \Delta t]$. This quantity can be obtained by utilizing the SPN output regarding the location probability of nodes j and d at time $t + \Delta t$. For the healthiness trust component, assuming that the "healthiness detection mechanism" in the protocol design is effective, $T_{i,j}^{encounter,healthiness}(t + \Delta t)$ can be approximated by the probability that place CN in node j does not contain any token at time $t + \Delta t$. Lastly, node i can observe node j's packet transmission signal strength over $[t, t + \Delta t]$ to estimate $T_{ij}^{encounter,energy}(t + \Delta t)$, which will be close to the ground truth energy status of node j and can be obtained from the SPN output by inspecting place $ENERGY$. Note that we predict $T_{i,j}^{encounter,X}(t + \Delta t)$ for theoretical analysis. In practice, node i would follow the protocol design to assess $T_{i,j}^{encounter,X}(t + \Delta t)$. Once $T_{i,j}^{encounter,X}(t + \Delta t)$ is obtained, node i can update its $T_{i,j}^X(t + \Delta t)$ based on Eq. 2, and subsequently, obtain $T_{i,j}(t + \Delta t)$ based on Eq. 1.

5   Results

In this section, we show numerical results and provide physical interpretation of the results obtained. For trust-threshold based routing (TTBR), we set $w_1 : w_2 : w_3 : w_4 = 0.25 : 0.25 : 0.25 : 0.25$. We setup 20 nodes with vastly different initial energy levels (in the range of $[12, 24]$ hours) in the system. Each node moves randomly in an 8×8 operational area with mobility rate being σ_0 in the range of $[1, 4]$ m/sec. Each of the 8×8 square regions is of the same size, with each side equal to $R = 250\ m$. There are three types of nodes, namely, good, uncooperative and malicious nodes. A bad node is either uncooperative or malicious, or both. Good nodes have zero compromise and uncooperative rates. Uncooperative nodes have a non-zero uncooperative rate $\lambda_{uncooper}$ (i.e., once per 300 sec). Malicious nodes have a non-zero compromise rate λ_{com} in the range of $[1/480\text{min}., 1/160\text{min}.]$. We set $\beta_1 : \beta_2 = 0.8 : 0.2$ to put high trust on direct observations over indirect recommendations. The initial trust level is set to ignorance (i.e., 0.5) for all trust components due to no prior interactions among nodes. We set the decay coefficient $\lambda_d = 0.001$, and the average encounter interval $\Delta t = 5$ min, resulting in $e^{-\lambda_d \Delta t} = 0.995$ to model small trust decay over time.

We consider a message forwarding case that a pair of source and destination nodes is picked randomly among good nodes in each run. We allow 30 min warm-up time for nodes to accumulate experiences about each other and start a message forwarding afterwards in each run. If a message carrier is malicious, the message is dropped (a weak attack). If the message carrier is uncooperative, the message delivery continues with 50% chance. The message delivery run is completed when the message is delivered to the destination node, or the message is lost before it reaches the destination node. Data are collected for 2000 runs from which the message delivery ratio, delay and overhead performance measurements are calculated. Here, the message overhead is measured by the number of copies forwarded to reach the destination node. For the message delay and the message overhead, we only consider messages that are delivered successfully.

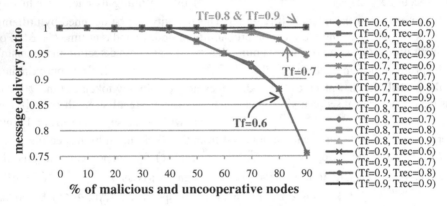

Fig. 2. Effect of T_f and T_{rec} on Message Delivery Ratio

First of all, we investigate the optimal values of T_{rec} and T_f under TTBR in DTNs. From Figs. 2-3, we see that $T_f = 0.9$ consistently performs better than the others in terms of all performance metrics over a wide range of bad node population. This is because with $T_f = 0.9$, TTBR behaves like a "direct delivery" approach with very little copies being passed around to intermediate message carriers, resulting in a more direct route to the destination node. More specifically, as the percentage of bad nodes increases, there may be an extreme case where node i stores a message and delivers it directly to the destination node because it could not encounter any node with trust higher than T_f. This is true in our DTN scenario where nodes can encounter each other with nonzero probability due to random movement. In situations where a node's movement is not random and the encountering probability may be zero or very small among certain nodes, $T_f = 0.9$ may not necessarily always perform the best. Our model helps identify the best T_f that minimizes the message delay/overhead. From Fig. 4, we see that $T_{rec} = 0.6$ has the shortest message delay and the lowest message overhead over a wide range of the percentage of bad nodes when T_f is fixed at 0.9. The reason is that the recommenders are all good nodes when $0.6 \leq T_{rec} \leq 0.9$ and $T_{rec} = 0.6$ not only allows more recommenders but also provides sufficiently correct recommendations, resulting in a more accurate indirect trust assessment based on Eq. 4.

In summary, we conclude that there can exist optimal T_f and T_{rec} in TTBR to best tradeoff message delivery ratio, message delay, and message overhead, adapting to application or network environmental conditions.

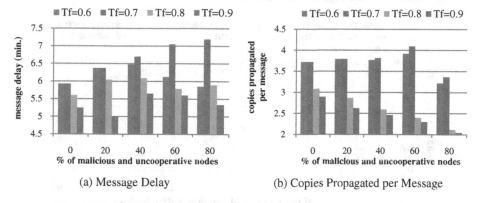

(a) Message Delay

(b) Copies Propagated per Message

Fig. 3. Effect of T_f on Message Delay and Message Overhead ($T_{rec} = 0.6$)

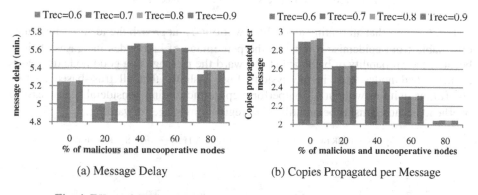

(a) Message Delay

(b) Copies Propagated per Message

Fig. 4. Effect of T_{rec} on Message Delay and Message Overhead ($T_f = 0.9$)

We also perform a comparative analysis of TTBR against epidemic routing, social-trust-based routing (STBR), and QoS-trust-based routing (QTBR). For STBR and QTBR, we set $w_1: w_2: w_3: w_4 = 0.5: 0.5: 0: 0$ and $0: 0: 0.5: 0.5$, respectively. Note that STBR and QTBR are special cases of TTBR, with STBR using only social trust metrics and QTBR using only QoS trust metrics for trust evaluation. Thus, the design concept of trust thresholds also applies to them. To show the effect of T_f, we evaluate the performance of these two routing algorithms with and without T_f.

Fig. 5 shows that the routing protocols with T_f outperform those without T_f in the delivery ratio. Also, TTBR with T_f and STBR with T_f perform better than QTBR with T_f and epidemic routing with delivery ratio approaching 1 over a wide range of bad node population. This is because TTBR and STBR are able to differentiate trustworthy nodes from bad nodes and select trustworthy nodes to relay the message. We also note that performance of epidemic routing deteriorates when there is a high bad node population because it does not select trustworthy message carriers. This result demonstrates the effectiveness of incorporating social trust into the decision making process for DTN message routing, as well as using T_f to select the next message carrier to yield high delivery ratio.

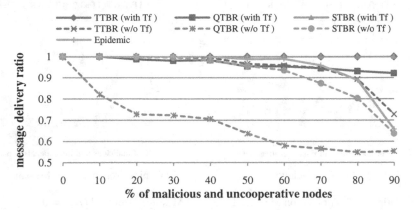

Fig. 5. Message Delivery Ratio $\left(T_{rec} = 0.6, \quad T_f = 0.9\right)$

Fig. 6 shows that all routing algorithms without T_f approach the ideal performance obtainable from epidemisc routing as the percentage of bad nodes increases. This is because the probability of being able to forward the message to a good node decreases as more bad nodes exist in the system. Fig. 7 shows that all trust-based routing algorithms, with or without T_f, outperform epidemic routing considerably in message overhead because trust is being utilized to regulate message forwarding.

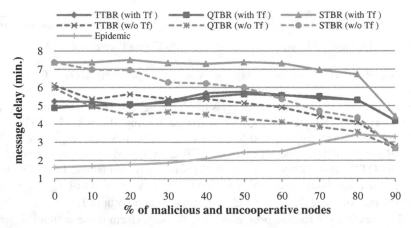

Fig. 6. Message Delay $(T_{rec} = 0.6, \quad T_f = 0.9)$

In Figs. 6-7, QTBR performs better than TTBR and STBR in terms of message delay and message overhead. This is because the path selected by TTBR or STBR may not be the most direct route as they attempt to avoid bad nodes when compared with QTBR that only uses the connectivity metric and the residual energy metric as the criteria to select a message carrier. This result indicates that if the objective is to minimize message delay or message overhead, we should set the weights associated with connectivity and energy considerably higher than those for healthiness and cooperativeness for TTBR to approach the performance of QTBR in message delay or message overhead.

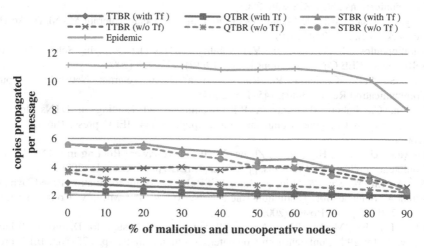

Fig. 7. Number of Copies Propagated per Message ($T_{rec} = 0.6$, $T_f = 0.9$)

In summary, from Figs. 5-7, we see that our proposed trust-threshold based routing algorithm operating under identified optimal T_f values can effectively trade off message overhead and message delay for a significant gain in message delivery ratio. Moreover, our analysis results reveal that there exists an optimal weight setting in terms of $w_1 : w_2 : w_3 : w_4$ (e.g., STBR vs. QTBR vs. TTBR) to best balance the effect of social trust metrics vs. QoS trust metrics to maximize the delivery ratio without compromising message delay and/or message overhead requirements.

6   Conclusion

We have proposed and analyzed a trust-threshold based routing algorithm with the design objective to maximize the message delivery ratio while satisfying the message delay and message overhead requirements. Our algorithm leverages a trust management protocol incorporating both social and QoS trust metrics for peer-to-peer trust evaluation, as well as trust thresholds for selecting recommenders for indirect trust evaluation and for selecting the next message carrier for message forwarding. Our performance analysis results demonstrate that when operating under proper trust thresholds and social vs. QoS trust weight settings as identified in the paper, TTBR can effectively trade off message delay and message overhead for a significant gain in message delivery ratio to achieve the design objective. In the future we plan to perform a more comprehensive comparative analysis with existing trust management protocols for DTN routing. We also plan to address quality assurance of subjective trust evaluation by extensive theoretical and experimental validation with trace data.

Acknowledgments. This work was supported by the National Research Foundation of Korea Grant funded by the Korean Government [NRF-2009-352-D00262] to Dr. Chang.

References

1. Fall, K., Farrell, S.: DTN: An Architectural Retrospective. Journal on Selected Areas in Communications 26(5), 828–836 (2008)
2. Daly, M., Haahr, M.: The Challenges of Disconnected Delay Tolerant MANETs. Ad Hoc Networks 8(2), 241–250 (2010)
3. Karaliopoulos, M.: Assessing the Vulnerability of DTN Data Relaying Schemes to Node Selfishness. IEEE Communications Letters 13(12), 923–925 (2009)
4. Jain, S., Fall, K., Patra, R.: Routing in a Delay Tolerant Network. Computer Communication Review 34(4), 145–158 (2004)
5. Nelson, C., Bakht, M., Kravets, R.: Encounter-based Routing in DTNs. In: 28th Conference on Computer Communications, pp. 846–854. IEEE press, Rio De Janeiro (2009)
6. Shevade, U., Song, H., Qiu, L., Zhang, Y.: Incentive-Aware Routing in DTNs. In: 16th Conference on Network Protocols, pp. 238–247. IEEE press, Orlando (2008)
7. Xu, A., Jin, Y., Shu, W., Liu, X., Luo, J.: SReD: A Secure Reputation-Based Dynamic Window Scheme for Disruption-Tolerant Networks. In: Military Communications, pp. 1–7. IEEE press, Boston (2009)
8. Chen, B., Chan, M.: MobiCent: A Credit-Based Incentive System for Disruption Tolerant Network. In: 29th Conference on Computer Communications, pp. 875–883. IEEE press, San Diego (2010)
9. Lu, R., Lin, X., Zhu, H., Shen, X.: Pi: A Practical Incentive Protocol for Delay Tolerant Networks. IEEE Transactions on Wireless Communications 9(4), 1483–1493 (2010)
10. Hui, P., Crowcroft, J., Yoneki, E.: BUBBLE Rap: Social-based Forwarding in Delay Tolerant Networks. In: MobiHoc, pp. 241–250. ACM press, Hong Kong (2008)
11. Daly, M., Haahr, M.: Social Network Analysis for Information Flow in Disconnected Delay-Tolerant MANETs. IEEE Transactions on Mobile Computing 8(5), 606–621 (2009)
12. Bulut, E., Wang, Z., Szymanski, K.: Impact of Social Networks on Delay Tolerant Routing. In: Global Communications Conference, pp. 1804–1809. IEEE press, Hawaii (2009)
13. Hossmann, T., Spyropoulos, T., Legendre, F.: Know Thy Neighbor: Towards Optimal Mapping of Contacts to Social Graphs for DTN Routing. In: 29th Conference on Computer Communications, pp. 866–874. IEEE press, San Diego (2010)
14. Mtibaa, A., May, M., Diot, C., Ammar, M.: PeopleRank: Social Opportunistic Forwarding. In: 29th Conference on Computer Communications, pp. 111–115. IEEE press, San Diego (2010)
15. Chen, I.R., Bao, F., Chang, M.J., Cho, J.H.: Trust Management for Encounter-based Routing in Delay Tolerant Networks. In: Global Communications Conference. IEEE press, Miami (2010)
16. Vahdat, A., Becker, D.: Epidemic Routing for Partially Connected Ad Hoc Networks. Technical Report, Computer Science Department, Duke University (2000)
17. Ren, Y., Chuah, M., Yang, J., Chen, Y.: Muton: Detecting Malicious Nodes in Disruption-tolerant Networks. In: Wireless Communications and Networking conference, pp. 1–6. IEEE press, Sydney (2010)
18. Giardo, G., Fricks, R.M., Mupplala, J.K., Trivedi, K.S.: Stochastic Petri Net Package Users Manual. Department of Electrical Engineering. Duke University, Durham (1999)

A Trust Management Framework for Detecting Malicious and Selfish Behaviour in Ad-Hoc Wireless Networks Using Fuzzy Sets and Grey Theory

Ji Guo, Alan Marshall, and Bosheng Zhou

The Institute of Electronics, Communications and Information Technology
Queens University Belfast, Belfast, UK
Belfast, United Kingom
{jguo04,a.marshall,b.zhou}@qub.ac.uk

Abstract. As wireless network applications evolve, they require interaction between many entities (protocols, middleware etc), and an increasing requirement for the design of secure applications among the entities is trust management. Consequently, many new attacks against networks are aimed at the trust management. In this paper, we develop a new trust management framework (TMF) for wireless networks. The proposed framework applies Grey theory combined with Fuzzy Sets to calculate a node's trust value based on observations from neighbour nodes'. The new TMF employs multiple rather than a single parameter to decide the resulting trust value. Simulations conducted in an 802.11 based wireless network show that the new framework can not only identify abnormal trust behaviour, but can also effectively find which aspect of the metrics used to establish the trust value for a node are abnormal, and hence identify the strategy the attacker is using against the TMF.

Keywords: trust management framework, Fuzzy Set, Grey theory, wireless networks.

1 Introduction

Wireless network technologies have greatly changed our daily lives by offering access to the Internet anywhere and anytime. However attacks and intrusions against wireless networks, Internet fraud and high-tech crimes have kept raising in recent years, and security has become a major concern for those who intend to use wireless technologies and Internet services. Substantial resources have been deployed to tackle this issue; firewalls, anti-virus software, encryption algorithms, and intrusion detection and prevention systems are examples of the tools to secure network applications. A networked application involves interactions among many entities, such as networking protocols from physical layer to application layer, middleware, various algorithms, etc. An essential challenge when designing a secure application is therefore to determine how one network entity can trust another network entity.

In today's business communications systems, trust plays an important role in virtual organizations, where it is used to counter uncertainty caused by the business

I. Wakeman et al. (Eds.): IFIPTM 2011, IFIP AICT 358, pp. 277–289, 2011.
© Springer-Verlag Berlin Heidelberg 2011

requirement for openness. The requirement seeks to make marketable services openly available to all potential, highly autonomous clients, which increases a service provider's vulnerability to an attack [1]. Especially in distributed environments, trust management can provide a basis for more detailed and better-informed authorization decisions, while allowing for a high level of automation. Researchers want to design trust management systems in order to establish trust relationships, dynamically monitor, and adjust any existing trust relationships [1][2]. In recent years, various models and algorithms for describing trust and designing trust management in distributed systems or wireless networks have been considered, such as policy language, public-key cryptography, the resurrecting duckling model, and the distributed trust model [1][2][3][4]. The distributed trust models are usually applied in peer-to-peer (P2P) systems and wireless ad hoc Networks; these networks rely on all participants actively contributing to network activities such as routing and packet forwarding. The particular characteristics of a wireless network's nodes, such as limited memory, battery power, and bandwidth, can provide incentives for them to act selfishly (refuse to participate in routing and provide services to other nodes, for example). Trust management can help mitigate nodes' selfish behaviors and advantage the efficient utilization of network resources. Recent research has considered how to evaluate the trust of communication entities in wireless networks, and various theories such as Probabilistic Estimation [1], Information Theory [4], Fuzzy theory, and Game theory have been used for designing the trust metrics [5][6]. For evaluating trust values from more aspects, some researchers introduce Grey theory to improve existing trust management or network performance [7][8][9][10].

In this article, we focus on designing a new trust management framework which uses algorithms based on Fuzzy Sets and Grey theory. Grey theory has been widely applied in many fields like economics, agriculture, aerographs, the environment and materials. In [7][9], Deng Julong proposed the grey relational analysis method to make a quantitative analysis of the dynamic development process of systems. The basic idea of Grey theory is to determine the relationship of different factors according to the degree of similarity between curves. The research presented here takes the idea of Grey theory in order to rank trust values. A major advantage of this method is that it does not require a high quantity of sample data. Moreover, it does not require the data to be consistent with any kind of distribution rule in order to produce very convincing results, which are consistent with qualitative analysis. In [8], Fu Cal *et al* applied an improved traditional analysis method to the problems mentioned above. This method can effectively deal with data that has multiple attributes, while obtaining grey relational grades that can be compared with each other, no matter what the units of the original data are [8]. It can therefore be considered a feasible method for risk assessment of peer nodes in P2P networks and wireless ad-hoc networks.

The rest of this article is organized as follows: first, the classification of trust relationships is introduced, then the application of Grey theory to the design of a new trust management framework is described. Several simulation cases are then described that use the proposed algorithms and their performance examined. Conclusions and further research are then detailed.

2 Trust Relationships

Current trust management research in wireless networks, usually views the neighbourhood from three levels [1][4][11]. For the neighbourhood of one node, according to the link conditions, we can classify as direct, indirect, and recommendation relationships, on behalf of node A's different neighbours' trust opinions.

Direct trust is established through observations on whether the previous interactions between the nodes have been successful [11]. For example, node A wants to know node B's information, for which observations from A to B are for direct trust.

Indirect trust can be transited through the third entities. For example, node E and F are the indirect trust nodes, which have interactions with B, but not with A.

Recommendation trust is a special type of trust relationships. We assume the nodes have a common node to communicate. This common node is denoted as the recommendation node. For example, nodes A and B have a common node C. If A wants to know the trust records of B from C, C will calculate the trust value of B based on the observations of interactions between B and C.

3 A New Trust Management Framework for Wireless Networks Using Fuzzy Set and Grey Theory

This section presents a TMF for a pure mobile ad hoc network environment, using Grey Theory. The TMF is designed to be robust against attacks that are aimed to deceive the trust relationships, such as Selective Misbehaviour attack, On-off attack, Conflicting attack, and Bad Mouthing attack [1][11]. In wireless ad-hoc and mesh, the links between communicating nodes can be one-hop, and multi-hop, only single-hop links are considered in this paper.

3.1 The framework

For a node in a distributed environment, such as in a wireless ad hoc network, the trust management of the network views the node as an agent for obtaining the trust information. The functional blocks of the framework are shown in Figure 1.

In Figure 1, the nodes in the TMF firstly collect the input information for subsequent computation of trust. Many existing trust models for distributed environments choose the probability of successful interactions, which is generally viewed as corresponding to the packet loss rate, as the main parameter in calculation of the trust value. However, in fact the probability of one node cooperating with other nodes is influenced not only by the packet loss rate, but also signal strength, data rate, and other physical factors that are not considered in current trust models.

For example, an attacker/selfish node may make use of the knowledge that the packet loss rate is the main parameter used in trust calculation. Due to this limitation, the attacker can obtain a very high trust value by just interacting with close neighbours, while dropping or abandoning communications with nodes far away. In comparison, normal behaving nodes will communicate with *all* neighbours (near and far). However when a normal node interacts with a far away neighbour, the packet loss rate may be higher than that of the attacker which communicates only with near neighbours. Thus, if only the packet loss rate is used as the deciding parameter, it will lead to a normal node's trust value being lower than the attacker's who intends to choose partners. This leads to the conclusion that any TMF should consider multiple parameters, including those involved in the communications processes in order to avoid such duplicity.

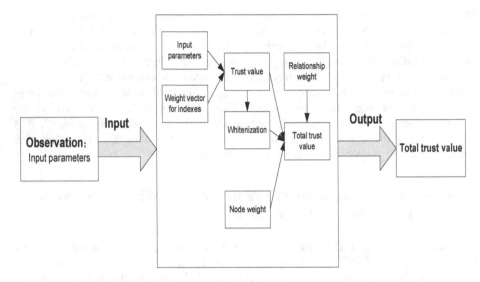

Fig. 1. Functional blocks of the TMF

The input parameters include: packet loss rate, signal strength, data rate, end-to-end delay, and throughput. These parameters are chosen as the basic minimum set of parameters required to cover all types of attacks against lower level protocols as they can easily be obtained from MAC, data link and network layer protocols.

3.2 Using Grey Theory

For multiple input parameters, we can use Grey Theory to proceed and calculate trust value. From Grey theory, let X be a grey relational set which is used as the evaluation index set, $X = \{ x_1,..., x_m \}$, while x_j is an evaluation index. Here, we assume that $X=\{packet\ loss\ rate,\ signal\ strength,\ data\ rate,\ delay,\ throughput\}$.

During a time period t $(t=1,2,...T)$, from the view of a node that observes its neighbouring node k's behaviour and calculates its trust values, k's value of the evaluated index x_j is $a_{kj}{}^t$ $(j=1,2,...,m)$. We can get node k's sample sequence $A_k{}^t= \{a_{kj}{}^t\}$, $j=1,2,...,m$, and the sample matrix for all the neighbouring nodes at t, $A^t= [a_{kj}{}^t]$, $j=1,2,...,m$, $k=1, 2,..., K$.

We define at period t, the best reference sequence $G^t=(g_1{}^t,..., g_m{}^t)$, while $g_j{}^t$ is the chosen best index from $\{a_{kj}{}^t\}$. From Grey theory, we can obtain the Grey Relational

Coefficient [6] between node k's sample and the best reference sequence about x_j at period t as:

$$\theta_{k,j}^{t} = \frac{\min_k \left| a_{kj}^{t} - g_j^{t} \right| + \rho \max_k \left| a_{kj}^{t} - g_j^{t} \right|}{\left| a_{kj}^{t} - g_j^{t} \right| + \rho \max_k \left| a_{kj}^{t} - g_j^{t} \right|} \qquad \ldots(1)$$

$\rho \in (0,1)$ is the distinguishing coefficient [8]. Also we define the worst reference sequence $B^{t} = (b_1^{t}, \ldots, b_m^{t})$, while b_j^{t} is the chosen worst index from $\{a_{kj}^{t}\}$. From Grey theory, we can obtain the Grey Relational Coefficient between node k's samples and worst reference sequence about x_j at period t as:

$$\phi_{k,j}^{t} = \frac{\min_k \left| a_{kj}^{t} - b_j^{t} \right| + \rho \max_k \left| a_{kj}^{t} - b_j^{t} \right|}{\left| a_{kj}^{t} - b_j^{t} \right| + \rho \max_k \left| a_{kj}^{t} - b_j^{t} \right|} \qquad \ldots(2)$$

$\rho \in (0,1)$ is distinguishing coefficient. From (1) and (2), when normally setting $\rho = 1/2$, the value area of a grey relational coefficient is from 0.33 to 1. In order to make the grey relational coefficient to be in [0, 1], it can convert the values by using the mapping $y = 1.5x - 0.5$ (x is the grey relational coefficient).

We define the index set X's weight vector $H = \{h_1, \ldots, h_m\}$, $\sum h_j = 1$. At period t, node k's Grey Relational Grades with best and worst reference sequence are $\theta_k^{t} = \sum_j h_j \theta_{k,j}^{t}$, $\phi_k^{t} = \sum_j h_j \phi_{k,j}^{t}$, respectively.

Then, by using the least-square methods [12], we can obtain the integrated expected value at period t as node k's trust value:

$$T_k^{t} = \frac{1}{1 + \dfrac{(\phi_k^{t})^2}{(\theta_k^{t})^2}} \qquad \ldots(3)$$

3.3 Overall Trust Value with Fuzzy Set and Whitenization Weight Function

The trust models currently used seldom consider the influence of different nodes' viewings; moreover, they also set the weights of the opinions as fixed values, usually average values. This means the important degrees of opinions about trust information from a normal node and a selfish node (or an attacker) are equal. Therefore, our approach is to set the weights as changeable parameters in order to express the degree of trust of a node or nodes, based on their historical behaviour.

We can obtain the trust assessment by using classes of grey clusters and a whitenization weight function. Grey whitenization weight function can be used to measure the utility value of expected revenue [9][13]. This means that whitenization weight functions can describe one value's weights in different clusters, which can be viewed as the degree of how much the value belongs to a cluster. We define n grey clusters $c_1, c_2, \ldots, c_n$ for evaluating trust degrees, the corresponding whitening functions $f_1(x), f_2(x), ..., f_n(x)$, and the threshold values $\sigma_1, \sigma_2, ..., \sigma_n$ [7]. Three classes of grey clusters are defined as shown in table 1.

Table 1. Grey clusters

c_1	Not quite trusted
c_2	Some trust
c_3	Quite trusted

The corresponding whitenization functions are as follows:

$$f_1(x) = \begin{cases} 1, x <= 0.25 \\ -4x/3 + 4/3, x > 0.25 \end{cases}, \sigma_1 = 0.25 \qquad ...(4)$$

$$f_2(x) = \begin{cases} 2x, x <= 0.5 \\ -2x + 2, x > 0.5 \end{cases}, \sigma_2 = 0.5 \qquad ...(5)$$

$$f_3(x) = \begin{cases} 4x/3, x <= 0.75 \\ 1, x > 0.75 \end{cases}, \sigma_3 = 0.75 \qquad ...(6)$$

When node A gets various trust values of node B from different neighbor nodes. The whitenization weight of a trust value T_{Bk} (node B's trust value evaluated by node k, also named as T_k) belonging to the j class c_j is $f_j(T_{Bk})$. According to $max_j\{f_j(T_{Bk})\}$, we can know the grey cluster class of *node B* based on T_{Bk}.

$$T_{total} = \frac{1}{2}(\max_j\{f_j(T_{direct})\})T_{direct} + \frac{1}{2}\frac{2N_R}{2N_R + N_I}\sum_k \frac{w_k}{\sum w_k}(\max_j\{f_j(T_k)\})T_k$$
$$+ \frac{1}{2}\frac{N_I}{2N_R + N_I}\sum_k \frac{w_k}{\sum w_k}(\max_j\{f_j(T_k)\})T_k \qquad ...(7)$$

Here, $\rho = 1/2$; Nr means the number of recommendation nodes, while Ni means the number of indirect nodes. The Nr and Ni can express the effect levels of different trust relationships, to compose relationship weights. w_k (or w_{kA}) is the weight value of node k that is set by node A. From $max_j\{f_j(T_{total})\}$, it can get the total grey cluster class for *node B*.

4   Simulation and Analysis

The experiment scenario used ns-2 to create a wireless environment, using 802.11 standards, to simulate 6 wireless nodes in a distributed MANETs like structure shown in Figure 2. *node 0* wants to get the trust value of *node 1* based on trust opinions from *node 0* and its neighbouring nodes *2, 3, 4 & 5*.The DSDV routing protocol is used.

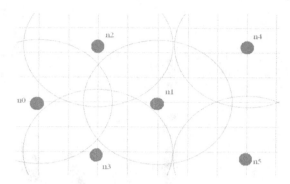

Fig. 2. Topology of the 6 wireless nodes

4.1 Direct and Recommendation trust values

In this part, the simulation sets 6 nodes and calculates 4 nodes' trust values from them. All the nodes are static. Each link from node i to node j has a 10-second CBR/UDP traffic. The size of each data packets is 220 Bytes. The parameters observed are: packet loss rate; received signal strength; delay; throughput; data rate (currently set as a fixed value 1.0Mbps, 802.11 basic data rate). Initially all parameters have equal importance (equal weight).

From Grey Theory, we can use the input parameters of a node to calculate the target node's (*node 1*) trust value, from the view of a specified node like *node 0*, compared with the neighbour nodes of *node 0*. That means by Grey Theory, we get *node 1*'s trust value from *node 0*, which has neighbouring nodes *node 2 and node 3*. The TMF gets the three nodes' (*node 1, 2, 3*) trust values for *node 0* over a period of 10 seconds, which is $T_{10}=0.44509$ as the direct trust value of *node 1*. Here $\rho=0.5$, $H=\{0.2,0.2,0.2,0.2,0.2\}$, $N_R=2$, $N_I=0$, which means the indirect nodes *4, 5* are not included. All the initial weight values w_{k0} are set to 1.

The framework also gets $T_{12}=0.22490$, and $T_{13}=0.20000$, which are the recommendation values from nodes *2* and *3* about node 1. After the whitenization functions, the total value of *node 1* for *node 0* with 3 neighbor nodes is $T_{10\text{-}3nodes}=0.30433$, as shown in Figure 3.

4.2 Direct, Recommendation and Indirect Trust Values

Here, the system calculates the trust values among 6 nodes, considering several additional links. $\rho=0.5$, $H=\{0.2,0.2,0.2,0.2,0.2\}$, $w_{k0}=1$, $N_R=2$, and $N_I=2$.

From the simulating data, we get $T_{10}=0.44509$, and $T_{12}=0.22490$, $T_{13}=0.20000$, $T_{14}=0.80000$, and $T_{15}=0.50000$. From these it is possible to calculate the total trust value with 5 neighbor nodes $T_{10\text{-}5nodes}=0.37726$, as shown in Figure 3. From max_j $\{f_j(T_{10\text{-}5nodes})\}$, we can know *node 1*'s grey cluster class is c_1.

4.3 Analysis

In Figure 3, there are the trust values of node 1 from node 0, 2, 3, 4, 5, and the total values with 3 nodes and 5 nodes, the average value $T_{10\text{-}average}$ of $T_{10}\text{~}T_{15}$.

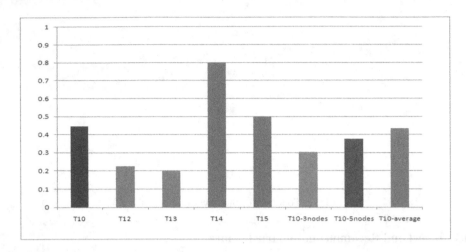

Fig. 3. Trust values

From the figure, the results show that taking different relationship factors will affect the total value. $T_{10\text{-}average}$ is higher than $T_{10\text{-}3nodes}$ and $T_{10\text{-}5nodes}$, due to not including the relationship weights. If the simulation just considers the opinions of nodes *0, 2, 3*, the result will be lower than that including nodes *0, 2, 3, 4, 5* because T_{15} is higher than T_{13}, and T_{14} is higher than T_{12}.

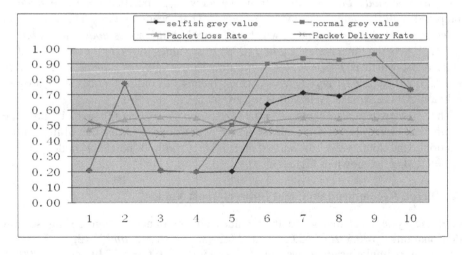

Fig. 4. Trust values calculated by grey theory and PDR

Figure 4 shows the trust values calculated by grey theory, and PLR (Packet Loss Rate) which is often the single metric selected by current TMF approaches such as OTMF (Objective Trust Management Framework) [1]. Existing trust management schemes like OTMF, often choose the probability of successful interactions as their input parameter in order to calculate their trust values.

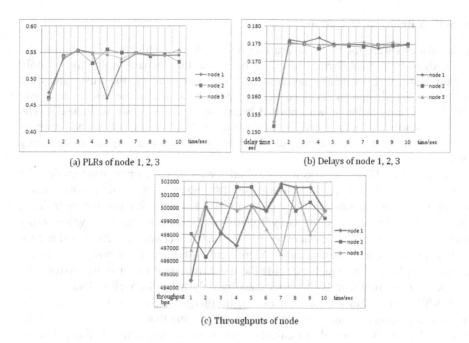

(a) PLRs of node 1, 2, 3   (b) Delays of node 1, 2, 3

(c) Throughputs of node

Fig. 5. Trust Parameters of nodes *1, 2, 3* for 10 seconds

For nodes *0, 1*, the simulation takes a 10-second CBR/UDP traffic from *node 0* to *node 1*. Every second as an interval, the simulator calculates and records the grey trust value of *node 1* from *node 0*, compared with the good-put trust values obtained from the packet delivery rate (PDR) of *node 1*. The good-put trust value obtained from the packet delivery rate is equal to *1-PLR* . T_{10} in Figure 3 is the grey trust value of *node 1* from *node 0* for the period of 10 seconds, while the good-put trust value of *node 1* for the period of 10 seconds is 0.463517. The result clearly shows that the individual good-put sample values are very close to the good-put value for the period of 10 seconds, while the grey values have significant variation from T_{10}. That means when PLRs are similar, trust values also tend to be similar, by using existed trust management schemes which choose PLR as the main parameter, though these schemes may process PLR with various formulas or algorithms, i.e., Bayesian approach. However, the new TMF described uses multiple parameters with Grey Theory to measure trust values. This is based on the assertion that any one node's behaviour, whether that interaction is successful or not, is affected by various factors, for example the node's signal strength, data rate, throughout, and delay. Therefore, the judgement on whether any node should be trusted, is not only determined by the probability of successful interactions, but also from various parameters in the physical and MAC layers.In fact, the packet loss rates of nodes *1, 2, 3* have little variance over the period, while the throughput and delay times of *node 1* are changing with time, compared with those of nodes *2 and 3*; this is shown in Figure 5. These changing parameters have a significant impact on the grey trust values.

4.4 Selfish Behavior Detection

The simulations were modified so that one node behaved selfishly. In operation, the node tends to be normal during the initial time, and then behaves selfishly, by only communicating with its nearby neighbours. Using Grey theory, the trust values are affected by the change in received signal strength, although the packet loss rate maintains the same value as with normal behaviours, this is shown in Figure 4. The main reason why the selfish node's trust value decreases is that its signal strength observed by the neighbour is increasing, leading to the drop in its signal strength grey value.

Currently Grey Theory has been considered for use in developing trust models for wireless networks that have fixed topologies [8]. Some of these new trust models consider just three parameters; they also set fixed weight vectors for their input parameters in calculation of the Grey Relational Grade and the trust value; other research [10] uses Grey Theory in other aspects such as network selection, and not for distributed network trust management. A problem with using fixed weight vectors is that once attackers know which aspect is the most important factor in the system, the malicious nodes can obtain high trust values by only behaving well in that specified aspect, while in fact they do not cooperate with other normal nodes. In this paper, the new TMF considers a greater number of input parameters that cover all aspects of the lower level network protocols to calculate the trust values, hence making it more difficult for any malicious node to replicate all of them. Moreover, it uses several weight vector groups in order to obtain different trust values for a node; this can identify which aspect of a node's behaviour is abnormal, compared with other neighbour nodes. With this idea, the new TMF can also deduce selfish nodes' behaviour strategies.

Different weight vectors H may be used to calculate the grey value, and the new TMF uses multiple weight vectors from which it can calculate various trust values. These different values can help to show differences between abnormal and normal behaviours; therefore in order detect the strategy that a selfish node employs, a range of vectors are used to identify the attempt to deceive the TMF. Figure 6 shows the results obtain when using the following vectors the : $H=\{0.2,0.2,0.2,0.2,0.2\}$ for (a), $H=\{0.6,0.1,0.1,0.1,0.1\}$ for (b), while $H=\{0.1,0.6,0.1,0.1,0.1\}$ for (c), and $H=\{0.1,0.1,0.1,0.6,0.1\}$ for (d), $H=\{0.1,0.1,0.1,0.1,0.6\}$ for (e), $H=\{0.1,0.1,0.6,0.1,0.1\}$ for (f). The weight configuration is such that for 5 input parameters, we use 6 vectors: one vector with equal weigh assigned to all input parameters, and 5 vectors each with one of the parameters having higher priority. Using this approach, we can not only detect general abnormal behavior, but also identify which of the input parameters are more responsible for it.

In Figure 6, the TMF sets different weight values for the signal strength and other parameters. The weight of signal strength is 0.2 Figure 6(a), 0.6 for Figure 6(c), while 0.1 for Figure 6(b), (d), (e) and (f). Generally, the system can find the difference in trust values between a normal node and a selfish one, when the five parameters have equal weight values, shown in Figure 6(a). Then, by using other weight vector groups, it can be clearly seen that there is a very large gap between normal and selfish trust values whenever the signal strength is set as the most important factor (weight value 0.6), in Figure 6(c). This reveals that the observed node is likely to be behaving selfishly on the aspect of signal strength, due to the abnormal value in Figure 6(c).

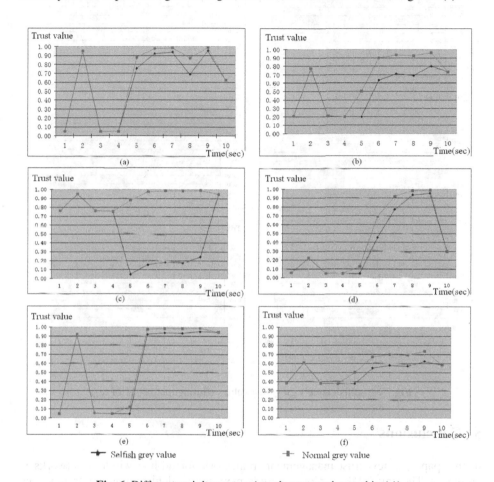

Fig. 6. Different weight vectors (attack strategy detected in (c))

By setting the weight vectors, the trust management framework can detect more covert (intelligent) selfish behavior. For example, a node may maintain the packet loss rate at a normal level, but just cooperate with other nodes less frequently compared with normal nodes. By using the new framework, the results in Figure 7 (a) show that a selfish node with lower throughput results in a lower trust value, when setting $H=\{0.2,0.2,0.2,0.2,0.2\}$. Moreover, if the framework uses $H=\{0.1,0.1,0.1,0.1,0.6\}$, it may be observed that the selfish behavior is largely linked with the parameter throughput, shown in Figure 7 (e). Similar results can be obtained for other selfish strategiies such as delaying packets.

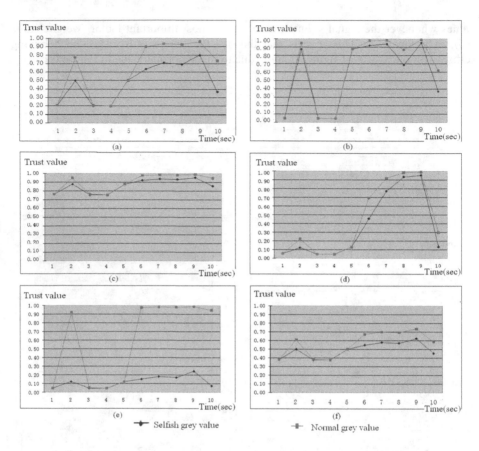

Fig. 7. A selfish node's grey trust values (throughput behavior (e))

5 Conclusions

In this paper, a new trust management framework for ad-hoc wireless networks is presented. The new TMF employs multiple metrics to calculate a node's trust values rather than current approaches such as OTMF that consider only one parameter. The approach also uses Grey theory and Fuzzy sets to improve the trust value generation algorithms. Unlike other trust management frameworks, the TMF described in this paper sets a weight vector for each of the input parameters. This provides a significant new benefit for the TMF as it can detect not only selfish or anomalous behaviour, but can also help identify the type of parameters used in the strategy of the attacker or selfish node.

Simulation results are presented that reveal the proposed framework can show clearly the difference in the trust values between a normal and selfish node on a specific parameter by setting an appropriate weight vector. In addition, the total trust value is calculated by using relation factors and weights of neighbour nodes, not just by simply taking an average value. Further research will test the proposed framework in more comprehensive environments with more network alternatives and selection criteria.

Acknowledgments. The authors would like to acknowledge the financial support from the China Scholarship Council (CSC) for this research. Also the authors would like to express their gratitude to Doctor F. Cai for offering useful information and constructive comments on the experiment studies this paper.

References

1. Li, J., Li, R., Kato, J.: Future Trust Management Framework for Mobile Ad Hoc Networks. IEEE Communications Magazine 46(2), 108–114 (2008)
2. Hu, Y.-C., Perrig, A., Johnson, D.B.: Ariadne: A Secure On-Demand Routing Protocol for Ad Hoc Networks. In: Proc. MobiCom 2002 (September 2002)
3. Li, H., Singhal, M.: Trust Management in Distributed Systems. IEEE Computer Society 40, 45–53 (2007)
4. Sun, Y.L., Yu, W., Han, Z., Ray Liu, K.J.: Information Theoretic Framework of Trust Modelling and Evaluation for Ad Hoc Networks. IEEE Journal of Selected Areas in Communications (J-SAC) 24(2), 305–317 (2006)
5. Tuan, T.A.: A Game-Theoretic Analysis of Trust Management in P2P Systems. In: First International Conference on ICCE 2006, pp. 130–134 (October 2006)
6. Qin, Z., Jia, Z., Chen, X.: Fuzzy Dynamic Programming based Trusted Routing Decision in Mobile Ad Hoc Networks, Embedded Computing. In: Fifth IEEE International Symposium on Embedded Computing, SEC 2008, pp. 180–185 (2008)
7. Julong, D.: Introduction to Grey Theory. Huazhong University of Science & Technology Press, Wuhan (2002)
8. Cai, F., Fugui, T., Yongquan, C., Ming, L., Bing, P.: Grey Theory Based Nodes Risk Assessment in P2P Networks. In: IEEE International Symposium on Parallel and Distributed Processing with Applications, pp. 479–483 (2009)
9. Deng, J.: A Course in Grey Systems. Huazhong University of Science and Technology Press, Wuhan (1990)
10. Song, Q., Jamalipour, A.: Network Selection in An Integrated Wireless LAN and UMTS Environment Using Mathematical Modeling and Computing Techniques. IEEE Wireless Communication, 42–48 (June 2005)
11. Sun, Y.L., Han, Z., Liu, K.J.R.: Defense of Trust Management Vulnerabilities in Distributed networks. IEEE Communications Magazine 46(2), 112–119 (2008)
12. Hong, L., Chen, W., Gao, L., Zhang, G., Fu, C.: Grey theory based reputation system for Secure Neighbor Discovery in Wireless Ad Hoc Networks. In: 2nd International Conference on Future Computer and Communication (ICFCC), vol. 2, pp. 749–754 (2010)
13. Liu, S., Lin, Y.: Grey Information: Theory and Practical Applications. Springer, London (2006)

Regulatory Impact of Data Protection and Privacy in the Cloud

Sakshi Porwal[*], Srijith K. Nair[**], and Theo Dimitrakos

Security Futures Practice, BT Innovate & Design,
Martlesham Heath, Ipswich IP5 3RE, United Kingdom
{sakshi.porwal,srijith.nair,theo.dimitrakos}@bt.com

Abstract. The use of cloud computing services has developed into a new method for deploying software and services and hosting data. The model has provided enormous social and economic benefits but at the same time it has also created potential privacy and security challenges for businesses, individuals and the governments. For example, the use of shared compute environment, data storage and access via internet has made information vulnerable to misuse, and thus, has made privacy a major concern for organisations adopting cloud services for storage and computation purpose. Generally, each country maintains their own laws and regulations to prevent frauds and protect their citizens from harm, including the potential dangers of data privacy, essential when internet and related technologies are involved. The European Union, for example, follows the overarching governmental regulations while the United States prefers the Sectoral Approach to Data Protection legislation, which relies on the combination of legislation, regulation and self regulation. This report discusses data protection issues related to cloud computing and identifies privacy laws enforced in the EU that can be applied to this model. Moreover, it also provides recommendations that cloud service providers can consider to implement in order to provide enhancements to their services and to demonstrate that they have taken all necessary measures to comply with the data protection principals in place.

Keywords: cloud computing, data privacy, data protection, regulations.

1 Introduction

Privacy of digital data has always been a critical concern of the IT industry. It occupies a central concern in the cloud computing service delivery model due to its unique multi-tenanted and resource-shared nature. Its richness in functionalities has exacerbated the concerns of individuals, organisations and government as there is a greater perceived probability of compromise of the privacy of personal data.

Many elements of regulations related to the traditional IT industry can be applied in order to protect information in a cloud environment, with little or no specialized provisions. However, the cloud model introduces additional complications in order to

---

[*] Work carried out during internship at BT.
[**] Corresponding author.

I. Wakeman et al. (Eds.): IFIPTM 2011, IFIP AICT 358, pp. 290–299, 2011.
© Springer-Verlag Berlin Heidelberg 2011

comply with some of these regulations. In addition, different nations have varying views on the regulation needed to protect data and private information and to whom these laws apply. One of the major reasons for this difference across countries is due to the fundamental difference in the role and relationships of government and the commercial sector.

While the European Union (EU) and the United States are each other's largest trading partners, they follow vastly different approaches to protect their personal information. In the EU, government actively participates along with the major industries to achieve public tasks. Moreover, it discusses regulatory and public interests, objectives and strategies to attain them. In contrast, US decision makers follow a more laissez-faire approach to corporate governance and emphasize on the role of private sectors in resolving challenges [1].

Cloud service providers, like any other IT service providers, have to architect their system in such a way as to obey their country specific laws and regulations. In the EU, the European Union Data Protection Directive is the central pillar of data privacy and in the US, several sector specific laws and regulations are collectively set forth to protect the privacy of cloud service consumer's personal data.

This paper looks at the data protection and privacy issues associated with the cloud computing model and goes on to examine the EU privacy laws related to this area with the aim of providing recommendations, with special emphasis on the point of view of cloud providers, in order for them to comply with country specific regulations. The structure of this paper is as follows: Section 2 provides a brief introduction of the cloud computing service model and identifies various areas that need special consideration from a regulatory point of view. The next section describes data protection and privacy laws applicable in the EU and with the help of different cloud scenarios discusses their applicability. Section 4 attempts to provide generic legal and regulatory recommendations distilled from the earlier section for cloud providers to consider in order to comply with their country-specific laws. The last section concludes the paper.

2 Cloud Computing

Cloud computing has emerged as a promising and challenging model for deploying software and services and hosting data. It utilizes two separate technological pillars-utility computing and service oriented architecture principles, to provide cloud service consumer with highly scalable, economic and everything-as-a-service delivery model. Cloud computing is rich in features such as scalability/elasticity, shared resource pooling, multi-tenant environment, ubiquitous network access and pay-as-you-go pricing. Its characteristics for providing faster, agile, robust and economic solution makes it a very attractive service delivery model from the customer's perspective.

The major players of the cloud computing ecosystem are Cloud Service Providers (CSP) that provides cloud services and Cloud Service Consumers (CSC) which makes use of (consumes) these cloud services. The CSC can be an individual, SME or a bigger enterprise.

While cloud computing has been characterized as one of the most game-changing IT models to emerge in recent years, its adoption carry a number of risks and threats, the general discussion of which is however beyond the scope of this papers. Here we concentrate on the data protection and privacy issues associated with the model.

Some aspects of cloud computing demands special attention because of the strong privacy concerns and legal requirements surrounding its use. To exemplify, data of various users is stored in a shared infrastructure environment, where faulty access control mechanisms can lead to unauthorised access to confidential data. Therefore, special mechanisms are needed to protect the sensitive data from such unwanted access. In order to secure their services, cloud providers have to comply with the legal and regulatory standards. Grey areas exist in the regulatory sphere. Concerns have been raised as to how the data will be transferred from the user's domain to the cloud and the associated legal issues if the cloud provider is based in a different country. Also, in the cloud model, providers have to provide assurance to their customers that they will respect the confidentiality of their data and integrity of their computation. In addition, the protection of intellectual property is another concern for service providers who provide flexible environment to cloud consumers to deploy their applications. Other issues which cloud providers have to consider in order to provide effective services to their customers includes risk allocation, privileged user access, data leakage, data recovering methods and key management.

Thus we see that there are several data protection and privacy issues that have to be considered by both the CSPs as well as the CSCs. In the next section we discuss the conceptions of privacy with respect to cloud computing model in the context of EU.

3   EU Perspective

The EU follows a single overarching privacy law which claims privacy as the fundamental right of a human being. It is the responsibility of the government in the EU to protect an individual's right to privacy and to actively participate with industries to achieve public tasks and discuss the regulatory and public interests, objectives and strategies. Furthermore, in the EU, use of personal data is proactively regulated which is refrained in the US [2, 3].

The Data Protection Directive [4] forms an important component of the EU privacy and human rights law and applies to the processing of information in electronic as well as manual forms and addresses both personal data and personally identifiable information. Its main purpose was to harmonize the privacy laws that existed in the different member states of the EU and to provide a basic standard on privacy protection. It consists of 32 articles, setting requirements on handling personal data and mandating the countries of the EU to implement them.

The EU directive is applicable to cloud providers that are established in the EU or "act as processor for a controller established in the EU." In other words, any cloud provider based in the EU or serving companies based or operating in the EU has to abide by its clauses. These include both the cloud provider as well as other service providers that use cloud providers for powering their service, based in the EU. It is also applicable if the cloud provider uses equipment (such as servers) that is located within an EU member state or act as processor for a controller using such equipment.

Furthermore, the EU Directive assumes the existence of cross border data flows and attempts to protect the data privacy rights of EU regardless of where the data is transferred or processed [5,6]. The Article 5 of the Directive mandates that participating states should ensure that the personal data of EU is protected with adequate level of protection when it is exported to and processed in countries outside EU.

The following legal and regulatory analysis covers the issues and solutions unique to cloud services with regards to data protection, confidentiality, intellectual property and outsourcing services and changes in control.

3.1 Data Protection

The services provided by cloud providers in a Software as a Service (SaaS) model generally consist of email, messaging, desktops, projects management, payroll, accounts and finance, CRM, sales management, custom application development, custom applications, telemedicine and billing., where personal data of the customer get processed[1]. This data may belong to a number of persons for example, employees, clients, suppliers, patients and, more generally, business partners.

From an analysis of Section 4 of the Data Protection Directive, it can be concluded that the place where the controller is established is relevant to the application of the Data Protection Directive, and the place of processing of the personal data or the residence of the data subject is less relevant. The Data Protection Directive will then apply if the Controller is established in the EU and also if the Controller is not established in the EU but uses equipment located in the EU for processing of personal data (e.g., data centers for storage and remote processing of personal data situated on the territory of a Member State, computers, terminals, servers), unless such equipment is used solely for the purpose of transit through the territory of the Community.

Once it is determined that the Data Protection Directive applies, the first question that needs to be clarified is the identity of the Controller and the Processor. The classification as a Processor or Controller greatly determines the very different compliance duties and obligations and related liabilities associated with the entity. In general, if the customer of the cloud provider determines the purposes and means of the processing of personal data, he is the Controller and if the cloud provider processes personal data on behalf of his customer, it is an External Processor. In this analysis it is assumed that the customer of the cloud provider is the Controller and the cloud provider an External Processor.

Some of the main duties and obligations for the Controller set forth in the Directive are:

a. Processing the personal data according to the principles of Fairness, Lawfulness, Finality, Adequacy, Proportionality, Necessity and Data Minimisation (Section 6 of the Data Protection Directive)
b. Processing the personal data after having provided the data subject with the necessary information (Section 10 of the Data Protection Directive);
c. Guaranteeing the data subject the rights laid down in Section 12 of the Data Protection Directive - e.g., to obtain confirmation as to whether or not data relating to the data subject is being processed, to obtain information on the purposes of the processing etc.

---

[1] Note that as far as the directive is concerned, storage is a form of process.

d. Implementing appropriate technical and organisational security measures to protect personal data against accidental loss, alteration, unauthorised disclosure or access and against all other unlawful forms of processing (Section 17 of the Data Protection Directive);

e. Choosing a Processor that provides sufficient guarantees with respect to the technical security measures and organisational measures governing the processing to be carried out, and ensuring compliance with those measures;

f. Transferring of personal data to 'third countries which do not ensure an adequate level of protection within the meaning of Section 25 (2) of the Data Protection Directive only in case the data subject has given the previous consent unambiguously to the proposed transfer or under the condition that other procedures are in place as per Section 26 (e.g., 'Standard Contractual Clauses' or – if the data are transferred to the United States – 'Safe Harbor Principles'[7,8]).

The data controller (cloud customer) should provide the data subjects (end-users of the cloud customer) with all the mandatory information related to data processing. The cloud customer will be required under the Directive to inform their customers about the circumstances of the transfer to the cloud provider, the quality of the cloud provider (external processor), and the purposes of the transfer. It is crucial that those who collect data subject to the Data Protection Directive ensure that they understand the application of the Directive to the use and transfer of that data. In this respect, controllers not currently engaging in cloud computing are advised to seek informed consent from the data subjects to data processing and transfer outside the European Economic Area. Those currently engaged in cloud computing are advised to ensure that this consent has been procured and that it adequately describes the nature and extent of processing and transfer. The alternative would be to have in place one of the procedures set forth in Section 26 (Standard Contractual Clauses or Safe Harbor Principles – if the data is transferred to the US and the cloud provider participates in such a program).

To apply the Data Protection Directive adequately, the availability and integrity of data are key, which leads the discussion to data security measures. There are unavoidable trade-offs here. More data security is likely to lead to reduced availability. The customer of the cloud provider may thus want to take a close look at the security measures the cloud provider has in place and the data availability guaranteed. It has to be born in mind that in most European countries there are mandatory data security requirements. The customer of the cloud provider needs to make sure that those measures are complied with.

It has to be clear at this point that the customer – when classified as sole data Controller - will be the entity responsible for the processing of personal data in relation to the data subjects. The customer will also be responsible for this data when such processing is carried out by the Cloud Provider in the role of external Processor. Failure to comply with the Data Protection Directive may lead to administrative, civil and also criminal sanctions, which vary from country to country, for the data controller.

Dealing with the issues

Various steps can be taken in order to deal with the various regulatory constraints imposed on the cloud provider and cloud customer by the EU directive. Here we discuss some of the prominent ones.

It is recommended that the Cloud provider use fine grained access control mechanisms that take into account location of data owner/ jurisdiction and also the organisational structure of customer.

At the Cloud consumer's side, it should look for the presence of Data Protection clause in the contract between them and the provider instead of ensuring themselves that the collected personal data is handled in compliance with Sections 7 and 10 of the Data Protection Directive. This clause should set forth the relevant parties' duties and obligations. The cloud provider should cooperate with the controller in order to assure that the latter can effectively guarantee the data subject's rights in accordance with Section 12 of the Data Protection Directive.

The cloud provider should also have in place adequate security measures pursuant to Section 17 of the Directive and it should promptly notify the controller of any breach of data security and cooperate swiftly to solve the problem.

The data protection clause between the provider and the consumer should be subject to negotiation. In addition, security measures may be addressed in annexes and SLAs. In addressing security issues, the parties should keep in mind that they may not be able to detail all security measures to be addressed. Because IT security is an ongoing race to deal with new issues, contract terms need to be free to develop accordingly.

It may also be advisable for the customer to negotiate adequate remedies for contractual damages should the Data Protection clause be breached. Also, if the cloud provider's breach is substantial it may be included in the list of instances which lead to unilateral termination of the agreement

In addition, if the cloud provider is in a country outside the European Economic Area and that country does not offer an adequate level of data protection, it is advisable to have in place procedures in accordance with Section 26 (e.g., 'Standard Contractual Clauses' or 'Safe Harbor Principles' – if the data are transferred to the United States and the cloud provider participates in such a programme), rather than basing the transfer on the consent of the data subject.

However, it has to be stressed that the transfer of data within the territory of Member States is not without problems. Indeed, despite the fact that personal data can freely circulate within Member States, the laws are not consistent across countries. This inconsistency may create obvious difficulties in compliance and thus liability issues. As the Data Protection Directive is currently under revision, it is hoped that the Commission would take steps towards the standardization of minimum data protection requirements in Europe.

3.2 Confidentiality

Confidentiality concerns are also raised by the scenarios considered in this paper. As secret information and 'know-how' may be processed in clouds, any leakage of information caused by voluntary communication by the Cloud Provider or cloud's security breach may jeopardise the customer business/services. It is crucial to distinguish between processing of data as in computational operations over that data, and the storage or transmission of data without altering it, since processing in this sense usually requires the data to be in unencrypted form, at least during the computation stage.

There do not seem to be any European regulations applicable to such scenarios. European regulations regarding know-how, defined as a body of information that is secret, substantial and identified in any appropriate form, apply principally to licensing and activities involving the transfer and exploitation of information.

Dealing with the issues

Keeping regulations in mind, and in order to preserve the economic value of know-how and secret information in general, including research results, customer and project-related information, it is recommended that customers seek contractual terms covering this issue. In fact, parties' duties and obligations to preserve such value could be specifically addressed in a 'confidentiality/non-disclosure clause'. Particular attention should be given to the boundaries of the responsibilities of parties and related liabilities.

The potential customer of the cloud provider should carefully analyse the confidentiality/non-disclosure clause to determine whether the cloud provider offers sufficient guarantees to protect the customer's secret information and know-how that will be placed in the cloud.

It is also recommended that the parties negotiate a provision that reflects the damage a party may sustain should confidential or secret information be disclosed. If the disclosure is substantial, this breach may be included in the list of instances which allow the company to unilaterally terminate the agreement.

3.3 Intellectual Property

Intellectual property may also be at risk when used within a cloud environment. Although an entity outsourcing services to the Cloud Provider may protect and enforce its intellectual property rights by means of the relevant legislation, which is similar in all the European Member States, a breach of Intellectual Property rights may cause immediate damage which will never be fully restored in a legal proceeding.

Moreover, in the unlikely case that the interactions between the customer and the cloud provider may give rise to joint results which can be object of intellectual property rights, it is wise to determine who will own these rights prior to engaging in cloud computing activities, and further determine the use that the parties can make of the objects of such rights.

Dealing with the issues

Intellectual Property rights should be regulated through dedicated contractual clauses: "Intellectual Property Clause" and "Confidentiality/Non Disclosure Clause". The Intellectual property clause should be detailed enough that it covers all the issues related to the Intellectual Property right. It should be explicitly mentioned in the contract that who owns various parts of the process- the data, the application, the result of the computation etc.

In addition, the potential customer of the cloud provider should carefully assess the value of its intellectual property and the risks related to cloud computing services. Having done so, the customer should carefully review any clauses governing intellectual property to determine whether the cloud provider offers sufficient guarantees and allows the customer appropriate tools to protect its information (e.g. through encryption of data), to protect the customer's assets. The cloud customer should ensure that the contract respects their rights to any intellectual property as far as possible without compromising the quality of service offered (e.g. the creation of backup copies may be a necessary part of offering a good service level).

It is also advisable that the customer negotiate a clause in which the cloud provider is penalized should the provisions governing intellectual property be violated. Substantial breaches by the cloud provider may be included in the list of instances allowing the company to unilaterally terminate the agreement.

3.4 Outsourcing Services and Changes in Control

The agreement between the company and the cloud provider is likely to be defined as a contract "intuitu personae". This contract is one in which a party chooses to contract with a company based on qualities that are unique to the company. For example, a customer may choose a particular cloud provider because of the services it offers, its reputation or professionalism, or its technical skills. As a result, the customer may be reluctant to see the cloud provider outsource all or part of the services to be provided to the customer.

Furthermore, the control of the cloud provider may also change and, as a result, the terms and conditions of the services provided by the cloud provider may change too.

Dealing with the issues

Cloud providers should explicitly state in the contract which of the processes it is outsourcing to a third party and maybe even allow the customer to choose from a list of potential outsourcing companies based on its preference.

Moreover, the customer should determine in advance whether services will be outsourced by the cloud providers and whether the cloud provider issues some guarantees or warranties relating to the performance of the services outsourced. However, it is recommended that the customer look to be able to restrict the outsourcing of services by the cloud provider. It is also advisable that the contract be reviewed to determine how the cloud provider will communicate changes in control to the customer. The customer may also want to consider whether the contract includes the right to terminate the contract if a change in control occurs.

Furthermore, the customer may choose to require that the outsourcing of services by the cloud provider be subject to the customer's prior authorisation. To make this decision, the customer will need to be informed about the type of services that the cloud provider intends to outsource and the identity of the company to whom these will be outsourced. Even if the customer agrees to the outsourcing, it may want the cloud provider to issue some guarantees or warranties relating to the performance of the services outsourced. By the same line of reasoning, the customer may also want to have the chance to approve a change of control, or to terminate or renegotiate the contract in case of a change in the control of the cloud provider. Such options may be carefully specified in the contract between the company and the cloud provider by means of a 'third-party outsourcing' clause, a 'warranties and indemnification' clause, a 'change in control' clause, or a 'termination of agreement' clause – again depending on the bargaining power of the parties.

5 Conclusions

In this paper we took a close look at the European Union regulations that we consider will have direct impact on the use of cloud computing based services. We analysed these impacts and made specific observations on how the cloud service provider as well as the consumer can take steps in order to comply with the regulations.

Based on the discussions in the preceding section, we conclude the paper with the following high level regulatory recommendations

- **Data Protection:** Cloud provider should provide sufficient technical security measures and organisational measures governing the processing to be carried out, and provide to the customer evidence ensuring compliance with those measures.
- **Data Security:** Cloud provider should pay attention to mandatory data security measures that potentially cause either the cloud provider or the customer to be subject to regulatory and judicial measures if the contract does not address these obligations.
- **Data Transfer:** Cloud service provider should also pay attention to what information is provided to the customer regarding how data is transferred within the cloud, outside that cloud, and within and outside the European Economic Area or the US territory.
- **Confidentiality and Non-disclosure:** Cloud provider should provide assurance to their customers that they will not disclose customer's data to any third party.
- **Law Enforcement Access:** Cloud provider should make available information about the jurisdiction in which data may be stored and processed and evaluate risks resulting from the jurisdiction to the customer.
- **Intellectual Property:** Cloud providers should ensure that the contracts with the customer acknowledge and respect their rights to any intellectual property or original works as far as possible without compromising the quality of service offered.
- **Risk Allocation and Limitation of Liability:** When reviewing their respective contract obligations, cloud provider and all other parties should underscore those obligations that present significant risk to them by including monetary remediation clauses, or obligations to indemnify, for the other party's breach of that contract obligation. Furthermore, any standard clauses covering limitations of liability should be evaluated carefully. The review should include both the liability of the cloud provider and the liability of the customer for data storage or processing that is performed by the cloud provider or on cloud provider's premises / infrastructure on behalf of the customer.
- **Change of Control:** Transparency should be ensured, cloud provider should honor their contract obligations in the case of a change of control, as well as any possibility to rescind the contract.
- **Audit:** As customers have no visibility into the cloud, cloud provider should take specific measures to audit and monitor customer's data and processes in the cloud.

References

[1] Farrell, H.: Constructing the international foundations of e-commerce: The EU-U.S. safe harbor arrangement. International Organisation 57, 277–306 (2003)
[2] Fromholz, J.M.: The European data privacy directive. Berkeley Technology Law Journal 15, 461–484 (2000)
[3] Schwartz, P., Reidenberg, J.: Data privacy law: A Study of United States data protection. Michie, Charlottesville (1996)
[4] European Commission, "Data Protection Legislative Documents", http://ec.europa.eu/justice/doc_centre/privacy/law/index_en.htm#directive
[5] Movius, L.B., Krup, N.: U.S and EU Privacy Policy: Comparison of Regulatory Approaches. International Journal of Communication 3, 168–187 (2009)
[6] Schriver, R.R.: You Cheated, You Lied: the Safe Harbor Agreement and Its Enforcement By the Federal Trade Commission. 70 Fordham L. Rev. 2777, 2779 (2002)
[7] Dubois, P., Wiles, N.: Solutions for cross-border transfers of personal data from EEA. In: IP&IT, vol. 2 Data Protection (2006/2007)
[8] Kobrin, S.: Safe harbors are hard to find: The transatlantic data privacy dispute, territorial jurisdiction and global governance. Review of International Studies 20, 111–131 (2004)

Assessment of the Trustworthiness of Digital Records

Jianqiang Ma[1,2], Habtamu Abie[2], Torbjørn Skramstad[1], and Mads Nygård[1]

[1] Department of Computer and Information Science,
Norwegian University of Science and Technology, Trondheim, Norway
{majian,torbjorn,mads}@idi.ntnu.no
[2] Norwegian Computing Center, Oslo, Norway
{Jianqiang.Ma, Habtamu.Abie}@nr.no

Abstract. It is easy enough to assert the trustworthiness or otherwise of a digital record, but it is far more difficult to present an objective basis for that assertion. A number of recent research efforts have focused on the trustworthiness of a digital record while paying scant attention to the record's evidential value as a measure of and a basis for the assessment of its trustworthiness. In this work, we study a model for the assessment of the trustworthiness of digital records based on their evidential values using the Dempster-Shafer (D-S) theory. The model is divided into three modules, (i) a knowledge-modelling module that models expert knowledge and consequent belief of evidence, (ii) an evidence-combination module that combines evidence from different sources in the face of uncertainty, and (iii) a trustworthiness assessment module that aggregates and integrates evidence, and assesses its trustworthiness. An example is presented to show how the model works.

1 Introduction

Due to the last century's developments in information technology, electronic documents are replacing paper documents to an ever-increasing degree. This technology enables electronic documents to be easily modified and transferred, which makes life easier for us in our digital businesses, but also makes it easier for malicious elements to compromise or tamper with them, which makes life more difficult for us. On receipt of an electronic document, one's first reaction is to question the document's trustworthiness. Current research into how to reduce the questionability of a document's trustworthiness is conducted in two areas, security and trustworthy repositories.

In the former area, in which most current research is conducted, research is concerned with the development of algorithms [17], protocols [19], and architectures [7, 8], whose purpose is to protect the electronic documents from tampering, and to ensure their trustworthiness. Even though the security methods such as digital signature and digital watermarking technology can protect digital records, they are not generally accepted in the area of digital library, as Boudrez [2] states, *"in general, the international archival community rejects the*

I. Wakeman et al. (Eds.): IFIPTM 2011, IFIP AICT 358, pp. 300–311, 2011.

preservation of encrypted documents". Thus, there is still a need for a method for assessing the trustworthiness of digital records preserved in digital libraries.

In the latter area, the emphasis is on the establishment of digital repositories, the trustworthiness of which is intended to be a guarantee of the trustworthiness of the digital records stored therein [3,5]. There is, however, a need to assess the trustworthiness of the digital records themselves, since they do not reside solely in the repository at all times.

Therefore, in this work, we study the trustworthiness of the digital records, using their evidential values as a measure of trustworthiness. Specifically, we look into Evidence-Keeping Metadata (EKM) [16] related to them. The EKM are a subset of the Recordkeeping Metadata [18], but limited only to the metadata which contain the evidence to proof the trustworthiness or untrustworthiness of a digital record. Note that the digital records we studied here are the records preserved in digital library; EKM of those records are dynamically documented by the digital library system and stored in a secure place. It is assumed that the EKM are not modified. The protection of the digital library system as well as the EKM is not covered in this paper. By combining the evidential values of EKM, the evidential value of a digital record can be deduced and used to assess the trustworthiness of the record. This work is a complement to the research on both security protections and trustworthy digital repositories.

The rest of this paper is organised as follows. First, we briefly describe related work in Section 2. After illustrating the assessment approach and how to apply this approach to the assessment of the trustworthiness of digital records in Section 3 and Section 4, respectively, we present an example to show how the assessment model works in Section 5. After discussing the challenges to the assessment model which we will investigate in our future work in Section 6, we present the conclusion in Section 7.

2   Related Work

Digital trust has become an increasingly important area of research. Of special importance is the estimation of trustworthiness of information and users. Extensive surveys and overviews of trust in IT (Information Technology) can be found in [1,9,12,23]. In this area, an often used methodology for trust management is the exploitation of the D-S theory of evidence [21] that defines a mathematical theory of evidence based on the belief function and plausible reasoning, which can combine separate evidence to compute the trustworthiness of an event.

There have been many attempts to apply the Dempster-Shafer (D-S) theory to the problem of assessing trustworthiness. Chen and Venkataramanan [4] applied D-S to intrusion detection in ad-hoc networks. They use D-S to combine observations on the trustworthiness of the suspected node from different nodes, and derive a number which shows the trustworthiness of the suspect node. Hu et al. [11] applied D-S to assess the trustworthiness of a digital image. They proposed a list of attributes that a digital image contains, and trained the classifier with 2000 images. Using the classifier in the experiments, their results show that the evaluation model is stable and robust. It is evident from these attempts that the D-S theory *offers a mathematical way to combine evidence from multiple observers without the need to know a priori or conditional probabilities as in the Bayesian approach* [4]. In this study, we apply D-S to assess the trustworthiness of digital records. To the best of our knowledge, no research has been conducted on the application of D-S to the assessment of the trustworthiness of digital records using their evidential values.

3   Our Approach

In this research, we adopt the D-S theory for assessing the trustworthiness of digital records for two reasons. First, the D-S theory can combine evidence from different sources, and achieves a degree of belief based on all the available evidence into consideration [6, 21]. Second, it can handle uncertainty without requiring a priori or conditional probabilities [4, 20].

In the D-S theory there is a set of mutually exclusive and exhaustive propositions denoted by Γ, called frame of discernment. A power set 2^{Γ} contains all possible subsets of Γ, as well as the Γ itself and the null set ϕ. A mapping function from 2^{Γ} to the interval between 0 and 1 is called the basic belief assignment (or mass function), which requires that:

$$m(\phi) = 0; and \sum_{A_i \subset \Gamma} m(A_i) = 1 \tag{1}$$

The mass function $m(A)$ expresses the proportion of evidence that supports the proposition set A, but not any subsets of A. Proposition set A may contain multiple propositions due to lack of information. In this case, the mass function $m(A)$ is the source of uncertainty in the D-S theory. In this work, the evidential values of EKM are initialised by a group of experts. That is because, first, it is often difficult, if not impossible, to find an expert who has professional knowledge of the complete EKM dataset. Second, in order to have more objective results when assessing the trustworthiness of digital records, we request a group of experts, instead of a single expert, to initialise the evidential values of EKM. This is inspired by the research work in the area of instrument development [15, 10] in which a panel of experts are always used in the judgement-qualification stage so as to validate content more objectively. The basic belief assignments are used to capture experts' knowledge of EKM's evidential values, which are assigned to numeric evidential values between 0 and 1 that are converted from linguistic evidential values initialised by experts.

A belief function in the D-S theory as defined in Equation (2) is the degree of belief that the proposition set A is true. It gathers all evidence that directly supports A. If proposition set A contains a single proposition, the belief function of A equals its mass function.

$$bel(A) = \sum_{B_i \subset A} m(B_i) \tag{2}$$

A plausibility function presents the possibility that proposition set A is not negated. The plausibility function gathers all evidence that support A or do not contradict A. It is defined as:

$$pls(A) = \sum_{B_i \cap A \neq \phi} m(B_i) \tag{3}$$

$bel(A)$ and $pls(A)$ are the lower bound and upper bound of the proposition set A, respectively. They are related to each other by:

$$pls(A) = 1 - bel(\overline{A}) \tag{4}$$

In this model, the belief function is used to model the quality of EKM that provide evidence that their high-level nodes are either trustworthy or untrustworthy, while the plausibility function is used to model the quality of EKM that provide evidence that their high-level nodes may be either trustworthy or untrustworthy.

Dempster's rule of combination is used to combine the basic belief assignments from different sources. Suppose there are two sources of evidence where the basic belief assignment functions are m_1 and m_2, respectively. Then, the rule of combination is defined as:

$$m_{12}(A) = m_1(A) \oplus m_2(A) = \frac{\sum_{B \cap C = A} m_1(B) m_2(C)}{1 - \sum_{B \cap C = \phi} m_1(B) m_2(C)} \tag{5}$$

The Dempster's rule of combination is used to combine the various assignments from different experts, and the evidence provided by the EKM, so as to assess the trustworthiness of digital records (as will be presented in Section 4). Based on the combined basic belief assignment, the corresponding belief and plausibility of the combined evidence can be obtained.

As described in Section 2, in the area of computer science, the D-S theory of evidence [21] is an often-used methodology for trust management [23]. A survey of its mathematical foundations, applications and computational analysis can be found in [14]. Since the D-S theory remains attractive because of its relative flexibility in reflecting uncertainty or lack of complete evidence and giving a convenient numerical procedure for fusing together multiple pieces of evidential data by its rule of combination [4], we use the D-S evidence theory in this paper. Despite the criticisms of the use of Dempster's rule of combination when encountering significant conflicting information [20,24], it is our considered opinion that it is suited to the assessment of the trustworthiness of digital records using evidential value as a measure of trustworthiness.

In the following section, we explain how the evidential values of EKM are used to assess the trustworthiness of a digital record in detail.

4   Assessment of the Trustworthiness of a Digital Record Using D-S Theory

In a previous work [16], we structured EKM of a digital record as a tree based on a proposed life-cycle model. The trustworthiness of the record is assessed from the leaves to the root of the tree, where the final assessment is made. The trustworthiness assessment model is divided into three modules, (i) a knowledge-modelling module that models expert knowledge and consequent belief of evidence, (ii) an evidence-combination module that combines evidence from different sources in the face of uncertainty, and (iii) a trustworthiness assessment module that aggregates and integrates evidence, and assesses its trustworthiness.

4.1   The Knowledge-Modelling Module

In order to obtain the evidential values of EKM, a set of experts are selected to provide their knowledge about the quality of all EKM used as evidence to prove the trustworthiness or untrustworthiness of the digital record. The knowledge-modelling module models knowledge from experts to the evidential value of EKM, which will later be used to assess the trustworthiness of the digital record. Each expert assigns a tuple set (EV, H) to EKM. $EV \in$ {Extremely High (EH), Very High (VH), High (H), Medium (M), Low (L), Very Low (VL), Extremely Low (EL)} [1], presents the evidential value of EKM assigned by the expert. H is a Boolean value that stands for the "trustworthy hypothesis", if it is true, it means the expert believes that the corresponding EKM provide evidence that their higher-level nodes are trustworthy. For example, if an expert assigns $(EH$, true) for an EKM, it indicates that the expert thinks these EKM provide strong evidence that their higher-level nodes are trustworthy. The linguistic values can then be mapped to numeric evidential values between 0 and 1. The numeric evidential values can be presented in percentage between 0 and 100%, Table 1 shows an example of the mapping.

Table 1. Mapping linguistic evidential values to numeric evidential values

Linguistic EV	extremely high	very high	high	medium	low	very low	extremely low	ϕ
Numeric EV	95%	80%	65%	50%	35%	20%	5%	0

After this step, the knowledge-modelling module models the experts' knowledge as a tuple set Ψ.

$$\Psi = \{\{(NEV_{11}, H_{11}), (NEV_{12}, H_{12}) \ldots (NEV_{1n}, H_{1n})\} \ldots$$
$$\{(NEV_{m1}, H_{m1}), (NEV_{m2}, H_{m2}), (NEV_{mn}, H_{mn})\}\} \quad (6)$$

where m is the index of EKM, n is the number of experts and NEV is the numeric evidential value. Assume that H_{ij} is true, then, tuple (NEV_{ij}, H_{ij}) only means expert E_j believes that EKM_i (a piece of EKM) supports the trustworthiness hypothesis that "its higher-level node is trustworthy" to the extent NEV_{ij}. It does not necessarily mean that expert E_j believes EKM_i supports the hypothesis that its higher-level node is untrustworthy to the extent $1 - NEV_{ij}$.

---

[1] $EV = \phi$ means that the EKM can be used to establish neither that their higher-level nodes are trustworthy nor that they are untrustworthy.

Note that aspects like what happen when no expert exist to provide the evidential values and the data are coming from a third party source, are not considered while it is a more realistic scenario. In addition, there is concern that some of the experts may be malicious, thus, attacks (such as bad mouthing attack, on-off attack, etc.) may be performed. In the p2p networks area, many defence mechanisms [13,22] have been proposed to detect malicious agents. Those solutions can also be adopted here to detect malicious experts. However, this will not be discussed any further in this paper.

4.2   The Evidence-Combination Module

After modelling all the experts' knowledge by the previous module, this module combines the assignments from all experts for each piece of EKM, so as to obtain the assessed evidential value of each piece of EKM.

Suppose the frame of discernment of EKM_i is $\Gamma = \{T, \overline{T}\}$, and N stands for the higher-level node of EKM_i, where T is the proposition set that $\{N$ is trustworthy$\}$, $\overline{T}$ is the proposition set that $\{N$ is untrustworthy$\}$, and U is the universal set that $\{N$ is trustworthy, N is untrustworthy$\}$. The expert E_j's assignment tuple (NEV_{ij}, H_{ij}) can then be mapped to the basic belief assignment. If $H_{ij} = \phi$, it means that EKM_i provides no evidence about the trustworthiness or untrustworthiness of N. Thus, in that case, $m_{ij}(T)$ and $m_{ij}(\overline{T})$ are equal to 0, and $m_{ij}(U)$ equals 1 (100%). In other cases, the mapping follows Equations (7) and (8) below.

$$\text{if } H_{ij} = true, \text{then} \begin{cases} m_{ij}(T) = NEV_{ij} \\ m_{ij}(\overline{T}) = 0 \\ m_{ij}(U) = 1 - NEV_{ij} \end{cases} \tag{7}$$

otherwise,

$$\text{if } H_{ij} = false, \text{then} \begin{cases} m_{ij}(T) = 0 \\ m_{ij}(\overline{T}) = NEV_{ij} \\ m_{ij}(U) = 1 - NEV_{ij} \end{cases} \tag{8}$$

As we stated at the end of Section 4.1, when H_{ij} is true, it does not mean that expert E_j believes EKM_i supports $\overline{T}$ to the extend $1 - NEV_{ij}$. Also, it is the same case when H_{ij} is false. Therefore, $1 - NEV_{ij}$ is assigned to $m_{ij}(U)$ to show that expert E_j is not certain that EKM_i supports T or $\overline{T}$ to the extent $1 - NEV_{ij}$.

By applying Dempster's rule of combination to the aggregated probabilities assigned to each piece of EKM by all experts, the evidence-combination module calculates the evidential value of each piece of EKM.

According to the mapping function presented in (7) and (8), the basic belief (i.e. $m_{ij}(T)$, $m_{ij}(\overline{T})$, $m_{ij}(U)$) assigned to each tuple is obtained. Then, using Equation (5), the basic beliefs assigned to EKM_i by all experts are calculated as follows.

$$m_{EKM_i}(T) = m_{i1}(T) \oplus m_{i2}(T) \oplus \ldots \oplus m_{in}(T)$$
$$m_{EKM_i}(\overline{T}) = m_{i1}(\overline{T}) \oplus m_{i2}(\overline{T}) \oplus \ldots \oplus m_{in}(\overline{T})$$
$$m_{EKM_i}(U) = m_{i1}(U) \oplus m_{i2}(U) \oplus \ldots \oplus m_{in}(U)$$

Based on Equation (2), the belief functions of EKM_i are:

$$bel_{EKM_i}(T) = m_{EKM_i}(T); \; bel_{EKM_i}(\overline{T}) = m_{EKM_i}(\overline{T})$$

The belief function of EKM_i presents its evidential value. To the experts' knowledge, the quality of EKM_i that provides evidence that its higher-level node is trustworthy is $bel_{EKM_i}(T)$, while the quality of EKM_i that provides evidence that its higher-level node is untrustworthy is $bel_{EKM_i}(\overline{T})$.

4.3   The Trustworthiness Assessment Module

The trustworthiness assessment module assesses the trustworthiness of the digital record by first aggregating the evidential values of EKM to assess the trustworthiness of their corresponding components. It then integrates the trustworthiness of components to assess the record's trustworthiness during each life-cycle phase. Finally, it integrates trustworthiness during life-cycle phases to deduce the trustworthiness of the digital record.

Dempster's rule of combination is also applied here to assess the trustworthiness of the digital record. The basic beliefs assigned to the digital record are arrived at by:

$$m_{record}(T) = m_{creation}(T) \oplus m_{modification}(T) \oplus m_{migration}(T) \oplus m_{retrieval}(T)$$
$$\oplus \, m_{disposal}(T) = m_{Originator}(T) \oplus m_{Creator}(T) \oplus m_{CreationAction}(T) \oplus \ldots$$
$$\oplus \, m_{DisposalExecutor}(T) \oplus m_{DisposalAction}(T) = m_{EKM_1}(T) \oplus \ldots \oplus m_{EKM_m}(T)$$
$$m_{record}(\overline{T}) = m_{EKM_1}(\overline{T}) \oplus \ldots \oplus m_{EKM_m}(\overline{T})$$
$$m_{record}(U) = m_{EKM_1}(U) \oplus \ldots \oplus m_{EKM_m}(U)$$

Accordingly, the belief and plausibility of the trustworthiness of the digital record are calculated respectively as follows:

$$bel_{record}(T) = m_{record}(T); \quad pls_{record}(T) = 1 - bel_{record}(\overline{T}) = 1 - m_{record}(\overline{T})$$

The belief function states that we can believe that the digital record is trustworthy to the extent that $bel_{record}(T)$. The plausibility function states that the digital record may be trustworthy to the extent that $pls_{record}(T)$. The trustworthiness of the digital record is a value within the interval from $bel_{record}(T)$ to $pls_{record}(T)$. However, to be conservative, we say that the trustworthiness of the digital record is $bel_{record}(T)$.

5 An Example of the Assessment of the Trustworthiness

In this section, we present an example showing how the assessment model works based on a proposed record's life-cycle model [16] with elaborated EKM required for the assessment. Here, we only describe the trustworthiness assessment during the creation phase as an example of the trustworthiness assessment of a digital record, since the approach is basically the same for the other life-cycle phases.

Suppose three experts E_1, E_2, and E_3 share their knowledge by assigning evidential values to EKM, as shown in Table 2. The numeric evidential values are given right after the linguistic evidential values and expressed as percentage for clarity.

Table 2. Assigned evidential values of EKM during creation

	EKM	Exp.1	Exp.2	Exp.3
Originator	Name	(EH (95%)), true)	(EH (95%), false)	(ϕ (0), ϕ)
	Affiliation	(VH (80%), true)	(L (35%), false)	(L (35%), false)
	Compose Time	(ϕ (0), ϕ)	(H (65%), false)	(H (65%), true)
Creator	Name	(H (65%), true)	(H (65%), false)	(VH (80%), true)
	Affiliation	(VH (80%), true)	(M (50%), false)	(L (35%), false)
Creation	Record's Name	(VH (80%), true)	(VH (80%), false)	(VH (80%), true)
	Time	(L (35%), true)	(H (65%), false)	(VH (80%), false)
	Environment	(H (65%), true)	(VH (80%), true)	(H (65%), false)
	Format	(EH (95%), true)	(EL (5%), true)	(M (50%), false)
	Source	(H (65%), true)	(H (65%), true)	(VL (20%), false)
	Reason & Purpose	(VH (80%), false)	(VH (80%), true)	(H (65%), false)

By mapping linguistic evidential values to numeric evidential values, the experts' knowledge during the creation phase is modelled as follows:

$$\Psi_{creation} = \{\{(95\%, true), (95\%, false), (0, \phi)\} \ldots$$
$$\{(80\%, false), (80\%, true), (65\%, false)\}\}$$

Then, using Equations (7) and (8), the basic beliefs of EKM during the creation phase can be assigned. As an example, the basic belief assigned to "name of originator" is given below:

$$m_{OName_1}(T) = 0.95; \quad m_{OName_1}(\overline{T}) = 0; \quad m_{OName_1}(U) = 0.05$$
$$m_{OName_2}(T) = 0; \quad m_{OName_2}(\overline{T}) = 0.95; \quad m_{OName_2}(U) = 0.05$$
$$m_{OName_3}(T) = 0; \quad m_{OName_3}(\overline{T}) = 0; \quad m_{OName_3}(U) = 1$$

The evidence-combination module then combines the experts' knowledge for each piece of EKM using Equation (5) as follows:

$$m_{OName}(T) = [m_{OName_1}(T) \oplus m_{OName_2}(T)] \oplus m_{OName_3}(T) \approx 0.4872$$
$$m_{OName}(\overline{T}) \approx 0.4872; \quad m_{OName}U \approx 0.0256$$

Since both proposition sets T and $\overline{T}$ only contain a single proposition, its belief function equals its mass function, as presented in Equation (2). Thus, $bel_{OName}(T) = m_{OName}(T) = 0.4872$, $bel_{OName}(\overline{T}) = m_{OName}(\overline{T}) = 0.4872$.

The belief function states that, based on the three experts' knowledge, the reliability score of the originator's name as evidence of the truth of the hypothesis "the originator is trustworthy" is 48.72%. It also states the reliability score of the originator's name as evidence of the hypothesis "the originator is untrustworthy" is 48.72%. This occurs due to the experts' conflicting knowledge and opinions. We address this issue in Section 5.1.

The combined results of all EKM during the creation phase are presented in Table 3.

Table 3. Combined results of experts' knowledge on EKM during creation phase

	EKM	$m(T)$	$m(\overline{T})$	$m(U)$
Originator	Name	0.4872	0.4872	0.0256
	Affiliation	0.6282	0.2147	0.1571
	Compose Time	0.3939	0.3939	0.2122
Creator	Name	0.8230	0.1150	0.062
	Affiliation	0.5652	0.2717	0.1631
Creation	Record's Name	0.8276	0.1379	0.0345
	Time	0.0363	0.8962	0.0675
	Environment	0.8230	0.1150	0.062
	Format	0.9094	0.0453	0.0453
	Source	0.8514	0.0297	0.1189
	Reason & Purpose	0.2188	0.7266	0.0546

The trustworthiness assessment module aggregates the evidence of attributes to their parent components to assess the trustworthiness of those components, as shown below.

$$m_{Originator}(T) = 0.6779; \quad m_{Originator}(\overline{T}) = 0.3197; \quad m_{Originator}(U) = 0.0024$$
$$m_{Creator}(T) = 0.8918; \quad m_{Creator}(\overline{T}) = 0.0940; \quad m_{Creator}(U) = 0.0142$$
$$m_{Creation}(T) = 0.9848; \quad m_{Creation}(\overline{T}) = 0.0152; \quad m_{Creation}(U) = 0$$

Based on the aggregated results, it integrates the trustworthiness of components into the parent level, where the trustworthiness of the digital record during the creation phase is obtained, as shown below.

$$m_{creation}(T) = 0.9991; \; m_{creation}(\overline{T}) = 0.0009; \; m_{creation}(U) = 0$$
$$bel_{creation}(T) = 0.9991; \; pls_{creation}(T) = 1 - bel_{creation}(\overline{T}) = 0.9991$$
(9)

Equation (9) states that, based on the experts' knowledge of the EKM during the creation phase, the trustworthiness score of the digital record is 99.91% after its creation.

Similarly, the trustworthiness of the digital record for the other phases of the life-cycle can be calculated. Finally, the trustworthiness of the digital record can be assessed by integrating its trustworthiness in all its life-cycle phases.

Below, we highlight three cases to present how the trustworthiness assessment of the experts' knowledge works.

5.1   Case One

As in the above example, Expert 1 and 2 agree that the originator's name has extremely high evidential value, which means it is a strong evidence for the trustworthiness or untrustworthiness of the component Originator. However, the knowledge of each individual expert concerning the trustworthiness hypotheses is in conflict with that of the other(s). Combining their knowledge, we arrived at $bel_{Exp_1 \& Exp_2}(T) = 0.4872$, $bel_{Exp_1 \& Exp_2}(\overline{T}) = 0.4872$, and $bel_{Exp_1 \& Exp_2}(U) = 0.0256$. As the belief functions show, due to the contradictory nature of the knowledge of the experts, although it is strong evidence in the experts' opinions, it can not be used to support the assertion of either the trustworthiness or untrustworthiness of the record in any way that has any high evidential value.

5.2   Case Two

To continue with the calculation of the trustworthiness of originator's name, due to the lack of information, Expert 3 believes that the originator's name can prove nothing about the trustworthiness or untrustworthiness of the component. Thus, he/she assigned basic belief with full uncertainty ($m_{Exp_3}(U) = 1$). When combining the knowledge of Expert 3 with the knowledge of other experts, assignments from Expert 3 have no impact on the combined result.

5.3   Case Three

About the EKM "affiliation of originator", Expert 1 believes that it supports the claim that the originator is trustworthy, while other experts have opposing opinions. If their knowledge is combined based on the majority-vote approach, the results will suggest that the originator is untrustworthy. However, from the perspective of Expert 1, the affiliation of the originator has very high evidential value, which means the evidence it presents is strong. The other experts regard the affiliation as having low evidential value, which means although it suggests that the originator is not trustworthy, the evidence is not strong enough. Thus, the combined results using D-S theory suggest that affiliation provides evidence that the originator's trustworthiness score is 62.82%, which acknowledges Expert 1's knowledge.

6   Discussion and Future Work

There have been many researches on the area of digital trust, however, they either focus on developing secure algorithms [17], protocols [19], and architectures [7, 8] to protect digital records, or pay attention to the establishment of trustworthy repositories [3,5], which are intended to be a guarantee of the digital records stored therein. To our knowledge, no research has been conducted into the calculation of the trustworthiness of digital records using evidential value as a measure of trustworthiness. In addition, not much research has been conducted into the value of the metadata around digital records as evidence of the trustworthiness of these records. Therefore, we look into the EKM of digital records. By using the D-S theory of evidence, we developed a model for the assessment of the trustworthiness of digital records. Our model demonstrates that the incremental improvement of experts' knowledge in the area of evidential value, and the adoption of a rigorous formal approach, make possible the objective assessment of the trustworthiness of digital records.

There still remain a number of challenges to be met, including (1) the impact on the assessment from the temporal aspect is a challenge which needs further research, (2) as one of the criticisms on the D-S theory, the way of handling conflicts between EKM in the assessment model needs further studies, (3) since EKM may have different importance to the assessment result, weighting difference within the model needs further investigation, and (4) some of EKM can be interrelated in the model, such as name and affiliation of an operator, thus, how to combine dependent EKM needs further studies.

7   Conclusion

In this paper, we have developed and described a model for the assessment of the trustworthiness of digital records using Dempster-Shafer (D-S) theory. It uses the records' evidential values as a measure of trustworthiness. This model consists of three modules, (i) a knowledge-modelling module, which models the experts' knowledge related to a digital record, (ii) an evidence-combination module, which combines experts' knowledge of evidential values of Evidence-Keeping Metadata (EKM), and (iii) a trustworthiness assessment module, which assesses the trustworthiness of the digital record by aggregating and integrating evidence of EKM. We have presented an example with three cases to show how this model works. We have also identified challenges to the assessment model, which we will investigate in our future work.

Our results show that by incrementally improving experts' knowledge about evidential values and applying a rigorous formal approach, the trustworthiness of digital records can be assessed objectively.

As mentioned in the previous section, in our future work, we will continue to investigate the temporal, conflict, weighting and dependency aspects of the trustworthiness assessment of digital records.

References

1. Blaze, M., Feigenbaum, J., Ioannidis, J., Keromytis, A.D.: The role of trust management in distributed systems security. In: Ryan, M. (ed.) Secure Internet Programming. LNCS, vol. 1603, pp. 183–210. Springer, Heidelberg (1999)

2. Boudrez, F.: Digital singatures and electronic records. Archival Science 7(2), 179–193 (2007)
3. Center for Research Libraries: Trustworthy repositories audit & certification: Criteria and checklist (2008), http://www.crl.edu/PDF/trac.pdf
4. Chen, T.M., Venkataramanan, V.: Dempster-Shafer theory for intrusion detection in ad hoc networks. IEEE Internet Computing 9(6), 35–41 (2005)
5. Consultative Committee for Space Data Systems: Reference model for an open archival information system (OAIS) (2002)
6. Dempster, A.P.: Upper and lower probabilities induced by a multivalued mapping. Annals of Mathematical Statistics 38, 325–339 (1967)
7. Gladney, H.M.: Trustworthy 100-year digital objects: Evidence after every witness is dead. ACM Transaction on Information System (TOIS) 22(3), 406–436 (2004)
8. Gladney, H.M., Lorie, R.A.: Trustworthy 100-year digital objects: durable encoding for when it's too late to ask. ACM TOIS 23(3), 299–324 (2005)
9. Grandison, T., Sloman, M.: A survey of trust in internet applications. IEEE Communications Surveys and Tutorials 3(4) (2000)
10. Grant, J.S., Davis, L.L.: Selection and use of content experts in instrument development. Research in Nursing & Health 20(3), 269–274 (1997)
11. Hu, D., Wang, L., Zhou, Y., Zhou, Y., Jiang, X., Ma, L.: D-S evidence theory based digital image trustworthiness evaluation model. In: MINES 2009 (2009)
12. Jøsang, A., Ismail, R., Boyd, C.: A survey of trust and reputation systems for online service provision. Decision Support Systems 43(2), 618–644 (2007)
13. Kamvar, S.D., Schlosser, M.T., Garcia-Molina, H.: The eigentrust algorithm for reputation management in p2p networks. In: WWW 2003, pp. 640–651 (2003)
14. Kohlas, J., Monney, P.A.: Theory of evidence - a survey of its mathematical foundations, applications and computational aspects. Mathematical Methods of Operations Research 39(1), 35–68 (1994)
15. Lynn, M.: Determination and quantification of content validity. Nursing Research 35(6), 382 (1986)
16. Ma, J., Abie, H., Skramstad, T., Nygård, M.: Development and validation of requirements for evidential value for assessing trustworthiness of digital records over time. Journal of Information (to appear, 2011)
17. Menezes, A., Oorschot, P., Vanstone, S. (eds.) Handbook of applied cryptography (1996)
18. National Archives of Australia: Australian government recordkeeping metadata standard. Tech. rep (2008)
19. Rescorla, E.: SSL and TLS: Designing and building secure systems. Addison-Wesley Professional, Reading (2000)
20. Sentz, K., Ferson, S.: Combination of evidence in dempster-shafer theory. Tech. rep. (2002)
21. Shafer, G.: A Mathematical Theory of Evidence. Princeton University Press, Princeton (1976)
22. Sun, Y.L., Han, Z., Yu, W., Liu, K.: Attacks on trust evaluation in distributed networks. In: CISS 2006, pp. 1461–1466 (2006)
23. Trcek, D.: A formal apparatus for modeling trust in computing environments. Mathematical and Computer Modelling 49(1-2), 226–233 (2009)
24. Zadeh, L.A.: A simple view of the dempster-shafer theory of evidence and its implication for the rule of combination. AI Magazine 7(2), 85–90 (1986)

Taste and Trust

Audun Jøsang[1], Walter Quattrociocchi[2], and Dino Karabeg[3]

[1] University of Oslo, Norway
josang@matnat.uio.no
[2] University of Siena, Italy
walter.quattrociocchi@istc.cnr.it
[3] University of Oslo, Norway
Dino.Karabeg@ifi.uio.no

Abstract. Although taste and trust are concepts on clearly distinct ontological levels, they are strongly interrelated in several contexts. For instance, when assessing trust, e.g. through a trust network, it is important to understand the role that personal taste plays in order to correctly interpret potential value dependent trust recommendations and conclusions, in order to provide a sound basis for decision-making. This paper aims at exploring the relationship between taste and trust in the analysis of semantic trust networks.

Keywords: Trust, Reputation, Taste, Recommender, Semantic, Opinion, Knowledge, Agents.

1 Introduction

Understanding the dynamics between social artifacts such as reputation and trust and their effects on both opinions formation, revision and decision making is an important challenge. Several studies have focused on modeling their interdependencies and on predicting their evolutions [3,15,19,18], e.g. focusing on how the dynamics of decisions are affected by the society in which the individual is immersed. In fact, the dynamic nature of social interactions is considered to play a fundamental role [11] in the formation of taste and trust. Taste as an aesthetic, sociological, economic and anthropological concept refers to a cultural patterns of choice and preference. The term "taste" is also commonly interpreted as the bio-chemical assessment of food. In this study we primarily consider the sociological interpretation of taste, i.e. where it reflects the subjective judgment of things such as styles, manners, consumer goods and works of art. Social inquiry of taste is about the human ability to judge what is beautiful, good and proper.

The social artifacts such as reputation and trust are built upon the acceptance (or refusal) of a social standard or norm. Dealing with decision making, either reputation or trust act as selection criteria in the mind of the individuals and, in turn, are based upon cognitive attitudes.

Social psychology offers an extensive literature on attitude change models, as reviewed by [13]. Most influential in social psychology is the "The Social Impact Theory" [16], according to which the amount of influence depends on the distance, number,

I. Wakeman et al. (Eds.): IFIPTM 2011, IFIP AICT 358, pp. 312–322, 2011.

and strength (i.e., persuasiveness) of influence sources. As stated in ([2]), an important variable, poorly controlled in current studies, is structure topology. Interactions are invariably assumed as either all-to-all or based on a spatial regular location (lattice), while more realistic scenarios are ignored.

Within this universe, in this paper we outline the role of taste relative to trust and reputation. We will start by describing two simple examples to illustrate the effect of taste in trust situations. For example, assume that a trusted (without being more specific) friend recommends watching a movie, but you find the movie so unpleasant to watch that you leave before the end. As a result your trust in your friend's movie recommendations will drop, but interestingly your friend might still insist that it was a good movie. It is perfectly plausible that your friend genuinely likes movies that you dislike, which is unproblematic, so your friendship is not challenged. Assume now a different situation where a trusted friend recommends a car mechanic for servicing your car, but you end up very disappointed because the mechanic left oil marks everywhere and charged an unreasonably high amount for a relatively simple job. In this situation it is not plausible that your friend claims that the mechanic did a good job, because oil marks and unreasonable prices are undisputedly negative, i.e. they are taste independent aspects. You would therefore not find it credible if your friend genuinely thinks that the mechanic did a great job, and if he did you might suspect that there are other motives behind. Not only would your trust in your friends ability to recommend car mechanics drop, you would also find your friend irrational which could cause you to distrust him in general and even damage your friendship. The only rational response from your friend would be to agree that the mechanic did a horrible job, and to apologize for having recommended such a bad mechanic, in which case you mutual trust and friendship would survive. These two examples show that people can very well agree to disagree on taste dependent aspects, but can not agree to disagree on taste independent aspects. Determining what is taste dependent or independent thus has implications for analysing trust networks.

The concept of trust is relatively well studied in the trust management literature, where authors mostly agree that it is a rather overloaded concept with many different meanings. In order to foster a meaningful discussion it is therefore useful to define the exact type of trust that is intended when the term is used. In this paper we will distinguish between so-called *evaluation trust* and *decision trust* that can be defined as follows[9].

- *Evaluation Trust*
  Evaluation trust is the subjective probability by which an entity, A, expects that another entity, B, fulfills a function on which A's welfare depends.
- *Decision Trust*
  Decision trust is the extent to which one party is willing to depend on something or somebody in a given situation with a feeling of relative security, even though negative consequences are possible.

Evaluation trust is conceptually much simpler than decision trust because evaluation trust only depends on assumed qualities of the trusted entity itself, whereas decision trust depends on additional parameters, such as utility and risk attitude of the trusting party, that in fact are external to the trusted entity.

Since taste and trust are both subjective, and they both express an entity's opinion about some concrete or abstract object there seems to be a close correspondence between the two concepts. A noteworthy aspect of trust is that it is typically assumed that relying party faces a (potential) risk exposure because of some value at stake with potential loss, and secondly that there is some uncertainty about whether the trusted object will fulfill its expected function. In case of taste, i.e. when the relying party likes or dislikes something, risk exposure or uncertainty are not normally assumed as important cognitive elements.

The term "trust" is both a verb and a noun, such as in *"Bob trusts the car mechanic"* and *"Bob has full trust in the car mechanic"*, which both have the same semantical basis in the expectation of quality service. The term "taste" is also both a verb and a noun, such as in *"Bob tastes the food"* and *"Bob has a taste for food"*, but which interestingly do not share the same semantic basis. To "taste the food" is the bio-chemical assessment of a particular food sample, whereas "taste for food" is the sociological ability to judge the quality of food in general. The verbs "to like" and "to dislike" correspond better to the sociological interpretation of taste as a noun, meaning that Bob's taste for food corresponds to which food he likes or dislikes. To say *"Bob likes the food"* would then express that the food has good quality according to Bob's sociological taste for food.

The concept "opinion" or more specifically the verb-like expression "to have an opinion about" is in many ways a generalisation of the verbs "to trust/distrust" and "to like/dislike". In that sense, the nouns "trust" and "taste" should be considered as subcategories of the more general noun "opinion". In this background we will consider "trust" and "taste" to be two variants of a more general concept which could be called "belief" or "opinion".

A *scope*[1] expresses what the opinion is about, e.g. the specific type(s) of trust or taste assumed in a given situation. In other words, the object is assumed to fulfill certain quality functions such as being reliable/unreliable or good/bad, and the scope is what the subject assumes those functions to be.

A scope can be narrow or broad. For example, a relatively broad trust scope could be "to be competent in car mechanics", whereas a relatively narrow trust scope could be "to know how to change wheels".

Trust transitivity means, for example, that if Alice trusts Bob who has a specific opinion about something, then Alice will tend to adopt the same opinion. This assumes that Alice is actually aware of Bob's opinion. This could e.g. be achieved through a *referral* or *recommendation* from Bob to Alice.

Let us assume two separate scenarios. In scenario 1) Alice needs to get her car serviced, so she asks Bob to recommend a good car mechanic. In scenario 2) Alice considers going to a rock concert, but she does not know the band, so she asks Bob about his opinion. This situation is illustrated in Fig.1.

In TNA-SL (Trust Network Analysis with Subjective Logic), there is a separation between functional and referral trust [8]. Alice's trust in Bob is considered to be referral, because Bob will not service the car or play the music, Bob will just refer to something

---

[1] The terms "trust context" [5], "trust purpose" [9] and "subject matter" [12] have been used in the literature with the same meaning.

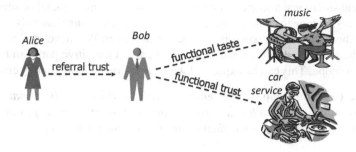

Fig. 1. Scenarios of recommended taste and trust

else. In contrast, Bob's trust in the mechanic and Bob's taste for the band is functional, because they will service the car and play the music respectively.

A recommendation is equivalent to a referral, and is precisely what allows trust to become transitive. At the same time, a referral always assumes the existence of a functional scope at the end of the transitive path, which in this example is about being a good car mechanic, or a good rock band.

A transitive trust path stops with the first functional taste/trust edge encountered when there are no remaining outgoing referral edges. It is, of course, possible for a principal to have both functional and referral trust in another principal, but that should be expressed as two separate trust edges.

In practice the last functional edge in a trust chain can very well be either described as "likes/dislikes" or as "trusts/distrusts", or in more general terms as *"has opinion about object Y."* The referral edges are clearly meaningful when interpreted as "trusts/distrusts", but their interpretation can also be generalised as *"has opinion about advice from entity X."* This seems reasonable because the main quality of a referral is to correctly recommend somebody's opinion, be it trust or taste. There is thus little room for taste dependence in the recommendations. However, the referral trust edge assumes that the relying party shares the same taste dependent scope as the functional edge.

The "referral" variant of a scope can be considered to be recursive, so that any transitive opinion chain, with arbitrary length, can be expressed using only one scope with two variants. This principle is captured by the following criterion.

Definition 1 (Functional opinion derivation). *Derivation of functional opinion (e.g. taste or trust) through transitive referrals requires that the last edge represents a functional opinion (e.g. about taste or trust), and that all previous edges represent referral opinions.*

When generalising "taste" and "trust" as two specific types of a subject entity's opinion about the quality of an object, it is possible to let any semantic opinion scope be part of a transitive trust path. This opinion scope can express trust, taste or other beliefs. Let the relying party be denoted by A, let the intermediate recommender agents be denoted by X_i and the target object by Y. Then a transitive semantic path can be expressed as:

$$A \xrightarrow{\substack{\text{referral} \\ \text{opinion}}} X_1 \xrightarrow{\substack{\text{referral} \\ \text{opinion}}} \cdots \xrightarrow{\substack{\text{referral} \\ \text{opinion}}} X_n \xrightarrow{\substack{\text{functional} \\ \text{opinion}}} Y \qquad (1)$$

In practical situations, a scope can be characterised by being general or specific. For example, knowing how to change wheels on a car is more specific than to be a good car mechanic, where the former scope is a subset of the latter. Whenever a given scope is part of all the referral and functional scopes in a path, a transitive path can be formed based on that scope. This can be expressed with the following consistency criterion.

Definition 2 (Opinion scope consistency). *A valid transitive opinion path requires that there exists a scope which is a common subset of all opinion scopes in the path. The scope of the derived opinion is then the largest common subset of all scopes along the path.*

Trivially, every edge in a path can carry the same scope. Transitive opinion propagation is thus possible with two variants (i.e. functional and referral) of the same opinion scope.

The examples above assume binary beliefs about the recommending agents along the transitive path, and about the target object. In reality an opinion is never absolute, and researchers have proposed to express trust as discrete verbal statements, as probabilities or other continuous measures. For example, in TNA-SL (Trust Network Analysis with Subjective Logic) [8] arguments are expressed as subjective opinions which can contain degrees of belief and uncertainty.

2   Trust and Reputation with Different Preference Cliques

It is common that different subjects express different scores and/or rankings of the same objects as a function of some quality criterion. When two subjects give a different assessment of the same object or observation there can be at least two explanations. One explanation is that they interpreted the observation differently so that the two subjects in fact perceived two different things, e.g. due to different observation conditions or cognitive capabilities. We will exclude this explanation in the analysis below, and assume that the observations are objective. The other explanation is then that the subjects have a different preferences for the same objects, e.g. due to a different internalised value set. The effect of different preferences is extensively used in collaborative filtering and recommender systems, where a group of users who express similar preferences is called a *clique* or *neighbourhood*. The existence of preference cliques is important for trust models and for the analysis of semantic trust networks.

The easiest situation to analyse is when all subjects belong to the same clique, i.e. they have the same value set when assessing objects. For example assume that a digital music file is corrupted so that it can not be played on any playback device. All persons would normally assess a corrupted mp3 file to be bad. This situation is illustrated in Fig.2 where agents A and B belong to the same preference clique.

Reputation systems work best in case of a homogeneous preference clique. When it can be assumed that observations are objective, and that assessments are based on the same value set, then global ranking of the quality of objects is meaningful. Working within a single clique also simplifies the the analysis of trust networks.

Situations of different cliques with different value sets are very common. Assume for example that two subjects A and B assess a piece of classical music and a piece of rock music, where A likes classical music but dislikes rock music, and B likes rock music

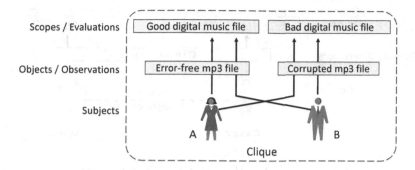

Fig. 2. Homogeneous preference clique

but dislikes classical music. In this situation, *A* and *B* clearly belong to different cliques regarding their taste for music. This is illustrated in Fig.3.

In this situation it would not be meaningful to let ratings from *A* and *B* be used to rank pieces of classical and rock music together because they have a different value set for judging music. Still, both *A* and *B* would normally respect and accept that other people have a different taste, and would therefore not question each other's moral integrity. The meaningful analysis of trust relationships between entities in different preference cliques would require to explicitly capture and express the difference in taste in the evaluation of trust opinions, so that a person would naturally distrust/discount a recommender who belongs to a different preference clique with respect to a specific scope. Several authors have proposed models inspired by this principle, e.g. [1,4,6,14,17,20].

Another situation is if *A* has had her car serviced, and the mechanic has left oil marks on the car seats, which *A* assesses to reflect horrible car service. Let us assume that *B* assesses oil marks on car seats to reflect great car service. In this situation it is likely that *A* will think there is something wrong with *B*'s judgment and might question his moral integrity, as illustrated in Fig.4.

In this situation it is plausible that the irrational assessment by *B* could make *A* suspicious about *B*'s moral integrity for other trust scopes in addition to car service, because

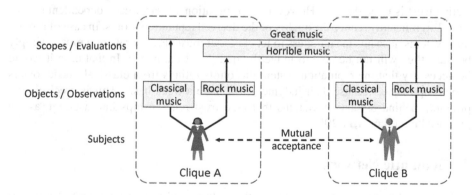

Fig. 3. Heterogeneous preference cliques with mutual acceptance

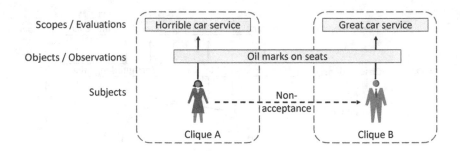

Fig. 4. Heterogeneous preference cliques with non-acceptance

if B clearly makes an irrational assessment within one scope it is likely that B might also be irrational for other scopes. A simple reputation system applied to this situation where ratings from A and B carry the same weight would not be very meaningful. Additional functionality would be needed to make it more useful, e.g. enabling ratings from B to be excluded or discounted. However, this principle would still not be useful in all situations, because it is *a priori* not evident whose ratings should be considered as irrational. In the case of election or voting for example, people often belong to different preference categories, but their votes carry the same weight. Voting systems allow people belonging to different preference cliques to cast their votes to decide who will be elected to political seats.

Trust functions can exhibit variability and still be the same type of function. For example, there can be an infinity of different movies that can all be judged as quality movies. Similarly, there can be an infinity of different music performances that can all be judged as quality performances, some being classical music and some being pop music.

In theory it might be possible refine variable scope functions so that in the end there is no room for variability, in which case it becomes a specific taste-independent scope. However, refining taste dependent scopes so that they become taste independent seems impractical, and nearly impossible in most cases.

Taste dependent scope seems to be manageable in case of trust systems where subjective trust is to be derived. However, for reputation systems, taste dependent scopes would significantly reduce the quality of the derived reputation scores. In case of reputation systems, it seems meaningless to let classical music lowers rate pop music, simply because they will not be able to judge the quality of the music. In that case it would be necessary that the reputation system discounts ratings from classical music lovers about pop music, because their judgment will have a weak basis. This is precisely the principle behind reputation systems that take trust relationships into account, as e.g proposed in [1,4,6,14,17,20].

3   Semantic Networks

Online social networks are growing fast these days, and it is fascinating to try understand their meaning and implications. All social networks have in common a set of three fundamental building blocks which are entities, pointers, and attributes. These are in essence the same fundamental building blocks required for the Semantic Web and for Semantic Networks which in general can represent relationships between concrete entities or abstract concepts, or both. An entity is something that exists, virtually or physically. It can be a person like you and me, an organisation, a Web site, a document, or a service. An abstract concept can be thought of as an object class, where an entity as an object instance.

An entity's identity serves as the pointer for accessing or navigating to the entity. Entities can point to other entities, and to each other, to form a graph. An entity pointing to another entity represents a directed edge in the graph and implicitly suggests a semantic relationship between the entities. A set of attributes can be used to describe the nature of the relationship, e.g. as "belongs to", "likes" or "trusts". Without attributes it would only be possible to define pure mathematical graphs. Equipped with attributes, the graphs come alive and can represent semantic and social networks as illustrated in the somewhat ego-centric example below.

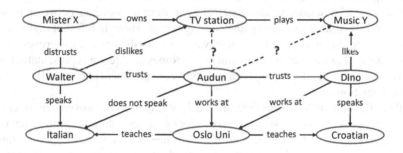

Fig. 5. Semantic Network

There is of course an infinity of entities and relationships out there, so it is impossible to formally represent them all. In the semantic network illustrated above, only Walter, Audun and Dino are person-entities, and they typically have some semantic relationship to each other. The Walter-Audun-Dino relationships are just a tiny part of the whole semantic network, which shows that semantic networks are much more than just social networks.

The fact that Audun trusts Walter and Dino can be very useful in the sense that it can help Audun to learn something from them. This now becomes a semantic trust graph derived from the underlying semantic network. In fact, the missing - but potential - link between Audun and Mister X's TV station in the diagram, or the missing link between Audun and music Y, can be derived from the existing semantic trust graph.

An example of an implementation of this type of semantic network is the social web-site Rummble.com that allows people to express their taste for various things, and where they also can express levels of trust in each other. The computational trust engine inside Rummble.com uses Subjective Logic which represents trust by the three parameters Trusted - Distrusted - Don't Know. Some people might find it strange to include "Don't Know", but this is really essential for representing trust. In fact, there is a default "Don't

Know" trust relationship between any pair of person-entities which in practice can take the value of the base rate trust between entities in the community. A link gets initialised with base rate trust, and then evolves dynamically with various degrees of trust.

4   Implications for Knowledge Management

We have a subjective view of the world philosophically seen. At the same time, we often strive towards a shared view, such as common knowledge. Wikipedia shows how technology may be combined with innovative social organization to establish a common body of knowledge from distributed subjective sources: Instead of only publishing distinct documents about a given subject, Wikipedia allows the global community to create and maintain a single document for each subject. While a single-document solution dramatically reduces effort and aggregates trust, Wikipedia-style unification is feasible only for undisputed facts, although various attempts have been made to add degrees of trust and/or reputation to Wikipedia [7] to reflect relative quality of contributions. Wikipedia therefore tends to exclude controversial content. Knowledge federation is a collaborative knowledge model aimed at exploiting possibilities between those two extremes. While aiming to identify and highlight that which is relevant and shared as community view, knowledge federation leaves room for dissent and difference of opinions. A federated organization of documents becomes in effect a representation of the collective state of mind, displaying both the points of agreement and the still contending individual positions.

While collaborative document federation *à la* Wikipedia is a proven way of creating shared documents, a specific value matrix object enables a complementary approach: by *crowdsourcing* or *federating* the information needed for corresponding judgment and decisions. A value matrix is an object – attached to a resource throughout its lifetime – that accumulates all data potentially useful for evaluating this resource [10]. The columns define the criteria and the rows define available ways of evaluating those criteria. Implemented as an object, the value matrix gathers and stores relevant information, and provides suitable functions for evaluating the resource. By separating data collection from decision making, a value matrix object accumulates every piece of data that may be of value when making a decision, without judgment or bias, and affords free choice of criteria, including the ones reflecting taste and trust. In a socio-technical system where every resource (author, user, document, idea) has an associated value matrix object, creative systemic analysi and derivation of taste and trust become accessible. The development of a suitable theory, technical tools and practices are the subjects for further research.

5   Conclusion

Trust and taste are closely related, and it is necessary to take differences in taste into account when analysing trust networks. We argue that trust and taste are specific types of the more general concepts of belief or opinion with a given smenatic scope, so that trust networks can be generalised as semantic opinion networks. The analysis of trust networks can therefore be generalised to the analysis of semantic opinion networks. In such networks it is possible, and necessary, to take differences in taste and preferences into account for modelling, analysis and decision making. This has important implicaitons e.g. for the collaborative management of knowledge.

References

1. Bhuiyan, T., Xu, Y., Jøsang, A., Liang, H., Cox, C.: Developing trust networks based on user tagging information for recommendation making. In: Chen, L., Triantafillou, P., Suel, T. (eds.) WISE 2010. LNCS, vol. 6488, pp. 357–364. Springer, Heidelberg (2010)
2. Castellano, C., Fortunato, S., Loreto, V.: Statistical physics of social dynamics. Reviews of Modern Physics 81(2), p. 591+ (2009)
3. Deighton, J., Grayson, K.: Marketing and seduction: Building exchange relationships by managing social consensus. Journal of Consumer Research: An Interdisciplinary Quarterly 21(4), 660–676 (1995)
4. Golbeck, J.: Generating predictive movie recommendations from trust in social networks. In: Stølen, K., Winsborough, W.H., Martinelli, F., Massacci, F. (eds.) iTrust 2006. LNCS, vol. 3986, pp. 93–104. Springer, Heidelberg (2006)
5. Grandison, T., Sloman, M.: A Survey of Trust in Internet Applications. IEEE Communications Surveys and Tutorials 3 (2000)
6. Hess, C., Schlieder, C.: Trust-based recommendations for documents. AI Communications - AICOM 21(2-3), 145–153 (2008)
7. Jensen, C.: Supporting multi-agent reputation calculation in the wikipedia recommender system. IET Information Security 4(4), 273–282 (2010)
8. Jøsang, A., Hayward, R., Pope, S.: Trust Network Analysis with Subjective Logic. In: Proceedings of the 29th Australasian Computer Science Conference (ACSC 2006), CRPIT, Hobart, Australia, vol. 48 (January 2006)
9. Jøsang, A., Ismail, R., Boyd, C.: A Survey of Trust and Reputation Systems for Online Service Provision. Decision Support Systems 43(2), 618–644 (2007)
10. Karabeg, D., Lachica, R.: Knowledge federation as a principle of social organization of knowledge creation and sharing. In: Proceedings of the First International Workshop on Knowledge Federation, CEUR, Aachen, Dubrovnik (October 2008)
11. Lorenz, J.: Continuous opinion dynamics under bounded confidence: A survey. Int. Journal of Modern Physics C 18(12), 1819–1838 (2007)
12. Mahoney, G., Myrvold, W., Shoja, G.C.: Generic Reliability Trust Model. In: Ghorbani, A., Marsh, S. (eds.) Proceedings of the 3rd Annual Conference on Privacy, Security and Trust, St. Andrews, New Brunswick, Canada (October 2005)
13. Mason, W.A., Conrey, F.R., Smith, E.R.: Situating social influence processes: Dynamic, multidirectional flows of influence within social networks. Personality and Social Psychology Review 11(3), 279 (2007)
14. Massa, P., Avesani, P.: Trust-aware recommender systems. In: Proceedings of the 2007 ACM conference on Recommender systems (RECSYS 2007) RecSys 2007, pp. 17–24. ACM, New York (2007)
15. McCombs, M.: Setting the agenda: the mass media and public opinion. Public Opinion Quarterly (2004)
16. Nowak, A., Latane, B., Szamrej, J.: From private attitude to public opinion: A dynamic theory of social impact. Psychological Review 97(3), 362–376 (1990)

17. O'Donovan, J., Smyth, B.: Trust in recommender systems. In: Proceedings of the 10th international conference on Intelligent user interfaces, pp. 167–174. ACM, New York (2005)
18. Quattrociocchi, W., Conte, R., Lodi, E.: Simulating opinion dynamics in heterogeneous communication systems. In: ECCS 2010 - Lisbon Portugal (2010)
19. Quattrociocchi, W., Paolucci, M.: Reputation and uncertainty. a fairly optimistic society when cheating is total. In: ICORE 2009 - International Conference on Reputation, Gargonza, Italy (2009)
20. Victor, P., Cornelis, C., Cock, M.D., Silva, P.P.D.: Gradual trust and distrust in recommender systems. In: Fuzzy Sets and Systems - FSS, vol. 160(10), pp. 1367–1382 (2009)

Trust Dynamics: A Data-Driven Simulation Approach

Olufunmilola Onolaja, Rami Bahsoon, and Georgios Theodoropoulos

The School of Computer Science, University of Birmingham, UK
{o.o.onolaja,r.bahsoon,g.k.theodoropoulos}@cs.bham.ac.uk

Abstract. Reputation and trust-based models have gained popularity recently because they have been shown to be promising in the area of trust management. Despite this fact, building reliable systems still remains a challenge. Proposed models focus on historical and online information to determine the reputation of domain members. However, the dynamic nature of reputation and trust requires an equally dynamic approach to computing and resolving trust related issues in any domain. This paper proposes a reliable and novel dynamic framework that utilises a data-driven approach for trust management. The framework uses past interactions, recent and anticipated future trust values of every identity in the domain. The proposed framework is critically evaluated and compared with existing work through experiments. The advantage of this proactive framework compared to other approaches is that informed decisions about the domain can be made before misbehaviour occurs.

Keywords: trust dynamics, trust management, reputation.

1 Introduction

In a social context, when a person is *trusted*, it implicitly means that the probability that the person will perform an action that is beneficial or at least not detrimental in the society, is high enough to consider engaging in some form of cooperation with the individual [5]. *Reputation*, on the other hand, is the opinion of one person about another; it is a measure of the trustworthiness of a person. Both trust and reputation have been used synonymously in literature.

Behavioural expectation in any domain can be motivated from a social perspective, where individuals are expected to behave in certain ways within the society. The behaviour of an individual, whether good or bad, will determine how others will cooperate with the individual. The expected behaviour of a sensor for example, in a Wireless Sensor Network (WSN) set up for monitoring, is to be cooperative in collecting and processing observed data with neighbouring sensors. *Misbehaviour* is the deviation from the expected behaviour in the domain and entities that misbehave are said to be untrusted.

Reputation and Trust-based Models (RTMs) [1,3,4,6,7,17] are described as systems that provide mechanisms to produce a metric encapsulating reputation for a given domain for each identity in the domain . This is referred to as *Trust*

I. Wakeman et al. (Eds.): IFIPTM 2011, IFIP AICT 358, pp. 323–334, 2011.

Value (TV) or trust ratings in this paper. Generally, RTMs aim to provide information to distinguish between trustworthy and untrustworthy members. The models encourage members to cooperate by providing incentives and discourage maliciousness by punishment schemes such as isolation and service denial. RTMs have been used extensively in various e-commerce and online communities such as YouTube, Amazon and eBay. Some literatures also suggest their use in domains ranging from Peer-to-Peer (P2P) to mobile networks [3,6,8,17].

Traditional RTMs rely on recommendations provided by entities in the domain to determine the reputation of others. Each of the models addresses some of the trust issues but not all of the problems, or in the process of solving one issue they introduce others. An example of the problem that arises from the reliance on these recommendations is *collusion*, where two or more entities team up to behave maliciously. Without countermeasures, the effects of this attack have shown to dramatically affect the network performance as evidenced in poor reliability and quality of service, higher overhead and throughput degradation [3]. Incentive policies that are used in P2P networks to ensure cooperation between peers are also generally susceptible to collusion attack [14].

Generally, RTMs make use of past events as a pointer for the future. However, for an RTM to be reliable and effective in trust management, trust has to be predictable. It is generally assumed that the predictive power of an RTM depends on the supposition that past behaviour is an indication of future behaviour [13]. This assumption might not be true with another malicious behaviour called *intoxication*. Intoxication occurs because the effect of past good behaviour outweighs the effect of current misbehaviour. Therefore, we argue that using historic (or past) interactions as the only basis for predicting the future TVs of identities in a domain is inadequate to provide a trusted system. Our framework extends the supposition further by not only considering past interactions but also anticipating possible future behaviour of members.

In previous papers [18,19], we described how trust decisions can be corrupted through recommendations made by members. We proposed a framework that is capable of providing dynamic trust ratings of members at runtime and predicting the future trust ratings. The framework does not rely on collective opinion and recommendations to determine the reputation of members. Instead, the framework predicts a potential compromise before it occurs. In this paper we present an extension to our original design, which uses predictions of future behaviour to determine trust ratings. We also present experiments comparing the results obtained with and without the use of prediction capabilities, confirming that the framework can provide more reliable predictions.

The rest of this paper is organised as follows: Section 2 describes significant RTMs in literature. The motivation for the use of dynamic data-driven paradigm in this research is discussed in Sect. 3 while Sect. 4 details the components of the framework. Section 5 presents a set of experimental results and analysis that shows that the predictive capability of our framework. Finally, we discuss and conclude in Sect. 6 and Sect. 7 respectively.

2   Related Work

Researchers proposed RTMs to solve trust related issues and the models have shown positive results. Some models that have contributed significantly to trust management in literature are discussed in this section.

Michiardi and Molva [17] proposed a model where reputation is formed and updated over time by direct observations and information provided by other members of the network. In their model, nodes have to contribute continuously to remain trusted or their reputation will be degraded until they are excluded from the network. The model gives a higher weight to past behaviour. The authors argue that a more recent sporadic misbehaviour should have minimal influence on a node's reputation that has been built over a long period of time.

A file-sharing P2P reputation system's algorithm: EigenTrust [10], similar to the popular PageRank aims to identify sources of inauthentic file and to prevent peers downloading from them. The algorithm assigns each peer a unique global TV, based on the peer's history of uploads. EigenTrust's susceptibility to collusion has been demonstrated in [14], where certain colluding peers are able to obtain high TVs.

Buchegger et al. [3] proposed a protocol that aims to detect and isolate misbehaving nodes, making it unattractive for any node to deny cooperation with others. In the protocol, each node maintains a reputation and a trust rating about every other node of interest. Only fresh reputation is propagated in the network, with more weight given to the current behaviour of a node over its past behaviour. Nodes monitor and detect misbehaviour in their neighbourhood by means of an enhanced *packet acknowledgment* mechanism; where the confirmation of acknowledgment comes indirectly by overhearing the next node forward the packet [2,20].

In the work of Ganeriwal et al. [6]; which is applicable to WSNs, each sensor node maintains reputation metrics. These metrics represent the past behaviour of other nodes and are used as an inherent aspect in predicting their future behaviour. The model relies on network members to maintain the reputation of others based on their experiences and uses this to evaluate their trustworthiness.

More recent studies on RTMs are discussed in [1,4,7]. A common problem seen in the models is the vulnerability to collusion attacks [9]. Models applicable in the mobile networks domain, make use of a component resident on each node called *watchdog* mechanism. This component monitors its neighbourhood and gathers data by *promiscuous observation*. By promiscuous observation we mean that each node overhears the transmission of neighbours to detect misbehaviour. Watchdog requires that every node report to the originator about the next node. Once misbehaviour is detected, a negative TV is stored. This detection mechanism also has a weakness of failing to detect a misbehaving device in case of collusions [16].

Let us consider a set of sensor nodes that are deployed along the roadside to monitor vehicular movement in order to obtain real traffic flow data and conditions. The sensors are equipped with wireless interfaces with which they form a network. Nodes collaborate to collect and process data that generate information about traffic conditions. When a sensor node receives information

Fig. 1. Sensor node can misbehave by colluding to deceive the network

from another, this is combined and fused with local information before being sent to a server to control traffic. Figure 1 depicts collusion attack showing a downside of the watchdog mechanism. Knowing that WSNs are vulnerable to attacks due to their nature, an adversary compromises a sensor node, which in turn compromises other nodes. Consider a normal situation, where for example, sensor node A forwards a message to node B and B forwards the message to C. Node C then forwards the message to node D. However, node C may decide to alter the message before sending it to D. With the watchdog mechanism, it is possible that B colludes with C and does not report to A when C alters message M, before forwarding the message. Misbehaving nodes do not only have the chance to collude but can also propagate false information. Therefore, trust decisions can be corrupted through recommendations made by such sensor nodes.

3   Why Dynamic Data-Driven Simulation?

A disreputable person could redeem himself through honest actions and a trusted person could become less reputable or untrustworthy if he misbehaves in a society. This analogy is applicable also in trust management and implies that trust can fluctuate over time, making it dynamic. This dynamic nature of trust therefore calls for an equally dynamic approach for identifying misbehaving members.

The missing element in traditional RTMs is the reliable prediction of future TVs of members to proactively prevent misbehaviour. The classification of members into different levels of risk is also an important missing element. This classification can potentially help the RTM to focus on members that are of high-risk in the domain. Hence, we propose an approach that

1. Predicts the future TVs using past events, recent events and possible future interactions
2. Provides information about members that are classified as high-risk
3. Prevents members' bias from influencing trust decisions
4. Provides dynamic TVs of domain members.

This fits within a more general emerging paradigm referred to as Dynamic Data-Driven Application Systems (DDDAS). The DDDAS approach is that of a symbiotic relationship between reality and simulations. The simulation is able to make predictions about how an entity would evolve and its future state. The predictions made can then influence how and where future data will be gathered from the system, in order to focus on areas of uncertainty [11].

DDDAS has been applied in the simulation of physical, artificial or social entities [12,15]. The application of DDDAS for trust management provides dynamism in the detection of misbehaving members and prediction of future ratings. The

data about behaviour of members is simulated to gain a better understanding
and a more accurate prediction of the level of trust for each member.

4   Dynamic Data-Driven Framework

This section introduces the framework and gives a comparative analysis with
pre-existing models using monitoring, simulation, dynamism, and prediction as
criteria. Figure 2 illustrates the relationship between the framework components.

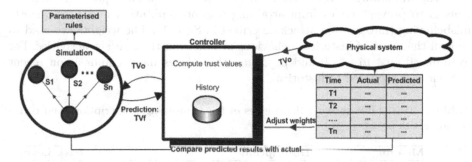

Fig. 2. Framework components showing how data is injected into the simulation and
the scenarios $s_1, s_2, ..., s_n$

4.1   Trust Computation

Trust computation is very difficult, as trust has to be defined precisely. This is
because the computation is crucial to the fulfilment of the functions in any trust-
based framework. Computing trust in RTMs has been described as an abstract
mathematical specification of how available information should be transformed
into a usable metric [8]. In this framework, the specification is made through
explicit equations.

A set of discrete TVs is assumed in the framework and each value represents a
degree of trust [19]. These discrete degrees of trust introduce flexibility into applications of our framework, as different behaviours correspond to different levels
of trust. Table 1 shows the trust table, the degrees of trust and corresponding
level of risk in this framework.

Captured qualitative data is converted to a quantitative value. Data collected
from the network (e.g. a P2P system, eBay, WSN etc) is transformed to a value
ranging from 0 to 5, where a score of 0 means a node is completely untrusted, 5
means a node is absolutely trusted and if $0 < TV < 5$, then it implies that the
node is trusted to a certain extent.

Using the notation tv^R, let the computed TV be

$$tv^R = \mu_h tv_h^R + \mu_o tv_o^R \tag{1}$$

where tv_h^R and tv_o^R are the average historical and recent online TVs respectively. Weights μ_h and μ_o are scaling factors of the TVs which can be varied and are introduced to allow for flexibility in the framework.

The simulation considers the possible scenarios a member may undertake in the future and the average of the ratings for the member determines the future tv_f^S. An predicted overall TV is computed as

$$TV = \mu_h tv_h^R + \mu_o tv_o^R + \mu_f tv_f^S \tag{2}$$

where μ_f is a scaling factor for the predicted value.

In the framework, recent behaviour has more weight than past interactions. This is to prevent nodes from attaining a good reputation and subsequently misbehaving (intoxication attack described in Sect. 1). The weights are used to control the effect of historical behaviour of nodes on their recent activities. For example, if $(\mu_o, \mu_h) > 0$ and $\mu_o > \mu_h$, this places more emphasis on recent behaviour as opposed to historical.

Table 1. Trust table showing the degrees of trust, meanings, descriptions and corresponding risk levels

TV	Meaning	Description	Risk Level
5	Complete trust	Trusted node with an excellent reputation	Low risk
4	Good trust level	Very reliable node	Low risk
3	Average trust level	Average value and somewhat reliable node	Medium risk
2	Average trust level	Average value but questionable node	Medium risk
1	Poor trust level	A questionable node	High risk
0	Complete distrust	Malicious node with a bad reputation	High risk

4.2 Simulation

In order for any RTM to fulfil its functions; observations, experiences and recommendations need to be captured and represented numerically. The simulation of the network runs concurrently with the real system itself. The aim of the simulation is to predict TV of members by using past interactions, current events and possible future scenarios. However, this component of the framework works ahead in time of the system. At specific time slots, the current state of the system is obtained and adapted to the simulation.

Data collected from the system are the online TV (tv_o^R) that represents the current rating of a member and the computed TV (tv^R) using the online ratings and past events. These values from reality are injected into the simulation at the start. The simulation runs for more time steps and considers different what-if scenarios in which a member may be in the future.

Possible outcomes in the what-if scenarios are simulated to anticipate possible fluctuations in member behaviour. This is because the behaviour of members generally in any network, domain or context is dynamic and changes with time. Examples of possible scenarios that can be considered by the simulation are collusion attacks such as altering a message, intoxication and normal expected behaviour. The resulting TV for a member in each scenario is considered and with this information, it is possible to compute and anticipate the future TV of the member. In the controller (a trusted framework component depicted in Fig. 2), the data from the simulation is combined with online and historical TVs in order to obtain an overall TV.

After some specified time intervals $T_1, T_2, ..., T_n$, the simulation state is observed and compared with the actual state; this comparison is done automatically in the controller. The framework is adaptive such that if there are any differences in the predicted values and the reality, the weights for the trust computation can be continually adjusted to reflect reality. Each instance of the adjustment always ensures that the condition $\mu_o > \mu_h$ holds. This means that an entity's most recent action has more impact on its TV than past actions; consequently preventing intoxication. The exact way the adjustment may be achieved is beyond the scope of this paper.

Table 2 compares the extended framework with the RTMs described earlier based on the criteria of monitoring, simulation, dynamism and prediction.

Table 2. Summary table comparing existing RTMs with framework

Models	[17]	[10]	[3]	[6]	Framework
Monitoring	Watchdog mechanism	Peer recommendation	Watchdog mechanism	Watchdog mechanism	Controller monitoring
Simulation	n/a	n/a	n/a	n/a	Simulation of possible future states
Dynamism	Ratings are not constant	Periodic iterations to compute global TVs	Periodically updated	Provides real time feedback	Online ratings and control at intervals
Prediction	n/a	Past interactions serve as an indication of TVs	n/a	Trust metric that is representative of a history, online and nodes' future possible future behaviour	Prediction of TVs using data from history, online and possible future behaviours

The framework performs better by predicting the future TVs of members. The prediction gives the network enough time for preventive measures, making the framework proactive compared to other models that are reactive. We refer to being proactive in terms of providing control such as downgrading of TV of suspect members that are predicted to be malicious before they can carry out an attack. This is contrary to how other approaches work, that only downgrade the TV as a reaction to misbehaviour. The assumption is that a member that has been compromised by an adversary exhibits a sequence of behaviour in order to misbehave. A hypothetical example is depicted in Fig. 3a and Fig. 3b which show the time difference in response time between the framework and other approaches. Figure 3a shows that the TV is only downgraded at time t_5 after the member exhibits maliciousness. The simulation in the framework predicts the maliciousness between time interval t_1 and t_2 and the TV is downgraded at time t_3 in Fig. 3b.

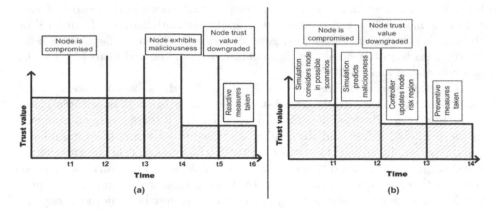

Fig. 3. Other approaches in (a) compared with the dynamic approach in (b)

5   Experiments

This section describes the simulation environment setup using Repast Simphony[1], an agent based simulation toolkit. The experimental analysis is to confirm the hypothesis described in Fig(s). 3a and 3b showing the reliability of the framework in providing timely predictions. Experiments were carried out using a P2P network scenario where the framework anticipates the behaviour of members in different network scenarios and predicts the TV of network peers.

The network is modelled with certain properties. Peers interact with others using the communication mechanism found in a P2P network, causing peer states to change. The peers are self-contained as they are uniquely identifiable with a set of characteristics, behaviours and attributes. Also, the peers function independently and interact with other peers by message transfer.

In each experiment, the network consists of dormant peers that do not participate in network activities, misbehaving peers and reputable peers that are active in file upload and download. The network parameters used are in Table 3. The simulation which runs concurrently with the network contains a snapshot of the network and is 20 *ticks* (a compression of time) ahead.

5.1   Implementation Environment

The experiments were carried out with and without the predictive capability of the framework. In the first experiment, trust computation was based on only the online data and past interactions with no predictions from the simulation.

The TV derived from nodes recent activities tv_o^R is updated every 5 ticks. The tv_o^R from the last update replaces the value of tv_h^R every 5 ticks. The set of past tv_h^Rs is stored in a database for records of historical TVs. With every observation k in the experiment, we compute tv_o^R with the formula $(tv_o^R)k^{th} =$

---

[1] http://repast.sourceforge.net/

Table 3. Simulation parameters

Parameter	Value
Total simulation time (in ticks)	100
Total number of nodes	100
Percentage of malicious nodes	4
Total number of messages transferred	27
Default trust values tv_o^R, tv_h^R	2.5
Online weight μ_o	0.5
Historical weight μ_h	0.3
Prediction weight μ_f	0.17

$((tv_o^R)k - 1^{th}) - \alpha$ and $(tv_o^R)k^{th} = ((tv_o^R)k - 1^{th}) + (\alpha + 0.5)$ for observed bad and good behaviour respectively, where α is set to 0.5.

From mathematical proofing, the weightings of the TVs serve as a scaling factor and must be such that $0 \leq 1/\mu_o + 1/\mu_h < 1$ for the overall TV to be within the range of 0 and 5. Also, in order for more emphasis to be placed on recent observations, $\mu_o > \mu_h$. For these experiments, the weights were kept at constant values of 0.5, 0.3 and 0.17 for μ_o, μ_h and μ_f respectively.

The simulation component in the second experiment considered 3 possible scenarios and the corresponding TVs for each scenario was obtained. The what-if scenarios considered are collusion, intoxication and failure to cooperate in forwarding of files. A scenario where the peer is active and behaves as expected is also considered. The average of the TVs (tv_f^S) from the scenarios was used and combined with tv_o^R and tv_h^R (of each peer) to compute the overall TV in the second experiment.

5.2   Preliminary Results

In the absence of prediction, the misbehaving nodes colluded and sent inauthentic files through the network at 60 ticks. With prediction, the framework detected and flagged the peer as malicious at 40 ticks and with a downgrade of its TV immediately. Figure 4 shows the TVs of one of the misbehaving peers, with and without the use of prediction. The figure shows the time gained with the use of prediction with a downgrade of the peer's TV immediately to below the allowed threshold of 2.

Ultimately in the experiment with prediction, the peer is isolated because its overall TV is below the threshold for other peers to want to cooperate with the peer. This averts the misbehaviour, unlike in the experiment without the prediction (similar to the models that do not anticipate future behaviour by simulation), where the TV was downgraded as a response to the attack. Figure 5 compares the predicted trust with actual TV for some peers. The graph shows the changes in the value of a peer exhibiting intoxication, an untrusted peer whose TV continues to drop and a trusted peer that is active with a high value.

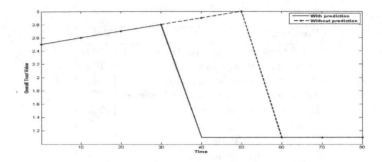

Fig. 4. P2P file-sharing network result (with and without prediction of TVs)

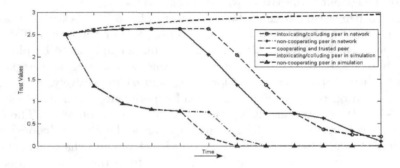

Fig. 5. TVs of a peer and the comparison of the values in the network and simulation

6   Discussion

Ad hoc networks are traditionally known to lack a central entity; therefore, this framework will be most applicable in semi-distributed contexts such as sensor networks, which lend themselves to centralised control.

By comparing the results from the simulation with those from the network, we observed some degree of variance and this might account for possible false-positives or false-negatives generated from the simulation. Hence, we shall explore approaches to improve the correlation of these trust values (i.e. simulated and actual) in the future. Approaches to parameterise the simulation rules for more dynamism in the framework will also be considered in the near future.

In this paper, our experimental study considers only the case of fixed number of identities in the network without random entry and exit of peers. In the future, we shall analyse the implication of dynamic admission and departure of nodes on accuracy of the predictive capability of our framework. Even though we have assumed a constant value for the TV weights, the simulation has a potential to be adaptive in a way that the feedback gathered from the system can help in the adjustments of the weights for future rounds.

7 Conclusion

This paper proposes a dynamic reputation and trust-based framework that is able to predict the behaviour of network members in the future. The framework anticipates future events and considers available information for prediction. Compared to other existing work on trust management, this framework has shown to have the potential to be useful in terms of providing timely information about the domain. This approach is not only useful at the network level but also at a higher level, providing adequate and timely information that allows for countermeasures and making security aware decisions in the network by stakeholders. It can therefore be concluded that the use of monitoring, simulation, and feedback in terms of prediction and control mechanisms, can potentially improve the reliability of systems that rely on trust management to function.

References

1. Balakrishnan, V., Varadharajan, V., Lucs, P., Tupakula, U.: Trust enhanced secure mobile ad-hoc network routing. In: Advanced Information Networking and Applications Workshops AINAW, vol. 1, pp. 27–33 (2007)
2. Buchegger, S., Le Boudec, J.: Self-policing mobile ad hoc networks by reputation systems. IEEE Communications Magazine 43(7), 101–107 (2005)
3. Buchegger, S., Le Boudec, J.: Performance analysis of the CONFIDANT protocol (Cooperation of nodes: Fairness In Dynamic Ad-hoc Networks). In: Proceedings of the International Symposium on Mobile Ad Hoc Networking and Computing, MobiHoc. pp. 226–236 (2002)
4. Chen, H., Wu, H., Hu, J., Gao, C.: Event-based trust framework model in wireless sensor networks. In: Proceedings of the International Conference on Networking, Architecture, and Storage, NAS, pp. 359–364. IEEE Computer Society, Los Alamitos (2008)
5. Gambetta, D.: Can we trust? trust: making and breaking cooperative relations edn. Basil Blackwell, New York (1988)
6. Ganeriwal, S., Balzano, L.K., Srivastava, M.B.: Reputation-based framework for high integrity sensor networks. ACM Transactions on Sensor Networks 4(3), 15:1–15:37 (2008)
7. He, Q., Wu, D., Khosla, P.: SORI: A secure and objective reputation-based incentive scheme for ad-hoc networks. In: Proceedings of WCNC Wireless Communications and Networking Conference, vol. 2, pp. 825–830. IEEE, Los Alamitos (2004)
8. Hoffman, K., Zage, D., Nita-Rotaru, C.: A survey of attack and defense techniques for reputation systems. ACM Computing Surveys 42(1), 1–31 (2009)
9. Hu, J., Burmester, M.: Lars - a locally aware reputation system for mobile ad hoc networks. In: Proceedings of the ACM SE Regional Conference, vol. 2006, pp. 119–123 (2006)
10. Kamvar, S., Schlosser, M., Garcia-Molina, H.: The eigentrust algorithm for reputation management in p2p networks. In: Proceedings of the 12th international conference on World Wide Web WWW, pp. 640–651. ACM, New York (2003)
11. Kennedy, C., Theodoropoulos, G.: Intelligent management of data driven simulations to support model building in the social sciences. In: Alexandrov, V.N., van Albada, G.D., Sloot, P.M.A., Dongarra, J. (eds.) ICCS 2006. LNCS, vol. 3993, pp. 562–569. Springer, Heidelberg (2006)

12. Kennedy, C., Theodoropoulos, G., Sorge, V., Ferrari, E., Lee, P., Skelcher, C.:
    AIMSS: An architecture for data driven simulations in the social sciences. In:
    Shi, Y., van Albada, G.D., Dongarra, J., Sloot, P.M.A. (eds.) ICCS 2007. LNCS,
    vol. 4487, pp. 1098–1105. Springer, Heidelberg (2007)
13. Kollock, P.: The production of trust in online markets. Advances in Group Pro-
    cesses 16 (1999)
14. Lian, Q., Zhang, Z., Yang, M., Zhao, B.Y., Dai, Y., Li, X.: An empirical study of
    collusion behavior in the maze p2p file-sharing system. In: Proceedings of the 27th
    IEEE International Conference on Distributed Computing Systems, vol. 56 (2007)
15. Madey, G., Szabo, G., Barabasi, A.: WIPER: The integrated wireless phone
    based emergency response system. In: Alexandrov, V.N., van Albada, G.D., Sloot,
    P.M.A., Dongarra, J. (eds.) ICCS 2006, Part III. LNCS, vol. 3993, pp. 417–424.
    Springer, Heidelberg (2006)
16. Marti, S., Giuli, T., Lai, K., Baker, M.: Mitigating routing misbehavior in mobile
    ad hoc networks. In: Proceedings of the Annual International Conference on Mobile
    Computing and Networking, MOBICOM, pp. 255–265 (2000)
17. Michiardi, P., Molva, R.: CORE: A collaborative reputation mechanism to en-
    force node cooperation in mobile ad hoc networks. In: Proceedings of the IFIP
    TC6/TC11 Sixth Joint Working Conference on Communications and Multimedia
    Security, vol. 100, pp. 107–121 (2002)
18. Onolaja, O., Bahsoon, R., Theodoropoulos, G.: An architecture for dynamic trust
    monitoring in mobile networks. In: Meersman, R., Herrero, P., Dillon, T. (eds.)
    OTM 2009 Workshops. LNCS, vol. 5872, pp. 494–503. Springer, Heidelberg (2009)
19. Onolaja, O., Bahsoon, R., Theodoropoulos, G.: Conceptual framework for
    dynamic trust monitoring and prediction. Procedia Computer Science 1(1),
    1241–1250 (2010); ICCS 2010
20. Srinivasan, A., Teitelbaum, J., Liang, H., Wu, J., Cardei, M.: Reputation and Trust-
    based Systems for Ad Hoc and Sensor Networks. In: Algorithms and Protocols for
    Wireless Ad Hoc Networks. Wiley & Sons, Chichester (2008)

Author Index